Systematic Screenings of Behavior to Support Instruction

FROM PRESCHOOL TO HIGH SCHOOL

Kathleen Lynne Lane
Holly Mariah Menzies
Wendy Peia Oakes
Jemma Robertson Kalberg

THE GUILFORD PRESS
New York   London

Library of Congress Cataloging-in-Publication Data

Systematic screenings of behavior to support instruction : from preschool to high school /
Kathleen Lynne Lane . . . [et al.].
      p. cm.
   Includes bibliographical references and index.
   ISBN 978-1-4625-0336-0 (pbk.)–ISBN 978-1-4625-0342-1 (hardcover)
   1. Behavioral assessment of children.   2. Classroom management.   I. Lane, Kathleen L.
   LB1124.S96 2012
   371.102′4—dc23

                                                                    2011031693

To my family:

> *Craig, my rock—thank you for your undying devotion and confidence (and I am so sorry I forgot our anniversary while writing this book!).*

> *Nathan and Katie—my blessings. As I watch you grow, I continue to marvel at the people you are—bright, compassionate, musical, funny, gracious, and tender-hearted. Thank you for loving me. I am so honored to be your mom. I treasure my time with you . . . the greatest part of my life continues to be our family.*

To the students we serve: I pray we can understand how to best identify and support you at the earliest possible juncture. May you feel respected and supported every day.

To my friends and colleagues: Thank you for writing this book with me—I love the way you bring balance and perspective to all that I do. I am forever thankful for you.
—K. L. L.

To all my students over these many years—from kindergarten to graduate school— who have made my work rewarding and interesting
—H. M. M.

To my family, who have allowed me the time and space to be fully committed to others' children:

> *Dan, my beacon, who has ensured my own children and many others were safe and loved*

> *Abigail, who inspires me in her creative perspective of the world, quest for knowledge, and unfailing acceptance of differences*

> *Katherine, who helps me remember to find joy in every moment*

> *My extended family, who have loved, supported, and accepted me always*

To my dear friends who have inspired me by their compassion and commitment to children and families

And to my coauthors, who have allowed me this opportunity
—W. P. O.

To the students of Classroom E, who give me a reason to keep learning
—J. R. K.

About the Authors

Kathleen Lynne Lane, PhD, BCBA-D, is Professor in the School of Education at the University of North Carolina at Chapel Hill. Prior to entering academia, Dr. Lane served as a classroom teacher of general and special education students for 5 years and provided consultation, intervention, and staff development services to five school districts in southern California for 2 years as a Program Specialist. Her research interests focus on school-based interventions (academic and behavioral) with students at risk for emotional and behavioral disorders (EBD). Dr. Lane has designed, implemented, and evaluated multilevel prevention models in elementary, middle, and high school settings to prevent the development of EBD and respond to existing instances. While at Vanderbilt University, she served as the Principal Investigator of a state-funded technical assistance grant, Project Support and Include, which provides professional development and technical assistance to schools in 17 counties, focusing on the design, implementation, and evaluation of comprehensive, integrated, three-tiered (CI3T) models of prevention. Dr. Lane also served as the Principal Investigator of federally funded projects, including Project WRITE, a Goal Area 2 Grant funded through the Institute of Education Sciences, focusing on the impact of writing interventions for students at risk for EBD who are also poor writers; a project directed by the Office of Special Education Programs (OSEP) studying positive behavior support at the high school level; and an OSEP field-initiated project studying prevention of EBD at the elementary level. She has expertise in school-based intervention and statistical analysis, including multivariate analysis of longitudinal data sets. Dr. Lane is coeditor of *Remedial and Special Education* and an associate editor of the *Journal of Positive Behavior Interventions* and *Education and Treatment of Children*; serves on several editorial boards, including *Exceptional Children*, the *Journal of Special Education*, and the *Journal of Emotional and Behavioral Disorders*; and has coauthored five books and published over 100 refereed journal articles and book chapters.

Holly Mariah Menzies, PhD, is Associate Professor in the Charter College of Education at California State University, Los Angeles, and the program coordinator in mild–moderate disabilities in the Division of Special Education and Counseling. She worked as both a general educator and special educator for over 10 years. Dr. Menzies has provided staff development in the areas of assessment, language arts, and schoolwide positive behavior support. Her scholarly interests focus on inclusive education and school-based interventions. She serves on the editorial board of *Learning Disabilities Research and Practice* and is an associate editor of *Remedial and Special Education.*

Wendy Peia Oakes, PhD, is Research Associate in the Department of Special Education at Peabody College of Vanderbilt University. She has over 10 years of special education teaching experience at the elementary and middle school levels in self-contained, resource, and inclusive classrooms. Dr. Oakes's research interests focus on the early identification of and support for students with behavioral and academic needs, early development of reading, preservice teacher education, and inservice teacher and administrator professional development. She is currently the project manager of Project Support and Include, providing professional development and technical assistance to schools in designing, implementing, and evaluating CI3T models of prevention with a focus on inclusive practices, including the use of screening procedures to identify and serve students with special educational needs. Dr. Oakes also serves on the editorial board of *Remedial and Special Education.*

Jemma Robertson Kalberg, MEd, BCBA, was most recently a consultant at the Seneca Center in San Leandro, California. Her research interests focused on supporting students who are at risk for and identified with EBD, both behaviorally and academically. In addition, she had been involved in designing, implementing, and evaluating schoolwide positive behavior support plans with academic, behavioral, and social components at the elementary, middle, and high school levels. Within the context of schoolwide positive behavioral support, she focused her efforts on using schoolwide screeners to identify students who were nonresponsive to the primary prevention model.

Acknowledgments

We begin by thanking . . .

Hill Walker for his firm commitment to identifying and supporting students with behavioral challenges. We so respect and admire your vision, mentorship, and commitment. We also extend our sincere appreciation and continued respect to Herb Severson, Ed Feil, T. Drummond, Robert Goodman, Randy Kamphaus, Cecil Reynolds, Frank Gresham (MML), and Steve Elliott for their work in systematic screening efforts. We have learned so much from each of you and hope that the content of this book captures the gifts you have given the research and teaching communities.

Heather Griller-Clark and Sarup Mathur for continuing the legacy of Robert B. Ruherford, Jr., at TECBD by gathering the community of educators committed to improving outcomes for students with EBD.

The teachers, staff, administrators, parents, and students of the many schools in Tennessee, California, Arizona, Missouri, and Illinois for teaching and inspiring us. Thank you for working with us to help find and assist those in need. Your images and efforts filled our thoughts as we filled these pages. We hold you all in high esteem.

Our editor at The Guilford Press, Rochelle Serwator, for allowing us this opportunity to provide what we hope is a very useful tool for the educational community.

Our families and our children (Nathan, Katie, Lucia, Abby, Katie O, Maisie, and Lachlan) for their time, inspiration, and perspective. We hope the tools in this book will help to meet your needs and the needs of other children.

We wish you all well as you search and serve.

Contents

CHAPTER 1

Systematic Screenings of Behavior to Support Instruction

An Overview

As former classroom teachers and behavior specialists, we are continually amazed and impressed by the multiple demands today's administrators, teachers, and support staff face on a daily basis. Within the course of a typical school year, these professionals are expected to welcome, educate, and support an increasingly diverse student population. Students pass through the schoolhouse doors with a wide range of skill sets in academic, behavioral, and social domains, coming from a wide range of home environments and an even wider range of ethnic, cultural, and socioeconomic backgrounds (Lane, Kalberg, & Menzies, 2009; Lane, Wehby, Robertson, & Rogers, 2007). Although such diversity is valued, the range of abilities students bring to the classroom can make it challenging for teachers to differentiate the curriculum sufficiently while meeting students' social and behavioral needs in a manner that allows students to meet increasingly rigorous state standards (Tomlinson, 2005; Tomlinson & McTighe, 2005).

Some students have the necessary skills and experiences to adapt easily to the school setting by successfully negotiating relationships with their teachers and peers. These students have acquired important skill sets such as listening to and following instructions the first time they are asked to do so, appropriately requesting support when they need assistance, being self-determined in their work, and resolving conflicts with others in peaceful ways (Carter, Lane, Pierson, & Stang, 2008; Elliott & Gresham, 2007b; Wehmeyer & Field, 2007). They have the skills in their repertoire to navigate the instructional process. These behaviors, in turn, support teachers' goals of providing meaningful, relevant instruction to enhance students' academic outcomes. Such harmony in the classroom is highly desirable because it allows teachers the opportunity to maximize academic engagement and overall instructional experiences (Lane, Menzies, Bruhn, & Crnobori, 2011; Sutherland & Wright, in press). When behavioral expectations are clear and students are explicitly taught and reinforced for meeting these expectations, teachers are able to maximize learning opportunities. In turn, teachers spend less time responding to problem behaviors and more time instructing all students, including those who require additional assistance beyond primary prevention (Tier 1) in the form of secondary (Tier 2) and tertiary (Tier 3) supports (Lane, Kalberg, & Menzies, 2009). Ultimately, student success is evidenced by improved academic performance while teachers meet their obligation of delivering opportunities for all students to demonstrate academic excellence, including those with exceptionalities, as established in the No Child Left Behind Act (2001) and Individuals with Disabilities Education Improvement Act (IDEA, 2004).

In contrast, other students arrive at school with less than optimal skill sets and are less able to meet the variety of demands required over the course of the school day (Lane, 2007; Walker, Ramsey, & Gresham, 2004). This is particularly true for students who have learning and behavioral challenges. Although many teachers indicate they feel well prepared to meet students' diverse academic needs, there is evidence to suggest that teachers feel less prepared to support students who demonstrate challenging behaviors, especially those with emotional and behavioral disorders (EBD). According to a Metropolitan Life survey of first-time teachers before beginning their first year of teaching, more than half (58%) of respondents reported they wished they had more practical training in classroom management skills before the school year began. This percentage increased slightly to 61% at the end of the first year of instruction, suggesting that "surviving" their first year of teaching did not change teachers' desire for additional knowledge and skills pertaining to preventing and responding to problem behaviors (Harris, 1991). Not surprisingly, teachers' self-efficacy with respect to classroom management skills actually predicted longevity in the field: Teachers who viewed themselves as less capable were more likely to leave education than those who viewed themselves as effective in their behavior management skills (Brouwers & Tomic, 2000). This is a concern given conservative estimates suggest that between 3 and 6% of the school-age population at some point have EBD (Kauffman & Brigham, 2009).

Students with EBD: Not a Special Education Issue

Although initial thoughts of EBD conjure images of students with serious acting-out behaviors such as verbal and physical aggression, coercive tactics, and even delinquent acts (externalizing behaviors), they also include internalizing behavior patterns that are less often recognized in the classroom (Achenbach, 1991; Crick, Grotpeter, & Bigbee, 2002; Walker et al., 2004). Internalizing behaviors include anxiety, depression, somatic complaints (e.g., stomachache, headache), social withdrawal, and eating disorders (Morris, Shah, & Morris, 2002). As you might imagine, externalizing behavior patterns are far more likely to be recognized by teachers because these behaviors disrupt the classroom environment and consequently impede instruction, whereas internalizing behaviors, which are no less harmful, go unnoticed. Although some might contend that problem behaviors are issues that should be dealt with by special education teachers, paraprofessionals, and mental health staff, in reality this is often not the case.

The truth is that less than 1% of school-age students across the K–12 continuum ultimately receive special education services under the label of emotional disturbance (ED) as defined in IDEA (2004). Even when identified for such supports, the goal is inclusive programming—to the greatest extent possible, students should be in the general education setting (MacMillan, Gresham, & Forness, 1996; Wagner et al., 2006). When we consider the small number of students served in special education with ED and the fact that the majority of students with EBD will not receive special education services, it becomes clear that general education teachers need the knowledge, skills, and confidence to identify and support students at risk for EBD at the earliest possible juncture. This way the necessary supports can be provided to prevent learning, behavioral, and social problems from becoming more firmly engrained and less amenable to intervention efforts (Kazdin, 1985; Lane, Kalberg, & Menzies, 2009). Behavior problems are not a special education problem or even a "within-child" problem—they are a schoolwide concern that cannot be ignored given that students with EBD and with ED pose significant challenges to the educational system as well as to society as a whole (Walker, 2003). These students struggle within and outside of school contexts, as evidenced by limited rates of academic engaged time, poor work completion, higher rates of school failure, retention in grade, school dropout, impaired social relationships, and even poor employment outcomes after they leave school (Bullis & Walker, 1994; Mattison, Hooper, & Glassberg, 2002; Reid, Gonzalez, Nordness, Trout, & Epstein, 2004; Wagner & Davis, 2006; Zigmond, 2006). Clearly, life is challenging for these students and their families (Kauffman, 2005; Quinn & Poirier, 2004).

Fortunately, many schools across the country are taking steps to coordinate academic, behavioral, and social supports for students by developing comprehensive, integrated, three-tiered (CI3T) models of prevention to better meet all students' multiple needs (Lane, Kalberg, & Menzies, 2009). This is encouraging given that learning and behavioral concerns do not occur in isolation from one another. Understanding the relation between the two has important implications for teachers and students alike (Lane & Wehby, 2002).

Responding with a Systems-Based Approach: Comprehensive, Integrated, Three-Tiered Models of Prevention (CI3T Model)

Across the United States, many schools, districts, and even states have shifted their perspectives, no longer subscribing to a "wait-to-fail" model (Horner & Sugai, 2000; Lane, Menzies, et al., 2011). Instead, they are embracing the concepts of *prevention* and *search and serve* (IDEA, 2004). With this approach, the goal is to design, implement, and evaluate multi-tiered models of prevention to focus on (1) preventing learning and behavior problems from occurring by providing primary prevention (Tier

1) efforts to all students and (2) responding to existing concerns by identifying and assisting students who require secondary (Tier 2) and/or tertiary (Tier 3) supports. Some models such as response to intervention (Fuchs & Fuchs, 2006; Gresham, 2002; Sugai, Horner, & Gresham, 2002) have focused primarily on academic domains, whereas models such as positive behavior interventions and supports (Lewis & Sugai, 1999; Sugai & Horner, 2002) have focused predominantly on behavior and social domains.

In each of these models, the entire student body participates in primary prevention efforts with a goal of preventing harm. The expectation is that this global level of support will reach approximately 80% of the student body (Sugai & Horner, 2006).

Data collected as part of regular school practices (e.g., report card grades, curriculum-based measures, formative assessments, behavior screenings, and office discipline referrals [ODRs]) are analyzed to determine which students need secondary supports (also referred to as Tier 2 and targeted supports), such as small-group interventions for those with common acquisition (can't do), fluency (have trouble doing), or performance (don't want to do) deficits (Elliott & Gresham, 2007b). Students receiving secondary supports are monitored closely using frequent, repeated assessment to determine patterns of responsiveness (Is this working? Is he reading with greater speed and accuracy? Is she more engaged during instruction? Is he completing more assignments?). Answers to these questions (as well as others) will guide the school-site leadership team to make decisions about whether or not to continue, modify, or move into maintenance of the secondary support; return solely to primary prevention efforts; or transition a student to even more intensive prevention efforts—tertiary supports.

Students exposed to multiple risk factors and those who need more intensive supports are provided with tertiary efforts. This level is the most exhaustive in terms of intensity, resources, and individualization. Again, students are monitored closely to determine patterns of responsiveness for the specific target behaviors of interest (e.g., decoding, work completion, social interactions, verbal aggression, and noncompliance).

Models that focus solely on reading or behavior may miss important aspects of students' complex individual needs. By not considering academic and behavioral needs together, critical information that can more fully inform intervention efforts and patterns of responsiveness may be overlooked. For example, if a student is identified as not responding to the primary reading curriculum as determined by Fall benchmark scores measured using AIMSweb® reading curriculum-based measurement probes (Pearson Education, 2008), he or she might be placed into a secondary support that involves an additional 30 minutes of reading instruction each day to improve fluency (e.g., repeated readings; Chard, Ketterlin-Geller, Baker, Doabler, & Apichatabutra, 2009). Yet if data regarding behavior concerns (e.g., excesses or deficits) are not also acquired, critical information that could be used to enhance intervention efforts and improve outcomes is lost. Consider the student who has high levels of inattention or impulsivity. This student would likely need behavioral support such as self-monitoring (Mooney, Ryan, Uhing, Reid, & Epstein, 2005) to help him or her access the additional instruction (Kalberg, Lane, & Menzies, 2010). In other words, just as teachers have been taught to differentiate academic instruction by modifying content, process, or product (Tomlinson, 2005), they must also learn how to differentiate along behavioral dimensions to help students access the core curriculum.

Slowly, a shift is occurring in which researchers and practitioners are recognizing the need for a CI3T model that uses multiple sources of data—academic and behavioral measures—to understand more fully students' multiple needs. In such models, the primary prevention plan contains three core components—academic, behavioral, and social—to better address students' total needs. For example, the primary prevention plan for academics may include a validated literacy program such as Open Court (Adams et al., 2002) or Harcourt Brace (Hiebert & Raphael, 1998). With this type of program, teachers provide evidence-based instruction in language arts skills 90 minutes per day 4 days a week. Instruction is aligned within and across grade levels as part of such a program, with the necessary assessments in place to monitor students' progress in Fall, Winter, and Spring to inform instruction and identify students who do not meet expected benchmarks and, therefore, may require secondary (Tier 2) or tertiary (Tier 3) levels of prevention. As part of the primary plan, treatment integrity data are collected to make certain the core elements of the plan are taught as designed. Without such data, it is not possible to evaluate accurately the impact of the program. In other words, if you are not certain that an intervention is being implemented correctly, how can you make accurate decisions about whether or not it is working for individual students?

The second component of the primary plan is a schoolwide positive behavior support (SWPBS) plan in which universal expectations are established and clarified among all adults for each key area in the school (e.g., classrooms, hallways, recreational areas). Teachers explicitly teach all students these expectations, providing them opportunities to practice and receive reinforcement for meeting the expectations. Reinforcement is delivered with behavior-specific praise to reinforce skills (e.g., effort) that will facilitate success. It is important to recognize that positive behavior support is a framework, not a curriculum. It is a method by which students can be directly taught the behaviors necessary to facilitate the instructional process and empower them to negotiate interactions with others (e.g., teachers, peers, other adults). Again, it is important to monitor the treatment integrity of the SWPBS prevention program to accurately identify students who may require additional supports. In the school setting, this allows teachers to gain instructional time by spending less time responding to problem behaviors and more time engaged in teaching not only the academic curriculum but also the social competencies development curriculum, the third component of the plan.

Ideally, the social component of the primary plan is a schoolwide program designed to promote students' character development (Person, Moiduddlin, Hague-Angus, & Malone, 2009) or social skills (Elliott & Gresham, 2007a). When selecting such a program, school-site leadership teams should consider the needs of the school. For example, if there are significant problems with bullying and other forms of aggression, it would be wise to incorporate a program that teaches students how to prevent violence. In this case, a program such as Second Step: Violence Prevention (Committee for Children, 2007; Sprague et al., 2001) might be useful. When considering this social component, you should reflect on the school's (or district's) vision for making its implicit curriculum explicit. Then select a validated, evidence-based program with sufficient proof to support implementation. It is imperative that precious resources (e.g., time, personnel, money) not be wasted implementing programs without evidence to support the specific outcomes you are seeking. This means that you must consider more than just, "Are there high-quality research studies to show that the program works?" Another important question to consider is, "Are there high-quality research studies to show that this program works to produce the outcomes we are looking for in our school or district?" Once an evidence-based program is selected (e.g., a character education program such as Positive Action [Flay, Allred, & Ordway, 2001]), then it too should be implemented consistently and monitored for treatment integrity to determine which students need more intensive supports.

In sum, these three components are not mutually exclusive but rather are interrelated. They are implemented as part of a unified system to better serve students. The SWPBS component is an instructional approach to behavior that teaches behavioral expectations (e.g., respect, responsibility, best effort). As students understand and meet behavioral expectations, teachers gain instructional time by not having to stop to respond to behavior problems. This affords teachers the time to provide instruction using evidence-based programs to develop students' academic (e.g., Open Court or Harcourt Brace) and social or character competencies (e.g., Social Skills Improvement System: Classwide Intervention Program [Elliott & Gresham, 2007a]; Positive Action [Positive Action Inc., 2008]). SWPBS is a data-driven framework that can be used to analyze multiple sources of data collected. However, the data collected using these monitoring systems must also be checked for procedural fidelity to make certain all individuals are using the assessment system correctly. These data are collected as part of regular school practices (e.g., academic progress monitoring, ODRs, attendance, and behavior screenings [the focus of this book]). Academic and behavioral data should be analyzed in tandem for accurate decision making and information sharing regarding (1) progress for schools as a whole and (2) identification and progress of students who require additional supports in the form of secondary (Tier 2) and tertiary (Tier 3) levels of prevention.

Systematic Screening

In a CI3T model of prevention, accurate measurement is a central feature. Decisions related to how a school improves student outcomes over time and identifies which students need additional supports in academic, behavioral, social, and combined areas are dependent on the accuracy of the data collected as part of school practices. To ensure accuracy in decision making, it is imperative that (1) reliable, valid tools be selected to measure student progress and (2) procedural fidelity data be collected at the school-site level to make certain the identified measurement system is being implemented consistently by all those involved. For example, the School-wide Information System (May et al., 2000) is a reliable, valid method of monitoring ODRs. This system offers clear guidelines as to which behaviors are viewed as major or minor offenses using operational definitions and indicates when a given infraction warrants an ODR. Yet the data generated from this system are only as valid as the extent to which the procedures for assigning ODRs are followed. If such tools and systems are selected and implemented with integrity, then measurement error is minimized and school-site decision-making teams can have confidence in the accuracy of the decisions made with respect to overall progress and the identification of students who need secondary (Tier 2) and tertiary (Tier 3) supports.

In terms of measurement, teachers have extensive experience and training in evaluating academic performance over time (Lane, Menzies, et al., 2011). For example, many schools use commercially available programs such as AIMSweb to monitor academic performance indicators for reading, math, and writing skills. As part of this academic assessment program, teachers administer probes to all students three times a year (Fall, Winter, and Spring) to monitor student progress and determine which students are above, at, or below benchmark levels for their respective grade. This information is often used by grade-level teams to make instructional decisions. Students below benchmark participate in secondary (Tier 2) interventions for additional instruction and are often grouped according to common deficits (often 30 minutes, three to four times per week). Secondary interventions are evidence-based programs or strategies provided in addition to the instruction in primary prevention (e.g., 90 minutes 5 days a week). Students receiving secondary interventions are monitored with increased frequency, meaning they participate in frequent, repeated assessments (e.g., weekly 1-minute oral reading fluency probes) that are analyzed each week to monitor incremental progress more closely. This practice is known as progress monitoring.

Yet teachers have less experience in implementing behavior screening tools. This is unfortunate given that behavior and academic learning are interrelated (Lane & Wehby, 2002). How students behave influences how we teach, and how we teach influences how students behave. Teachers need information on behavioral patterns—externalizing, internalizing, and otherwise—so that this information can be used to inform instruction. For example, the student who has excessive shyness, high levels of inattention, or low tolerance for frustration may need positive behavior supports to access instruction at each level of prevention. Without information on behavioral performance, teachers lack important information that can inform instruction and help interpret patterns of responsiveness (Kalberg et al., 2010).

Also, teachers are in a unique position to observe behavior. In truth, teachers often spend more waking hours per day with students than many of the parents and siblings. Teachers have the honor, opportunity, and responsibility to watch over students as they grow and develop as learners and citizens. Accordingly, teachers are privy to knowledge that parents are not—they can see how students respond to challenging academic tasks within a group and individually. For example, teachers may notice some students respond with high levels of frustration or avoidance when asked to complete tasks that are too challenging or even too easy. Other students avoid tasks by demonstrating behaviors that manifest as social withdrawal, such as requesting to go to the nurse's office, saying that they are too ill to give a presentation or participate in the role-play activity.

In addition to providing valuable information to inform educational programming, behavior screenings provide students with equal access to secondary and tertiary supports. Behavior screenings, when implemented within the context of three-tiered models of prevention, can identify and support students who show soft signs of behavior problems before behavior patterns become more firmly engrained and are less amenable to intervention efforts. By providing sometimes simple (e.g., increased opportunities to respond; Brophy & Good, 1986) and other times more complex (functional assessment-based interventions; Kern & Manz, 2004; Umbreit, Ferro, Liaupsin, & Lane, 2007) behavioral supports, teachers can improve educational outcomes for a range of students.

Behavior screenings also provide support for teachers by eliminating the pressure of potentially missing a student who needs additional support. As mentioned at the beginning of this chapter, teachers are confronted with many demands over the course of a given school day and across the academic year. It is simply unrealistic (and creates too much pressure!) to expect teachers to be aware of all types of behavior concerns and then independently evaluate whether each student has each concern. A key benefit of behavior screening systems is that they protect and support students and teachers alike.

Purpose

We encourage every school-site leadership team to incorporate behavior screening tools as part of their regular school practices to inform educational programming and protect students and teachers. The central question is not "Should we use behavior screening tools?" but rather "Which screening tool or system should we adopt as part of regular school practices?" given that systematic screening is an essential component in the identification of and support for students with and at risk for EBD and the teachers who serve them. However, we do strongly encourage you to review your state laws and policies regarding screening practices, particularly as they relate to behavioral screening. Rules and regulations do vary across states (see Chapter 8 for further discussion).

We offer this book as a guide for researchers and practitioners in selecting a screening tool or system that is both psychometrically sound and feasible based on the identified goals and resources of a school, district, or research study. In terms of psychometric consideration, effective systematic screening tools ideally meet certain core features (Gresham, Lane, & Lambros, 2000; Lane, Kalberg, Parks, & Carter, 2008; Lane, Parks, Kalberg, & Carter, 2007). First, to correctly identify students who do (or do not) have certain conditions such as externalizing, internalizing, or hyperactivity, it is important for a screening tool to have reliable and valid cut scores.

These scores are important in reducing the proportion of false positives (students who are identified as having a given concern when, in fact, the concern is not present) and false negatives (students identified as not having a given concern when, in fact, they do have such a concern). In prevention efforts, false negatives—overlooking a student who actually needs assistance—are the greater concern (Kauffman & Brigham, 2009). The validity of a tool is defined by the evidence (both empirical and logical) that supports the use and interpretation of test scores (American Educational Research Association [AERA], American Psychological Association [APA], & National Council for Measurement in Education [NCME], 1999).

Before decisions can be made as to whether or not a tool is valid, its reliability must be established. There are many different types of reliability (see Table 1.1 to relive the joy of your college measurement and statistics classes!). In brief, reliability refers to the extent to which a given measure, when administered two or more times or from different perspectives, will yield the same (or very similar) results (Hatcher & Stepanski, 1994).

In Table 1.1 you will see definitions of different psychometric properties, including internal consistency (the manner in which items hang together on a test, meaning they are measuring the same construct), test–retest stability (correlations between the same scores from the same rater over time), interrater reliability (correlations between ratings from two different raters who completed the same measures [or similar versions] at the same time), convergent validity (correlations between one tool and other established tools measured at the same time), positive predictive power (the probability that a student who scores above a given cut score is actually a member of the target group) and negative predictive power (the probability that a student who scores below the given cut score selected is a member of the control group), as well as specificity (proportion of the comparison group not identified as having a certain condition given the same cut score) and sensitivity (proportion of the target population correctly identified; AERA, APA, & NCME, 1999; Hatcher & Stepanski, 1994; Lane, Kalberg, Parks, et al., 2008; Lane, Parks, et al., 2007; Lanyon, 2006). These properties are central in making accurate decisions about how student risk status is shifting over time in a building or across schools in a district. They are equally important in determining which students need which types of supports. As we stated previously, the decisions that school-site leadership teams make on a daily basis are only as good or as precise as the accuracy of the data used to make instructional decisions. But equally important is the issue of feasibility. Speaking from experience, we know that it does not matter how strong an instrument is psychometrically if the tool is too difficult to implement given the multitude of responsibilities teachers shoulder each day.

A systematic screening tool must also be feasible in terms of practical considerations. For example, it must be reasonable in terms of time, effort, and cost when it comes to issues of preparation, administration, scoring, and interpretation (Lane, Kalberg, Parks, et al., 2008; Lane, Parks, et al., 2007). From our perspective, the ideal screener cannot be unreasonable when it comes to a cost–benefit comparison. It needs to be both scientifically rigorous with respect to issues of validity and reliability and reasonable in terms of the cost, financial and otherwise.

TABLE 1.1. Psychometric Properties

Psychometrics	Definition
Construct validity	"A term used to indicate that the test scores are to be interpreted as indicating the test taker's standing on the psychological construct measured by the test. A construct is a theoretical variable inferred from multiple types of evidence, which might include the interrelations of the test scores with other variables, internal test structure, observations of response processes, as well as the content of the test. In the current standards, all the scores are viewed as measures of some construct, so the phrase is redundant with validity. The validity argument establishes the construct validity of a test" (AERA, APA, & NCME, 1999, p. 174). A term used to indicate that the test scores are to be interpreted as accurate for the construct measured (AERA, APA, & NCME, 1999).
Content validity	"A term used in the 1974 Standards to refer to a kind or aspect of validity that was 'required when the test user wishes to estimate how an individual performs in the universe of situations the test is intended to represent' (p. 28). In the 1985 Standards, the term was changed to content-related evidence emphasizing that it referred to one type of evidence within the unitary conception of validity. In the current Standards, this type of evidence is characterized as 'evidence based on test content' " (AERA, APA, & NCME, 1999, p. 174). A term used to refer to the validity of the score on the present test as an indicator of how well the individual performs in all situations for which the test represents (AERA, APA, & NCME, 1999).
Convergent validity (convergent evidence)	"Evidence based on the relationship between test scores and other measures of the same construct" (AERA, APA, & NCME, 1999, p. 174). A term referring to the relation between the scores on the current test and other tests that measure the same construct (AERA, APA, & NCME, 1999).
Internal consistency coefficient	"An index of the reliability of test scores derived from the statistical interrelationships of responses among item responses or scores on separate parts of the test" (AERA, APA, & NCME, 1999, p. 176). A term used to describe the consistency of items within a test to measure the intended construct (AERA, APA, & NCME, 1999).
Interrater reliability (interrater agreement)	"The consistency with which two or more judges rate the work or performance of test takers; sometimes referred to as *inter-rater reliability*" (AERA, APA, & NCME, 1999, p. 177).
Test–retest reliability (test–retest stability)	"A reliability coefficient obtained by administering the same test a second time to the same group after a time interval and correlating the two sets of scores" (AERA, APA, & NCME, 1999, p. 183).
Validity	"The degree to which accumulated evidence and theory support specific interpretations of test scores entailed by proposed uses of a test" (AERA, APA, & NCME, 1999, p. 184).

Conditional probabilities statistics		Proficiency (outcome)	
		Below (risk present)	At or above (risk not present)
	Identified by a given screening tool (risk indicator present)	*a*	*b*
	Not identified by a given screening tool (risk indicator absent)	*c*	*d*

(cont.)

TABLE 1.1. *(cont.)*	
Psychometrics	**Definition**
Negative predictive power	"The proportion of those classified as low risk who do not develop the outcome and equals" the number who were not found to be at risk when, in fact, they were not divided by the number of students not found to be at risk when, in fact, they were plus the number of students not found to be at risk who were not (Severson & Walker, 2002, p. 38): $NPP = d/(c + d)$.
Positive predictive power	"The proportion of those classified as high risk who develop the outcome and equals" the number who were identified at risk and were, in fact, at risk, divided by the number found to be at risk who were at risk plus those found to be at risk when, in fact, they were not (Severson & Walker, 2002, p. 38): $PPP = a/(a + b)$.
Sensitivity	"In classification of disorders, the proportion of cases in which a disorder is detected when it is, in fact, present" (AERA, APA, & NCME, 1999, p. 182). The proportion equals the number who were found to be at risk and were at risk divided by the number who were found to be at risk and were not plus those who were found to be at risk and were (Severson & Walker, 2002): True positive rate = $a/(a + c)$.
Specificity	"In classification of disorders, the proportion of cases in which a diagnosis of disorder is rejected when rejection is warranted" (AERA, APA, & NCME, 1999, p. 182). The proportion equals the number who were found not to be at risk and were not divided by the number who were found to be at risk and were not plus those who were found to be at risk and were (Severson & Walker, 2002): True negative rate = $d/(b + d)$.
Base rate	Prevalence = $(a + c)/(a + b + c + d)$
Percentage of accuracy in classification	Hit rate (accuracy) = $(a + d)/(a + b + c + d)$

Note. Based on American Educational Research Association, American Psychological Association, and National Council for Measurement in Education (1999) and Severson and Walker (2002).

Because each school and each district have varying resources and needs in terms of specific behavioral challenges (e.g., violence toward others [externalizing behaviors] and anger turned inward [internalizing behaviors]), we cannot advocate for one specific screening tool. Instead, we write this book to help guide the decision-making process for which screening tool to adopt. Currently, there are *no* books available to the research and teaching communities that offer an overview of validated systematic behavior screening tools providing descriptions; procedures for administering, scoring, and interpreting; benefits and limitations; and illustrations of each measure. The intent of this book is to address this void. We have written a straightforward, practical, user-friendly book that synthesizes the information available on screening tools.

In this chapter, we provided you with an overview of the importance of conducting systematic screenings for behavior, and explained how to implement these tools within the context of three-tiered models of prevention. We emphasized the importance of analyzing academic and behavioral data in tandem with one another in a user-friendly manner.

In each of the next six chapters, we feature a validated screening tool: Chapter 2, Systematic Screening for Behavior Disorders (Walker & Severson, 1992); Chapter

3, Early Screening Project (Walker, Severson, & Feil, 1995); Chapter 4, Student Risk Screening Scale (Drummond, 1994); Chapter 5, Strengths and Difficulties Questionnaire (Goodman, 1997); Chapter 6: BASC-2 Behavior and Emotional Screening System (Kamphaus & Reynolds, 2007b); and Chapter 7, Social Skills Improvement System: Performance Screening Guide (Elliott & Gresham, 2007b). We then conclude with Chapter 8: Getting Started: A Few Concluding Thoughts to Guide the Decision-Making Process, to assist you as you select a screening tool and begin this process.

We begin each chapter with a description of the screening tool and instructions on how to complete the screener. Next, we synthesize the supporting research for each measure to provide the reader with information on reliability and validity. We then provide an evenhanded discussion of the strengths and challenges of preparing, administering, scoring, and interpreting the findings of each screening tool. We conclude each chapter with illustrations of how to use screening data to (1) monitor the overall level of risk over time and (2) inform instruction, including how to provide students with evidence-based secondary (Tier 2) or tertiary (Tier 3) supports. Illustrations are offered from preschool through high school as appropriate for each screening tool. In reading the illustrations provided, we want you to be aware that while some illustrations are completely fictitious, others are adapted from actual studies conducted as part of ongoing school–university partnerships with Vanderbilt University and Arizona State University. When appropriate, we refer readers wanting more details to the actual studies. Also, some illustrations are written primarily for the teaching community and others more for the research community, with the latter emphasizing how to conduct experimental studies (using single-case and group methodologies) within the context of CI3T models.

In Chapter 8, we provide information on how to select a screening tool that is psychometrically sound, socially valid, and responsive to your school's culture, needs, and values characteristic of their given context (e.g., a rural middle school interested in identifying a student with antisocial tendencies). We included a set of self-assessment questions to be used by school-site leadership teams to guide the decision-making process.

In terms of how to read this book, one option is to read from cover to cover. Another option is to (1) read Chapter 1 to obtain an overview of the main considerations when selecting a behavior screening tool, (2) read the chapters dedicated to the two or three behavior screeners you are interested in learning more about before making a decision, and (3) conclude by reading Chapter 8 to assist with your decision making. Whether you move to Chapter 2 or Chapter 7 or read the book cover to cover, we encourage you to grab a cup of green tea and read on!

Systematic Screening
for Behavior Disorders

This chapter introduces the Systematic Screening for Behavior Disorders (SSBD; Walker & Severson, 1992), a multiple-gating system designed to detect elementary-age students in first through sixth grades who have either internalizing or externalizing behavior patterns. Since its introduction, the SSBD has been hailed as the gold standard of systematic screening in that it uses a graduated input system (Kauffman, 2001). This instrument holds particular benefit in that it was one of the first highly practical tools available to detect students with internalizing behaviors—an often overlooked group of individuals who tend to suffer quietly in the school setting (Morris et al., 2002).

In essence, this instrument, like other screening tools, holds the potential to help school-site leadership teams move away from reactive response and toward proactive service delivery approaches (Walker et al., 2004). Rather than waiting until student behavior exceeds teacher tolerance levels before making a referral for assistance, school-site leadership teams have tools such as the SSBD to search for (and ultimately support) students who show soft signs of behavior problems that are predictive of future negative outcomes (Lane, 2007). In this way, teachers can access support before their motive shifts from "refer–consult–intervene" to "refer–test–place elsewhere" (Lane, Mahdavi, & Borthwick-Duffy, 2003).

To this end, the SSBD was developed based on seven fundamental assumptions (Walker & Severson, 1992), briefly outlined here:

1. Teachers are far more likely to recognize and refer students with externalizing behaviors for assistance compared with those with internalizing behaviors. Even still, students with externalizing behavior problems tend to be under-referred.
2. Teachers are excellent tests; teacher judgments of student behavior are accurate, valid, cost-effective (and underutilized) resources for identifying students with externalizing or internalizing behaviors (Lane, 2003a).

3. It is possible to conduct relatively simple screening procedures in school settings that make it possible to (1) capitalize on the numerous opportunities teachers have to make observations and judgments about students' full range of behavior in a variety of settings and (2) provide all students with an equal opportunity to be identified as having externalizing or internalizing behavior patterns (Severson & Walker, 2002).

4. The combination of teacher ranking and ratings (of adaptive and maladaptive behaviors) as well as direct observations is important in adequately assessing students' behavior in terms of screening, identification, and determining supports.

5. Academic engaged time (AET) is an index of teacher-related adjustment in the classroom setting and students' social behavior is an index of peer-related adjustment in recreational settings, with both being equally important markers of adjustment in the school setting (Walker, Irvin, Noell, & Singer, 1992; Walker, McConnell, & Clarke, 1985).

6. Externalizing and internalizing behaviors are broad-band dimensions of behavior concerns that include most of the typical behavior disorders observed in the school setting (Achenbach, 1991).

7. Given the long-term stability of maladaptive behaviors and the deleterious outcomes that confront students with externalizing and/or internalizing behaviors who do not receive support, early detection is critical because it is the first step to receiving supports (Walker, Golly, McLane, & Kimmich, 2005).

The SSBD is a feasible and effective method in which the screening process embodies each of these assumptions, with an overall goal of preventing the development of emotional and behavioral disorders (EBD) that may (or may not) require supports through the Individuals with Disabilities Education Improvement Act (2004) under the label of emotional disturbance (ED). This tool capitalizes on the strengths of the general education teacher to detect students who may need additional supports beyond the primary prevention plan in the form of secondary and tertiary levels of prevention (Lane, Kalberg, & Menzies, 2009).

We begin this chapter with an overview of the SSBD, including step-by-step directions for how to complete this multistage assessment and responses to frequently asked questions regarding logistical considerations. Next, we synthesize the supporting research conducted with the SSBD, including studies (1) examining the reliability and validity of this tool as well as (2) demonstrating how to use the SSBD to identify students who might require secondary (Tier 2) or tertiary (Tier 3) supports. Then we provide a balanced discussion of the strengths and considerations associated with preparation, administration, scoring, and interpretation. We conclude this chapter with three illustrations. The first illustration explains how to monitor the overall level of risk over time. The second demonstrates how to use the screening data in a three-tiered model of support in an elementary school to identify students for targeted supports (Tier 2). The third illustration shows how to use academic and behavioral data in tandem to identify and support students with dual challenges.

An Overview of the SSBD

We begin by describing each of the three stages constituting this screening tool. Then we provide information on logistical considerations such as preparing, administering, scoring, and interpreting.

Description

The SSBD is a cost-effective, empirically validated multiple-gating system designed to detect elementary-age students in first through sixth grades with externalizing or internalizing behavior disorders. The instrument includes three stages: nomination and rank ordering, teacher ratings, and direct observations. The process begins with classroom teachers evaluating all students in their classroom on two dimensions—externalizing and internalizing behaviors—with the use of operational definitions, examples, and nonexamples. Moreover, initial stages begin with teacher nominations and ratings followed by independent observations in structured (seatwork) and non-structured (playground) settings in subsequent stages (see Figure 2.1). Each teacher is given a packet that includes (1) Stage 1 nomination procedures (four pages copied on white paper), (2) three sets of Stage 2 ratings for students with internalizing behaviors (four pages each × three copies on green paper), and (3) three sets of Stage 2 ratings for students with externalizing behaviors (four pages each × three copies on blue paper). Stage 3 papers are not distributed to the teacher.

Stage 1: Nomination and Rank Ordering

In Stage 1, each classroom teacher is given the full set of instructions describing the three stages. Then the teacher reads information on how to rank-order the internalizing and externalizing dimensions. Specifically, the teacher reads the full description of internalizing behaviors, including the definition, examples, and nonexamples. Then, in the first column, the teacher enters the names of 10 students in the class whose *characteristic behavior patterns* are most like internalizing behaviors.

Next, the teacher rank-orders his or her students on the internalizing list from *most like* (receiving a score of 1) to *least like* (receiving a score of 10) the dimensions. This step is done to determine which students' characteristic behavior patterns correspond most closely with the description of internalizing as provided in the behavioral profiles.

This two-step process of nominating and ranking is repeated to rank-order students on the externalizing dimension. It is important to note that students can appear on only one list (internalizing or externalizing). The end result is two rank-ordered

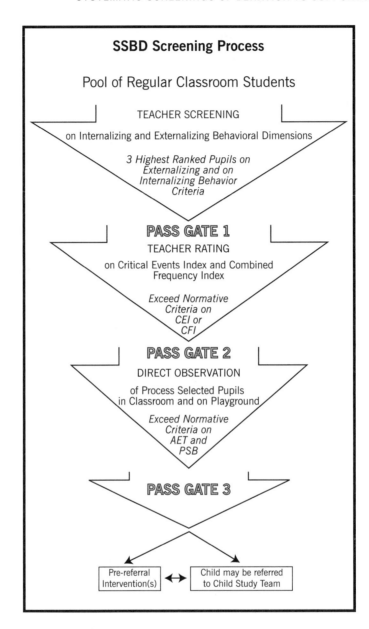

FIGURE 2.1. SSBD multiple-gating assessment procedure for identification of students with behavior disorders. From Walker and Severson (1992, p. 4). Copyright 1992 by Sopris West, Inc. Reprinted by permission.

lists: one for students with internalizing behaviors and a second for students with externalizing behaviors.

The six highest ranked students (three on each dimension) pass through Gate 1 into Stage 2. However, if a teacher feels additional students warrant consideration (e.g., students ranked in the fourth or fifth position for a given dimension), they could be moved through Gate 1 as well.

Stage 2: Teacher Ratings

In Stage 2, teachers complete additional measures on only the students who passed through Gate 1. Specifically, they complete two rating scales, the Critical Events Index (CEI) and the Combined Frequency Index (CFI), to gain a more complete picture of these students' typical behavior patterns on both rarely and frequently occurring behaviors. Both instruments are nationally normed tools that offer cutoff scores for identifying students as at risk for behavior or learning difficulties.

The CEI is a teacher-completed checklist of 33 high-intensity, low-frequency behaviors (e.g., *steals*, *sets fires*, *vomits after eating*). After filling in brief demographic information (including the date, teacher name, school name, student name, gender, grade, and Stage 1 SSBD ranking [1, 2, or 3]), teachers evaluate each student on the 33 items, recording the presence of any behavior known to have occurred in the last 6 months by placing a checkmark next to the behavior. Two blank spaces (Items 34 and 35) are provided to allow teachers to write in any other extreme behaviors that do not appear previously in the checklist among Items 1–33.

The CFI, another teacher-completed checklist, assesses low-intensity, high-frequency behaviors on adaptive (12 items) and maladaptive (11 item) domains. Sample adaptive items include *follows established classroom rules*, *does seatwork as directed*, and *initiates positive social interactions with peers*. These items are rated on a 5-point Likert-type scale ranging from 1 (*never*) to 5 (*frequently*), with total scores ranging from 12 to 60. Sample maladaptive items include *manipulates other children and/or situations to get his/her own way*, *is excessively demanding*, and *pouts or sulks*. These items are rated on the same Likert-type scale, with total scores ranging from 11 to 55.

Data from the CEI and CFI are used to determine whether students exceed normative criteria. Students exceeding normative criteria pass through Gate 2 into Stage 3, the final and most intensive level of screening. However, it should be noted that often schools implement only Stages 1 and 2 of the SSBD because of the level of resources required for Stage 3, as described next (Kalberg et al., 2010; Lane, Kalberg, Bruhn, Mahoney, & Driscoll, 2008; Lane, Little, et al., 2009).

Stage 3: Direct Observation

In Stage 3, a professional other than the classroom teacher conducts formal, systematic observations of students who pass through Gate 2 to confirm teacher ratings. This person may be a behavior specialist, a special education teacher, a school psychologist, or other site-level or district-level person with sufficient training and expertise to learn and implement the direct observation procedures according to the training guidelines provided (which includes a video training component).

The direct observations occur in two settings: classroom and playground. There should be two 15-minute observations in each setting conducted on separate days (e.g., one classroom and one playground observation on a given day), ideally not in the same week. In the classroom, the amount of AET is recorded on two separate occasions during seatwork time. On the playground, the quantity and quality of peer social behavior (PSB) are observed. The quantity of social interactions refers to the frequency of initiations and responses to peers, whereas the quality refers to the extent to which these initiations and responses are positive, negative, or neutral in nature. The manual includes a detailed, research-based approach to conducting these structured observations, including procedures for ensuring the reliability of the direct observation data collected. Information on each student's classroom and playground behavior is compared with the normative levels provided by age and gender. The SSBD norming sample is a national standardization sample, which allows for greater confidence in interpreting direct observation data. Students whose classroom and playground behavior deviates substantially from other same-gender and same-age students pass through the final gate and may be referred to the prereferral intervention team.

It should be noted that there is an optional procedure designed to further evaluate target students' behavior in relation to their peers. Namely, the authors recommend the classroom and playground observations also be conducted on a same-gender peer who is not referred for support who the teacher views as having typical behavior. This can be used as comparison information to evaluate the performance levels of students who do—and do not—pass through Stage 2. It is important that the teacher (and not the observer) select the typical peer for comparison purposes.

Logistical Issues

A number of logistical considerations require discussion. In the following sections, each consideration is framed in the form of a question, followed by recommendations from the technical manual as well as our own work.

When Should We Administer the SSBD?

The SSBD should be completed by teachers a minimum of 30 days after they have worked with students (Walker & Severson, 1992). This is a minimum time frame to make certain that they have enough familiarity with students' behavior before conducting the screening process.

Walker and Severson (1992) recommend conducting the screenings twice a school year: in the Fall and after Winter break. In this way, students are given two opportunities to be identified for additional supports, and it also facilitates screening of students who move into a school site after the onset of the academic year or whose behavior patterns change during a school year (Lane, Kalberg, et al., 2011).

In our school-based intervention work, we actually recommend conducting systematic screenings three times per year: 6 weeks after the onset of the school year, before Winter break, and again prior to the end of the academic year (Kalberg et al., 2010; Lane, Kalberg, Bruhn, et al., 2008; Lane, Kalberg, et al., 2011; Lane, Kalberg, Parks, et al., 2008). Fall data can be used to establish interventions immediately after the first screening is conducted. Another option is to use Winter data to determine responsiveness to the primary prevention plan. For example, students who still screen as exceeding normative criteria for either internalizing or externalizing behaviors can be identified as nonresponsive to primary prevention efforts (see Illustration 2). If screenings are conducted and analyzed prior to Winter break, secondary (e.g., social skills groups for students with internalizing behavior; Elliott & Gresham, 2007b) or tertiary (e.g., functional assessment-based interventions for students with externalizing behaviors; Umbreit et al., 2007) supports can be planned for the beginning of the Spring semester when students return from break. Spring screening data can be used to inform not only year-end performance but also plans for next year, such as class placements (e.g., making sure that not all students with higher than average externalizing behaviors are placed in the same fifth-grade classroom; Lane, Oakes, & Menzies, 2010).

We encourage school-site leadership teams to develop an assessment schedule (see, e.g., Table 2.1) that depicts the time frames for all assessments that occur as part of regular school practices. This information should be shared with teachers and support staff to facilitate their instructional planning.

How Do We Prepare Materials to Conduct the SSBD?

The SSBD kit contains all of the forms necessary to conduct the screening. Each teacher will need a packet that includes (1) Stage 1 materials to conduct the nominations and rankings (four pages for the entire class) and (2) Stage 2 materials that include the CEI and CFI rating scales (four pages for each of the six students who pass through the first gate). Stage 2 materials are color coded (as previously described), with the CEI and CFI materials copied on green paper to evaluate the top three ranked students on the internalizing dimension and on blue paper to evaluate the top three ranked students on the externalizing dimension.

Teachers will need this packet of materials along with a current class roster for each screening conducted (Fall, Winter, and Spring). It is very important that teachers have a current roster to ensure that all students are considered in the screening process because it is essential that all eligible students (e.g., enrolled at least 30 days) are evaluated at each screening time point.

Stage 3 materials are more involved, requiring training of professionals other than the classroom teacher who will conduct the direct observations of AET in the classroom and PSB on the playground. As with Stages 1 and 2, the SSBD kit includes all necessary information and materials to conduct Stage 3 activities, including

TABLE 2.1. WES Monthly Assessment Schedule

	Aug	Sept	Oct	Nov	Dec	Jan	Feb	Mar	Apr	May
		Quarter 1			Quarter 2		Quarter 3		Quarter 4	
School demographics										
Student demographics		×			×		×		×	
Academic measures										
STAR reading (Renaissance Learning, 2010)		× (2–5)			× (1)				× (1–5)	
AIMSweb reading		×				× (Jan)			×	
Writing prompt		× (K–5)			× (K–5)		× (K–4; 5 = State)		× (K–4; 5 = State)	
State achievement assessment									×	
Behavior measures										
Screener: SRSS (Drummond, 1994)		×			×				×	
Screener: SSBD (Walker & Severson, 1992)		×			×				×	
ODRs		×			×		×		×	
Attendance (tardies/absences)		×			×		×		×	
Referrals										
Special education General education intervention team		×			×		×		×	
Program measures										
Social validity (Primary Intervention Rating Scale: Lane, Kalberg, Bruhn, et al., 2009; Lane, Robertson, et al., 2002)		×					×			
School-Wide Evaluation Tool (Sugai, Lewis-Palmer, Todd, & Horner, 2001)							×			
Teacher-completed ratings of treatment integrity		×			×		×		×	
Direct observations of treatment integrity by an objective observer		×			×		×		×	

Note. From Lane, Kalberg, and Menzies (2009, Table 5.1, p. 105). Copyright 2009 by The Guilford Press. Adapted by permission.

operational definitions, data collection forms, training video, audio recording tape, and quizzes to establish conceptual mastery of the target behaviors. The only additional item necessary to purchase is a stopwatch that does not attract attention (i.e., does not beep or is not a flamboyant color).

How Do We Administer the SSBD?

Stages 1 and 2 can be conducted during a regularly scheduled faculty meeting. It is highly recommended that all teachers be together in a room to learn how to conduct the screening, answer any questions, and monitor the procedural fidelity with which the screening occurs (Walker & Severson, 1992). For example, it is important to make certain that (1) students are placed on either the internalizing or the externalizing list (not both); (2) students are ranked from *most like* (1) to *least like* (10); (3) the CEI and CFI are completed on the top three students with internalizing behavior patterns and the top three students with externalizing behavior patterns; (4) all items on the CEI and CFI are answered (if more than one item is omitted, it compromises the validity of the measure; Walker & Severson, 1992); (5) the CEI and CFI are scored using the correct criteria for students on the internalizing or externalizing dimension because the criteria are different for the two constructs; and (6) reliability is conducted on the scoring procedure to make certain that accurate decisions are made regarding the students who do and do not pass through Gate 2 to Stage 3. These are just a few common errors that warrant specific attention. It is important for the school-site facilitator to read the entire SSBD manual before beginning the screening process to ensure proper implementation (and, yes, we really do think the manual should be read in full before beginning the process).

After teachers become fluent in the process, it is not necessary to come together as a full faculty; instead, teachers can complete the screening Stage 1 and 2 forms on their own. However, it will be important to have a procedure at the school site for working with new teachers to complete the screening tools as intended.

In terms of Stage 3, the procedures are more intensive. However, as mentioned previously, the SSBD manual provides very thorough directions for Stage 3 procedures. There are procedures in place to make certain the individuals conducting PSB and AET observations have a firm conceptual and behavioral mastery of the material. First, conceptual mastery is demonstrated using quizzes to make certain the observers are clear on the conceptual piece (e.g., do they know what counts as engaged or not engaged?). Then, after the observers have demonstrated 100% accuracy on the conceptual component, there are steps to ensure mastery of the behavioral component. These include role-playing techniques, videotaped practice, and in vivo classroom and playground sessions, occurring in this order. The authors also recommend that agreement levels between observers (interobserver agreement [IOA]) be monitored carefully and continuously to make certain the data are accurate. There are different methods of getting the observers to become reliable in their direct observations. In general, it is best to establish observer accuracy against a standard and then move forward with determining IOA among observers (Walker & Severson, 1992).

How Do We Score and Interpret the SSBD?

Stage 1 does not require any scoring because the process involves rank ordering students whose behavior is most characteristic of either the internalizing or the externalizing dimension. Although there is no addition to verify, we do recommend confirming that students are placed on only one list (internalizing or externalizing) and the correct top three students on each dimensions are passed through Gate 1 to Stage 2.

After teachers have completed the CEI and CFI on the six students in Stage 2, each rating scale needs to be scored. For the CEI, checked items are summed, with total score ranging from 0 to 35. The CFI yields two total scores: one for the maladaptive domain (range: 12–60) and a second for the adaptive domain (range: 11–55). Before moving forward with the remaining steps in determining students who should move through Gate 2 to Stage 3 direct observations, we encourage people to confirm the scoring for each of these three total scores to ensure reliability. The SSBD scoring and administration manual provides two decision flowcharts, one for students nominated on the internalizing dimension and a second for students on the externalizing dimension. Using these flowcharts (also referred to as decision trees), scores are reviewed to determine whether students exceed normative criteria for the given dimension. If so, they are moved into Stage 3 for direct observations. It should be noted, however, the occurrence of even just one critical event listed on the CEI is cause for concern and warrants consideration (Walker & Severson, 1992). Also, the manual provides tables for converting raw scores to a standard score and percentile ranking for each Stage 2 measure (a useful tool for researchers as well as practitioners).

In Stage 3, there are extensive directions with checks to ensure direct observation data in the classroom (AET) and playground (PSB) settings are reliable. We encourage you to review the specific procedures for not only collecting direct observation data but also for IOA to ensure the data collected are accurate. When evaluating data from Stage 3 direction observations, students' AET scores and PSB (percentage of time spent in parallel play, percentage of time alone, and total percentage of time involved in negative behavior) are used to determine whether or not they pass through Gate 3, which results in a referral to the prereferral intervention team. Although more detailed information is provided in the manual, it is important for all teachers to know that academic engagement in typical general education classrooms ranges from 65 to 80% (Walker & Severson, 1992).

We cannot emphasize enough how important accuracy of the data collected in each stage is because the decisions made at each stage directly impact the extent to which students are considered at subsequent stages in the SSBD screening process. Also, we highly recommend the school-site leadership team devote sufficient time to reviewing the more detailed guidelines for interpreting the scores at each stage in this multiple-gating screening process. Ultimately, this information is used to make decisions regarding how to (1) identify students who require supports beyond primary prevention efforts and (2) monitor the overall level of performance over time at a given school. We refer you to illustrations presented later in this chapter that depict both uses.

How Can We Use This Information at Our School Site?

Information from the SSBD can be used in a number of ways. First, it can be used to identify students who may require additional supports in the form of secondary or tertiary prevention efforts: either students who exceed normative criteria by passing through Gate 2 or, as described in the SSBD manual, students who pass through Gate 3. Second, the information can also be used to monitor risk over time for the school as a whole as well as for individual students. At the end of this chapter, we provide three illustrations adapted from actual schools whose school-site leadership teams elected to implement the SSBD data as part of regular school practices. The illustrations provide concrete examples of how to (1) monitor the overall level of risk present over time at a given school and (2) analyze data from the SSBD (independently [Illustrations 1 and 2] and in conjunction with academic data [Illustration 3]) to identify students for secondary and tertiary levels of prevention within the context of a comprehensive, integrated, three-tiered (CI3T) model of prevention.

How Much Does the SSBD Cost, and Where Can I Order It?

The SSBD is a low-cost instrument available for purchase from Cambium Learning/Sopris West (*store.cambiumlearning.com*). The full kit costs less than $150 (the screening forms less than $20) and includes (1) the instruments (which are reproducible), (2) the users' guide and administration manual, (3) observer training manual (inclusive of a videotape and audiotape), and (4) technical manual. All materials come in a large three-ring binder, which makes preparation activities quite simple.

Next, we provide an overview of the supporting research for the SSBD, specifically, information on the psychometric features of the SSBD as well as on how the SSBD has been used in research studies to identify students who are nonresponsive to primary prevention efforts.

Supporting Research

Reliability and Validity

Several field trials of the SSBD screening procedures have demonstrated the instrument to be reliable, valid, and feasible (e.g., Lane, Little, et al., 2009; Walker, Severson, Nicholson, Kehle, Jenson, & Clark, 1994; Walker et al., 1990). Collectively, these findings have established the reputation of the SSBD as a leading tool for use at the elementary level (Gresham et al., 2000; Kauffman, 2001). The SSBD is sensitive in distinguishing between students with externalizing, internalizing, or certified emotional disturbances and typically developing students (e.g., Walker et al., 1990, 1994).

The SSBD technical manual provides extensive information on the initial development and field-testing activities as well as replication studies conducted by Walker and colleagues in a number of sites across the country. The validation and norming of the SSBD were supported (in part) by an Office of Special Education Programs field-initiated grant to Hill Walker and Herb Severson. It is beyond the scope of this chapter to reiterate the instrument's development procedures and validation studies for Stage 1, 2, and 3 tools. However, we have summarized a few of the reliability and validity studies published in peer-reviewed journals (see Table 2.2).

The collective findings from initial studies conducted by Walker and colleagues suggest that instruments in each stage are reliable, as evidenced by test–retest stability estimates for Stage 1 and 2 instruments, interrrater agreement for Stage 1 and 2 instruments, and IOA for Stage 3 direct observation measures (Todis, Severson, & Walker, 1990; Walker et al., 1988, 1990).

Furthermore, findings of these studies indicate that the SSBD is also valid. For example, studies have established the discriminative validity of Stage 2 measures in differentiating among students with externalizing, internalizing, and typical (control) behavior patterns (Walker et al., 1988). Also, convergent and concurrent validity with a number of measures has been established. For example, concurrent validity has been established with the Child Behavior Checklist on the externalizing dimension for (1) Stage 2 measures as well as (2) AET, negative social interaction, PSB, and positive social interaction (Walker et al., 1988). More recent studies also showed evidence of convergent validity with the SSBD and the Scale for Assessing Emotional Disturbance (SAED; Epstein & Cullinan, 1998), Behavioral and Emotional Rating Scale (BERS; Epstein & Sharma 1998), and the Student Risk Screening Scale (SRSS; Drummond, 1994). Specifically, results of a study of 123 kindergarten and first-grade students as rated by 21 teachers from three elementary schools in a small midwestern city yielded correlation coefficients ranging from a low of .105 (SAED Unhappiness/Depressed and SSBD Maladaptive) and a high of .810 (SAED Inappropriate Behavior and SSBD Maladaptive). SAED Overall Competence and Unhappiness/Depression subscales did not correlate significantly with SSBD Maladaptive (Esptein, Nordness, Cullinan & Hertzog, 2002). Adequate convergent validity was also established between the BERS and SSBD in a study of 220 kindergarten and first-grade students as rated by 37 teachers in three elementary schools in a medium-size city in the Midwest (Epstein, Nordness, Nelson, & Hertzog, 2002). Namely, there was a moderate to high relation between all subscales, with a low of –.263 (BERS Intrapersonal Strengths and SSBD Maladaptive) and a high of –.798 (BERS Interpersonal Strengths and SSBD Maladaptive), with BERS strengths items more related to externalizing behaviors. Finally, two studies of concurrent validity of the SSBD and SRSS (one with 562 K–2 students in seven inclusive elementary schools in middle Tennessee and a second with 2,588 K–5 students in five inclusive schools in middle Tennessee) indicated similar findings. Both studies indicated the SRSS is more accurate for detecting externalizing (improving change estimates by approximately 45%) than internalizing (improving change estimates by approximately 26–30%) behavior, as measured by the SSBD (Lane, Little, et al., 2009; Lane, Kalberg, Lambert, Crnobori, & Bruhn, 2010).

Collectively, these studies provide evidence that the SSBD is a reliable and valid tool for use in the elementary setting. Furthermore, a few studies conducted in the last few years suggest that a modified version of the SSBD may also hold promise for

TABLE 2.2. Reliability and Validity Studies of the SSBD

Citation	Purpose	Description of participants and schools	Reliability	Validity
Walker et al. (1988)	Provides a rationale for and description of the SSBD. Reports results of (1) development activities and (2) a year-long trial test of the efficacy in one elementary school	Year-long trial: $N = 454$ students; 1–5 grades; ethnicity not reported; $N = 18$ teachers Year-long trial: 1 elementary school: Springfield, OR	**Development research** Stage 1: Established interrater agreement and test–retest stability Stage 2: Introduced extensive item development procedures Stage 3: Established IOA for AET (.90–.99) and PSB (.78–90) **Year-long trial** Stage 1: Established test–retest stability for (1) students placed in same grouping and (2) between Time 1 and Time 2 teacher rankings Stage 2: Established stability of top three ranked students (.88 adaptive; .83 maladaptive) and internal consistency (.85 and .88 adaptive; .82 and .87 maladaptive) Stage 3: Established IOA for AET (.96) and PSB (.84)	**Development research** Stage 1: Established sensitivity, with 9 of 10 students with BD being within the highest three ranked on externalizing dimension Stage 3: AET discriminated between 16 antisocial (68%) and 19 at-risk control (85%) fifth-grade students **Year-long trial** Stage 2: Discriminative validity (externalizing, internalizing, controls); concurrent validity with CBCL on externalizing dimension; Stage 3: Discriminative validity among externalizing and internalizing students and controls on AET, alone, positive social interaction, negative social interaction, total positive behavior, total negative behavior Concurrent validity with CBCL externalizing dimension for AET, negative social interaction, and positive social interaction
Todis et al. (1990)	Describes the critical events that characterize students identified as having internalizing or externalizing in SSBD Stage 1	Study 1: 158 teachers rated > 850 students in grades 1–5 on Stages 1 and 2; $N = 33$ students (18 externalizing; 15 internalizing); 15 elementary schools in one district in Springfield, OR		Study 1: Results offer profile of behavior patterns of students with externalizing and internalizing behaviors Study 2: 10 items discriminated between students with externalizing

(cont.)

TABLE 2.2. *(cont.)*

Citation	Purpose	Description of participants and schools	Reliability	Validity
Todis et al. (1990) *(cont.)*	Study 1: Original form of CEI (separate lists for items) Study 2: Subsequent form (all items on one list)	Study 2: Teachers rated 912 students in grades 1–5; $N = 41$ students (27 externalizing; 14 internalizing) Two samples: one from Springfield (five elementary; 33% F/ RP lunches) and one from Parkrose (five elementary, 35% F/RP lunches), OR		(ignores teacher reprimands; is physically aggressive; damages other's property; steals; uses obscene language, swears; has tantrums; makes lewd or obscene gestures; demonstrates obsessive–compulsive behavior) and internalizing (exhibits painful shyness; is teased, neglected by peers); highlights need to assess both types of students on items that are descriptive of these dimensions
Walker et al. (1990)	Two studies reported focusing on validation, replication, normative information Study 1: Normative and validity questions (factorial, criterion-related, and discriminant) Study 2: Replication and validity	Study 1: 158 teachers rated > 850 students in grades 1–5 on Stages 1 and 2 15 elementary schools in one district in Springfield, OR (33% F/ RP lunches) Study 2: 40 teachers, 216 general education students in grades 1–5, 54 students with SED who were mainstreamed 17 schools in 2 districts: one urban and one suburban, WA	Study 2: Established test–retest stability of SSBD Stage 1 and 2 measures for 40 teachers	Study 1: Provided evidence of discriminative validity (subject group differences) and criterion-related validity between SSBD and archival school record profiles Study 2: Replicated the results of Study 1 and established SSBD's sensitivity to behavioral characteristics of students previously certified as ED who were mainstreamed
Epstein, Nordness, Cullinan, et al. (2002)	Two studies reported Study 1: Long-term test–retest stability of the SAED Study 2: Convergent validity of the SAED with subscales of the SSBD*	$N = 123$ students; K–1 grade; $N = 21$ teachers Three elementary schools in small midwestern city		Convergent validity: results of correlation coefficients ranged from a low of .105 (SAED Unhappiness/Depressed and SSBD Maladaptive); and a high of .810 (SAED Inappropriate Behavior and SSBD Maladaptive); SAED Overall Competence and Unhappiness/ Depression subscales did not correlate significantly with SSBD Maladaptive

(cont.)

TABLE 2.2. *(cont.)*

Citation	Purpose	Description of participants and schools	Reliability	Validity
Epstein, Nordness, Nelson, et al. (2002)	Two convergent validity studies reported Study 1: BERS with subscales of the SSBD* Study 2: BERS with subscales of the SAED	$N = 220$ students; K–1 grade; $N = 37$ teachers Three elementary schools in medium-size city in Midwest		Adequate convergent validity established; there was a moderate–high relationship between all subscales, with a low of −.263 (BERS Intrapersonal Strengths and SSBD Maladaptive) and a high of −.798 (BERS Interpersonal Strengths and SSBD Maladaptive), with BERS strengths items more related to externalizing behaviors
Lane, Little, et al. (2009)	Examine extent to which SRSS is equally sensitive and specific in identifying students with externalizing and internalizing behaviors as measured by SSBD	$N = 562$ students; K–2 grades; 94.77% white; $N = 84$ teachers Seven inclusive elementary schools in middle TN; 0.08–19.4% economic disadvantage rate		Concurrent: ROC curve, conditional probabilities, and kappa coefficients suggest SRSS is more accurate for detecting externalizing than internalizing behavior as measured by the SSBD; predicting externalizing: AUC .95; predicting internalizing: AUC .80
Lane, Kalberg, et al. (2010)	Internal consistency and test–retest stability of the SRSS over three administrations in one academic year; concurrent validity of SRSS and SSBD	$N = 2,588$ students in K–5; 90.68% white; $N = 131$ teachers Five inclusive elementary schools in middle TN; 5.50–10.57% of students received special education; 6.9–32.9% were economically disadvantaged	Internal consistency: .80, .82, .81 Test–retest stability: .73 (8 weeks, Fall to Winter); .68 (24 weeks, Fall to Spring); .74 (16 weeks, Winter to Spring).	Concurrent: ROC curves suggest SRSS is more accurate for detecting externalizing than internalizing behavior as measured by the SSBD; predicting externalizing: AUC .95, .95, .96; predicting internalizing: AUC .76, .78, and .82

Note. Asterisks (*) indicate only results relevant to the SSBD are reported. IOA, interobserver agreement; AET, academic engaged time; PSB, peer social behaviors; BD, behavior disorders; CBCL, Child Behavior Checklist (Achenbach, 1991); CEI, Critical Events Index; F/RP, free and reduced-price; SED, serious emotional disturbance; ED, emotional disturbance; SAED, Scale for Assessing Emotional Disturbance (Epstein & Cullinan, 1998); BERS, Behavioral and Emotional Rating Scale (Epstein & Sharma, 1998); ROC, receiver operating characteristics; AUC, the area under the curve.

use in the middle school setting (Caldarella, Young, Richardson, Young, & Young, 2008; Richardson, Caldarella, Young, Young, & Young, 2009).

Applications of the SSBD

We now highlight a few applications of the SSBD as presented in published, peer-reviewed articles to demonstrate how the SSBD has been used in the research community to identify and support students who require supports beyond primary prevention efforts (see Table 2.3). Specifically, in Table 2.3, you will see studies conducted within the context of three-tiered models of prevention using the SSBD as one of the measures to identify and support students beyond the primary prevention plan. For example, studies focus on secondary (Tier 2) supports in the area of reading (Lane, Little, Redding-Rhodes, Phillips, & Welsh, 2007), writing (Lane, Harris, et al., 2008), and social–behavioral skills (Cheney, Flower, & Templeton, 2008). In addition, there is one study reported focusing on tertiary (Tier 3) supports, in this case two first-grade boys (one identified as at risk for EBD according to the SSBD and a second receiving services for ED) who benefited from functional assessment-based interventions implemented by teachers who were job-sharing (Lane, Eisner, et al., 2009). We encourage you to examine the core features of these studies highlighted in Table 2.3, including (1) the students identified for the extra support (e.g., grade level) as well as the characteristics of the schools in which the secondary and tertiary supports were conducted (e.g., locale); (2) a brief description of the intervention, including the name of the intervention and the frequency with which it was conducted and by whom (e.g., teacher, paraprofessional, research assistant); (3) the specific schoolwide data collected as part of regular school practices analyzed to identify nonresponders who might benefit from the extra support (note the precision of this information—very necessary!); (4) the design used to determine whether the intervention resulted in changes in student performance, the specific behaviors (academic, behavioral, or social) measured to determine responsiveness to the secondary support, treatment integrity data (to see the degree to which the intervention was implemented as intended; Lane & Beebe-Frankenberger, 2004), and social validity data (to see what people thought about the goals, procedures, and outcomes; Kazdin, 1977; Wolf, 1978); and (5) a brief statement of the results. This information can be very useful in gathering some ideas about how to implement and evaluate practices (especially those that are evidence based) at your school site.

In addition, there are other applications of the SSBD for use within three-tiered models of prevention. For example, Walker, Cheney, Stage, and Blum (2005) used the SSBD with three schools involved in the BEACONS Project at the University of Washington. Each school implemented positive behavior supports for a minimum of 3 years, with the primary prevention plan well established. Teachers at each school completed Stages 1 and 2 of the SSBD in October. School-site teams used the information from the SSBD along with information on office discipline referral (ODR) earned and academic performance to link students to programs and supports that already existed in their schools (e.g., homework clubs, tutoring, social skills groups, school counseling).

				Design and	
Study	Participants and setting	Support and description	Schoolwide data: Entry criteria	monitoring procedures	Results
Lane, Little, et al. (2007)	Seven first-grade students; all white Two general education classrooms in two schools that subscribed to inclusive education in rural middle TN	Reading intervention: Peer-Assisted Learning Strategies (Fuchs, Fuchs, Mathes, & Simmons, 1997); identified students meet 3 days/week during literacy block in which classroom teachers conducted 30-minute lessons 4 days/week over 7-week period (14 intervention hours)	Students were either (1) in control condition of a Tier 2 intervention during kindergarten ($n = 4$) or (2) nonresponsive to a Tier 2 reading intervention administered during kindergarten ($n = 2$) or did not maintain gains over Summer ($n = 1$) Reading: WJIII ≤ 25th percentile reading cluster Behavior: SSBD (externalizing or internalizing); SRSS (moderate or high risk); or TRF (aggression; borderline or clinical)	Multiple baseline Academic behavior: DIBELS: decoding (NWF) and ORF Behavior: academic engagement using direct observation procedures Treatment integrity Social validity	Sustained improvements in ORF, with four students demonstrating improvements in engagement
Lane, Harris, et al. (2008)	Six second-grade students; four white, two black Large inclusive elementary school in rural middle TN	Writing intervention: Self-Regulated Strategy Development for story writing (Graham & Harris, 2005); identified students meet 3 days/week when deemed appropriate by teachers and administrators, during which research assistants conducted 30-minute lessons 3–4 days/week over 3- to 6-week period (10–15 sessions)	Identified using schoolwide data: Writing: TOWL-3—story construction ≤ 25th percentile Behavior: SSBD (externalizing or internalizing Stage 2); or SRSS (moderate or high risk)	Multiple probe during baseline Academic behavior: writing prompts Treatment integrity Social validity	Sustained improvements, story completeness, length, and quality for all students
Cheney et al. (2008)	127 K–3 receiving CCE who were in treatment condition 11 schools in three districts in WA, where CCE intervention was implemented	Social-behavior intervention: CCE CCE coach met with students in the morning (20–40 minutes); tracked their progress using DPRs; conducted period checks in the classroom, playground, and cafeteria; and met with students at end of day to check progress (20–40 minutes); minimum of 80 days participation, with minimum of 64 days of DPR completed over 1 school year	Identified for participation using SSBD (meeting or exceeding criteria on Stage 2)	Withdrawal design behavior: DPR; problem behavior (Social Skills Rating System; [Problem Behavior Scale] Gresham & Elliott, 1990); special education eligibility Treatment integrity	Results indicated 67% of students responded; 91% of responders were not identified for special education and > 50% showed decreases in problem behaviors

TABLE 2.3. Applications of the SSBD: Identifying and Supporting Students

(cont.)

TABLE 2.3. *(cont.)*

Study	Participants and setting	Support and description	Schoolwide data: Entry criteria	Design and monitoring procedures	Results
Lane, Eisner, et al. (2009)	Two first-grade students; one general education and one special education services for ED One general education classroom where teachers job-shared, in middle TN	Behavior intervention: Functional Assessment-Based Intervention (Umbreit, Ferro, Liaupsin, & Lane, 2007) Identified students received intervention designed (1) based on function of their undesirable behavior (2) to improve the environment, as both students were capable of performing the tasks but environment could benefit from modifications Interventions included (1) antecedent adjustments, (2) reinforcement adjustments, and (3) extinction components	Teacher nominations confirmed by behavior screening data Behavior: SSBD (externalizing) and SRSS (high risk)	Withdrawal design Behavior: off-task and AET behavior using direct observation procedures Treatment integrity Social validity	Results indicated functional relation between introduction of intervention and changes in AET, with increased AET sustaining into maintenance phase

Note. WJIII, Woodcock–Johnson Test of Achievement III (Woodcock, Mather, & McGrew, 2001); TRF, Teacher Report Form (Achenbach, 1991); DIBELS, Dynamic Indicators of Basic Early Literacy Skills (Good & Kaminski, 2002); NWF, nonsense word fluency; TOWL-3, Test of Written Language–3 (Hammill & Larsen, 1996); CCE, Check, Connect, and Expect; DPR, daily progress reports; ORF, oral reading fluency; AET, academic engaged time.

Kamps and colleagues also used the SSBD in their research. Specifically, they used the SSBD to identify students at risk for EBD and then compared the extent to which the primary prevention program was effective for students with or at risk for EBD (Kamps, Kravits, Rauch, Kamps, & Chung, 2000; Kamps, Kravitz, Stolze, & Swaggart, 1999). The primary prevention program included classroom behavior management, social skills training, and peer tutoring in reading. Results indicated the intervention was successful, with direct observation data indicating significant differences between treatment and wait-list control groups in on-task, positive recess interaction and play, aggression, and out-of-seat behaviors. Also, teachers indicated the following improvements for students in the intervention groups: requesting attention appropriately, following directions, and reducing disruption (Kamps et al., 1999).

Furthermore, First Step to Success (Walker et al., 1997), a manualized program to identify and support students at risk for EBD, incorporates systematic screening to identify students appropriate for this tertiary support. The program contains three components: (1) screening and early detection procedures (including four approaches), (2) a school-based intervention component, and (3) a parent training component (HomeBase). The SSBD is one of the four procedures that can be used to identify kindergarten, first-grade, and second-grade students who are having difficulty meeting behavioral expectations in the school setting (Walker, Golly, et al., 2005; Walker et al., 1997, 1998).

The SSBD can also be used outside of a three-tiered model of prevention to identify students who may require additional supports (e.g., Lane, 1999). However, it is
very important to recognize that parent consent is required to conduct systematic
screenings if they are not universally conducted at the school site as part of regular
school practices. This is a point we revisit in Chapter 8.

In the next section, we present an evenhanded discussion of the strengths and
considerations associated with using the SSBD in elementary schools.

Strengths and Considerations

Strengths

As we mentioned at the onset of this chapter, the SSBD is viewed by many researchers to be the gold standard of systematic screening (Kauffman, 2001; Lane, Little, et
al., 2009). In fact, it is the only tool designed to explicitly detect elementary students
with either externalizing or internalizing behavior patterns. The SSBD has several
strengths, five of which we highlight next.

First, the SSBD was conceptualized to identify students with internalizing behaviors as well as those with externalizing behaviors by providing teachers with uniform
standards to examine risk. Given that students with internalizing behaviors often
go undetected by teachers and other adults because of the covert or overcontrolled
nature of their defining characteristics, it is critical that instruments identify not only
students with overt and undercontrolled behaviors but also those internalizing behaviors (Achenbach, 1991; Walker et al., 2004). The SSBD accomplishes this charge by
considering all students across these two dimensions.

Second, the psychometric properties of each stage are well established. Therefore, school-site teams can be confident that when the screening tool is implemented
as intended, the decisions made regarding which students do (and do not) require
additional considerations or supports are accurate. The goal of all screening is accurate identification, with careful attention to avoid false negatives (students who actually do have either internalizing or externalizing behaviors but who were overlooked;
Kauffman & Brigham, 2009; Lane, Oakes, Ennis, et al., in press).

Third, the SSBD is a relatively simple, cost-effective, user-friendly tool that combines teacher ranking and rating with direct observations when appraising students'
behavior, requiring very limited time commitments in Stage 1 and 2 activities (Lane,
Little, et al., 2009), taking actually less than 1 hour to complete. The process becomes
more time intensive in Stage 3, when direct observations occur; however, this is only
for a small number of students who pass through Gate 2 and is typically completed
by specialists other than the classroom teachers.

Fourth, the SSBD can be highly useful in systematically monitoring school
adjustment and behavioral performance of students within a given school and across
multiple school years, as demonstrated in the illustrations presented in the next section. It can also be used as a method of "matching students to available interventions
and existing school-based services" (Walker & Severson, 1992, p. 79), and the initial

rank-order position as well as Stage 2 status could provide a simple, nonintrusive, indirect measure of behavioral gains or changes over time to determine patterns of responsiveness (Lane, Kalberg, et al., 2010).

Fifth, information gleaned from the SSBD has been used by some school sites and districts for establishing need and securing resource allocations. For example, principals have used Stage 2 data (e.g., the percentage of students in the building who exceed normative criteria on the externalizing and internalizing dimensions) to acquire resources either in terms of personnel (e.g., social workers or counselors) or monies to support schoolwide efforts to teach and reinforce behavioral expectations.

In sum, the SSBD is a feasible, accurate instrument that allows all students to be considered for additional supports for internalizing or externalizing behaviors (the two most global and common disorders characteristic of school-age students).

Considerations

In terms of limiting factors, there are a few key characteristics that should be considered. First, the SSBD typically allows for just six students—three with externalizing behaviors and three with internalizing behaviors—to past through Gate 1 for subsequent evaluation. Although the instructional manual indicates that teachers may nominate additional students to pass through Gate 1, the initial guideline is six students, which may be a limiting factor for teachers who have classrooms with a larger number of students with either internalizing or externalizing (please buy this teacher a cup of decaf!) behavior patterns.

Second, and conversely, when conducting Stage 1 activities, teachers often express concern that they do not have 10 students who should appear on the initial list for externalizing or internalizing behaviors. They are highly concerned that by writing students' names on this list, it would cause students to be noticed when there is not actually a concern. However, in our work, once teachers received the result as to which students meet the criteria to pass through Stage 2, their concerns are quelled as they realize that students are not passing through Gate 2 unless their behavior patterns truly suggest cause for concern.

A third consideration is that the SSBD does not specifically address students with comorbid behavior concerns. Given that internalizing and externalizing behavior patterns tend to occur with a moderate degree of comorbidity (Achenbach, 1991), this is a limiting characteristic of the tool. Teachers also recognize this co-occurrence, sometimes expressing concern that they have a student who should be placed on both the externalizing and internalizing lists. However, this is not possible; students must be placed on one list only—externalizing or internalizing.

Finally, on a cautionary note, the authors make it very clear that the SSBD is a screening tool. As such, the SSBD alone does not (and was not intended to) provide sufficient information to make decisions about whether or not special education services are warranted under the ED label. This is a screening tool. Other measures will need to be completed after securing parental consent to more fully evaluate students, including those measures necessary to more fully describe complex social, behavioral, and academic problems (Walker & Severson, 1992).

In sum, the SSBD is a cost-effective, efficient tool for systematic screening at the elementary level with only two cautionary features: (1) a limited number of students intended to pass through Gate 1 (typically six; however, teachers may nominate more students) and (2) inability to detect students with co-occurring behaviors (externalizing and internalizing).

In the next section, we provide illustrations to offer you further guidance as to how to use the SSBD as part of regular school practices to monitor overall progress in the building and to identify and support students requiring additional supports.

Illustrations

The following three illustrations involve the elementary level because this is the target population for the SSBD. These illustrations are adapted from public schools that have participated in training and evaluation studies at Vanderbilt University in an ongoing effort to support schools in designing, implementing, and evaluating CI3T models of prevention. We use citations throughout the illustrations to refer interested readers to the original applications of these practices.

An Illustration at a Small-Town Elementary School: Woodridge Elementary School

Woodridge Elementary School (WES) is located in a southern state within 10 miles of an urbanized area. It serves approximately 500 K–5 students. The student population is predominantly white, with 7.8% representing other ethnicities. Approximately 15% of the student body received special education services, and 38.8% were economically disadvantaged.

Building a CI3T Model of Prevention

A school-site leadership team from WES participated in a year-long training series at a local university during the 2006–2007 school year. Throughout the training series, the school team (principal, guidance counselor, special education teacher, general education teacher, and parent representative) designed a CI3T model of prevention. Their primary plan (Tier 1) integrated three key areas: academics, behavior, and social skills. The school team identified three schoolwide behavioral expectations: Be Ready, Be Responsible, and Be Respectful. These expectations aligned with the school's mission and purpose statement to "create a safe and caring environment that cultivates and nurtures the development of each child socially, behaviorally, and academically." To solicit ongoing feedback from faculty and staff regarding their primary prevention plan, they built in measures to assess the social validity (significance of the goal, acceptability of the procedures, and importance of effects) (Primary

Intervention Rating Scale: Lane, Kalberg, et al., 2009; Lane, Robertson, & Wehby, 2002) and treatment integrity (the degree to which they implemented their plan as designed; see Table 2.1).

ACADEMIC COMPONENT

WES expected all students to "strive to do their best at all times" and, therefore, set clear, high expectations for all learners. Teachers were responsible for teaching rigorous content as specified in the state and district standards. Without a specific reading program adopted by the district, WES elected to use multiple resources for reading instruction. STAR™ reading (Renaissance Learning, 2010) was used to identify each reader's instructional level (zone of proximal development; Vygotsky, 1978) through a computer-based assessment. The Accelerated Reader™ program (Renaissance Learning, 2010), a companion to the STAR assessment, was used to monitor each student's reading progress through comprehension tests. Students earned points based on accuracy of assessments and number of books completed. Furthermore, WES adopted the AIMSweb® (Pearson Education, 2008) Web-based assessment and data management system to monitor reading skill growth over time. The curriculum-based measures were used to monitor early literacy skills (letter-naming fluency, phoneme segmentation fluency) in kindergarten and first grade and reading skills (oral reading fluency) in second through fifth grades. Students identified as below benchmark participated in additional instruction and practice with the classroom teacher during the schoolwide reading intervention block (30 minutes per day 4 days per week). Teachers were offered professional development, team planning time, and administrative support for planning rigorous and relevant instruction. Lesson plans were structured with starting and closing activities to maximize learning time and minimize time-off-task behavior. Academic expectations fostered a positive learning environment. By 2009, 97% of WES students were proficient or advanced in math and reading according to the state achievement assessment.

BEHAVIORAL COMPONENT

The behavioral component of the primary prevention plan supported students in meeting the identified schoolwide expectations (Be Ready, Be Responsible, and Be Respectful) using an instructional approach to behavior. First, an expectation matrix was drafted by the school-site leadership team to clearly define the expectations for all school settings (e.g., classroom, bus, cafeteria; see Table 2.4). Teachers were aligned their classroom procedures (e.g., homework policies, turning in completed assignments, bathroom procedures) with the other classes in their grade level to maintain consistency and predictability. Teachers reinforced students who demonstrated the expected behaviors through a schoolwide ticket system with behavior-specific praise (e.g., PAWS [Positive Actions of Woodridge Students]). For example, a teacher would hand a student a PAWS ticket and say "Thank you for showing respect on the bus by talking quietly with your seatmate."

TABLE 2.4. WES Expectation Matrix

Expectation	Classroom	Bus	Cafeteria	Playground	Hallway	Bathroom
Be ready	• Be on time • Complete assignments • Have materials and school supplies on hand • Be positive about learning • Be a good listener	• Be on time • Walk to and from bus • Stay clear of roadway	• Get all items the first time • Line up quickly and quietly	• Use restroom before going outside • Stay away from mud, water, and puddles • Wear appropriate clothes and shoes	• Line up quietly • Stay in line	• Wait your turn
Be responsible	• Follow directions • Make good choices • Be a good example to others	• Stay in seat • Talk quietly with neighbor • Keep aisles clear • Only bring school supplies and approved items • Keep hands and feet inside the bus	• Keep hands and feet to self at all times • Eat your own food • Walk • Clean area around tray and seat	• Stay in playground area • Bring in anything you took out • Report unsafe objects • Report unsafe behaviors and actions	• Walk at all times • Keep up in line • Keep hands and feet to self • Eyes forward • Stay on task • Stay on the right	• Use facilities appropriately • Flush and clean up after oneself • Flush toilet paper and throw all paper towels in the trash • Wash hands • Report messes
Be respectful	• Follow directions • Use kind words • Use kind actions • Control temper • Stop, think, and choose • Cooperate with others • Use inside voices	• Obey the bus driver at all times • Talk quietly with neighbor • Keep hands and feet to self	• Talk quietly • Keep hands and feet to self • Use good manners • Obey cafeteria staff and monitors at all times • Raise hand for permission to get up • Saving seats for friends is not allowed	• Play cooperatively • Follow game rules • Use kind words • Invite others to play • Use playground equipment for intended use	• Quietly walk down the hall • Stay on the right • Keep hands to self	• Allow privacy • Wipe off the seat

Note. From Walker, Ramsey, and Gresham (2004, Figure 2.4, p. 138). Copyright 2004 by Wadsworth, a part of Cengage Learning, Inc. Reproduced by permission. *www.cengage.com/permissions.*

SOCIAL SKILLS COMPONENT

The social skills component of the primary prevention plan was a district-adopted program, Character Under Construction (Forrest, 2000), to teach students desired character traits. While the classroom teachers taught the behavioral expectations for each setting using the expectation matrix, the school's guidance counselor taught the social skill lessons weekly or biweekly to each K–5 class. All faculty and staff modeled and reinforced the social skills taught by the counselor using the PAWS ticket system. A second district-adopted social skills program for bullying prevention (Olweus et al., 2007) was also in place. The bullying prevention program was taught in partnership with Students Taking a Right Stand (STARS; Hazeldon/Johnson in partnership with Rodger Dinwiddie).

Measures

As part of the CI3T model, the leadership team used multiple sources of data to measure the school's overall progress and identify students for secondary (Tier 2) and tertiary (Tier 3) supports (see Table 2.1). Academic outcome measures monitored included the STAR reading assessment (Renaissance Learning, 2010; administered twice per year or as students enrolled), districtwide writing prompts (quarterly), and the statewide achievement assessment (annually). Behavioral outcome measures included attendance and discipline data (ODRs), which were collected daily and monitored quarterly at the school level. These measures were considered reactive as students had to have already earned the ODRs or were tardy or absent too often. WES conducted schoolwide behavior screenings at three time points throughout the school year—Fall, Winter, and Spring—to monitor the overall level of risk in their building and identify students for secondary and tertiary supports. The school elected to complete both the SSBD (Walker & Severson, 1992) and the SRSS (Drummond, 1994) for the first 3 years of their CI3T model because they were undecided as to which of the screening tools to select. The leadership team liked the appeal of the SRSS because of the ease of preparation, administration, and scoring (see Chapter 4 for information on the SRSS). However, they were also very concerned about being able to identify and support students with internalizing behavior patterns the SRSS might not detect. Therefore, the leadership team presented the full faculty with the option of completing two screeners (SRSS and SSBD) to ensure the identification of students with internalizing behavior patterns and to work with the local university to determine how many students would have been overlooked at the end of the 3 years had the SSBD not been implemented. The leadership team also felt this would give adequate time for the teachers to make an informed decision as to which screening to continue with following the first 3 years of implementation. The faculty agreed with these priorities and felt that spending about 1 hour, three times per year, to identify and monitor their students was well worth the investment. Finally, the school monitored referrals to the general education intervention team (prereferrals) and for special education because they were interested to see if prereferral interventions would increase and referrals to special education would decrease over time after implementing their CI3T model.

The following questions guided WES in their use of their SSBD data to (1) monitor level of risk at their school and (2) to supplement their primary plan with secondary (Tier 2) and tertiary (Tier 3) support systems.

Has the Overall Level of Risk Changed at WES after 3 Years of Implementing the Primary Prevention Plan?

As mentioned previously, WES monitored schoolwide data over time to evaluate their schoolwide prevention plan. Figure 2.2 illustrates the change of the overall level of risk over a 3-year period, focusing on the Winter time point (2007, 2008, and 2009). The WES leadership team focused on the Winter time point to (1) identify students who continued to have elevated risk after participating in the primary prevention plan for the first semester and (2) show the shifts in the proportion of students at risk during this time frame relative to previous years. The leadership team presented this information for each time point (Fall, Winter, and Spring) during faculty training on schoolwide screeners so new (and returning) faculty would see shifts in risk status —the utility to the behavioral screeners—and, therefore, understand the importance of accurately completing the screeners at each of the three times during the school year.

Figure 2.2 displays the percentage of students who exceeded normative criteria in both the externalizing and the internalizing categories in Winter 2007, 2008, and 2009. The first three bars reflect the students nominated in the externalizing risk category (students who passed through Gate 1 and were rated in Stage 2). During Winter 2007, 60 students were nominated as at risk in the externalizing category while only 13 (6.81% of the school) exceeded normative criteria in Stage 2 as determined by their total scores on the CEI and CFI, as explained earlier in this chapter. During the Winter screening time point the following school year (2008), 69 students were nominated in the same category; however, only seven exceeded normative criteria based on their CEI and CFI scores. The percentage of students exceeding normative criteria from Winter 2007 to Winter 2008 dropped substantially, from 6.81 to 3.5%. This pattern continued for the next school year, when the student body increased in number, resulting in a small drop in the percentage of students determined to be at risk in the externalizing category to 3.18% of the student body.

The last three bars contain information about students who were nominated in the internalizing risk category. During Winter 2007, again 60 students (three from each of the 20 classrooms) were nominated in Stage 1, as per the screener's directions. Seventeen (8.9% of students) exceeded normative criteria for Stage 2, as determined by their CEI and CFI scores. During the Winter screening time point the following school year (2008), 13 (6.5% of the school) students exceeded normative criteria. An additional and more pronounced decrease occurred between the Winter time point in 2008 and 2009, from 13 (6.5%) to 6 (2.73%). The faculty were encouraged

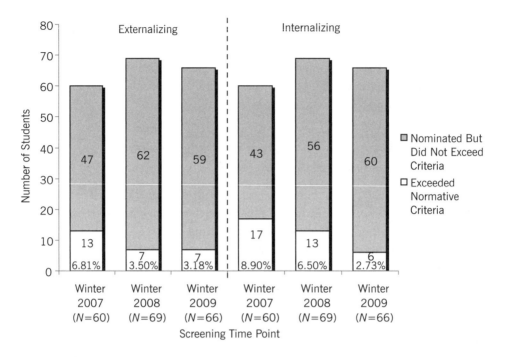

FIGURE 2.2. WES SSBD results comparing the percentage of students nominated and exceeding normative criteria for both externalizing and internalizing behavior disorders over a 3-year period. From Lane, Kalberg, and Menzies (2009, Figure 6.7, p. 142). Copyright 2009 by The Guilford Press. Adapted by permission.

by these data showing their primary prevention plan was sufficient for the majority of students (about 94%) in reducing and/or maintaining low behavioral risk, with particular benefits for students with internalizing patterns. However, the leadership team was careful to not draw causal conclusions regarding the information shared, as there was not an experimental design in place. The SSBD data also suggested that WES's CI3T model of prevention was addressing the needs of students with internalizing and externalizing behavior concerns. They felt they were now able, with the resources available in their building, to focus efforts on those students (about 6%) who needed additional supports. While certainly teachers had already provided classroom supports (e.g., differentiated instruction, parent conferences, small groups with the guidance counselor, support of the behavior specialist), they were ready to move toward a more coordinated data-driven model for providing secondary and tertiary supports (see Lane, Kalberg, & Menzies, 2009, for additional directions on how to establish these supports).

How Can This Information Be Used to Support Individual Students?

The school team at WES used the Winter screening time point data across the first 3 years (Figure 2.2) to answer the question, "How can we support students beyond the primary plan?" The team was encouraged by the continued decrease in the level of risk for internalizing behavior patterns. However, the team noted that the relatively stable number of students exceeding normative criteria for externalizing behavior patterns could be an area for improvement. In other words, the team chose to focus on secondary supports (see Table 2.5) for students with externalizing behavior concerns and consider tertiary supports for the few students with the most intensive needs (behavioral and academic).

The school-site team chose three new secondary supports, confident that teachers would continue to use low-intensity strategies within the classrooms (e.g., strategies to develop intrinsic motivation, differentiated instruction, clear classroom procedures). The first new strategy was a study skills group that met 2 days per week to teach specific skills such as time management and goal setting and strategies such as outlining, flash cards, and mnemonics. Students who met the academic and behavioral criteria would be considered for this secondary support (see Table 2.5). To specifically address the concern about the students demonstrating externalizing behavior patterns, the team chose two research-based programs: the Behavior Education Program (Crone, Horner, & Hawken, 2004) for students in grades 4 and 5 and the Incredible Years Training for Children (Webster-Stratton, 2000) for students in kindergarten through grade 3. Since these programs were new to the school, the team decided that they would research, plan for professional development, and prepare and organize the materials for the new interventions. They planned to begin with the supports in Fall 2010 using the Spring 2010 screening and academic data. This would allow adequate time to ensure they were fully prepared to be successful with the use of these secondary supports.

Summary

WES serves as one illustration of a school that established systematic behavioral screening practices to monitor the number and percentage of students exceeding normative criteria in both externalizing and internalizing risk categories across 3 school years. The school leadership team used data to keep the faculty and staff informed of how their prevention efforts were impacting behavioral risk for their students from year to year (Figure 2.2). Data were displayed and shared in such a way that the faculty and staff easily understood the changes in risk level and responded accordingly (i.e., coordinating the secondary supports for the externalizing group to improve risk status).

An Illustration at a Large Suburban Elementary School: Price Elementary School

Price Elementary School (PES), a large suburban elementary institution located in middle Tennessee, served students in kindergarten through fourth grade. The school population was approximately 498 students, 70% of whom were white. Twenty-three percent of the students were classified as economically disadvantaged and 7.46% received special educational services.

TABLE 2.5. WES Secondary Intervention Grid

Support	Description	Schoolwide data: Entry criteria	Data to monitor progress: Schoolwide data? Other?	Exit criteria
Study skills group	Study skills needed are targeted by classroom teachers Guidance counselor identifies curricula and teaches paraprofessionals to teach these skills to students using recommended practices (see Pashler et al., 2007, for Institute for Educational Sciences practice guide: Organizing Instruction and Study to Improve Student Learning) Target skills for the small group include: • Creating to-do lists • Time management strategies • Creating a study space • Goal setting and monitoring progress • Outlining strategies • Using graphic organizers to review content • Using flash cards and mnemonics to memorize facts Students meet with trained paraprofessional 2 days/ week for 30-minute lesson in study skills; lessons are conducted during regular school day during intervention block	Academic: 1. One or more grade below average (C or N, needs improvement) in an academic or study skills area *or* 2. Missing 30% of class work in given month *and* Behavior: 1. SRSS: moderate (4–8) or high (9–21) risk; *or* 2. SSBD: exceed normative criteria for internalizing or externalizing using Stage 2	Assignments completed: Teachers complete school–home note with percentage and accuracy of assignments completed each week in area of concern *and* Behavioral checklist matching each learned strategy (developed during instruction for each strategy taught) Students complete checklists weekly and review with instructing paraprofessional	Three consecutive weeks of 90% or better work completion with 80% or better work accuracy Academic progress monitored until next behavior screening shows reduced levels of risk on the SRSS and/or SSBD

(cont.)

TABLE 2.5. *(cont.)*

Support	Description	Schoolwide data: Entry criteria	Data to monitor progress: Schoolwide data? Other?	Exit criteria
Behavior Education Program (Crone et al., 2004)	Designed for students with persistent behavior concerns that are not dangerous; provides a daily check-in/check-out system that helps teachers provide students with (1) immediate feedback on behavior by completing a daily progress report and (2) additional opportunities for positive adult interactions Parents participate by signing off on daily sheets: fourth- and fifth-grade students are assigned mentors to check in and out with daily Students meet with mentor for 10 minutes at the beginning and end of day	Academic: 1. Report cards: earned N on study skills or a C– or lower in any academic content area *or* 2. Below proficient on curriculum-based measures *or* Behavior 1. SRSS: moderate (4–8) risk *or* 2. SSBD: exceed normative criteria for externalizing using Stage 2	Daily progress monitoring forms collected by teacher and viewed by parents/guardians	Moves into the maintenance self-monitoring phase when goals are met for 3 consecutive weeks Self-monitoring phase ends when next academic reporting period and behavior rating results indicate absence of risk following same criteria for inclusion
Incredible Years training for children (Webster-Stratton, 2000)	Curriculum builds skills in anger management, friendship skills, school success, and interpersonal problem solving; is delivered in a small-group format in designated classroom or office (see Blueprints for Violence Prevention, *www.colorado.edu/news/r/d12190 a32eb6b4545b7fd66147693 362.html* for further details); K–3 students	**Behavior:** Meets one of following criteria 1. SRSS: moderate (4–8) risk 2. SSBD: exceed normative criteria for externalizing using Stage 2 3. Two or more bullying referrals turned in during one quarter 4. Three or more ODRs for aggressive behaviors during one quarter	Information pertinent to elements of intervention is established, and self-assessment checklists used to evaluate progress Students meet individually with teacher to assess weekly progress ODRs and bullying referrals monitored weekly by teacher	Students complete curriculum components and then are assessed and compared with initial inclusion criteria At the next screening time point: 1. SRSS low-risk range (0–3) 2. SSBD does not meet normative criteria on externalizing dimension if passed to Stage 2 No bullying or ODRs for aggressive behavior for 3 consecutive weeks during same rating period

Note. From Lane, Kalberg, and Menzies (2009, Table 6.1, pp. 130–131). Copyright 2009 by The Guilford Press. Adapted by permission.

Building a CI3T Model of Prevention

PES built a CI3T model during a year-long training series held at Vanderbilt University in 2006. The schoolwide prevention plan was implemented the following school year (2007–2008) and continues to be part of regular school practices. The primary prevention plan included three components designed to address the academic program, positive behavior supports, and social skills instruction.

ACADEMIC COMPONENT

The academic program was guided by state and district standards and recommended programs. Teachers worked together to plan consistent instruction across grade-level teams. Student progress was monitored by classroom performance and assessment practice (described later). As such, teachers were expected to model and teach expectations, provide rigorous content instruction, provide a structure to increase student engagement in academic activities (i.e., starting and closing activities), be prepared and organized to teach, communicate with parents, be patient, and link lessons to district standards. For students the academic component of the primary prevention plan detailed expectations designed to allow full benefit from the academic instruction, such as completing all assignments on time, remaining attentive, and having a positive attitude.

BEHAVIORAL COMPONENT

The school identified three schoolwide behavioral expectations: Respect, Responsibility, and Participation and Best Effort. Expectations were defined and taught in all school settings (e.g., classroom, hallway, bathroom, cafeteria). In addition, students were encouraged to report unsafe behavior and to accept responsibility for their actions. Students earned Tiger tickets paired with behavior-specific praise for meeting expectations in behavioral, academic, and social skills domains. These tickets were used to access reinforcers such as class parties and school assemblies.

SOCIAL SKILLS COMPONENT

The social skills component of the primary prevention plan was based on Elliott and Gresham's (1991) Social Skills Intervention Guide. Teachers rated the 30 skills listed in the Social Skills Rating System on a 3-point Likert-type scale as follows: 0 = *not important*, 1 = *important*, 2 = *critical*. The top 10 skills rated by the majority of teachers as critical for success became the focus of the schoolwide social skills component. Lesson plans from the Social Skills Intervention Guide were modified for use as whole-class lessons (rather than small groups as originally designed). Each month teachers taught the social skill of the month using these lessons, which included "tell," "show," and "do" phases. The social skills were practiced and reinforced using the Tiger tickets, as described previously.

Measures

PES gathered and used various types of data to evaluate students' academic and behavioral performance as well as other aspects of the program. A complete list of measures and a schedule of collection time points are provided in Table 2.6. The behavior screeners implemented at PES included the SRSS (Drummond, 1994) and SSBD (Walker & Severson, 1992). They administered the screenings three times during the school year: Fall, Winter, and Spring.

How Did Risk Shift at PES during the First Year of Implementing Their CI3T Prevention Plan?

The faculty and staff at PES were curious to see whether there were any short-term changes in the level of risk at their school after only 3 months of implementing their primary plan. The leadership team looked at the number and percentage of students

TABLE 2.6. PES Monthly Assessment Schedule				
Measure	**Quarter 1**	**Quarter 2**	**Quarter 3**	**Quarter 4**
Student demographics	×	×	×	×
Academic measures				
State achievement assessment				×
District math assessment				×
District writing assessment	×			×
District reading assessment	×			×
Behavior measures				
Screener: SRSS (Drummond, 1994)	September	December		April
Screener: SSBD (Walker & Severson, 1992)	September	December		April
Attendance: tardies/absences	×	×	×	×
Out-of-school suspensions	×	×	×	×
Referrals				
Special education referrals	×	×	×	×
Support team referrals	×	×	×	×
Program evaluation measures				
Treatment integrity:				
School-Wide Evaluation Tool (Sugai et al., 2001)				
Social Validity (Primary Intervention Rating Scale: Lane, Kalberg, et al., 2009; Lane, Robertson, et al., 2002)				

Note. From Lane, Kalberg, and Menzies (2009, Table 5.1, p. 105). Copyright 2009 by The Guilford Press. Adapted by permission.

exceeding normative criteria on the SSBD screener for both internalizing and externalizing behavior patterns. Figure 2.3 displays change in level of students at risk for
both internalizing and externalizing behavior patterns from Fall to Winter 2007. The
first two bars show the number and percentage of students who exceeded normative
criteria for externalizing behavior patterns, the first representing Fall 2007 and the
second Winter 2007, 6 weeks after the fall screening time point. The percentage of students exceeding normative criteria decreased between the Fall and Winter screening
administrations, from 6.23 to 5.17%. The next two bars show the percentage of students exceeding normative criteria in the internalizing category, which also dropped
between Fall and Winter, from 3.65 to 1.29%. This graph demonstrates the level
of risk between two time points and allows the school to monitor the changes that
occurred and use these data to make an action plan (Lane, Kalberg, et al., 2011).

How Can This Information Be Used to Support Students with the Most Intensive Behavioral Needs?

The reduction in the number of students at risk was encouraging to the faculty and
staff. The team then turned their attention to supporting the students who were identified to be at the highest level of risk based on Winter 2007 data. They chose to

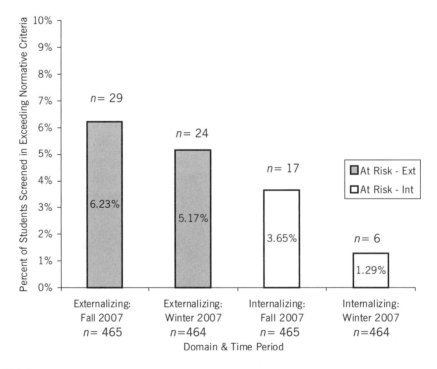

FIGURE 2.3. PES SSBD data over time at the elementary school level: comparing the percentage
of students at risk for internalizing and externalizing behavior concerns between Fall 2007 and
Winter 2007 screening time points, Year 1 of implementation. From Lane, Kalberg, et al. (2011,
Figure 3, p. 13). Copyright 2011 by Sage Publications, Inc. Reprinted by permission.

focus on this group of students because they felt, given the positive changes in just the first half of Year 1, they could monitor the responsiveness of the students at moderate risk who were receiving secondary supports that were part of regular school practices, such as differentiating academic assignments, contacts with parents, using classroom procedures to facilitate transitions, loss of privileges, and verbal redirection. The data represented in Figure 2.3 provided useful information to the school leadership regarding students who were at the greatest risk of increased behavioral and academic difficulties. Administrators created two lists: one of students at risk for internalizing behaviors and a second list of those at risk for externalizing behaviors. Using the Winter screening data, the administrators and faculty were able to consider students who were in need of tertiary supports (Tier 3; see Table 2.7).

In partnership with the university researchers, PES students were offered services under Project Function (Lane, Oakes, & Cox, 2011). Project Function offers support to the community by using a systematic process for designing, implementing, and

TABLE 2.7. PES Tertiary Intervention Grid: Sample Intervention

Support	Description	Schoolwide data: Entry criteria	Data to monitor progress: Schoolwide data? Other?	Exit criteria
Functional assessment-based intervention (Project Function; Lane, Oakes, & Cox, 2011)	Individualized intervention is developed 1. Information collection from a review of student records, student interview, teacher interview, parent interview, direct observation of target behavior, and SSRS (Gresham & Elliott, 1990) is used to identify target behavior and inform intervention 2. Information is placed in the function matrix (Umbreit et al., 2007) 3. Function of behavior is identified with decision model (Umbreit et al., 2007) 4. Intervention is developed with three components: (1) antecedent adjustments, (2) reinforcement, and (3) extinction Data are collected daily; procedural fidelity is assessed and data are graphed to determine effect of the intervention (see Lane, Eisner, et al., 2009)	Students who (1) are nonresponsive to secondary intervention in first 5 months of school; (2) are referred by teacher; and (3) had behavior screening data indicating high risk: SSBD—exceeding normative criteria on externalizing dimension or SRSS—high risk (score of 9–21)	Data collected on both (1) undesirable behavior and (2) desirable replacement behavior	Intervention will be faded and generalization monitored once undesirable and desirable behaviors reach specified goal levels Students will be monitored until next screening time point if they no longer meet screening criteria for intervention

Note. From Lane, Kalberg, and Menzies (2009, Box 6.3, pp. 134–135). Copyright by The Guilford Press. Adapted by permission.

evaluating functional assessment-based interventions (Umbreit et al., 2007). Individualized behavior plans or functional assessment-based interventions were developed, implemented, and monitored by research assistants and school staff to further support such struggling students. For example, two first-grade students participated in Project Function. They were both in one classroom, which was job-shared by two general education teachers. Although both students were initially nominated by teachers for participation in this project, their behavior screening data were used to confirm the need for such intensive interventions. Both students exceeded normative criteria on the SSBD and were in the high-risk group on the SRSS (see Table 2.7 for entry criteria). The target behavior of being off task was identified as a concern for both students, although the manifestations were unique to each student. Replacement behaviors were identified and an intervention was developed to teach, reinforce, and plan for generalization of the new behavior. For both boys, engagement was identified as the replacement behavior. Single-case methodology was used to evaluate intervention outcomes (see Figure 2.4). In brief, Figure 2.4 presents intervention outcomes for both boys (Derek and Mark). For both, the level of engagement increased with the introduction of the functional assessment-based interventions. When the interventions were withdrawn, engagement declined. When the interventions were reintroduced, engagement again increased and subsequently was maintained over time. See Lane, Eisner, and colleagues (2009) for a full description of the functional assessment-based intervention process and outcomes.

Summary

PES provides an illustration of one large suburban elementary school that monitored changes in level of risk of students after the first 3 months of implementing their primary prevention plan. While implementing schoolwide prevention efforts in their first year, they used the information from the SSBD to identify students who might benefit from tertiary support to more fully meet the needs of their student population.

An Illustration at a Rural Elementary School: Brighton Elementary School

Brighton Elementary School (BES) is located in a rural area of a southern state and serves 650 students in grades kindergarten through 5. BES is predominantly white (90%), with an economically disadvantaged rate of 12%. It is located in a district that adopted a full-inclusion model; and 9% of students received special education services in the general education setting.

Building a CI3T Model of Prevention

BES developed a CI3T model during a year-long training series held at a local university in 2005. The school administrators were extremely proactive in seeking practices

A: Derek's Intervention Outcomes: Percentage of Academic Engagement

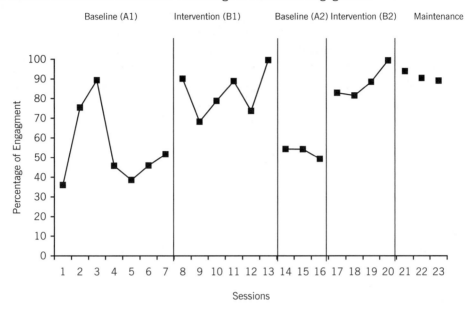

B: Mark's Intervention Outcomes: Percentage of Academic Engagement

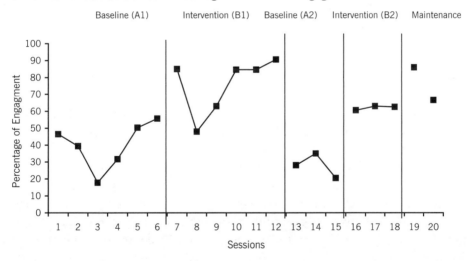

FIGURE 2.4. Functional assessment-based intervention outcomes for Derek (A) and Mark (B). For both boys, the level of engagement increased with the introduction of the functional assessment-based interventions. When the interventions were withdrawn, engagement declined. When the interventions were reintroduced, engagement again increased and subsequently maintained over time. From Lane, Eisner, et al. (2009, Figures 1, p. 594, and 2, p. 595). Copyright 2009 by the authors. Reprinted by permission.

that would increase the rigor of their educational program and create a safe, inclusive, welcoming environment for students to learn and families to belong. BES was one of the first schools in the district to adopt response to intervention and positive behavior supports in conjunction with their character development program. Through their CI3T model, they systematically screened, monitored progress, and addressed the academic, behavioral, and social needs of students in an integrated approach, with all stakeholders' (e.g., students, teachers, parents) assuming various responsibilities. This schoolwide prevention model was adopted by the faculty and staff and implemented the following school year.

ACADEMIC COMPONENT

Teachers prepared engaging and interactive lessons aligned with grade-level, state, and district standards; used starting and closing activities; arrived to class on time and prepared; provided positive praise and timely feedback to students; communicated expectations clearly; and used ongoing data to monitor student progress. Meanwhile, students were responsible for giving their best effort, arriving to class on time and prepared, participating in instruction and completing all assignments. Parents were asked bring students to school on time and avoid early dismissals when possible. Furthermore, parents were invited to review assignments with their child using the daily agenda, schedule appointments with teachers when needed, and participate in the parent–teacher organization.

BEHAVIORAL COMPONENT

During the training, three schoolwide expectations were identified—Respect, Responsibility, and Cooperation—which were defined for each location in the school. The team surveyed the faculty and staff to determine the behaviors most important for students to be successful. The expectation matrix was developed to clearly communicate the desired behaviors for each location (see Table 2.8). Furthermore, teachers modeled and taught schoolwide expectations and reinforced appropriate behaviors. At the start of the school year, each teacher taught lessons specific to each setting. This schoolwide effort allowed for any adult in the building to reinforce student behavior with the same language and reinforcement system. BES designed Dragon dollars and called their expectations Dragon Traits. Students demonstrating the desired behaviors were given Dragon dollars paired with behavior-specific praise. Dragon dollars were then traded for a variety of tangible (e.g., ice cream) and nontangible (e.g., assemblies, class recognition on the announcements) reinforcers.

SOCIAL SKILLS COMPONENT

The school leadership team chose to use monthly social skill lessons from Elliott and Gresham's (1991) Social Skills Intervention Guide linked to their expectations, as described in the previous illustration. Lessons were taught schoolwide within the

TABLE 2.8. BES Expectation Matrix

Expectation	Setting					
	Classroom	Hallway	Cafeteria	Playground	Arrival	Dismissal
Respect	• Take necessary materials to classroom • Take care of materials • Follow expectations • Listen while others are talking	• Keep hands, feet, and belongings to self • Walk in hallway • Stay on the right side of the hallway • Report visitors without stickers to teacher • Lead others by setting a good example	• Follow procedures • Keep hands, feet, and food to yourself • Low voice • Know what to order • Get necessary items (napkins, condiments, drinks, etc.) • Raise hand if you or someone else has needs	• Use equipment appropriately • Return property to its appropriate place • Follow game rules • Play approved activities	• Sit with grade level • Talk in low voice • Remain in seat until dismissed by teacher or adult	*Car riders* • Sit with grade level • Remain quiet • Listen for name to be called *Bus riders* • Sit with bus lines • Remain quiet • Listen for your bus to be called
Responsibility	• Dress appropriately • Respect belongings (yours and others) • Listen while others are talking • Speak in a quiet voice • Follow expectations • Respect school property	• Keep hands, feet, and belongings to yourself • Be mindful of activities in other classrooms and the hallway	• Low voice • Leave tables clean • Use "please" and "thank you" • Use good table manners • Stay in assigned seat	• Stay in established area • Respond immediately when teacher/adult calls • Be kind to peers while playing games	• Stay in established area • Respond immediately when teacher/adult calls	*Car riders* • Respond immediately when your name is called *Bus riders* • Respond immediately when your bus is called
Cooperation	• Follow expectations • Listen and support others' ideas • Work together/share • Be willing to give your best effort	• Follow rules consistently • Work together to keep everyone safe • Be considerate of others' safety and learning	• Follow expectations/ adult instructions • Clean up, keeping hands, feet, and food to yourself • Check table and floor for trash • Use quiet voices	• Keep each other safe • Share • Play approved games • Follow rules	• Keep hands, feet, and belongings to self • Listen for your bus to be called • Keep all materials in backpack	• Keep hands, feet, and belongings to self • Listen for your bus to be called • Keep all materials in backpack

same time period (e.g., week or day) during each month. This was important for consistency within the building. All school personnel could reinforce the socials skills using the same language when providing praise and corrective feedback. Not only were expectations and social skills taught directly, but prompts such as posters were displayed, and students demonstrating these skills were recognized and rewarded with Dragon dollars.

Measures

The BES school leadership team selected several types of data to monitor student performance with regard to both schoolwide and individual progress and needs (see Table 2.9). Academic outcome measures included district reading and writing assessments, ThinkLink Reading and Math, a formative assessment used to predict achievement on the state assessment and inform instruction, AIMSweb reading to monitor progress on reading skills, and statewide assessments (Tennessee Comprehensive Assessment Program). ODRs and attendance data were also monitored to assess behavioral performance. Furthermore, schoolwide behavior screeners were completed three times a year BES chose two behavior screeners—SRSS and SSBD— to monitor the level of risk. As part of their CI3T model, the school leadership team and grade-level teams looked at behavioral and academic data together.

How Can Academic and Behavioral Data Be Analyzed Together to Inform Intervention Efforts?

AIMSweb reading scores and the SSBD were completed three times during the school year (Fall, Winter, and Spring). SSBD scores determined whether students did or did not exceed normative criteria on the externalizing or internalizing behavioral dimensions. AIMSweb reading provided Fall and Winter benchmark scores for established, emerging, or deficient performance in reading. Established performance means the student met the minimum benchmark for grade-level reading skills, whereas emerging performance refers to scores approaching grade-level reading performance. Deficient performance indicates that meeting the end-of-year benchmark is unlikely. Students scoring in the deficient range should be closely monitored for growth to ensure that the chosen intervention is effective for their individual needs.

In their fourth year of implementation, the school team was interested in looking at the reading and behavioral risk data together in a more detailed manner given that they were now familiar with both screening tools and had interventions in place to address students' multiple needs. They had supplemental reading and behavioral supports available and wanted to ensure they were targeting the correct students for these supports. Furthermore, they were using behavioral strategies such as self-monitoring and behavioral contracting within their Tier 2 reading groups (Altmann, 2010).

TABLE 2.9. BES Monthly Assessment Schedule

	Aug	Sept	Oct	Nov	Dec	Jan	Feb	Mar	Apr	May
School demographics										
Student demographics		×	×		×			×		×
Academic measures										

District reading assessment
    Kindergarten: Winter
    Grades 1–3: Fall and Winter
			×		×					

ThinkLink: reading and math (ThinkLink Learning, 2000)			×		×			×		×
District writing prompt					×					×
AIMSweb reading (Pearson Education, 2008)			×		×					×
Tennessee Comprehensive Assessment Program (state achievement assessment)										×
Behavior measures										
Screener: SRSS (Drummond, 1994)		×			×					×
Screener: SSBD (Walker & Severson, 1992)		×			×					×
ODRs			×		×			×		×
Attendance (tardies/absences)			×		×			×		×
Referrals										
Special education			×		×			×		×
General education intervention team			×		×			×		×
Program evaluation measures										
Social validity: Primary Intervention Rating Scale (Lane, Kalberg, et al., 2009; Lane, Robertson, et al., 2002)	×					×				
Treatment integrity: School-Wide Evaluation Tool (Sugai et al., 2001) and interval ratings						×				

Note. From Lane, Kalberg, and Menzies (2009, Table 5.1, p. 105). Copyright 2009 by The Guilford Press. Adapted by permission.

Figure 2.5 displays how they organized both AIMSweb and SSBD data to be examined in tandem (Kalberg, Lane, & Menzies, 2010). This graph represents a third-grade classroom with 21 students (hence 21 data points). Their Fall (Time 1) and Winter (Time 2) scores are plotted as coordinates on the scatterplot graph. Each data point (dot) represents one student's scores. The solid vertical line represents the Fall benchmark score (77) for established reading scores, and the dashed vertical line represents the Fall benchmark score (54) for emerging performance in reading. The horizontal lines represent the Winter benchmarks for established (92) and emerging (67) reading scores. As mentioned previously, established reading benchmarks are the minimum score necessary for a student to be considered as meeting grade-

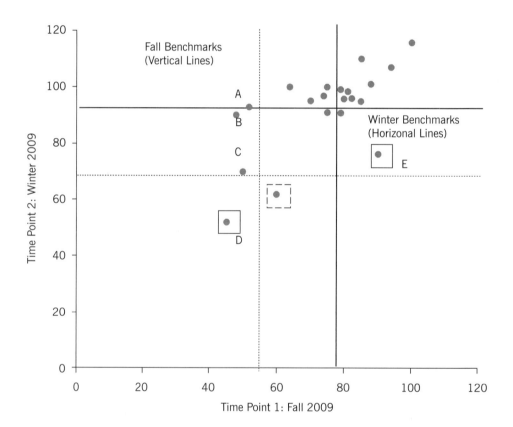

FIGURE 2.5. BES illustration considering students' academic reading scores plotted on an *xy* graph with their at-risk status according to the SSBD in a third-grade classroom in a rural setting. Solid squares indicate a student who exceeded normative criteria on Stage 2 of the SSBD on the externalizing dimension during Time 2 (Winter) administration. Dashed squares indicate a student who exceeded normative criteria on Stage 2 of the SSBD on the internalizing dimension during Time 2 administration. The solid vertical line represents the Fall benchmark score (77) for established reading scores, and the dashed vertical line represents the Fall benchmark score (54) for emerging performance in reading. The horizontal lines represent the benchmarks for established (92) and emerging (67) reading scores for Winter.

level reading requirements at the specified time point and, therefore, on track for meeting the end-of-year benchmark. Emerging performance is the minimum score for a student to be considered as approaching grade-level requirements in reading and may indicate the need for additional supports to meet the end-of-year reading goal. This graph allows you to have an overview of how students have progressed between Fall and Winter time points. For example, Students A, B, C, and D were below the emerging level (vertical dashed line) in the Fall, indicating deficient reading skills at that time. However, at the Winter assessment Student A scored in the established benchmark range (92) and Students B and C scored at the emerging level (67). Student D was still deficient. Take a moment and see if you can identify the four students who were in the emerging range in Fall and who scored in the established range in Winter.

Before looking at the behavior data, we want to point out that, in addition to examining individual students' performance, this figure allows the classroom teacher to have a better idea of where the majority of his or her students fall at a glance. For example, the teacher can see that the vast majority of his or her students are now established readers.

In terms of the behavior data, the Winter behavior screening data are displayed by the solid and dashed squares used in Figure 2.5. The solid squares indicated a student who exceeded normative criteria on Stage 2 of the SSBD on the externalizing dimension during Time 2 (Winter) administration. The dashed square indicated a student who exceeded normative criteria on Stage 2 of the SSBD on the internalizing dimension during Time 2 administration. When behavioral screening data are considered in tandem with the academic screening data, this combined set of information provides a better understanding of which students have multiple sets of concerns. For example, Student E (the student with a solid square indicating he or she exceeds normative criteria on the externalizing dimension of the SSBD) met the establishing benchmark following the Fall administration but *not* the Winter administration and may benefit from a behavior support such as increased reinforcement. In other words, the teacher may conclude that this student requires behavioral support (in the form of a reinforcement plan, gaining positive attention from the teacher) rather than supplemental reading support (see Table 2.10). However, Student D, who did not meet establishing benchmark for Fall or Winter, may actually require academic support in the form of one-on-one or small-group instruction as well as a behavioral support to encourage participation or increase engagement in the supplemental instruction (Altmann, 2010).

By plotting reading and behavior data, teachers can have a clear picture as to which students should be considered for reading and/or behavioral support. It also enables teachers to have a snapshot view of the relationship between reading and behavior performance in their class. The leadership team at BES used curriculum-based reading data as part of their schoolwide primary prevention plan to track students' academic progress and identify those in need of additional support and/or enrichment.

TABLE 2.10. BES Secondary Interventions Grid

Support	Description	Schoolwide data: Entry criteria	Data to monitor progress: Schoolwide data? Other?	Exit criteria
Increased attention and praise from teacher focused on reading growth—using self-graphing	Increased use of reinforcement and attention from teacher After the weekly AIMSweb reading probes, students will graph their own reading progress on monitoring graph while sitting with teacher, who will provide positive feedback about effort and growth Teacher will write praise note to parents (age appropriate) and give to student to take home; this may be used with behavioral contracting with reinforcement planned at home as well, at parents' discretion (see Lane, Menzies, Bruhn, & Crnobori, 2011, for procedures for behavioral contracting) Weekly one-on-one with teacher	Academic AIMSweb reading—met benchmark in Fall but not in Winter *and* Behavior SSBD—exceeded normative criteria for internalizing or externalizing dimension	Weekly AIMSweb reading probes with self-graphing of progress monitored with teacher Weekly praise note sent home with reading progress	Academic AIMSweb—meet reading benchmark at Spring timepoint Behavior SSBD—no longer exceeds normative criteria at Spring time point
Stepping Stones to Literacy (Nelson, Cooper, & Gonzalez, 2004)	Supplemental reading program to address rapid automatic naming, print awareness, alphabetic phonics, phonological awareness, listening comprehension K–3 students Small-group (< 5) or one-on-one format Five days/week for 15–20 minutes	K–3 students Academic AIMSweb reading—deficient or emerging in Fall and Winter *and* Behavior SSBD—exceeded normative criteria for internalizing or externalizing dimension	Weekly reading probes–AIMSweb	Academic AIMSweb—meet reading benchmark at Spring time point

(cont.)

TABLE 2.10. BES Secondary Interventions Grid				
Support	Description	Schoolwide data: Entry criteria	Data to monitor progress: Schoolwide data? Other?	Exit criteria
Read 180® (Hasselbring & Goin, 1999; Scholastic Inc., 1997)	Supplemental reading program provides for computerized instruction and practice, literature for independent reading at instructional level, and direct instruction; skills addressed include word recognition, fluency, comprehension, vocabulary, spelling

Students participate in small-group instruction 3 days/week for 30 minutes; individually on the computer 3 days/week for 30 minutes; and read independently for 60 minutes/week (assigned at home) | Fourth- and fifth-grade students

Academic AIMSweb reading—deficient or emerging in Fall and Winter

and

Behavior SSBD—exceeded normative criteria for internalizing or externalizing dimension | Weekly reading probes—AIMSweb

Reading assessments—AIMSweb; Read 180 program assessments | Academic AIMSweb—meet reading benchmark at Spring time point

Passing scores on district reading assessments |
| Reading program: Stepping Stones to Literacy or Read 180 as appropriate for grade level, with self-monitoring (Lane, Menzies, Bruhn, et al., 2011) | Description of reading programs (above)

Self-monitoring—students will use component checklist of reading intervention to self-monitor their own reading participation (during instruction, independent computer instruction or independent reading practice); checklists will include items such as participation, completion, and accuracy as appropriate, completion of checklists will be monitored for accuracy and completion with teacher; students who meet preset goals for self-monitoring checklist will receive teacher praise and Dragon dollars | Academic AIMSweb reading—deficient or emerging in Fall and Winter

and

Behavior SSBD—exceeded normative criteria for internalizing or externalizing dimension | Achievement of daily/weekly self-monitoring goals (levels of participation and completion)

Reading assessments—AIMSweb; Read 180 program assessments | Academic AIMSweb—meet reading benchmark at Spring time point

Passing scores on district reading assessments

Behavior SSBD—not exceeding normative criteria on Spring screening time point |

Note. From Lane, Kalberg, and Menzies (2009, Table 6.1, pp. 130–131). Copyright 2009 by The Guilford Press. Adapted by permission.

Summary

BES is an example of a school that compared academic and behavioral data and used informed instruction to make decisions on selecting students for appropriate secondary and tertiary support systems. Once BES established their comprehensive plan, which addressed academics, behavior, and social skills, and had systems in place to review their schoolwide data, they were able to focus resources to look at multiple data sources together that more clearly described student needs. Their school leadership team focused on all of the information they had about their students to create a positive and rigorous learning environment.

Summary

Perhaps Walker and Severson (1992) captured the importance of the role of the teacher in the systematic screening process best when they said, "Classroom teachers, with their extensive knowledge of the social, behavioral, and academic characteristics of children in their classes, are in the best position to participate fully in this process at the initial screening level. However, their expertise and considerable knowledge are rarely effectively utilized in this context" (p. 2). We encourage the use of the information provided in this chapter to help school-site personnel to recognize the value of and formalize the use of the SSBD within the context of regular school practices.

To assist with these goals, we provided an overview of the SSBD, including step-by-step directions on how to complete this multistage assessment and responses to frequently asked questions regarding logistical considerations. Then we provided you with the supporting research conducted with the SSBD, including studies (1) examining the reliability and validity of this tool as well as (2) demonstrating how to use the SSBD to identify students who might require secondary (Tier 2) or tertiary (Tier 3) supports. To assist you in the decision-making process, we provided a balanced discussion of the strengths and challenges associated with preparation, administration, scoring, and interpretation. We concluded this chapter with three illustrations to demonstrate how the SSBD can be used to monitor the overall level of risk in a building and inform targeted intervention efforts for students regarding additional supports beyond the primary prevention program. In Chapter 3, we introduce the downward extension of the SSBD—the Early Screening Project: A Proven Child Find Process (Walker, Severson, & Feil, 1995), designed for use with preschool and kindergarten students.

Early Screening Project

A Proven Child Find Process

This chapter introduces the Early Screening Project: A Proven Child Find Process (ESP; Walker et al., 1995), a downward extension of the Systematic Screening for Behavior Disorders (SSBD; Walker & Severson, 1992). Whereas the SSBD was developed for use with elementary-age students in first through sixth grades, the ESP is a multiple-gating system for use with preschool and kindergarten children between 3 and 5 years of age. Specifically, the ESP "incorporates the proactive, universal screening standard for emotional and behavioral problems required by Head Start Performance Standards and ensures that all children are screened for the presence of these problems" (Feil, Walker, Severson, & Ball, 2000, p. 14).

When children begin their preschool and kindergarten years, there are two main milestones to negotiate. First, this is their initial experience in learning how to interact socially with same-age children in a formal setting. Second, this is also the first time they must learn to meet a teacher's expectations. How preschool children negotiate these peer and adult relationships predicts important outcomes not only during the preschool years but also into adolescence and adulthood (Coie, Terry, Lenox, Lochman, & Hyman, 1995; Patterson, Reid, Dishion, 1992; Walker et al., 1990, 1995). For example, children who experience early peer rejection have higher rates of school adjustment difficulties, which result in higher rates of school dropout, psychiatric disorders, and poor academic and social outcomes (Coie, Lochman, Terry, & Hyman, 1992; Parker, Rubin, Erath, Wojslawowicz, & Buskirk, 2006). Poor teacher–student relationships have been associated with poor peer relationships, aggressive behavior, and poor academic outcomes up to 8 years later (Hamre & Pianta, 2001).

Given the importance of the early school years, it is essential to support these very young students in learning how to navigate the preschool and kindergarten years. Because there is such a limited window of opportunity to intervene successfully in preventing problem behaviors from manifesting and becoming stable, a focus on detecting behavioral issues in the preschool and kindergarten years is particularly necessary and important (Serna, Nielsen, Lambros, & Forness, 2000). Central to providing early intervention efforts is accurate detection of children who require additional supports. The ESP is a proactive tool designed to detect children with both externalizing (e.g., acting out; Kazdin, 1993a, 1993b) and internalizing (e.g., socially withdrawn; Morris et al., 2002) behavior patterns. Like the SSBD, the ESP screening process includes three progressively more intensive procedures, which increase in time and intensity. The overall goal of the ESP is to identify preschool- and kindergarten-age children who require early intervention to prevent the development of emotional and behavioral disorders (EBD) that may require services through the Individuals with Disabilities Education Improvement Act (IDEA, 2004) under the label of emotional disturbance (ED). However, it is important to remember that less than 1% of the school-age population is apt to qualify for special education services under the ED label. Given that 2 to 20% of school-age children may have an EBD at some point in their educational careers, it is important to implement systematic child find procedures to identify and support those who show soft signs of adjustment problems given what is acceptable developmentally (IDEA, 2004; Wagner & Davis, 2002; Walker et al., 2004). From very young (e.g., preschool) to older (e.g., high school age) students, early detection procedures are needed to identify those who may require intervention efforts (e.g., secondary [Tier 2] and tertiary [Tier 3] supports) beyond those provided in the primary prevention program (Lane, Kalberg, & Menzies, 2009).

In this chapter, we begin with an overview of the ESP, including step-by-step directions on how to complete this multistage assessment, and provide responses to frequently asked questions regarding logistical considerations. Next, we synthesize the supporting research conducted with the ESP, including studies (1) examining the reliability and validity of this screening tool as well as (2) demonstrating how to use the ESP to identify students who might require secondary (Tier 2) or tertiary (Tier 3) supports. Then we provide a balanced discussion of the strengths and challenges associated with preparation, administration, scoring, and interpretation. We conclude this chapter with two illustrations. The first explains how to monitor the overall level of risk and then use that information to provide individual supports in a large preschool setting. The second illustration demonstrates how to use the data from the screening tool in a three-tiered model of support in an elementary school kindergarten program to identify students for a manualized tertiary support, First Step to Success (Walker et al., 1997).

An Overview of the ESP

In this section, we begin by describing each of the three stages of the ESP. Then we provide information on logistical considerations regarding the ESP, such as preparing, administering, scoring, and interpreting.

Description

The ESP is a low-cost, effective, empirically validated multiple-gating system designed to detect preschool and kindergarten students between 3 and 5 years of age with externalizing or internalizing behavior patterns. Modeled after the SSBD (see Chapter 2), the ESP includes three stages: nominations and rank ordering, teacher ratings, and direct observations and parent questionnaire, with the last stage being optional. The process begins with preschool or kindergarten teachers evaluating all children in their class on two dimensions: externalizing and internalizing behaviors. The ESP contains operational definitions, examples, and nonexamples of externalizing and internalizing behavior patterns to assist with this process. The process begins with teacher nominations and ratings followed by the option of independent observations in nonstructured settings (e.g., home living center; see Figure 3.1).

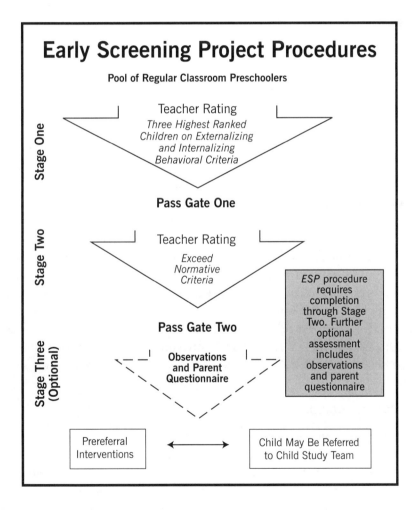

FIGURE 3.1. ESP multiple-gating assessment procedure for identification of students with behavior disorders. From Walker, Severson, and Feil (1995, p. 4). Copyright 1995 by Sopris West, Inc. Reprinted by permission.

Each teacher is given the following materials to complete the initial rating process: (1) Stage 1 nomination procedures (four pages of copies), (2) three sets of Stage 2 ratings for students with externalizing behaviors (five pages each × three copies), and (3) three sets of Stage 2 ratings for students with internalizing behaviors (five pages each × three copies). However, unlike the SSBD, the ESP includes scales unique to children with externalizing (aggressive behavior scale) and internalizing (social interaction scale) behavior patterns, which are described in greater detail next. Stage 3 papers are not distributed to the teacher.

Stage 1: Nomination and Rank Ordering

In Stage 1, each classroom teacher is given the full set of instructions describing the three stages constituting the ESP screening process. The teacher begins by reading the guidelines on how to rank-order the externalizing and internalizing dimensions. Specifically, the teacher reads the full description of externalizing behaviors, including the definition, examples, and nonexamples. Then, in the first column, the teacher enters the names of five children in his or her class whose *characteristic behavior patterns* are most like externalizing behaviors.

Next, the teacher rank-orders the five students on the externalizing list from *most like* (receiving a rank of 1) to *least like* (receiving a rank of 5) the dimensions. This step is done to determine which students' characteristic behavior patterns correspond most closely with the description of externalizing as described in the provided behavioral profiles.

This two-step process of nominating and ranking is repeated to rank-order students on the internalizing dimension. Students' names may appear on only one list (externalizing or internalizing); they cannot be nominated on both lists even if the teacher believes they show some behaviors from each dimension. A choice must be made as to which set of behaviors most closely fits the students' overall characteristic behavior pattern. The final result is two rank-ordered lists: one for students with externalizing behaviors and a second for students with internalizing behaviors.

The six highest ranked students (three on each dimension) pass through Gate 1 into Stage 2. However, if a teacher feels that additional students warrant consideration (e.g., students ranked in the fourth or fifth position for a given dimension), they could be passed through Gate 1 as well.

Stage 2: Teacher Ratings

In Stage 2, teachers complete additional measures on only the students who passed through Gate 1. First, teachers complete rating scales for each of three students with externalizing behavior patterns who passed through Gate 1 into Stage 2. Specifically, for each student, they complete a brief demographic questionnaire to record basic information (e.g., date the rating scale was completed, the name of the school, the classroom, the teacher's name). Then the teacher completes four rating scales—the Critical Events Index (CEI), the Aggressive Behavior Scale (ABS), the Combined

Frequency Index Adaptive Behavior (CFI-A), and the Combined Frequency Index Maladaptive Behavior (CFI-M)—on each student who passed through Gate 1 to gain a more complete picture of their typical behavior patterns on both rarely and frequently occurring behaviors. After all students nominated in the externalizing dimension are rated, the teacher evaluates those who were nominated on the internalizing dimension using the same procedures described previously. The same instruments are again completed, with the exception of the ABS. Instead of the ABS, the top three-ranked children on the internalizing dimensions are evaluated using the Social Interaction Scale (SIS). Each instrument is nationally normed, providing cutoff scores for identifying students as at risk for behavior or learning difficulties.

The CEI is a teacher-completed checklist of 15 high-intensity, low-frequency behaviors. Sample items include *exhibits painful shyness, steals, sets fires*. Teachers record any behavior known to have occurred during the school year. There is one open blank (Item 16) available for teachers to write in any other extreme behavior that does not appear in Items 1–15. First, the teacher circles the student's Stage 1 ESP ranking [1, 2, or 3]) and then evaluates the student on the 15 items provided and writes in any additional serious behavior that was not included in the 15 items.

The ABS is a rating scale for children with externalizing behaviors. It includes a list of nine aggressive behaviors (e.g., *has tantrums*; *physically assaults adults*; *is teased, neglected, and/or avoided by peers*) rated by the teacher on a 5-point Likert-type scale ranging from 1 (*never*) to 3 (*sometimes*) to 5 (*frequently*) to determine the frequency with which each item occurs.

The SIS, a rating scale for children with internalizing behaviors, includes a list of eight social behaviors (e.g., *shares laughter with classmates, verbally responds to a peer's initiation, verbally initiates to a peer or peers*) rated by the teacher on a 7-point Likert-type scale ranging from 1 (*not descriptive or true*) to 4 (*moderately descriptive or true*) to 7 (*very descriptive or true*) to determine the frequency with which each item occurs.

The CFI-A, a rating scale for all children passing through to Stage 2, includes eight adaptive behaviors (e.g., *follows established classroom routines, cooperates with other children, initiates positive social interactions with peers*) rated by teachers on a 5-point Likert-type scale ranging from 1 (*never*) to 3 (*sometimes*) to 5 (*frequently*), with total scores ranging from 8 to 40. Teachers use their knowledge of the child during the past 30 days to estimate the frequency with which each item occurs.

The CFI-M, a rating scale for all children passing through to Stage 2, includes nine maladaptive behaviors (e.g., *refuses to participate in games or activities with other children during free [unstructured] play, is very demanding of teacher attention, pouts or sulks*) rated by teachers on a 5-point Likert-type scale ranging from 1 (*never*) to 3 (*sometimes*) to 5 (*frequently*), with total scores ranging from 9 to 45. Teachers use their knowledge of the child during the past 30 days to estimate the frequency with which each item occurs.

The authors developed both normative comparison measures (CEI, ABS, and SIS) and clinical measures (CFI-A, CFI-M, as well as the Parent Questionnaire in Stage 3) so the ESP could be used for screening purposes as well as to provide assessment information that furnishes a complete picture of the child's behavior. The normative comparison measures determine the extent to which the child should be referred for additional assessment and supports within the context of a comprehensive, integrated, three-tiered (CI3T) model of prevention (e.g., secondary [Tier 2] or tertiary [Tier 3]) or as part of the prereferral intervention process. The clinical measures offer more nuanced information that can be used with other assessment activities (e.g., a structured interview) (Walker et al., 1995, p. 5).

Stage 3: Direct Observations and Parent Questionnaire—Optional

Stage 3 includes direct observations and the Parent Questionnaire, both of which require informed consent from the parents. We first describe the Parent Questionnaire, followed by the procedures for conducting the direct observations, as the questionnaire is completed before the observations occur.

PARENT QUESTIONNAIRE

The Parent Questionnaire enables information to be obtained from the parent perspective to determine whether the child's behaviors of concern are also noticed by the parent. This information offers the teacher and the school-site team insight on how the child navigates other settings beyond the classroom environment. If the child is struggling in multiple areas, then the intervention will need to focus on these multiple settings (Walker et al., 1995). The Parent Questionnaire includes 12 items representing three domains: (1) playing with other children (e.g., "If given a choice, does your child choose to play with other children?"), (2) getting along with caregivers (e.g., "Does your child follow your instructions and directions?"), and (3) playing with materials and self-care (e.g., "How often does your child break or destroy toys or household items?"). All items are adapted from those included in the Stage 2 measures described previously, with the majority of items phrased positively.

To complete the Parent Questionnaire, a meeting is scheduled by the school team with the parent of each child who passes through Stage 2 to (1) complete this questionnaire and (2) sign the informed consent to obtain parental or caregiver permission to conduct the social behavior observations. It is important to be sensitive to caregivers' feelings about the meeting's purpose because this may be the first time anyone has approached them regarding their child's behaviors. Remember: There is nothing more personal to most parents than their children. It is important to be cautious, non-confrontational, and respectful as you explain that (1) their child has been identified using a systematic screening tool conducted as part of regular school practices and (2) you would like additional information (from the questionnaire and direct observations) to help support their child within the context of the secondary and tertiary supports. It is also important to reassure parents that the child is not being referred for special education, but that additional information is being requested to help support the child in the school setting and, if necessary, at home.

After they have signed the consent form, encourage the parents to complete the Parent Questionnaire before they leave so you can answer any questions that might arise. Another option is to administer the Parent Questionnaire as an interview conducted by the teacher.

DIRECT OBSERVATIONS

Direct observation of the child's behavior (referred to as the Social Behavioral Observation) is designed to take place-during a free-play activity to see how the child behaves when playing with his or her peers. These are unstructured (but not unsupervised) settings within the school day that are sampled to provide an independent confirmation of the teacher-completed information in Stages 1 and 2.

It is important that the person conducting the observations have sufficient training and expertise to learn and implement the social behavior (SB) observation procedures according to the training guidelines provided (which includes a video training component). The SB observations will occur during free-play or unstructured activities, with each of the two 10-minute SB observations occurring on separate days.

During each session, the person conducting the observations will use duration recording procedures with the provided stopwatch to record two categories of social behavior: (1) antisocial or nonsocial behavior and (2) prosocial behavior. The first category includes both antisocial behavior (negative social engagement and disobeying established rules) and nonsocial behavior (tantrums and solitary play). The second category, prosocial behavior, includes positive social engagement, parallel play, and following established rules (Walker et al., 1995).

As with the SSBD, the ESP manual includes a detailed, research-based approach to conducting SB observations, including procedures for ensuring the reliability of the direct observation data collected. SB is compared with the normative levels provided by gender. The ESP norming sample is a national standardization sample, which allows for greater confidence in interpreting direct observation data. Students whose SB deviates substantially from other same-gender children may be recommended for secondary or tertiary levels of prevention available within the context of the school-site three-tiered model of prevention or referred to the prereferral intervention team.

Logistical Issues

In this section we address a number of logistical considerations. Each consideration is framed in the form of a question, followed by recommendations from the technical manual as well as our own work.

When Should We Administer the ESP?

The ESP should be completed by teachers no less than 30 days after they have worked with each child (Walker et al., 1995). This is a minimum time frame to make certain that they have enough familiarity with the child's behavior before conducting the screening process. If the child started school fewer than 30 days before the regularly scheduled screening date, the teachers should not rate the child at this screening time point.

Walker and colleagues (1995) recommend conducting the screenings twice each school year: in the Fall (October/November) and after Winter break (February/March). In this way, children are given two opportunities to be identified for additional supports. Also, it supports the screening of children who begin preschool after the onset of the traditional academic year or those whose behavior patterns change during a school year.

In our school-based intervention work at the elementary level, we recommend conducting systematic screenings three times per year: 6 weeks after the onset of the school year, before Winter break, and again prior to the end of the academic year (Kalberg et al., 2010; Lane, Kalberg, Menzies, Bruhn, et al., 2008; Lane, Kalberg, et al., 2011). Fall data can be used to establish interventions immediately after the first screening is conducted. Winter data can be used to determine responsiveness (if students still screen as at risk, it suggests they are not responding to primary prevention efforts) and establish secondary (e.g., friendship groups) or tertiary (e.g., functional assessment-based interventions for students with externalizing behaviors) (Umbreit et al., 2007) interventions. Spring data can used to inform year-end performance and plans for the coming year (e.g., class placements).

How Do We Prepare Materials to Conduct the ESP?

The ESP kit contains all forms necessary to conduct the screening. As previously explained, each teacher will need (1) Stage 1 nomination procedures (four pages of copies), (2) three sets of Stage 2 ratings for students with externalizing behaviors (five pages each × three copies; CEI, ABS, CFI-A, and CFI-M), and (3) three sets of Stage 2 ratings for students with internalizing behaviors (five pages each × three copies; CEI, SIS, CFI-A, and CFI-M).

Teachers will need this packet of materials along with a current class roster for each screening conducted (Fall, Winter, and/or Spring). It is very important to make certain that teachers have a current roster to ensure that all children are considered in the screening process, including those who have enrolled since the previous screening was conducted (provided the child has been at school for at least 30 days).

Stage 3 materials are more involved and require training on how to conduct the direct observations of SB. The ESP contains all necessary information and materials to conduct Stage 3 activities, including operational definitions, data collection forms, training video, audio recording tape, a stopwatch, and quizzes to establish conceptual mastery of the target behaviors.

How Do We Administer the ESP?

Walker and colleagues recommend administering Stages 1 and 2 in a group format with the entire preschool or kindergarten. In this case, all classroom teachers would be together in a room to learn how to conduct the screening, answer any questions, and monitor the procedural fidelity with which the screening occurs. Furthermore, they recommend all instructions be read aloud by the person(s) overseeing the screening process. Some common areas that need particular attention include making certain that (1) children are placed on either the internalizing or the externalizing list (not both); (2) children are ranked from *most like* (1) to *least like* (5); (3) the Stage 2 screenings take place on the correct six children (the top three children with externalizing and the top three with internalizing behaviors); (4) children with externalizing behaviors are evaluated using the ABS, the children with internalizing behaviors are evaluated using the SIS, and all children are rated using the CEI, CFI-A, and CFI-M; (5) all children with externalizing behaviors are rated first, followed by all children with internalizing behaviors; (6) all items on each measure are complete; (7) Stage 2 scales are scored correctly; and (8) reliability is conducted on the scoring procedure (a double-checking of addition and cutoff scores) to make certain that accurate decisions are made regarding the students who do and do not require additional supports. These are just a few areas that warrant attention; it is highly important that the ESP manual be read in its entirety (yes, really) before beginning the screening process to ensure proper implementation.

After teachers become fluent in the process, it may not be necessary to come together as a full faculty. Instead, teachers can complete Stage 1 and 2 forms on their own time or as time permits during their workday (Lane, Oakes, & Menzies, 2010). However, it will be important to have a procedure in place at the school site for working with new teachers to complete the screening tools as intended.

Like the SSBD, the ESP Stage 3 procedures are more intensive. However, as mentioned previously, the ESP manual provides very thorough directions for administering Stage 3 procedures. These include steps that ascertain whether the individuals conducting the SB observations have conceptual and behavioral mastery of the material. First, conceptual mastery is demonstrated using a quiz to make certain the observers are clear on conceptual pieces (e.g., do they know what counts as parallel play vs. alone play?). Then, after the observer has demonstrated conceptual mastery, there are steps (e.g., videotaped practice) to ensure mastery of the behavioral component. The authors also recommend that agreement levels between observers (interobserver agreement [IOA]) be monitored carefully and continuously to make certain the data are accurate. There are different methods of ensuring that observers become reliable in their direct observations. In general, it is best to establish observer accuracy against a standard and then move forward with determining IOA among observers.

How Do We Score and Interpret the ESP?

Stage 1 does not require any scoring in the sense that there are no values to be summed for each of the five students placed on either the externalizing or internalizing dimensions. However, we recommend two checks by confirming that (1) children are placed on only one list (externalizing or internalizing) and (2) the correct top three children on each dimension are passed through Gate 1 to Stage 2.

After teachers have completed the CEI and CFI on the six students in Stage 2, each rating scale needs to be scored. For the CEI, checked items are summed, with total scores ranging from 0 to 16. The ABS (used only for students with externalizing behaviors) requires scores for each item to be summed, with total scores ranging from 9 to 45. The SIS (used only for children with internalizing behaviors) requires scores for each item to be summed, with total scores ranging from 8 to 56 (remember, these items are rated on a 7-item Likert-type scale). The CFI-A includes eight items (score range: 8–40) and the CFI-A includes nine items (score range: 9–45), with all children passing to Stage 2 rated on these two scales along with the CEI. Before moving forward with the remaining steps in determining which students should move through Gate 2 to Stage 3 direct observations, the scoring of these total scores should be confirmed to ensure reliability. The ESP scoring and administration manual provides two normative comparison tables (one for boys and one for girls). These tables give you the criteria to determine whether a given child is (1) at risk, (2) at high risk, or (3) at extreme risk relative to the same-gender students in the norming sample for each rating scale. Also, there is a table (p. 47) for converting risk status scores to corresponding *T*-scores. (This is useful for researchers who might wish to examine the predictive validity of the ESP.)

In Stage 3 (which is optional), the Parent Questionnaire is examined at the item level to compare each item with corresponding items on Stage 2 teacher assessments. This requires careful attention to make accurate comparisons between the parent- and teacher-completed information. Yet this process holds great potential to inform intervention in the school—and potentially the home—setting.

There are extensive directions with checks to ensure the SB observation data are reliable. We encourage you to review the specific procedures for collecting both direct observation data and IOA to ensure that the data collected are accurate. When evaluating data from Stage 3, SB observations are averaged together to obtain an estimate of the total antisocial behavior and nonsocial time across the two (or more) observation sessions. The manual includes normative comparisons for boys and girls to determine the extent to which the antisocial/nonsocial behavior suggests (1) at risk, (2) high risk, or (3) extreme risk.

Finally, the ESP contains a form (p. 48) to organize the ESP assessment information from each stage. Children who exceed normative criteria on only the CEI may not be sufficiently different to warrant further assessment. However, if a child exceeds normative criteria on "several (but not all) scales, . . . [he or she] may or may not be at risk" (Walker et al., 1995, p. 48). Thus, the decision-making process for the ESP is not as explicit as that for the SSBD regarding how to (1) identify students who require supports beyond primary prevention efforts and (2) monitor the overall level of performance over time at a given school. The illustrations later in this chapter will be helpful in deciding how to proceed with the ESP assessment information.

How Can We Use This Information at Our School Site?

Information from the ESP can be used in several ways. First, it can be used to identify children who may require additional supports in the form of secondary or tertiary prevention efforts for those who exceed normative criteria by passing through Gate 2 (see Illustrations 1 and 2). Second, the information can also be used to monitor overall level of risk for a preschool center as a whole as described in Illustration 1. We encourage you to examine both illustrations at the end of this chapter for two demonstrations of how to use ESP.

How Much Does the ESP Cost, and Where Can I Order It?

The ESP is a very-low-cost instrument available for purchase from Applied Behavior Science Press. The full kit costs less than $100 and includes (1) the instruments (which are reproducible); (2) a spiral-bound users' guide and administration manual, inclusive of technical information on the test construction and norming procedures; and (3) a videotape and stopwatch. All materials come in a plastic case.

In the next section, we provide an overview of the supporting research for the ESP. Specifically, we provide information on the psychometric features of the ESP as well as how it has been used in research studies to identify students who are nonresponsive to primary prevention efforts.

Supporting Research

Reliability and Validity

Recognizing the value of the SSBD for identifying elementary-age students with EBD, researchers decided to modify the SSBD for use with preschool-age children (Feil & Becker, 1993; Sinclair, Del'Homme, & Gonzalez, 1993). For example, Sinclair and colleagues (1993) modified the SSBD by beginning with teachers nominating and ranking only seven children with externalizing and seven with internalizing behaviors (rather than 10 each) and making adjustments in the decision rules as to which children would pass through subsequent stages (to account for higher levels of parallel play for this age group). Also, they eliminated the academic engaged time (AET) component of the Stage 3 observation system because this was not developmentally appropriate for preschoolers. Instead, they included direct observations of peer SB during free play in the classroom (two 10-minute sessions) and on the playground (two 10-minute observations). Feil and Becker also explored modifications of the SSBD that included three hierarchical stages increasing in intensity and effort: (1) teacher rankings, (2) teacher ratings, and (3) direct observations. Specifically, they modified the SSBD to have teachers nominate five children with externalizing and five with internalizing behavior patterns. The Stage 2 behavior checklists were modified substantially to make them appropriate for the preschool level. For example, wording was simplified, and approximately half of the occurrence/nonoccurrence items were modified to a 5-point Likert-type scale to better assess frequency and intensity. Also, items pertaining to academics were omitted. Stage 3 direct observations involved a modified peer SB code, and AET observations were replaced with structured-activity engaged time. They also established concurrent validity of this modified tool with the Behar Preschool Behavior Questionnaire (Behar & Stringfield, 1974) and the Conners Teacher Rating Scale (Conners, 1989). In brief, studies that examined the initial modifications of the SSBD for use with preschool-age children indicated that the systematic revisions were effective in identifying very young children at risk for EBD (Feil & Becker, 1993).

After extensive work, Walker and colleagues (1995) produced the ESP. Field trials of the ESP screening procedures reported positive findings, suggesting that the instrument is reliable, valid, and feasible within the preschool context (e.g., Feil, Severson, & Walker, 1995, 1998). As you will note in Table 3.1, Feil and colleagues (1995) had an extensive norming sample (N = 2,853). The details of their development procedures and psychometric findings are presented in this study and in the technical manual. In brief, quantitative procedures were used to aggregate items to scales, making important modifications to develop a screening tool appropriate for this young population. Interrater reliability of teachers' and teaching assistants' ratings were established at Stage 1 with initial nominations, yielding kappa coefficients of .70 for externalizing behavior and .48 for internalizing behavior. A similar pattern was observed with Stage 2 rating scales in the sense that more negatively valenced items such as those on the Critical Events, Aggressive Behavior, and Maladaptive Behavior subscales had greater reliability between raters compared with more positively valenced scale items such as those on the Adaptive Behavior subscale (range: .58–.74). Interrater reliability was also established at Stage 3 for observations of SB, with interrater reliabilities calculated from a random sample of 20% indicating an average of .87 for interval agreement and .93 for duration procedures (Feil et al., 1995).

Test–retest stability was also established. Stage 1 nominations were repeated 6 months after the initial rankings, yielding kappa coefficients of .63 for the externalizing dimension and .35 for the internalizing dimension. Stage 2 measures also demonstrated high test–retest stability, with Pearson correlation coefficients ranging from .74 (CEI) to .90 (ABS; Feil et al., 1995).

Walker and colleagues (1995) also established the validity of the ESP as evidenced by content validity, concurrent validity, and discriminative validity. We refer interested readers to the technical manual because it is beyond the scope of this text to provide a full discussion of all psychometric studies. In brief, there is evidence to support convergent validity between the ESP and (1) the Preschool Behavior Questionnaire (Behar & Stringfield, 1974), (2) Conners' Teacher Rating Scale (Conners, 1989), and (3) Achenbach's Child Behavior Checklist—Teacher Report Form (TRF; Achenbach & Edelbrock, 1987; see also Feil et al., 1995, for validity findings). These findings were replicated and extended in a study by Feil and colleagues (2000) that established concurrent validity between the ESP and teacher and parent versions of the Social Skills Rating System (Gresham & Elliott, 1990) and the TRF of the Child Behavior Checklist (Achenbach, 1997) with a cross-cultural sample of 954 children between the ages of 3 and 4 in a Head Start program. Also, results of discriminative function analyses indicated that the ESP has a very low false-positive rating, meaning there is a very slim chance of a child being identified as at risk for EBD who is not actually at risk. This is an important consideration in the issue of overidentification of students from underrepresented populations. With a low false-positive reading,

TABLE 3.1. Reliability and Validity Studies of the ESP				
Citation	Purpose	Description of participants and schools	Reliability	Validity
Feil & Becker (1993)	To revise the SSBD for preschool children	121 preschool children between 3–6 years of age rated by 17 teachers and assistant teachers Five preschools in one district	Interrater reliability (teacher assistant and teacher ratings): externalizing, .71; internalizing, .55; critical events–A, .79; critical events–B, .83; adaptive, .60; maladaptive, .59; PBQ, .61; Conners hyperactivity, .59; Conners inattention, .56 Test–retest stability—Stage 1: externalizing, .64; internalizing, .49. Stage II: critical events–A, .77; critical events–B, .91; adaptive, .75; maladaptive, .79; Stage III structured-activity engaged time, .20; peer social behavior–positive, .22; peer social behavior–negative, .22; PBQ, .79, Conners hyperactivity, .82; Conners–inattention, .61	Concurrent validity: correlations between ESP and PBQ (Behar & Stringfield, 1974) and Conners Rating Scale (Conners, 1989) ranged from .25 to .84. Critical events–B, adaptive, and maladaptive scales showed substantial concurrent validity Discriminative validity: ESP has high levels of sensitivity and specificity (low false-positive and false-negative rates)
Feil et al. (1995)	To study the effectiveness of a functional screening and identification system for behavior problems among preschool children ages 3–5	National norming sample; $N = 2,853$ children; 3–6 years of age Enrolled in typical and special education preschool and kindergarten classrooms in Oregon, California, Texas, Utah, Kentucky, New Hampshire, Nebraska, and Louisiana between 1991–1994	Quantitative procedures were used to aggregate items to scales Interrater reliability of teacher-teacher assistant ratings Stage 1: nominations: kappa; coefficients: externalizing, .70; internalizing, .48 Stage 2: Pearson correlation coefficients ranged from .58 to .74, with more negatively valenced items (e.g., critical events, aggressive behavior, and maladaptive behavior) apparently more salient to the teachers than more positively valenced scale items (e.g., adaptive) Stage 3: observations of social behavior; interrater reliabilities calculated from a random sample of 20%: interval agreement, .87; duration procedures, .93	Discriminative validity: discriminative function and MANOVA indicated ESP is accurate in predicting problem behaviors among preschoolers in this norming sample, with very low chance of overidentification (small chance of a false positive) Concurrent validity assessed using the PBQ (Behar & Stringfield, 1974), Teacher Rating Scale (Conners, 1989), and CBCL–TRF (Achenbach & Edelbrock, 1987), with correlations ranging from .18–.89 and all statistically significant

(cont.)

TABLE 3.1. *(cont.)*

Citation	Purpose	Description of participants and schools	Reliability	Validity
Feil et al. (1995) *(cont.)*			Test–retest stability Stage 1: nominations 6 months later: kappa coefficients: externalizing, .63; internalizing, .35 Stage 2: ESP Stage 2 measures: Pearson correlation coefficients ranged from .74 (CEI) to .90 (ABS)	
Feil et al. (1998)	This study reports findings of a child find system	N = 2,797 children; 2.4 to 6 years of age Enrolled 64 preschool and kindergarten programs from 160 classrooms in California, Kentucky, Louisiana, Nebraska, New Hampshire, Oregon, Texas, Utah, Washington		Preschool teachers nominated, ranked, and rated children on externalizing and internalizing behaviors; these behaviors were independently confirmed with direct observations. Gender differences were established, with a majority of boys represented in externalizing category and a majority of girls in internalizing category Convergent validity established with Conner's hyperactivity and inattention and CBCL aggression and withdrawal
Feil et al. (2000)	To explore cross-cultural psychometric characteristics and validity of a multiple-gating screening process used by ESP to screen and identify children at risk for behavior problems in Head Start centers	954 children between 3 and 4 years of age in Head Start programs rated by teachers from 40 classrooms Rural and urban sites in Oregon		Concurrent validity: established between ESP and teacher and parent versions of the Social Skills Rating System (Gresham & Elliott, 1990) and the CBCL-TRF (Achenbach, 1997) Coefficients ranged from .91 to .83 between ESP aggressive and CBCL and SRSS externalizing (teacher); coefficients ranged from .53 to .44 between ESP adaptive and social interaction and CBCL internalizing; no significant differences among ethnic groups, suggesting generalizability

Note. Asterisks (*) indicate the study for which results are reported in the table. CEI, Critical Events Index; ABS, Aggressive Behavior Scale; SRSS, Student Risk Screening Scale (Drummond, 1994); PBQ, Behar Preschool Behavior Questionnaire; CBCL-TRF, Child Behavior Checklist Teacher Report Form; MANOVA, multivariate analysis of variance.

it is unlikely that students will be identified as a result of differences in cultural perceptions or English learner status.

In addition to reviewing the content provided in the ESP technical manual, we encourage you to see Table 3.1 for a summary of some of the reliability and validity studies published in peer-reviewed journals. Collectively, the findings from Walker, Severson, and Feil suggest instruments in each stage are reliable as evidenced by test–retest stability and interrater reliability estimates (Feil et al., 1995, 1998, 2000; Walker et al., 1995). Furthermore, findings of these initial studies indicate that the ESP is also valid as established by the several types of validity described previously.

In the next section, we discuss the numerous ways in which the ESP has been used, not only in identifying nonresponders but also as outcome measures in treatment studies.

Identification of Nonresponders

We highlight a few applications of the ESP as presented in published, peer-reviewed articles to demonstrate how the ESP has been used in the research community to identify and support young children in preschool and kindergarten who require more than primary prevention efforts (see Table 3.2). Specifically, in Table 3.2 you will see treatment–outcome studies that used the ESP to identify students who required secondary and tertiary interventions.

For example, you will notice the ESP has been used in a number of studies to identify preschool- and kindergarten-age students at risk for EBD to participate in an early intervention, First Step to Success (FSS; Walker et al., 1997). FSS is a combined intervention program for school and home support to assist very young children who show emerging signs of developing antisocial behavior. We refer you to Table 3.2 for a sample of FSS studies implemented in kindergarten classrooms, including one twin study. There have been several other studies of FSS conducted in the kindergarten setting using the ESP in the initial screening process to identify students for support in this comprehensive, intensive intervention designed to promote the development of prosocial behavior by focusing on teaching skills students need for a positive entry into the school environment (e.g., Beard & Sugai, 2004; Sprague & Perkins, 2009). This program involves a school-based component and a home-based component, which are implemented with the assistance of a behavioral consultant. If you are interested in reading more about this program, see Cambium Learning (*store. cambiumlearning.com*) for ordering materials and Lane, Walker, and colleagues (in press) for a review of the FSS literature. Overall, results have been quite favorable. A recent study even suggested there may be collateral benefits for other students with behavioral challenges in the classroom and improved teacher–student interactions. However, results are preliminary (Sprague & Perkins, 2009).

In addition to identifying students for support using FSS, the ESP has been used in other treatment–outcome studies to identify students with reading and behavioral problems for participation in a prereading intervention such as Stepping Stones to Literacy (Nelson, Cooper, et al., 2004). In these studies J. Ron Nelson and colleagues

TABLE 3.2. Applications of the ESP: Identifying and Supporting Students

Study	Participants and setting	Support and description	Schoolwide data: Entry criteria	Design and monitoring procedures	Results
Walker et al. (1998)	Two cohorts of 24 and 22 kindergarten students Kindergarten teachers in one district conducted screenings	First Steps to Success (Walker et al., 1997), a combined intervention program for school and home to support K–1 students; 3-month implementation period with kindergarten teacher and parent (or caregiver)	Students identified using ESP, with students in Stage 3 AET scores averaging ≤ 65% and > 1 SD above mean on CBCL aggression	Randomized, experimental wait-list control group design ESP adaptive, maladaptive, AET observations TRF aggression, withdrawn Treatment integrity mentioned	Detectable intervention effect for both cohorts, with gains maintaining into primary grades
Golly et al. (1998)	20 kindergarten students attending 10 different schools	First Steps to Success (Walker et al., 1997), a replication of combined intervention program for school and home to support at-risk kindergartners who show emerging signs of developing antisocial behavior (social skills program focusing on teaching skills contributing to positive entry into school environment)	High aggression scores on CBCL (Achenbach, 1991) Teacher ratings on ESP adaptive (low) and maladaptive (high) behavior rating scales Lower than average recordings of AET	Pre–posttest for treatment group, no untreated control group ESP adaptive, maladaptive, AET observations TRF aggression, withdrawn Social validity	Replication study showed comparable outcomes to Walker et al. (1998)
Golly et al. (2000)	Two sets of kindergarten twins, 5 years of age, white Two elementary schools in one suburban school district in southern Oregon	First Steps to Success (Walker et al., 1997)	Students identified using ESP: predetermined cutoff scores on Stage 2 teacher-report measures and Stage 3 observational measures	Multiple baseline design across participants: baseline, intervention, maintenance AET Classroom behaviors: talk out loud, out of seat, touch other, touch property, noncompliance	Strong changes occurred and maintained

(cont.)

TABLE 3.2. *(cont.)*

Study	Participants and setting	Support and description	Schoolwide data: Entry criteria	Design and monitoring procedures	Results
Sprague & Perkins (2009)	Four students from each classroom: 1 FSS student, 1 problem behavior peer, 1 typical peer, and classroom teacher Four kindergarten classrooms located in four elementary schools in Pacific Northwest	First Steps to Success (Walker et al., 1997)	Students identified using ESP: each student highest ranked for externalizing behavior patterns invited (top two in each class); typical students could not have been nominated in Stage 1	Multiple baseline design across participants: baseline, intervention, maintenance AET Student classroom behaviors Teacher-delivered positive and negative interactions with FSS student and whole class Treatment integrity Social validity	Students showed improvements in problem behavior, AET, and teacher ratings of behavioral adjustment Authors also examined collateral effects on classroom peer and teacher behavior, which suggested increased AET and moderate behavioral improvements for peers with behavior challenges and improved positive teacher–student interactions Teacher ratings of classroom ecology improved pre to post
Nelson, Benner, et al. (2005)	36 kindergarten students (18 intervention; 18 control) at risk for emotional disturbance and reading problems; 34 boys, two girls; 22 white, 10 black; three Hispanic, one Asian American Seven elementary schools, medium-sized midwestern city	Stepping Stones to Literacy (Nelson, Cooper, et al., 2004) 1:1 instruction by trained paraprofessional-level tutors (project staff) during school day; 25 lessons daily lessons lasting 10–20 minutes	ESP: Stage 1: nomination and ranking of externalizing and internalizing Stage 2: adaptive and maladaptive T-score $\geq$ 60 DIBELS: LNF < 27 and PSF < 18, indicating some risk according to benchmarks	Pre–post experimental– comparison group Phonological awareness: CTOPP PA; DIBELS ISF, PSF Word reading: DIBELS NWF RN; CTOPP RN; DIBELS LNF Treatment integrity	Students in intervention group showed significant improvement in PA, word reading, and RN skills compared with control group
Nelson, Stage, et al. (2005)	63 kindergarten students at risk for behavior disorders and reading problems; 75% boys; 47 white, nine black, six Hispanic, one Asian American	Stepping Stones to Literacy (Nelson, Cooper, et al., 2004) 1:1 instruction by trained paraprofessional-level tutors (project staff) during the school day;	ESP: Stage 1: nomination and ranking of externalizing and internalizing Stage 2: CEI, ABS, and MBS T-score $\geq$ 60	Pre–post experimental– comparison and nonspecific treatment group design PA: CTOPP PA; word reading: WRMT-R WI and WA	Students in intervention group showed significant improvement in reading skills compared with control group; improvements in teacher ratings

(cont.)

TABLE 3.2. *(cont.)*

Study	Participants and setting	Support and description	Schoolwide data: Entry criteria	Design and monitoring procedures	Results
Nelson, Stage, et al. (2005) *(cont.)*	27 kindergarten classrooms in 10 Midwest elementary schools	25 lessons daily lasting 10–20 minutes	DIBELS: LNF < 7, indicating risk	Letter-naming speed: DIBELS LNF Rapid automatic naming: CTOPP RN; social behavior: BERS (Epstein & Sharma, 1998) Treatment integrity	of classroom competence, self-control skills, and self-confidence were not statistically significant
Gunn et al. (2006)	16 students; 81% boys, all white Teachers in eight Head Start classrooms in two Oregon communities	Social skills intervention: First Steps to Success (Walker et al., 1997) Literacy intervention: early literacy essentials (oral language and vocabulary, print knowledge, and phonemic awareness) 3 days/ week for 15- to 20-minute sessions over 10-week period	ESP: Stage 1: nomination and ranking of externalizing and internalizing Stage 2: adaptive and maladaptive Parents of children with the highest teacher rankings on two scales were approached	Both intervention groups were combined (literacy only and literacy + social skills) and compared with control group (*n* = 8) Social Skills Rating System (Gresham & Elliott, 1990) Peabody Picture Vocabulary Test (Dunn & Dunn, 1997)	Results indicated improvements in social skills and receptive vocabulary for intervention group, as evidenced by large effect sizes, but not statistical significance (due to small cell sizes) Parent ratings of social skills were higher for comparison group
Upshur et al. (2009)	47 children with externalizing behaviors and their families (treatment) and 89 controls; matched sample of 19 intervention and 19 control children 37 teachers from four preschool programs and one Head Start program serving children ages 3–5	Early childhood mental health consultation: Together for Kids Classroom observations and teacher training, individual children assessment and therapy, family assessment and support, and referrals for other family needs	ESP: Fall and Spring ratings Normative data in ESP manual were used to identify children whose scores were in the at-risk level (2 *SD* above mean) on at least two ESP scales; children were prioritized in a meeting with director, and families were invited	Pre–post experimental design Teacher-rated aggressive behavior, maladaptive behavior, adaptive behavior Suspension and termination rates Social validity	Intervention was associated with statistically significant (1) improvements in classroom aggressive and maladaptive behavior, (2) improvements in adapted behavior, and (3) reductions in suspension and expulsion

Note. AET, academic engagement time (Walker & Severson, 1992); CBCL, Child Behavior Checklist (Achenbach, 1991); TRF, CBCL, Teacher Report Form (Achenbach, 1991); DIBELS, Dynamic Indicators of Basic Early Literacy (Good & Kaminski, 2002); ISF, initial sound fluency; PSF, phoneme sound fluency; CTOPP, Comprehensive Test of Phonological Awareness (Wagner, Torgesen, & Rashotte, 1999); PA, phonological awareness; NWF, nonsense word fluency; RN, rapid naming; LNF, letter-naming fluency; WRMT-R, Woodcock Reading Mastery Test–Revised (Woodcock, 1988); WI, word identification; WA, word attack; BERS, Behavioral and Emotional Rating Scale (Epstein & Sharma, 1998); FSS, First Steps to Success; CEI, Critical Events Index.

used Stages 1 and 2 of the ESP in conjunction with Dynamic Indicators of Basic Early Literacy Skills (DIBELS; Good & Kaminski, 2002) to identify kindergarten students with behavioral and academic challenges (e.g., Nelson, Benner, & Gonzalez, 2005; Nelson, Stage, Epstein, & Pierce, 2005; see Table 3.2). Furthermore, the ESP and DIBELS tools have been used in tandem to identify how early elementary-age students with academic, behavioral, and combined risk factors respond to different reading curricula (Kamps & Greenwood, 2005; Kamps et al., 2003). Kamps and colleagues (2003) applied a systematic screening approach to determine the risk status of 383 K–2 students from five urban schools to assess their progression in terms of reading growth over a 3-year period. As part of this study, Kamps and colleagues compared the following reading programs: Reading Mastery (Reading Mastery, 1995), Success for All (Success for All Foundation, 1999), and a literature-based curriculum. One finding of this elegant study was that students with academic or behavioral risk progressed more slowly than those not identified as at risk, whereas students with both academic and behavioral risk made the least progress in reading. (Please read this study if you are wondering which curriculum was most effective!) Furthermore, this study illustrated it was possible to reliably implement systematic screenings for academic and behavior in urban schools using commercially available tools, which in this case included the ESP for use with kindergarten students, the SSBD for first- and second-grade students, and DIBELS for all students.

Components of the ESP were used as both independent and dependent variables in a study conducted by Upshur, Wenz-Gross, and Reed (2009) to examine the impact of early childhood mental consultation, called Together for Kids. This program included classroom observations and teacher training, individual child assessment and therapy, family assessment and support, and referrals for other family needs. Results were favorable, suggesting the intervention was associated with (1) improvements in classroom aggressive and maladaptive behavior, (2) improvements in adapted behavior, and (3) reductions in suspension and expulsion. However, the limitations of this study should be considered carefully before generalizing results.

Components of the ESP have also been used as dependent variables in various group-design studies, including one in Head Start classrooms that focused on class-wide approaches to developing adaptive social and behavioral skills (Serna et al., 2000), another that looked at the functioning of preschool-age children with attention-deficit/hyperactivity disorder (DuPaul, McGoey, Eckert, & Van Brakle, 2001), a randomized trial of an early elementary school intervention to reduce conduct problems (Barrera et al., 2002), and a randomized trial of positive behavior support procedures in Head Start classrooms to improve school readiness (Feil et al., 2009). Furthermore, modified versions of the SB observation system have also been used as a dependent variable in single-case design studies (McGoey & DuPaul, 2000).

In addition to these applications, the ESP has been used to identify children for participation in (1) validation studies of behavioral assessment tools for use with preschool-age children, such as the Preschool and Kindergarten Behavior Scales (Jentzsch & Merrell, 1996); (2) studies characterizing the profiles of young children identified by their teachers as at risk for emotional disturbance (Trout, Epstein, Nelson,

Reid, & Ohlund, 2006) as well as students served in early intervention programs for behavior disorders (Trout, Epstein, Nelson, Synhorst, & Hurley, 2006); and (3) studies exploring risk factors that predict problem behavior of students at risk for EBD (Nelson, Stage, Duppong-Hurley, Synhorst, & Epstein, 2007).

As you can see, the ESP has been widely used, making the instrument useful for researchers and practitioners alike. In the next section, we discuss the strengths and areas for consideration when using the ESP.

Strengths and Considerations

Strengths

Beginning with the passage of Public Law 99-457, local education agencies were required to implement "search-and-serve" practices to detect very young children who demonstrated behavior challenges. This mandate was encouraging given that behavioral performance during the preschool years is highly predictive of important future outcomes (e.g., poor peer relations, aggressive behavior, and poor academic attainment; Hamre & Pianta, 2001). Early behavior problems increase the likelihood of peer and adult rejection and isolation, leading to a host of school adjustment difficulties (Coie et al., 1992; Parker at al., 2006). The ESP provides a practical, low-cost option for meeting this charge, sharing many of the same strengths offered by the SSBD (Feil et al., 2000).

First, the ESP allows for accurate detection of preschool-age children with either externalizing or internalizing behavior patterns. Too often internalizing behaviors go unrecognized and consequently are unaddressed by school-site professionals, given the covert and overcontrolled nature of these characteristic behavior patterns (Achenbach, 1991; Walker, Sprague, et al., 2005). A strength of the ESP is that it is designed to detect children with externalizing and internalizing patterns.

Second, the ESP is a reliable, valid tool with sufficient research conducted to establish the psychometric properties of each stage. As such, school-site teams can be confident when using data derived from each stage to inform the decision-making process. Namely, the ESP can be used to determine accurately—and in a timely manner (Feil et al., 2000)—preschool- and kindergarten-age students who may (or may not) require secondary or tertiary levels within the existing three-tiered model of support at the preschool center or elementary school.

Third, the ESP is a feasible tool in the sense that it is relatively inexpensive and requires less than 1 hour of teacher time to complete Stages 1 and 2. Furthermore, it provides the necessary materials to conduct all activities, including the optional direct observations and Parent Questionnaire constituting Stage 3. Collectively, this proven child find process combines teacher rankings, rating, and direct observations to appraise students' behavior, requiring very limited time commitments in Stage 1 and 2 activities (Walker et al., 1995). Like the SSBD, the process becomes more time intensive in Stage 3, when direct observations and the parent questionnaire are introduced. Yet this later stage is optional and is reserved for only a small number of children who pass through Gate 2.

Fourth, information generated from the ESP can be used to systematically monitor school adjustment and behavioral performance of students within a given school year and across multiple school years. The illustrations offered later can be used as a guide to assist your school site with information sharing regarding the level of risk evident in a given preschool center and identifying students for available supports (secondary and tertiary) beyond the regular school program (primary prevention efforts).

Fifth, there is initial evidence to support the use of the ESP within the context of ethnically and culturally diverse settings, such as those characteristic of Head Start programs (Feil et al., 2000). Specifically, Feil, Walker, Severson, and Ball (2000) report that their results "showed no significant differences in the number of referrals when using the ESP among ethnic groups" (p. 21). This speaks to the generalized use of the ESP.

Finally, there may be benefits for teachers in preschool settings whose experience and training vary widely. Specifically, Feil and colleagues (2000) reported that one preschool director stated that she expected "that the use of the ESP increases the credibility of the staff when they make referrals to local early childhood special education programs" (p. 18). In addition, several site coordinators who participated in the field testing of the ESP indicated they felt that the screening procedures served an educational capacity for teachers. Moreover, many of the teachers benefited "in their teaching and management from exposure to the explicit behavioral descriptions contained in the ESP" (Feil et al., 1995, p. 202).

In sum, the ESP is a feasible, accurate instrument for conducting child find procedures specified in federal legislation (IDEA, 2004). This tool allows all students to be considered when looking for those with internalizing or externalizing behaviors—the two most global and common disorders characteristic of school-age children.

Considerations

In terms of the limiting factors of the ESP, there are a few points that should be considered. First, the ESP allows a limited number of students (three with externalizing and three with internalizing behaviors) to pass through Gate 1 for subsequent evaluation. While the instructional manual indicates teachers may nominate additional students to pass through Gate 1, the initial guideline accounts for just six students, which may be a limiting factor for teachers who have classrooms with a large number of students with either internalizing or externalizing behavior patterns.

Second, when conducting Stage 1 activities, teachers sometimes are concerned with the initial ranking of students, indicating they do not have five students who should appear on the initial list for externalizing or internalizing behaviors. They are highly concerned that by placing students' names on this list, it would cause them to be noticed when there is not actually a concern. If such concerns arise, reassure the teachers there is a very low possibility of false-positive screens (Walker et al., 1995).

Third, like the SSBD, the ESP does not specifically address students with comorbid considerations. Given that internalizing and externalizing behavior patterns tend to co-occur (Achenbach, 1991), this is a limiting characteristic of this tool. Teachers also recognize this co-occurrence, sometimes expressing concern that they have a student who should be placed on both externalizing and internalizing lists. However, this is not possible. Teachers must decide whether the child is more externalizing or more internalizing in terms of his or her overall characteristic behavior pattern.

In sum, the ESP is a cost-effective, efficient tool for use in the early detection of preschool and kindergarten children. As with the SSBD, the ESP has two features that should be considered with caution: (1) a limited number of students intended to pass through Gate 1 (typically six; however, teachers may nominate more students) and (2) an inability to screen for students with co-occurring behaviors (externalizing and internalizing).

In the next section, we provide illustrations to provide further guidance in using the ESP as part of regular school practices to monitor overall progress in the building and identify and support students requiring additional assistance. The first illustration takes place in a preschool setting and the second in a kindergarten context.

Illustrations

An Illustration in a Large Suburban Public Early Childhood Center: Clark Early Childhood Center

Clark Early Childhood Center (CECC) is located in a large suburb of a midwestern city. CECC offered half-day programs for students (212 boys, 124 girls) ages 3–6 in preschool and prekindergarten classrooms. Students attending CECC were predominantly white (77%). Classrooms were inclusive, serving students with and without disabilities. Students without disabilities paid tuition to attend a 2-, 3-, or 4½-day/week program. Programs for students with disabilities were designed by the individualized education program (IEP) teams. Special education services available on site included speech and language and physical and occupational therapies. A school psychologist, diagnosticians, a board-certified behavior analyst and assistant, and a social worker were also on staff to support families and teachers. Approximately 53% of the students attending CECC were eligible for special education services.

Building a CI3T Model of Prevention

CECC began its schoolwide positive behavior intervention and support (PBIS) program in Fall 2008. In the first year of implementation, the school was recognized by the state department of education for excellence in implementation—bronze level. Criteria for this award included completion of all schoolwide evaluation surveys; regular leadership team meetings; ongoing data collection and sharing of information with faculty, community, and families; evidence of ongoing implementation; and achievement of 80% or higher on the School-wide Evaluation Tool (SET; Sugai et al., 2001). The cornerstone of their primary plan was four schoolwide expectations: Take Care of Yourself, Take Care of Each Other, Take Care of Your School, and Take Care of Your World. All classrooms and common areas displayed posters of the expectations with pictures of students who were engaged in behaviors that exemplified the expectations (e.g., wearing a jacket outside, helping a friend, putting away materials in the classroom, recycling). Expectations were directly taught to students (not just expected from them) through lessons, modeling, puppet shows, invited performances, class community meetings, and storytelling. Expectations were reinforced by distributing Helping Hands, paper tickets that specifically stated which of the expectations the student had demonstrated and how (e.g., Shanda showed care for her school by helping to clean the glue off the tables after art time).

THE FAMILY CONNECTION

The schoolwide expectations were communicated to parents through the *Positive Post* newsletter. Information about the four expectations was organized under a corresponding heading. For example, under the section Take Care of Your World might be information on a volunteer opportunity at a local hospital, or Take Care of Each Other might advertise a parent information evening presenting the topic of developing sibling relationships. Parents were given Helping Houses paper tickets to use at home to reinforce their children when they demonstrated any of the expectations at home. The parent–teacher organization (PTO) supported the PBIS philosophy with a purpose statement about their commitment to PBIS. PTO events were planned to bring together parents as a school community.

Detailed information on the preschool curriculum (e.g., communication, technology literacy, social/emotional development) was offered to families in a parent handbook. It included the goals for students (e.g., work collaboratively with children and adults, show curiosity, practice healthy behaviors), a description of the assessment tools, and discussion of how families could assist in the attainment of these goals (e.g., allowing students to freely express their opinions, following a consistent routine).

As part of the early childhood services, the school district funded a Parents as Partners program to teach parents to work with their very young children (birth to age 5). Parent educators worked directly with families to teach developmentally appropriate behaviors; observe and support parenting; conduct meetings on education, networking and support; and provide developmental screenings (see Table 3.3). These developmental screenings were offered for children from birth to 3 years of age by the Parents as Partners program and continued during preschool and pre-K to ensure that students were received appropriate educational experiences. Screening information was used by the school to evaluate the level of educational risk in their student population over time as well as monitor implementation of their overall school–home program (PBIS, academic, and social skill components).

Measures

CECC gathered screening information to report progress to parents and to monitor their overall program effectiveness. They chose three measures. First, the Ages and Stages Questionnaire, Third Edition (ASQ-3; Brookes Publishing, 2009) was used to

TABLE 3.3. CECC Assessment Schedule

	July	Aug	Sept	Oct	Nov	Dec	Jan	Feb	Mar	Apr	May
Student demographics											
Student demographics Special education status	×	×	×	×	×	×	×	×	×	×	×
Developmental growth											
ASQ-3 (Brookes Publishing, 2009)	×	×	×	×	×	×	×	×	×	×	×
		Completed at the appropriate age interval for each child—information reviewed monthly by the team									
DIAL-3 (Mardell-Czudnowski & Goldenberg, 1998)			×	×	×	×	×	×	×	×	×
			Completed within 90 days of school entry—information reviewed monthly by the team								
ESP (Walker, Severson, & Feil, 1995)			×				×				×
			Completed for all students enrolled for a minimum of 4 weeks prior to screening date								
Other student measures											
Progress on curricular goals	×	×	×	×	×	×	×	×	×	×	×
Parent participation in the Parents as Partners program	×	×	×	×	×	×	×	×	×	×	×
Health, hearing, and vision screening	×	×	×	×	×	×	×	×	×	×	×
School attendance		×	×	×	×	×	×	×	×	×	×
Program measures											
SET (Sugai et al., 2001)						×				×	
Social validity surveys	×	×				×				×	

Note. From Lane, Kalberg, and Menzies (2009, Table 5.1, p. 105). Copyright 2009 by The Guilford Press. Adapted by permission.

evaluate development among young children (1–66 months). It covered communication, gross motor, fine motor, problem solving, and personal social skills. Parents or educators who spent at least 15 hours per week with the child completed the measure. The tool used empirically derived criteria with three cut points for scores falling below the expected level of performance in each area to recommend (1) further evaluation, (2) close monitoring, or (3) sharing results with the child's parents or pediatrician. Cut scores were based on a national sample of more than 15,000 children. Second, the Developmental Indicators for the Assessment of Learning—Third Edition (DIAL-3; Mardell-Czudnowski & Goldenberg, 1998) assessed motor skills (fine, gross), concepts (color knowledge, counting), language (expressive, receptive, phonemic awareness), self-help development, and social development (sharing, self-control, empathy) of children ages 3 years to 6 years, 11 months. Percentile ranks were used for comparison with recommendations of "potential delay" and in need of further assessment or "okay and developing satisfactorily." Third, the teachers administered the ESP (Walker et al., 1995) to screen all students three times per year to determine the types of behavioral supports that they might need beyond the schoolwide PBIS plan. The CECC teachers screened all students in their classes regardless of how many days per week they were enrolled and without regard to disability status, a truly inclusive practice. Stages 1 and 2 were used for the purpose of screening. Stage 3 was used by the diagnosticians or school psychologist when additional information was needed. CECC offered health, hearing, and vision screenings at school entry and periodically throughout the year as needed. Students entered school at different times in the school year depending on their birth date; therefore, all screening data were reviewed at monthly leadership team meetings. Students not enrolled at the time of the ESP screening were not screened until the next time point provided they had been in school for at least 4 weeks. Parents were notified immediately by the school nurse of the results from the medical screenings. Together, these screening tools offered a comprehensive developmental picture of each student enrolled and facilitated instructional planning and home–school partnerships.

Schoolwide information was also collected and reviewed monthly by the leadership team. Student progress on curricular goals (academic, behavioral, and social) was monitored through teacher assessments and direct observation. The team monitored family participation in the Parents as Partners program and student attendance to ensure families had the supports they needed.

Implementation of the schoolwide PBIS program was monitored through the SET (Sugai et al., 2001). Social validity surveys were used to assess parental acceptability and level of satisfaction with the program, including the appropriateness of the program goals, opportunities for parent involvement, fairness of the program, and communication to meet the behavioral and social needs of students. Teachers and paraprofessionals also completed social validity surveys to measure their perceptions of the schoolwide program goals (see Lane & Beebe-Frankenberger, 2004, for examples). The leadership team used this information to provide support and training for teachers.

What Was the Behavioral Risk after 1 Year of Implementation?

To monitor behavioral patterns in the CECC after 1 year of implementation, the school team examined the schoolwide ESP screening data. Because this was the only measure collected at fixed intervals (e.g., every Fall, Winter, and Spring), it was used as a snapshot view of school risk at three times during the school year. All students screened participated in the schoolwide program for a minimum of 4 weeks, which gave teachers ample opportunity to observe behavior in the school environment. Figure 3.2 displays the Fall 2009 results of the ESP screening. Three hundred thirty-six students were considered for Stage 1 (the total school population at the time of screening). Twenty-eight classes were screened (15 morning and 13 afternoon) with 124 girls (see Figure 3.2A) and 212 boys (see Figure 3.2B) considered at Stage 1. Fifty-

A: Results for Girls (n = 124)

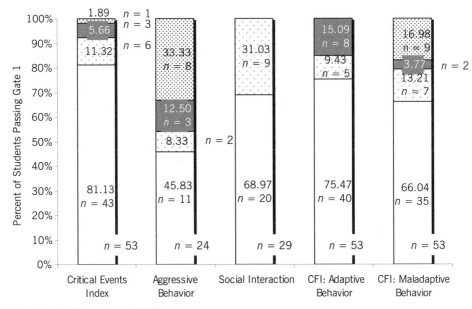

B: Results for Boys (n = 212)

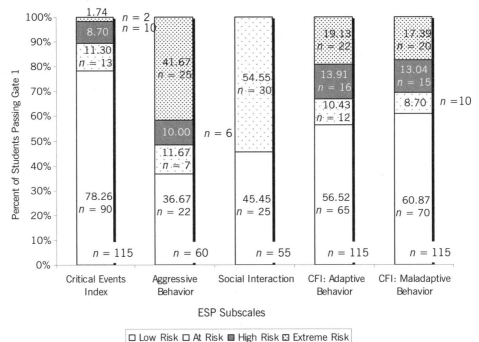

FIGURE 3.2. ESP screening results for CECC (*N* = 336; classes = 28), Fall 2009, Year 2 of implementation.

three girls and 115 boys passed through the first gate (top three ranked on the internalizing and externalizing lists: 28 classes × six students = 168 boys and girls, with 115 boys and 53 girls). Teachers completed the CEI for all six nominated students, the ABS for the three students on the externalizing list, the SIS for the three students on the internalizing list, and the CFI-A and CFI-M for all six nominated students (see Figure 3.1 for the screening process). Then scores were added for each subscale. Next, the cut scores for each subscale (see manual, pp. 25–26) were used to identify students who met the criteria for the four risk categories (low risk, at risk, high risk, extreme risk) except the SIS, which has two risk categories (low risk, at risk). The results are displayed in Figure 3.2, which shows the percentage of students ranked in each risk group. The team intended to build a similar graph for each time point to monitor changes over time. The team also decided to determine the number of students who scored in any risk category on the CEI and either the ABS or the SIS (see Table 3.4). These were used to determine students with elevated risk for externalizing (CEI and ABS) or internalizing (CEI and SIS) behavior patterns. The percentage of students was based on the total number of enrolled boys or girls. Twenty-five students (7.44%) were determined to be at elevated risk for externalizing behavior patterns and 10 (2.93%) with internalizing behavior patterns. The school leadership team decided to provide additional supports for these students in response to the Fall 2009 screening time point (onset of Year 2). Other students who met criteria on any scale were monitored monthly and schoolwide program supports were planned (e.g., parents invited to Parents as Partners, increase in Helping Hands reinforcement paired with behavior-specific praise, instruction of schoolwide expectations, differentiated instruction, multiple opportunities to respond; see Lane, Menzies, et al., 2011).

How Are Students Supported Beyond the Primary Schoolwide Program?

After their first year of implementation and achieving excellence at the bronze level (primary plan in place), the leadership team felt confident in adding secondary (Tier 2) supports for students who demonstrated need based on the schoolwide screening ESP data and other screening measures (see Table 3.3). The team discussed

TABLE 3.4. Number and Percentage of Students with Elevated Levels of Risk as Measured by the ESP

Risk category	Boys n (%)	Girls n (%)
Externalizing: CEI + aggressive behavior	19 (8.96)	6 (4.83)
Internalizing: CEI + social interaction	6 (2.83)	4 (3.22)

Note. CEI, Critical Events Index. Percentage represents the percentage of students in the category out of the total number of boys or girls enrolled.

adding tertiary supports but decided to focus their resources on secondary supports in the second year of implementation given the small number of students at risk (25 externalizing and 10 internalizing) and the additional resources they had (e.g., board-certified behavior analyst and assistant, school psychologist, and social worker). The team felt confident in implementing a strong secondary prevention plan in Year 2. They anticipated, based on students' response to the primary plan alone, that most of the students currently at risk would respond to secondary supports, leaving very few in need of tertiary supports. The team worked together to identify secondary supports that were already available and could easily be added to the existing structure. They also considered professional development options available in their district during the current school year. The leadership team developed a secondary supports grid listing what was available in the building and adding a few that they did not currently employ but had the knowledge and resources to offer (see Table 3.5 for a partial listing). Because they planned to add the secondary supports grid to the implementation manual (see Lane, Kalberg, & Menzies, 2009) was provided to all teachers, they included a description of the support, the criteria to be considered for the support, how they planned to monitor progress, and the exit criteria. Once this grid was completed, they looked at their screening results to determine which students would benefit from each support. To identify the students who met the criteria for each support, the team began by creating a table (see Figure 3.3 for a sample list) of students who passed through Gate 1 and their results of the Stage 2 screening on the ESP. Then, for students with elevated risk on the ESP (any risk level above low), teachers reviewed the DIAL-3 and ASQ-3 results to determine which students met the criteria. They planned to begin the secondary supports at the start of the second quarter. This allowed time to identify students, contact parents to share the results, offer the secondary supports, and create a schedule for the support delivery.

Summary

CECC is an illustration of a schoolwide comprehensive, integrated model of prevention that considers all students for additional supports regardless of disability status. One common misconception is that students receiving special education services do not need to be included in the three-tiered model of increasing supports because they have an IEP to address their specific individual needs. This is not necessarily the case. To be a truly inclusive school, all students should be screened and considered for supports within the general education program, as is the practice of CECC. Furthermore, this school serves as a model of how to design and implement a schoolwide prevention model. They established a strong schoolwide program in Year 1 and added the secondary supports in Year 2. In Year 3, when they design tertiary supports, they will see the benefit of this decision as they will have fewer students in need of Tier 3 support and will have created a schoolwide environment that promotes the new behaviors that replace undesirable behaviors. Finally, the practice of collecting data on how the program is implemented and on social validity helps the leadership team

TABLE 3.5. CECC Secondary Intervention Grid Sample Items

Support	Description	Schoolwide data: Entry criteria	Data to monitor progress	Exit criteria
Sharing and Caring with Words and Actions (social skills play group) taught by social worker and speech/language pathologist	Structured play group with the school social worker Using play to teach appropriate school behaviors; school contexts used such as art and music time, sitting on the carpet with friends, recess play (asking to play with others, sharing toys), snack time	Behavior: ESP: elevated risk on aggression scale (at, high, or extreme risk) *and* Language: DIAL-3: potential delay in language areas *or* IEP goals for expressive language development or social (pragmatic) language	Progress on curricular goals: Social/behavioral: exhibits self-control; works cooperatively with other children and adults Language: uses language to communicate ideas, feelings, questions or to solve problems Data collection of daily progress	Demonstrating appropriate interactions during classroom and outdoor contexts. Behavior: ESP in low-risk range for aggressive behavior Language: mastery of social language goals
Read with Me! Stress-Free Strategies for Building Language and Literacy (Robertson & Davig, 2002) Taught by Parents as Partners educators and one of their behavior support staff (board-certified behavior analyst, assistant, school psychologist, social worker)	Parent education program to facilitate language and literacy for young children. Strategies include (1) echo reading, (2) pair reading, (3) questioning, (4) predicting Parents participate with their preschool child one time per week. Parents meet for 1 hour while their child is in regular class. Parents learn and practice: • The focus reading strategy for that week • Helping their child choose books of interest • Strategies to keep child engaged in book time (teaching and reinforcing listen and engagement behaviors) Followed by 30 minutes of choosing books and applying reading and behavioral strategies with child. Snack and book discussion as a group at the end of the session. Focus on modeling language, engagement behaviors, and children using language to talk about text to build early literacy skills. Parent educators coach and provide support to parents.	Parents accept invitation to participate in Parents as Partners program Literacy: ASQ-3 communication score in the closely monitor or share results with parents/doctor categories *or* DIAL-3 potential delays in language *and* Behavior: ESP elevated risk for either internalizing or externalizing behavior patterns	Progress on curricular goals: Literacy: listen for different purposes; express ideas with topic-related vocabulary; demonstrate early reading skills Social/behavioral: takes turns with adults or peers; engages in tasks as requested by an adult (e.g., stays on carpet for instruction, completes academic activities, stays at chosen play center) Data collection on daily progress	Completion of program Parents are invited to attend again if they are interested and if students continue to meet entry criteria at following screening time points

Note. IEP, individual education plan. From Lane, Kalberg, and Menzies (2009, Table 6.1, pp. 130–131). Copyright 2009 by The Guilford Press. Adapted by permission.

Student name	Nominated in Stage 1	Stage 2				
		Critical Events Index	Aggressive Behavior Scale	Social Interaction Scale	Combined Frequency Index Adaptive Behaviors	Combined Frequency Index Maladaptive Behaviors
Nicolas M.	Internalizing	Low risk	—	Low risk	Low risk	Low risk
Luci T.	Internalizing	At risk	—	At risk	Low risk	At risk
Dana J.	Internalizing	Low risk	—	Low risk	Low risk	Low risk
Thomas L.	Externalizing	Extreme risk	High risk	—	High risk	High risk
Kelley M.	Externalizing	At risk	High risk	—	At risk	High risk
Christopher R.	Externalizing	High risk	High risk	—	High risk	High risk

FIGURE 3.3. Sample class list of students passing through Gate 1 of the ESP.

ensure that the program they are evaluating is happening as planned and is acceptable to all stakeholders. This information is critical to the success of any plan.

An Illustration in a Small Suburban Elementary School Kindergarten Program: Oakdale Elementary School

Oakdale Elementary School (OES) is located in a small suburb outside of a major metropolitan area in a Middle Atlantic state. The public school served 795 PreK–5 students (401 boys, 394 girls). The student population was 70.06% black, 17.99% white, and 11.96% other ethnicities. A full range of special education learning environments were offered (e.g., inclusion, resource, self-contained classes). There were five kindergarten teachers with eight half-day kindergarten classes and one full-day class serving 116 kindergarten students (56 boys, 60 girls) in 2009–2010. Each kindergarten class was supported by a teaching assistant. Speech and language services were provided in the general education setting 1 hour per week so that the therapist could work on improving students' pragmatic skills with their peers. The full-day class was inclusive, and both students with and without disabilities attended. All related services (e.g., physical, occupational, and speech/language therapies and adaptive physical education) were provided within the context of the general education program. Approximately 10% of the students attending OES participated in special education programs.

Building a CI3T Model of Prevention One Level at a Time

In 1996, the district established a districtwide program for character education, Character Counts!® (Josephson Institute Center for Youth Ethics, 2010). The mission of the nonprofit that developed this program was "to improve the ethical quality of society by changing personal and organizational decision making and behavior" (*Josephsoninstitute.org*). This mission aligned with the district philosophy that character education should be taught directly to students (not taken for granted) and the program must be grounded in skills (e.g., self-determination skills; Stang, Carter, Lane, & Pierson, 2009) with observable and measurable outcomes (behaviors). They believed that a proactive approach to character education would reduce problem behaviors in schools and have a positive effect on the morale and stance (looking for the positive responding to the negative) of its administrators, faculty, and staff, which would improve student–teacher and family–school relationships.

As a next step, the district offered training to schools to design and implement PBIS plans. They invited nationally known researchers in the field of PBIS to conduct these trainings with state funding. Of the 42 schools currently in the district, 30 had established schoolwide plans. OES attended a 6-month training process in the 2007–2008 school year and implemented it the following year. The school leadership team established two schoolwide expectations: Respect and Responsibility. They also established schoolwide procedures for teaching the behaviors that would demonstrate Respect and Responsibility. They chose to integrate these lessons into their Character Counts! lessons so that PBIS was not perceived or treated as a separate component but rather was an integrated and natural part of their current schoolwide program. The team established schoolwide procedures to reinforce students for meeting expectations and demonstrating the character traits taught (e.g., honesty, trustworthiness, respect). They integrated the reinforcement systems (one for the school, not for each program) so all faculty and staff (including bus drivers, office staff, substitute teachers, and cafeteria staff) could reinforce students. The school team designed Acorns for reinforcement, small acorn-shaped tickets printed with the school expectations and a place to write the reason why the student received the reinforcer. Acorns were used by students to access special privileges (entry into quarter assemblies and celebrations) and tangibles (items available from the Acorn Market, such as pencils and stickers). They also held weekly Acorn drawings for special prizes and privileges. All teachers were asked (and agreed) to use a coordinated approach to reinforcement and eliminate all other class-level systems.

As part of the state requirement for PBIS models, the school collected and looked at data the school already generated (see Table 3.6). Although the focus was initially on reviewing behavioral data (e.g., office discipline referrals, suspensions, attendance, referrals to special education for behavior), the school-site leadership team noticed that the students with behavioral difficulties often had academic difficulties as well. The team decided to look at behavioral and academic data together. During their training, the leadership team learned that early-onset behavioral difficulties (e.g., aggression, antisocial behaviors) are often persistent and associated with negative outcomes, including limited reading skills, school drop out, and incarceration (Lane, 2004; Wagner & Davis, 2006; Walker et al., 2004). They also learned that students are more amenable to prevention efforts at younger ages (Bullis & Walker, 1994). As a result, the kindergarten team searched for a way to find students at risk for these behavioral difficulties as early as possible.

Measures

In addition to the currently collected schoolwide measures (see Table 3.6), the kindergarten teachers and their principal decided to use a systematic screener for behavior specifically for young children, the ESP (Walker et al., 1995). Because they were not planning to screen all students in the school during the first year of implementation, the administrator decided to inform parents of this new screening procedure with the opportunity to "opt out." This meant that all students would be screened as part of the regular kindergarten program unless their parents requested that they not be included. None of the parents made such a request. This practice was considered similar to the vision, hearing, and dental screening provided at the school. The purpose of the screening was to monitor how the kindergarteners were responding to the primary plan and to inform prevention efforts.

TABLE 3.6. OES Assessment Schedule									
	Sept	Oct	Nov	Dec	Jan	Feb	Mar	Apr	May
Student demographics									
Student demographics Special education status	×	×	×	×	×	×	×	×	×
Hearing and vision screening	×	×	×	×	×	×	×	×	×
Behavioral measures									
DIBELS (Good & Kaminski, 2002) (reading CBM)		×			×			×	
Attendance	×	×	×	×	×	×	×	×	×
Office discipline referrals	×	×	×	×	×	×	×	×	×
Suspensions		×				×			
Academic measures									
DIBELS (Good & Kaminski, 2002) (reading CBM)	×				×				×
AIMSweb® (Pearson Education, 2008) (math CBM)	×				×				×
Report card grades (progress report and quarterly grades)		×	×	×		×	×	×	×
Maryland school assessment (reading, math, science; grades 3–5)	× (Results)					× (Test)			
Program evaluation measures									
Treatment integrity: SET (Sugai et al., 2001)			×					×	
Social validity (Primary Intervention Rating Scale: Lane, Kalberg, Bruhn, et al., 2009; Lane, Robertson, et al., 2002)	×				×				×

Note. From Lane, Kalberg, and Menzies (2009, Table 5.1, p. 105). Copyright 2009 by The Guilford Press. Adapted by permission.

How Did the Kindergarten Teachers Use the Data from the Primary Prevention Efforts to Determine Which Students Needed More Support?

To establish a baseline and determine immediate student needs, the teachers completed the ESP in October 2008. There were a total of 116 students (60 girls and 56 boys) enrolled and screened in Stage 1. Fifty-four students (six per each of nine classes) passed through Gate 1 to Stage 2 for further consideration. Figure 3.4 shows the results of the fall screening. As can be seen in Figure 3.4A, 24 of the 60 girls were nominated and passed to Stage 2 for consideration. Of those, nine were nominated with externalizing and 15 with internalizing behaviors. The bars display the percentage of students who were placed in each category of risk for each subscale. For example, the first bar represents the CEI (all 24 girls rated). Of those rated, 75% (N = 18) were at low risk, 16.67% (N = 4) were at risk, and 8.33% (N = 2) were at high risk. None of the girls rated were at extreme risk on this subscale. The second bar represents the ABS. Only the nine girls who were nominated with externalizing behaviors were screened on this scale, and of those 55.56% (N = 5) were at low risk, 11.11% (N = 1) at risk, 22.22% (N = 2) at high risk, and 11.11% (N = 1) at extreme risk. After reviewing the names of the students in any category of elevated risk, the kindergarten team (five teachers) determined that 11 girls were at some level of risk across all nine classes (including special and general education).

As can be seen in Figure 3.4B, of the 56 of boys enrolled, 30 passed through Gate 1 to Stage 2 for further screening. Eighteen boys were nominated with externalizing behaviors and 12 with internalizing behaviors. According to the CEI, 76.67% (n = 23) were at low risk on this subscale, 13.33% (n = 4) were at risk, 6.67% (n = 2) were at high risk, and 3.33% (n = 1) were at extreme risk. After reviewing the names of the boys at some level of increased risk on the ESP, the teachers determined that 15 boys needed additional supports.

The kindergarten team found a total of 26 students (11 girls, 15 boys) who were at increased risk of persistent behavior problems after 6 weeks of participation in the primary plan (Character Counts!, PBIS, academic instruction, and in some cases additional services through special education). Because intervention is critical for students with early-onset behavior difficulties, the team decided not to wait for additional time in the primary plan for these 26 students. Therefore, they collected the other data as part of regular school practices and offered secondary and tertiary supports in place at the school.

Given the extreme negative outcomes associated with aggression and the fact that aggressive behavior becomes increasingly resistant to intervention efforts (Bullis & Walker, 1994; Kazdin, 1993a, 1993b; Moffitt, 1993; Walker et al., 2004), the teachers decided to incorporate a new intervention focusing on supporting the boys and girls who showed high risk (three boys, two girls) and extreme risk (one boy, one girl) on the ABS. For these seven students, the teachers decided to move directly to tertiary support.

A: Results for Girls (n = 60)

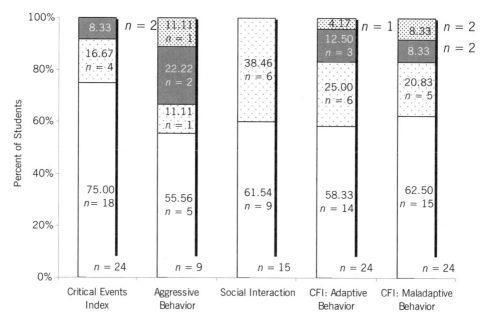

B: Results for Boys (n = 56)

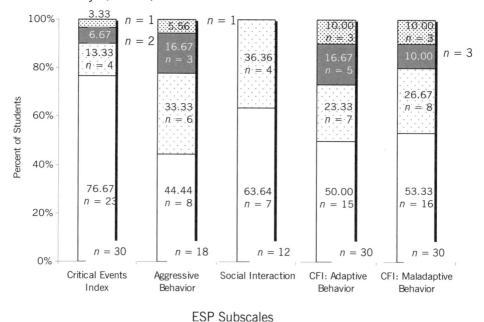

ESP Subscales

☐ Low Risk ☐ At Risk ■ High Risk ☒ Extreme Risk

FIGURE 3.4. ESP screening results for OEIS–kindergarten, Fall 2008, Year 1 of implementation.

How Are Students Supported at the Tertiary Level?

Teachers worked together at weekly team meetings to review the published literature to choose a research-based program to address aggression. They agreed to add only one new support that they would implement with fidelity for the one student in their class who was most in need, as determined by the ESP ABS. On the basis of the evidence reviewed, they decided the FSS program (Walker et al., 1997) would fit their identified needs.

In brief, FSS is a manualized program offering school-based and home-based instruction on specific social skills necessary for academic success by involving the essential social change agents in the child's life. These people include teachers, parents, and peers. The goal is to interrupt the progression of antisocial behavior tendencies for at-risk students upon school entry (Colvin, 2004; Walker et al., 1998). The FSS program contains three components: (1) proactive universal screening (such as the ESP), (2) school intervention, and (3) parent training. A school professional coordinates and delivers the program acting in the role of behavioral coach to the teacher and parents (i.e., FSS consultant).

After students are identified and the parents have consented, the school component begins. The school component includes an adapted version of the Contingencies for Learning Academic and Social Skills (CLASS) Program for Acting-Out Child (Hops & Walker, 1988). CLASS includes (1) frequent adult monitoring of student performance, with a heavy emphasis on praise; (2) points given to the student based on program guidelines and student performance; and (3) individual, group, and home rewards. This program is behavioral, including strategies such as frequent monitoring and feedback, positive reinforcement, and group contingencies that facilitate positive social involvement from peers.

The CLASS component involves two 20-minute sessions each day, one in the morning and another in the afternoon. These sessions are initially led by a consultant who is a behavior specialist, school psychologist, or other individual well versed in the FSS program. The consultant sits by the student to monitor his or her behavior and to provide feedback. Two cards (one red, one green) are used to give the student a signal regarding his or her behavior and to allocate points according to the program guidelines. The student's performance goals shift over time to help shape the desired behavior. Over time, the program is extended to half day or full day. After Day 6 of the program, the teacher takes over implementation. The program requires a minimum of 30 days to complete; however, the actually length depends on the amount of time it takes each student to master each phase (Walker et al., 1997, 1998). There is a formal maintenance phase used to fade out classroom reinforcement, leaving just the schoolwide program in place following FSS program completion.

There is also a parent component, referred to as homeBase. HomeBase typically begins on Day 10 of the CLASS component, lasting about 6 weeks. Parents work with the consultant to learn how to teach their child important school success skills such as accepting limits, cooperation, and problem solving. The program includes lessons, guidelines, and games and activities that parents can use. Parents teach and reinforce skills being taught in the school-based CLASS component, requiring about 10–15 minutes each day. The intent here is to establish a strong partnership to help provide the students with consistent feedback in terms of acceptable behavior and improve home–school communication (Epstein & Walker, 2002). By participating in this program, the parents learn parenting skills and eliminate coercive interaction patterns responsible for aggressive behavior (Patterson et al., 1992).

It is beyond the scope of this chapter to provide all details of this program. However, you can order the FSS kit for a nominal fee to learn more about the details of implementation and evaluation.

The OES teachers decided on the FSS program for several reasons. First, they reviewed the evidence, and the results achieved in previous studies gave them confidence they could be successful with this program (for a review of FSS studies conducted, see Lane, Walker, et al., in press). The authors of the ESP were also developers of FSS, which offered continuity between screening and support. Second, the program included a parent component, which teachers had previously determined to be a priority. Third, the program—cost-effective and time-efficient—could be implemented by the teachers and support staff.

After selecting this program, the teachers created the structure for their tertiary supports grid (see Table 3.7; Lane, Kalberg, & Menzies, 2009). Since they planned to add additional supports over time, they wanted to keep track of the supports they offered. They also hoped it would serve as a model for the rest of the school after the first year of schoolwide implementation when they moved the focus to developing other Tier 3 supports.

Because this was an extra support, it was necessary to secure parent permission before beginning the program. The teachers decided who would draft the letter to be sent to the parents from the teacher and principal to inform them that this support would be offered to their child. They did not expect any of the parents to refuse this support but felt strongly that they should be included as partners. The

TABLE 3.7. OES Tertiary Intervention Grid

Support	Description	Schoolwide data: Entry criteria	Data to monitor progress	Exit criteria
FSS (Walker et al., 1997): implemented by classroom teachers and support staff	Teacher and assistants work together to establish target behaviors for each eligible student. School intervention (CLASS): establish behaviors, direct feedback for desired target behaviors (green card), and corrective feedback for undesired behaviors (red card). Proximity and feedback faded as behavior is shaped.	Kindergarten students Behavior: ESP ratings at high or extreme risk on aggression	Behavioral measures: daily goals met on FSS card Academic measures: DIBELS (early literacy skills), AIMSweb (early numeracy skills)	Successful completion of program (approx. 30 school days) Behavior: ESP in low-risk range for aggression

Note. AIMSweb (Pearson Education, 2008). From Lane, Kalberg, and Menzies (2009, Box 6.3, pp. 134–135). Copyright 2009 by The Guilford Press. Adapted by permission.

kindergarten team wanted to make a special effort to partner with parents early so they could develop a positive working relationship (Epstein & Walker, 2002). Of the seven parents offered this extra support for their child, all agreed. In this school, the board-certified behavior analyst and assistant served as consultants working with the teachers, parents, and students to implement the program as designed. It is very important when implementing such programs that they not be modified; otherwise, it is no longer an evidence-based program.

Finally, the tertiary supports grid contained data that would be monitored to evaluate the students' response and an exit criteria set (Table 3.7). It is important to review student progress and either graduate the student once the goals are achieved or adjust the interventions if the results are not sufficient.

Summary

The OEIS kindergarten program is an illustration of a CI3T model of prevention. The staff moved forward at a rate that offered the opportunity for meaningful change. The school leadership incorporated the behavioral component (PBIS) into the existing character education program so that adding PBIS practices did not feel like a new program or "one more thing to do," but was a natural part of the total program to support all learners in their social, behavioral, and academic development. The school staff felt that they were helping students have positive school experiences and were promoting important lifelong outcomes, OEIS's mission.

Summary

This chapter introduced the ESP, a low-cost, multiple-gating screening tool for use with very young children and offered step-by-step directions on how to complete it. Research conducted with the ESP was synthesized to (1) examine the reliability and validity of this tool for use in the preschool and kindergarten settings as well as (2) demonstrate how to use the ESP to identify students who might require secondary (Tier 2) or tertiary (Tier 3) supports. Then an evenhanded discussion of the strengths and considerations associated with preparation, administration, scoring, and interpreting findings of the ESP was provided. The chapter closed with illustrations of how to use the ESP in preschool and kindergarten settings as part of regular school practices.

In the next chapter, we introduce a no-cost screening tool: the Student Risk Screening Scale (Drummond, 1994). We encourage you to read on to learn about a tool initially developed for use in the elementary setting that now has evidence to support its use in middle and high schools.

CHAPTER 4

Student Risk Screening Scale

In this chapter, we introduce the Student Risk Screening Scale (SRSS; Drummond, 1994), a no-cost, one-page universal screening tool initially developed to detect elementary-age students at risk for antisocial behavior patterns. Antisocial behavior is the opposite of prosocial behavior and includes aggressive, coercive behaviors that often impede the development of positive relationships with peers and adults. In short, antisocial behavior can be thought of as persistent violations of normative (typical) behavior that impedes the development of meaningful social interactions (Coie & Dodge, 1998; Walker et al., 2004).

Although initially developed for use with elementary-age students, recent validation studies have confirmed the use of this measure at the elementary school (Lane, Kalberg, et al., 2010; Lane, Little, et al., 2009; Oakes et al., 2010), middle school (Lane, Bruhn, Eisner, & Kalberg, 2010; Lane, Parks, et al., 2007), and high school (Lane, Kalberg, Parks, et al., 2008; Lane, Oakes, Ennis, et al., 2011) levels. There has even been a first attempt to validate a downward extension (SRSS: Early Childhood) for use at the preschool level (Lane & Oakes, 2011) and an extended version (SRSS: Internalizing and Externalizing [SRSS-IE]; see Lane, Oakes, Harris, Menzies, Cox, & Lambert, 2011) to detect students with internalizing behavior patterns (e.g., anxiety, social withdrawal, depression) as well as externalizing behaviors (e.g., aggression, defiance, bullying; Walker et al., 2004). While the usefulness of adapted versions of the SRSS remains to be seen, the SRSS is a valuable tool for identifying school-age students with externalizing behaviors.

We begin with an overview of the SRSS, including step-by-step directions on how to complete this multistage assessment. Next, we synthesize the supporting research conducted with the SRSS, including studies (1) examining the reliability and validity of this tool as well as (2) demonstrating how to use the SRSS to identify students who might require secondary (Tier 2) or tertiary (Tier 3) supports. Then we provide a balanced discussion of the strengths and considerations associated with preparation, administration, scoring, and interpreting findings of the SRSS. We conclude with three illustrations. The first depicts how Crafton Elementary School's leadership team used information from the SRSS to determine which students required supplemental support and to inform classwide instructional decisions. The second illustration explains how Foster Middle School's team used the SRSS in conjunction with other data collected as part of regular school practices to (1) monitor the overall level of risk over time and (2) make decisions about secondary and tertiary supports. The third illustration demonstrates how Liberty High School used the SRSS to examine changes in the level of risk present in the building over 2 consecutive academic years. In addition, information is provided on how to support students for whom primary prevention efforts are insufficient as well as teachers who might need professional development in terms of differentiating instruction and refining classroom management skills.

An Overview of the SRSS

In this section, we begin by describing the SRSS. Then we provide information on logistical considerations such as preparing, administering, scoring, and interpreting the SRSS.

Description

In contrast to the Systematic Screening for Behavior Disorders (SSBD; Walker & Severson, 1992) and the Early Screening Project (ESP; Walker et al., 1995), which are characterized by a three-stage multiple-gating system, the SRSS is a one-stage universal screening tool (Drummond, 1994), initially designed as a simple and accurate means to identify elementary-age students (K–6) with antisocial behavior patterns.

The SRSS is easy to prepare, administer, score, and interpret (Lane, Kalberg, & Menzies, 2009; Oakes, Wilder, et al., 2010). It requires one page (or Excel worksheet) to rate an entire class. As seen in Figure 4.1, the instrument contains a list of all students (names and/or district identification numbers) on a teacher's roster in the first column. The seven items constituting the SRSS are listed across the top row as follows: (1) steal; (2) lie, cheat, sneak; (3) behavior problem; (4) peer rejection; (5) low academic achievement; (6) negative attitude; and (7) aggressive behavior. Teachers rate students individually on each item using a 4-point Likert-type scale: *never* = 0, *occasionally* = 1, *sometimes* = 2, *frequently* = 3. The ratings for each item are added together, producing a total score ranging from 0 to 21. Drummond (1994) used these total scores to create three categories of risk: low (0–3), moderate (4–8), and high (9–21). These levels can be used to determine the types of support (secondary, tertiary) students may require. Additionally, total scores can be used to monitor the level of risk over time, as shown in the illustrations appearing at the end of this chapter. Approximately 10 minutes of teacher time is required to screen an entire class of about 25 students (Lane, Kalberg, Bruhn, et al., 2008, 2009).

TEACHER NAME

Student Risk Screening Scale (SRSS)

0 = Never
1 = Occasionally
2 = Sometimes
3 = Frequently

Use the above scale to rate each item for each student

Student ID	Student Name	Steal	Lie, Cheat, Sneak	Behavior Problem	Peer Rejection	Low Academic Achievement	Negative Attitude	Aggressive Behavior	Total
1111	Smith, Sally	0	0	3	1	3	3	3	

FIGURE 4.1. Illustration of the SRSS. From Walker, Ramsey, and Gresham (2004, Table 3.5, p. 98). Copyright 2004 by Wadsworth, a part of Cengage Learning, Inc. Adapted by permission.

Logistical Issues

In this section we present a number of logistical considerations, framed in the form of a question, followed by recommendations based on our 10 years of experience using the SRSS in school-based intervention and professional development work.

When Should We Administer the SRSS?

If your school-site leadership team elects to implement the SRSS as part of regular school practice, it should be completed by teachers 6–8 weeks after the onset of the academic year. This time frame is consistent with recommendations for the SSBD and the ESP. Unlike curriculum-based measures, behavior screening tools should not be implemented as soon as students begin the school year because teachers need sufficient time to become familiar with students' characteristic behavior patterns before conducting the screening process. Six to 8 weeks is considered ample time for this process to occur.

When we work with school-site teams to develop assessment plans, we recommend conducting systematic screenings three times per year: 6 weeks after the onset of the school year, before Winter break, and again prior to the end of the academic year (Kalberg et al., 2010; Lane, Kalberg, Bruhn, et al., 2008; Lane, Kalberg, et al., 2011; Lane, Kalberg, Parks, et al., 2008). As mentioned in previous chapters, Fall data can be used to identify students for secondary (Tier 2) and tertiary (Tier 3) supports immediately after the first screening is conducted. Winter data can be used to examine how students respond to primary prevention efforts. For example, students who still score in the moderate- or high-risk categories can be identified as nonresponsive to primary prevention efforts (see Illustration 1 of Crafton Elementary School, Illustration 2 of Foster Middle School, and Illustration 3 of Liberty High School). If screenings are conducted and analyzed prior to Winter break, secondary (e.g., self-regulation strategies for students at moderate risk for antisocial behavior; Mooney et al., 2005; Vanderbilt, 2005) or tertiary (e.g., functional assessment-based interventions for students at high risk; Umbreit et al., 2007) supports can be introduced when students return. Furthermore, Winter data can also be used as exit criteria for students who were placed in secondary and/or tertiary support programs immediately following the Fall assessment point. Spring screening data can be used to inform year-end performance as well as to plan for the following year (e.g., Lane, Oakes, & Menzies, 2010).

We encourage school-site leadership teams to develop an assessment schedule (see Table 4.1 for Crafton Elementary School Table 4.2 for Foster Middle School, and Table 4.3 for Liberty High School) to illustrate all assessments (and their timing) administered as part of regular school practices. This information should be shared with teachers and support staff to facilitate their instructional planning; it is important to ensure that assessments are strategically chosen to provide needed information so as to not take too much precious time away from teaching!

TABLE 4.1. CES Monthly Assessment Schedule

	Aug	Sept	Oct	Nov	Dec	Jan	Feb	Mar	Apr	May
School demographics	×	×	×	×	×	×	×	×	×	×
Academic measures										
Reading: DIBELS (Good & Kaminski, 2002) benchmark	×				×					×
District writing assessment	×		×		×		×		×	
Math/language arts: Tungsten Formative Assessment		×	×	×	×	×	×	×		
Report cards			×		×		×			×
State achievement assessment									×	
Behavior measures										
Screener: SRSS (Drummond, 1994)		×			×		×			
Discipline: ODR	×	×	×	×	×	×	×	×	×	×
Attendance: tardies/absences	×	×	×	×	×	×	×	×	×	×
Report card comments			×		×		×			×
Referrals										
Special education Child study team Social work	×	×	×	×	×	×	×	×	×	×
Program measures *for consented teachers only—second grade*										
Social validity surveys for secondary reading intervention	×							×		
Treatment integrity (reading program—primary and secondary)	×	×	×	×	×	×	×	×		

Note. From Lane, Kalberg, and Menzies (2009, Table 5.1, p. 105). Copyright 2009 by Guilford Press. Adapted by permission.

How Do We Prepare Materials to Conduct the SRSS?

The SRSS is not something to be purchased; it can be created in an Excel file or Word document, as illustrated in Figure 4.1. It is very important to check the accuracy of the document after it is finished, making sure, for example, that all items are present (e.g., did not get printed on a second page or were inadvertently left off) and that they are worded exactly as in Figure 4.1. If you add, delete, or modify items, then the instrument is no longer validated. Likewise, it is important to use only the Likert-type scale (0–3) provided. Again, the rating scale cannot be modified without impacting the psychometric rigor of the instrument. Teachers and administrators have asked, "Can we delete the 'steal' item and add in 'disruption'?" and "Can we change the

TABLE 4.2. FMS Monthly Assessment Schedule										
	Aug	Sept	Oct	Nov	Dec	Jan	Feb	Mar	Apr	May
School demographics	×	×	×	×	×	×	×	×	×	×
Academic measures										
Report cards 　GPA 　Course failures		×		×			×		×	
District writing assessment		×					×			×
State achievement assessment (Tennessee Comprehensive Assessment Program)									×	
Behavior measures										
Screener: SRSS (Drummond, 1994)		×			×				×	
Discipline: 　ODRs 　Suspensions/expulsions 　Alternative learning center	×	×	×	×	×	×	×	×	×	×
Attendance: tardies/absences	×	×	×	×	×	×	×	×	×	×
Referrals										
Special education Gen. ed. intervention team Students Taking a Right Stand (STARS) 　counseling	×	×	×	×	×	×	×	×	×	×
Program measures *for consented teachers only*										
Social validity (PIRS: Lane, Kalberg, Bruhn, et al., 2009; Lane, Robertson, et al., 2002)	×					×				
SET (Sugai, Lewis-Palmer, Todd, & Horner, 2001)						×				
Teacher-completed ratings of treatment integrity						×				
Direct observations of treatment integrity by an objective observer						×				

Note. From Lane, Kalberg, and Menzies (2009, Table 5.2, p. 106). Copyright 2009 by The Guilford Press. Adapted by permission.

TABLE 4.3. LHS Monthly Assessment Schedule

	Aug	Sept	Oct	Nov	Dec	Jan	Feb	Mar	Apr	May
School demographics	×		×			×		×		×
Academic measures										
Report cards										
GPA						×				×
Course failures			×			×		×		×
Behavior measures										
Screener: SRSS (Drummond, 1994)		×			×				×	
Discipline: ODRs			×			×		×		×
Attendance: tardies/unexcused absences			×			×				×
Referrals	×		×		×			×		×
Special education Prereferral intervention team Counseling or social work										
Program measures *for consented teachers only*										
Social validity (PIRS: Lane, Kalberg, Bruhn, et al., 2009; Lane, Robertson, et al., 2002)	×							×		
SET (Sugai et al., 2001)						×				
Teacher-completed ratings of treatment integrity						×				
Direct observations of treatment integrity by an objective observer						×				

Note. From Lane, Kalberg, and Menzies (2009, Table 5.2, p. 106). Copyright 2009 by The Guilford Press. Adapted by permission.

scale to a 'yes or no' rating?" In both cases, the answer is no. Others have asked for anchors to operationally define what is a 0 or a 1 for each item. Again, this is not necessary for this particular tool. A strength of the SRSS rests in its simplicity. Despite requiring so little time, it is a highly reliable and valid instrument that predicts important behavioral and academic outcomes for students (Drummond, Eddy, & Reid, 1998a, 1998b; Drummond, Eddy, Reid, & Bank, 1994).

While some school-site teams prepare printed hard copies of the SRSS, others have developed electronic versions on a secured shared drive or server. Security is highly important. Consequently, we recommend that completed screeners be kept at the school site and, if prepared electronically, not be e-mailed to avoid unintentionally sending it to someone who does not have permission to view it.

Many school-site teams work with an attendance secretary or staff person to import student names and identification numbers from each teacher's class so teachers will not have to spend time writing in names and identification numbers (which would increase the administration time). Teachers should compare the screening tool with their current class roster at each screening time point (Fall, Winter, and Spring) to make certain all students are included in the screening process.

How Do We Administer the SRSS?

Like Stages 1 and 2 of the SSBD and the ESP, the SRSS can be completed during a regularly scheduled faculty meeting. We recommend all teachers come together in one room (e.g., library or computer lab after students are dismissed) to learn how to conduct the screening and have their questions answered. This will also ensure that the procedural fidelity of the screening can be monitored. However, teachers are not permitted to discuss their scores with each other as parent permission is required before a team meeting is held regarding a student (see *www.privacyrights. org/fs/fs29-education.htm#3* for information on students' privacy rights). Because the instrument is so brief, it is also possible to have teachers add the total scores after rating each student. Some schools have teachers bring in laptops, log in to the secured server, rate each student, and compute total scores using formulas in Excel.

If scoring by hand, please double-check the addition. If scoring electronically using formulas, please double-check the accuracy of the formulas. We suggest that a second person complete a quick reliability check to ensure accuracy of formulas. This person should not review your scores, but only look at the formulas to make certain the number are added correctly. Important decisions are made using these data; therefore, assessment results must be accurate so that the decisions made about which students require extra support are also accurate. In addition, make certain that (1) all students in the class are rated, provided they have been in school for at least 6 weeks; (2) all items are completed; and (3) reliability is conducted on the scoring procedures.

After teachers become fluent in the process, it is not necessary to come together as a full faculty. Instead, the SRSS forms can be distributed to teachers to complete on their own (e.g., Lane, Oakes, Ennis, et al., 2011). It is important to have a procedure in place for working with new teachers to be certain the screening tools are completed as intended.

How Do We Score and Interpret the SRSS?

Scoring and interpretation of the SRSS are straightforward. Simply add the scores for each item for each student. Each student's score should be between 0 and 21. Total scores are used to classify students into one of three risk categories: 0–3, low risk; 4–8, moderate risk; and 9–21, high risk. As evident from the illustrations later in this chapter, the information is used to make decisions regarding how to (1) identify and support students who require supports beyond primary prevention efforts and (2) monitor the overall level of performance over time at a given school.

How Can We Use This Information at Our School Site?

As with the SSBD and the ESP, information from the SRSS can be used in a number of ways. First, it can be used to identify students who may require additional supports. Students scoring in the moderate- or high-risk categories should receive secondary or tertiary supports. Second, the information can be used to monitor risk over time for the school as a whole and for individual students. In the illustrations presented at the end of this chapter, we provide three examples (one each at the elementary, middle, and high school levels) adapted from actual schools whose school-site leadership teams elected to implement the SRSS as part of regular school practices. The illustrations provide concrete examples of how to (1) monitor the overall level of risk present over time at a given school (Illustrations 2 and 3), (2) analyze data from the SRSS in conjunction with academic data to identify students for secondary and tertiary levels of prevention within the context of three-tiered models of prevention (Illustration 1), and (3) offer strategies to support teachers (Illustration 3).

How Much Does the SRSS Cost, and Where Can I Order It?

The SRSS has the best possible price—it is free! Simply create the instrument as described previously, referring to Figure 4.1 to check for accuracy. Then follow the scoring directions provided in this chapter.

In the next section, we provide an overview of the supporting research for the SRSS. We provide information on the psychometric features of the SRSS as well as on how the tool has been used in research studies to identify students who are nonresponsive to primary prevention efforts.

Supporting Research

Reliability and Validity

There have been several studies of the SRSS to determine its reliability and validity (see Table 4.4 for peer-reviewed studies). Initial validity studies of the SRSS conducted by Drummond and colleagues indicated that it is a reliable tool for use in distinguishing between elementary students who do and do not demonstrate antisocial tendencies (Drummond et al., 1998a, 1998b, 1994). Studies also indicated important findings regarding SRSS scores: (1) They predicted negative behavioral and academic outcomes for students from 1.5 to 10 years later (Drummond et al., 1994) and (2) were correlated ($r = .79$) with the Aggressive Behavior subscale of the Child Behavior Checklist (Achenbach, 1991), suggesting convergent validity with a well-established, often-used measure.

More recent validation studies conducted with elementary-age students established the convergent validity of the SRSS with the SSBD. Lane, Little, and colleagues (2009) conducted a study to determine whether the SRSS screening tool was equally sensitive and specific in identifying students with both externalizing and internalizing

TABLE 4.4. Reliability and Validity Studies of the SRSS

Citation	Purpose	Description of participants	Description of schools	Reliability	Validity
Lane, Parks, et al. (2007)	Provide initial evidence to support use of SRSS at middle school level	Study 1: $N = 500$ students; grades 6–8; 97.60% white; rated by 38 teachers Study 2 $N = 528$ students; grades 5–8; 49.43% white; rated by 40 teachers	Study 1: One rural middle school in middle Tennessee; 30.8% economic disadvantage rate; 20% special education Study 2: One urban middle school in middle Tennessee; 46.6% economic disadvantage rate; 18.6% special education	Study 1: Internal consistency: .78, .85, .85 Test–retest stability: .66 (14 weeks; Fall–Winter); .56 (34 weeks, Fall–Spring); .80 (20 weeks, Winter–Spring) Study 2: Internal consistency: .83 for Fall and Winter time points Test–retest stability: .71 (11 weeks; Fall–Winter)	Study 1: Convergent: Pearson correlation coefficients suggest convergent validity between SRSS and all SDQ subscale scores and total score at each time point Predictive validity: results of MANOVAs indicated students with low-, moderate-, and high-risk status per SRSS could be best differentiated on behavioral variables (e.g., ODRs, in-school suspensions) and less so on academic variables (did not differentiate between moderate- and high-risk groups)
Lane, Kalberg, Parks, et al. (2008)	Provide initial evidence to support use of SRSS at high school level	$N = 674$ students; grades 9–12; 96.67% white; rated by 41 teachers	One rural high school in middle Tennessee; 17.2% economic disadvantage rate; 12.02% special education	Internal consistency: Instructional raters: .79, .81, .84, .82, .86, 78; Noninstructional raters: .84, .82, .84, .79, .81, .79 Test–retest stability: Instructional raters: .22–.71; noninstructional raters: .30–.73 Interrater reliability: Statistically significant correlations between raters, .19–.50	Convergent: Pearson correlation coefficients suggest convergent validity between SRSS and all SDQ subscale scores and total score at each time point for both raters, with more pronounced effects for noninstructional raters Discriminative validity: for both raters, low-risk group could be differentiated from moderate- and high-risk groups on behavior (ODRs) and academic (GPA) outcomes; the two risk groups were not differentiated

(cont.)

TABLE 4.4. *(cont.)*

Citation	Purpose	Description of participants	Description of schools	Reliability	Validity
Lane, Little, et al. (2009)	Examine extent to which SRSS is equally sensitive and specific in identifying students with externalizing and internalizing behaviors as measured by SSBD	$N = 562$ students in grades K–2 attending a K–5 school; 94.77% white	Seven inclusive elementary schools in middle Tennessee; .08–19.4% economic disadvantage rate	Internal consistency: .83	Concurrent: ROCs, conditional probabilities, and kappa coefficients suggest SRSS is more accurate for detecting externalizing than internalizing behavior as measured by the SSBD. Predicting externalizing: AUC, .95; predicting internalizing: AUC .80
Lane, Kalberg, et al. (2010)	Internal consistency and test–retest stability of SRSS over three administrations in 1 academic year; concurrent validity of SRSS and SSBD	$N = 2,588$ students in grades K–5; 90.68% white	Five inclusive elementary schools in middle Tennessee; 5.50–10.57% received special education; 6.9–32.9% economic disadvantage rate	Internal consistency: .81, .82, .81. Test–retest stability: .73 (8 weeks, Fall–Winter); .68 (24 weeks, Fall–Spring); .74 (16 weeks, Winter–Spring)	Concurrent: ROCs suggest SRSS is more accurate for detecting externalizing than internalizing behavior, as measured by SSBD. Predicting externalizing: AUC, .95, .95, .96; predicting internalizing: AUC, .76, .78, .82
Menzies & Lane (in press)	Internal consistency and test–retest stability of SRSS over three administrations in 1 academic year; predictive validity with ODR, SSRS (Gresham & Elliott, 1990) self-control teacher rating, attendance rate, and language arts proficiency	$N = 286$ students in grades K–6; 53% Hispanic	One diverse suburban school in southern California	Internal consistency: .87, .85, .86. Test–retest stability: .78 (≈15 weeks, Fall–Winter); .69 (≈43 weeks, Fall–Spring); .79 (≈28 weeks, Winter–Spring)	Predictive: regression analyses indicated that Fall SRSS scores predicted year-end teachers' rating of self-control, ODRs earned, and language arts performance scores. Correlation coefficients suggest significant relations between behavior and academic measures; no significant relation found for attendance rates
Ennis et al. (in press)	Internal consistency, test–retest stability, convergent validity of SRSS with SDQ and SSBD over three administrations per year across 2 school years; predictive validity of SRSS with year total suspension rates (K–4) and state achievement	Study 1: $N = 448$ (2006–2007) and $N = 497$ (2007–2008) students in grades K–4; 50% white. Study 2: $N = 449$ (2007–2008)	Study 1: One diverse, urban, elementary school in middle Tennessee; 9.80% (2006–2007) and 9.46% (2007–2008) received special education; 32.4% (2006–2007) and 27.2% (2007–2008) economically disadvantaged	Study 1: Internal consistency: .82, .78, .85, .83, .82, .83. Test–retest stability: conducted between each of the 15 time points (range, 13–82 weeks); all correlations were significant at $p < .0001$; 13 of 15	Study 1: Convergent: Pearson correlation coefficients suggest convergent validity between SRSS and all SDQ subscales and total scale for all administrations. Predictive: SRSS risk status in Fall 2006 predicted year-end suspension rates 1

(cont.)

TABLE 4.4. (cont.)

Citation	Purpose	Description of participants	Description of schools	Reliability	Validity
Ennis et al. (in press) (cont.)	test outcomes (3rd grade)	and $N = 491$ (2008–2009) students in grades K–4; 71.77% white	Study 2: Urban elementary school in middle Tennessee; 7.46% (2007–2008) and 7.77% (2008–2009) received special education; 23.8% (2007–2008) and 21.9% (2008–2009) economically disadvantaged	comparisons held moderate stability, with coefficients from .60 to .78 Study 2: Internal consistency: .81, .83, .87, .86, .86, .87 Test–retest stability: comparing each time point with all successive time points (13–84 weeks) moderate to high correlations (.62–.86) among all comparisons	and 2 years later and for TCAP achievement scores at year end Study 2: Convergent: ROCs of .95–.98 externalizing; .58–.78 internalizing; logistic regression odds ratios and point-biserial correlations were significant with moderate magnitude for externalizing behavior and low magnitude for internalizing behavior Predictive: SRSS risk status in Fall predicted suspension rates at end of Years 1 and 2 with a moderate positive relationship; correlation coefficients suggested moderate negative relationship with risk status and TCAP outcomes
Oakes, Wilder, et al. (2010)	Internal consistency and test–retest stability of SRSS over three administrations during 1 school year; predictive validity of SRSS with year total ODRs earned and Spring ORF scores, as measured by DIBELS (Good & Kaminski, 2002)	$N = 1,142$ students in grades K–5 (school C) and K–6 (schools A, B); 17.73–81.27% black (across three schools); $N = 53$ teachers	Three diverse, urban, elementary schools in midwestern city; 25.5–52.9% free and reduced-price lunch	Internal consistency: .82 and .81 Test–retest stability: .86 (31 and 22 weeks, Fall–Spring)	Predictive validity: Fall SRSS scores predicted year-end ODRs and DIBELS ORF; increased SRSS risk level related to increased ODRs and decreased DIBELS ORF outcomes
Lane, Bruhn, et al. (2010)	Findings extend literature on reliability and validity for urban schools at middle school level; as well as reliability, predictive validity was established for 2	Study 1: $N = 534$ students in grades 5–8; 58.43% white, 36.89% black; Ns = 7 (Fall), 18 (Winter),	Study 1: Urban middle school in middle Tennessee; 41.4% free and reduced-price lunch; 18.6% received special education services	Study 1: Internal consistency: .89, .84, .87 across three administrations in 1 academic year Test–retest stability: Pearson correlation coefficients were	Study 1: Significant differences found between low-risk group on SRSS and moderate- and high-risk groups for ODRs earned and GPA

(cont.)

TABLE 4.4. *(cont.)*

Citation	Purpose	Description of participants	Description of schools	Reliability	Validity
Lane, Bruhn, et al. (2010) *(cont.)*	years; social validity of screening process was measured	28 (Spring) teachers Study 2: *N* = 528 students in grades 5–8; 45.27% black; *N* = 40 teachers	Study 2: Large metropolitan middle school in middle Tennessee; 46.6% free and reduced-price lunch; 18.18% received special education services	significant for all three time points Study 2: Internal consistency: .83, .83, .84, .88, .86 across five administrations in 2 academic years Test–retest stability: yielded significant correlations between all time points	Study 2: Significant differences found between low-risk group and moderate- and high-risk groups on out-of-school suspensions and unexcused absences; there were low-magnitude differences between moderate- and high-risk groups; same pattern was found for predicting academic (GPA and CF) measures For Year 1 Fall SRSS rating predicting Year 2 year-end outcomes, significant differences were found between low-risk and moderate/high-risk groups; thus, risk status (high risk) predicted behavioral and academic outcomes 2 years later
Lane, Oakes, Ennis, et al. (2011)	Findings extend literature on reliability and validity at high school level; as well as reliability, predictive validity was established for 2 years	*N* = 1,854 students in grades 9–12; 90.12% white	Urban fringe high school in middle Tennessee; 7.14% (*n* = 127) of students received special education services; 13% of students classified as economically disadvantaged	Results suggest high internal consistency (.76–.87), test–retest stability (.23–.75), and interrater reliability (.28–.43)	Predictive validity was established across 2 academic years Spring SRSS scores differentiated students with low-, moderate-, and high-risk status on ODRs, GPAs, and CFs during following academic year Teacher ratings evaluating students' performance later in course of school day were more predictive than those conducted earlier in day

Note. MANOVA, multivariate analysis of covariance; TCAP, Tennessee Comprehensive Assessment Programs; CF, course failure; ORF, oral reading fluency.

behaviors as measured by the SSBD. Their sample included 562 K–2 students. Results suggested that when students' SRSS scores in the low- versus high-risk categories were compared, the SRSS was highly accurate for predicting both externalizing and internalizing problems as measured by the SSBD. However, the SRSS was more accurate for detecting externalizing relative to internalizing behaviors, improving chance estimates by 45% for externalizing behaviors and 30% for internalizing behaviors. This is expected as the SRSS was not designed to detect students with internalizing behavior patterns. Teachers should keep this limitation in mind when selecting the SRSS as a behavior screener. It is hoped the extended version, the SRSS-IE, will fill this void and be a reliable and valid tool to identify both externalizing and internalizing behavior patterns in students of varying ages.

Findings from the Lane, Little, and colleagues (2009) study were confirmed in a study of 2,588 elementary students in middle Tennessee (Lane, Kalberg, et al., 2010). Results suggested the SRSS was a reliable tool, as evidenced by strong internal consistency (> .80) and test–retest stability (.68–.74). Also, findings again indicated the SRSS is more accurate for detecting externalizing (exceeding chance estimates by 45–46%) than internalizing (exceeding chance estimates by 26, 28, and 32%) behaviors, as measured through Stage 2 of the SSBD, at three time points across 1 academic year.

There have also been studies that explored the extent to which SRSS scores predicted behavioral and academic outcomes of elementary students. For example, Menzies and Lane (in press) conducted a study of 286 students in a diverse suburban school in California to examine the SRSS on behavioral (office discipline referrals [ODRs] and teacher ratings of self-control skills) and academic outcomes (language arts skills). Results found SRSS scores predicted end-of-year ODRs ($r = .48, p < .0001$) as well as year-end self-control skills (SSRS; Gresham & Elliott, 1990, $r = -.59, p < .0001$) and language arts proficiency ($r = -.23, p = .02$). Collectively, results indicated that students' initial behavior patterns at the beginning of a school year predicted not only how many ODRs they would earn in a school year but also teachers' perceptions of self-control skills and reading competency at year's end.

These findings were confirmed by Oakes, Wilder, and colleagues (2010) in another study of three ethnically, culturally, and economically diverse urban midwestern elementary schools using the SRSS as part of regular school practices. Their results also supported strong internal consistency (.81–.82) and test–retest stability (.86). Furthermore, Fall SRSS scores predicted year-end ODR rates and Spring oral reading fluency scores. Like the Menzies and Lane study (in press), students with higher levels of risk at the onset of the academic year were likely to end the year with more ODRs and, to a lesser extent, lower oral reading fluency proficiency levels.

There have also been psychometric studies conducted at the middle and high school levels establishing the utility of the SRSS for use with students in sixth through 12th grades. For example, Lane, Parks, and colleagues (2007) conducted an initial investigation of the reliability and validity of the SRSS for use at the middle school level. Results of the first study conducted with 500 middle school students in sixth through eighth grade in a rural setting yielded high internal consistency, test–retest stability, and convergent validity with the Strengths and Difficulties Questionnaire (SDQ; Goodman, 1997). Short-term predictive validity of the SRSS was established; students in low-, moderate-, and high-risk categories earned significantly different numbers of ODRs and in-school suspensions, with students in higher risk categories earning more of both. Academic variables, which included grade point average (GPA) and number of course failures, differentiated between students with moderate or high risk and students with low risk (but not between the two elevated risk groups). Students in the low-risk group had higher GPAs and few course failures. Results of the second study conducted with 528 students in fifth through eighth grade in an urban setting also established the internal consistency and short-term test–retest stability. However, predictive validity was not addressed in the urban setting.

To address this absence of information, Lane, Bruhn, and colleagues (2010) conducted another series of studies to explore the reliability and validity of the SRSS in urban middle schools. In addition to confirming the reliability of the SRSS (alpha coefficients = .84–.89), the first study (N = 534) supported predictive validity of the SRSS in distinguishing students in the low-risk category from students with moderate- to high-risk status on behavioral (ODR) and academic (GPA) measures. In this study, students in the moderate- and high-risk categories were collapsed into one group as a result of low sample sizes. Results of the second study (N = 528) also supported reliability (internal consistency, .83–.88, and test–retest stability, .41–.71, over a 2-year period) and predictive validity. Specifically, initial Fall SRSS scores predicted behavioral and academic outcomes up to 2 years following initial SRSS status. Students in the low-risk category had statistically significantly fewer out-of-school suspensions, fewer unexcused absences, and higher GPAs relative to students with risk.

The utility of the SRSS was examined at the high school level. Lane, Kalberg, Parks, and Carter (2008), in their study of 674 ninth- through 12th-grade students attending a rural high school, provided initial evidence of the reliability and validity of the SRSS for use with high school students. Results revealed high internal consistency (.79–.86), test–retest stability over a 2-year period, and interrater reliability between instructional and noninstructional raters. In addition, both convergent validity and predictive validity were established. Specifically, convergent validity was established between SRSS total scores and subscale scores of the SDQ (Goodman, 1997). Predictive validity was established over 2 academic years. High school students at low risk for antisocial behavior differed on ODRs and GPAs from students with moderate and high levels of risk. However, neither variable could distinguish between students placing in the moderate- or high-risk status.

Lane, Oakes, Ennis, and colleagues (in press) explore the utility of the SRSS at the high school levels with a sample of ninth- through 12th-grade students (N = 1,854, 2008–2009; N = 1920, 2009–2010) in a large suburban high school. Results confirmed the utility of the SRSS at the high school levels with high internal consistency (.76–.87) and test–retest stability over a 2-year period. Furthermore, predictive validity was established across 2 academic years. Spring SRSS scores differentiated students with low-, moderate-, and high-risk status on ODRs, GPAs, and course failures during the following academic year. Teacher ratings evaluating students' performance later in the course of the school day were more predictive than teacher ratings conducted earlier in the day.

Collectively, these studies provide evidence to suggest that the SRSS is a reliable and valid tool for use in the elementary setting. Furthermore, there is initial evidence to support the utility of this measure for use in the middle school (Lane, Bruhn, et al., 2010; Lane, Parks, et al., 2007) and high school (Lane, Kalberg, Parks, & Carter, 2008; Lane, Oakes, Ennis, et al., in press) settings.

Identification of Nonresponders

In this section, we highlight a few applications of the SRSS as presented in published, peer-reviewed articles to demonstrate how this screening tool has been used by the research community to identify and assist students who require targeted supports when primary prevention efforts are not enough. Table 4.5 presents studies conducted in the context of multi-tiered models of prevention using the SRSS as one piece (and in some cases the sole source) of information to determine responsiveness. For example, there are studies focused on secondary (Tier 2) or tertiary (Tier 3) supports in the area of reading (Lane, Little, et al., 2007; Lane, Menzies, Munton, Von Duering, & English, 2005; Lane, Wehby, et al., 2002; Oakes, Mathur, & Lane, 2010), writing (Lane, Harris, et al., 2008), social skills (Kalberg, Lane, & Lambert, in press; Lane, Wehby, et al., 2003; Robertson & Lane, 2007), and behavioral (e.g., functional assessment-based interventions; Lane, Eisner, et al., 2009; Lane, Rogers, et al., 2007) skills. Similarly, the SRSS can also be used outside a formal three-tiered model of prevention to determine when to use commercial, manualized programs such as First Step to Success (Diken & Rutherford, 2005).

The table includes information about the core features such as (1) the students identified for the extra support (e.g., grade level) as well as the characteristics of the schools in which the secondary and tertiary supports were conducted (e.g., rural, urban, or suburban settings); (2) a brief description of the intervention and the frequency with which the intervention was conducted and by whom (e.g., teacher, paraprofessional, research assistant); (3) the specific schoolwide data collected as part of regular school practices analyzed to identify nonresponders who might benefit from the extra support (please note the precision of this information—very necessary!); (4) the design used to determine whether the intervention results in changes in student performance, the specific behaviors (academic, behavioral, or social) measured to determine responsiveness to the secondary support, treatment integrity data (to see how well the intervention was implemented as intended; Gresham, 1989; Lane & Beebe-Frankenberger, 2004), and social validity data (to see what people thought about the goals, procedures, and outcomes; Kazdin, 1977; Wolf, 1978); and (5) a brief statement of the results. This information can be very useful in deciding how to implement and evaluate practices (especially those that are evidence based) at your school site. As you review the studies in Table 4.4, consider how you might construct similar supports at your school or in your research project. Think about supports you currently offer: How are students identified for such supports? How will these

TABLE 4.5. Applications of the SRSS: Identifying and Supporting Students

Study	Participants and setting	Support and description	Schoolwide data: entry criteria	Design and monitoring procedures	Results
Lane et al. (2005)	$N = 1$ kindergarten general education student, Hispanic, male From a school implementing schoolwide intervention program with literacy and behavioral components	Early literacy skills: Shefelbine's (1998) phonics chapter books Identified students meet 3–4 days/week in school library during traditional school day in small groups with 2 other students (non-at-risk, low achieving), with the school-site literacy leader conducting 30-minute lessons 3–4 days per week over 9-week period (15 intervention hours)	Identified using schoolwide data: Behavior: SRSS (Drummond, 1994; high risk); continued to place in high-risk category at Fall and Winter screening time points Academic: performed below average in academic arena according to teacher report	ABAAA, with three follow-up phases (1 week, 4 weeks, 3 months) Academic behavior: DIBELS (Good & Kaminski, 2002): OF and LNF Behavior: TDB in classroom and NSI on playground using direct observations procedures Treatment integrity Social validity	Improvements in phonemic awareness were associated with lower levels of disruptive behavior in classroom and improved social interactions on playground
Lane, Wehby, et al. (2002)	$N = 7$ first-grade students: 4 white, 2 black, and 1 Hispanic American From one school implementing a schoolwide intervention program with literacy and behavioral components	Early literacy skills: Shefelbine's (1998) phonics chapter books Identified students meet 3–4 days/week in general education classroom during traditional school day in small groups, with school literacy leader conducting 30-minute lessons 3–4 days/week over 9-week period (15 intervention hours)	Identified using schoolwide data: Behavior: SRSS (moderate or high risk) Academic: bottom third of class in terms of early literacy skills according to teacher report	Multiple baseline Academic behavior: DIBELS: NWF and ORF Behavior: TDB in classroom and NSI on playground using direct observations procedures Treatment integrity Social validity	Although there was initial variability in decoding skills and problem behaviors, all students improved word attack skills and had lower levels of disruptive behavior in classroom
Lane, Little, et al. (2007)	$N = 7$ first-grade students, all white Two general education classrooms in two schools that subscribed to inclusive education in rural middle Tennessee	Reading intervention: PALS (Fuchs, Fuchs, Mathes, & Simmons, 1997) Identified students meet 4 days/week during literacy block in which classroom teachers conducted 30-minute lessons over 7-week period (14 intervention hours)	Students were either (1) in control condition of Tier 2 intervention during kindergarten ($n = 4$) or (2) nonresponsive to Tier 2 reading intervention administered in kindergarten ($n = 2$) or did not maintain gains over Summer ($n = 1$) Reading: WJIII ≤ 25th percentile	Multiple baseline Academic behavior: DIBELS: decoding (NWF) and ORF Behavior: academic engagement using direct observations procedures Treatment integrity Social validity	Sustained improvements in ORF, with 4 students demonstrating improvements in engagement

(cont.)

TABLE 4.5. *(cont.)*

Study	Participants and setting	Support and description	Schoolwide data: entry criteria	Design and monitoring procedures	Results
Lane, Little, et al. (2007) *(cont.)*			Behavior: SSBD (Walker & Severson, 1992; externalizing or internalizing); or SRSS (moderate or high risk); or CBCL-TRF (Achenbach, 1991; aggression—borderline or clinical)		
Oakes, Mathur, et al. (2010)	$N = 9$ second-grade students: 4 white, 4 Hispanic, 1 black Large suburban elementary school in southwestern city	Reading: Fundations: Wilson (2002) Language Basics for K–3©, Blastoff to Reading (Voyager Expanded Learning, 2004), and response–cost behavior support plan, similar to Teacher–Student Learning Game (Nelson, Benner, & Mooney, 2008) Identified students meet 4 days/week for 30 minutes/day for 8 weeks of three-part intervention with school-site reading specialist	Identified using schoolwide reading data: DIBELS ORF in Fall Students met criteria if (1) they were at-risk readers based on DIBELS Fall scores; (2) their ORF scores did not improve with 5 weeks of classroom supplemental instruction (30 minutes/day, 4 days/week); (3) classroom instruction was delivered with 80% procedural fidelity	Multiple baseline Reading: weekly DIBELS ORF progress monitoring probes SRSS used to evaluate effect of intervention with students with and without behavioral risk (high risk) Treatment integrity Social validity	Improvements demonstrated in ORF for 8 students
Lane, Harris, et al. (2008)	$N = 6$ second-grade students: 4 white, 2 black Large, inclusive elementary school in rural middle Tennessee	Writing intervention: SRSD for story writing (Graham & Harris, 2005) Identified students meet 3 days/week during time deemed appropriate by teachers and administrators during which research assistants conduct 30-minute lessons 3–4 days/week over 3- to 6-week period (10–15 sessions)	Identified using schoolwide data: Writing: TOWL-3 (Hammil & Larson, 1996)—story construction ≤ 25%th percentile Behavior: SSBD (externalizing or internalizing Stage 2); or SRSS (moderate or high risk)	Multiple probe during baseline Academic behavior: writing prompts Treatment integrity Social validity	Sustained improvements in story completeness, length, and quality for all students

(cont.)

TABLE 4.5. *(cont.)*

Study	Participants and setting	Support and description	Schoolwide data: entry criteria	Design and monitoring procedures	Results
Lane, Wehby, et al. (2003)	*N* = 7 first-grade students: 2 black, 5 Hispanic From one school implementing a schoolwide intervention program with literacy and behavioral components	Social skills: Social Skills Intervention Guide (Elliott & Gresham, 1991) Identified students meet outside of classroom during traditional school day in small groups, with school psychology doctoral students for 30-minute lessons 2 days/week over 10-week period (10 intervention hours)	Identified using schoolwide data: Behavior: students in high-risk status after 4 months of school year according to SRSS scores	Multiple baseline Behavior: TDB and AET in classroom as well as NSI on playground using direct observations procedures Treatment integrity Social validity	Results indicated lasting improvements in disruptive behavior in classroom, NSI on playground, and increases in academic engagement
Robertson & Lane (2007)	*N* = 65 students in grades 6–8, majority white Inclusive rural middle school	Conflict resolution and social skills Study skills (*n* = 34), including strategies to acquire and demonstration knowledge Study skills + conflict resolution skills (*n* = 31), Productive Conflict Resolution Program Teachers taught each section (one for each grade level for each condition [six classes]), and school counselors were available for support; students received instruction daily, for 56 lessons, including 30 minutes of instruction and 20 minutes of applied practice over 21-week period (28 hours)	Identified using schoolwide data collected during Fall semester Academic: Quarter 2 GPA ≤ 2.7 or 1+ failing grade Behavior: moderate or high risk on SRSS November screening or ≥ 1 ODR within first 4 months of school Exclusionary criteria: those participating in Read 180 (Scholastic Inc., 1997)	Randomized trial; pre–postexperimental design Proximal: knowledge of study skills Knowledge of conflict resolution skills Distal: Study Habit Inventory (Jones & Slate, 1990); ConflictTalk (Kimsey & Fuller, 2003) Treatment integrity Social validity	Despite high fidelity, only nominal changes in outcome measures were achieved

(cont.)

TABLE 4.5. *(cont.)*

Study	Participants and setting	Support and description	Schoolwide data: entry criteria	Design and monitoring procedures	Results
Kalberg et al. (in press)	*N* = 45 students in grades 7–8; majority white Inclusive rural middle school	Conflict resolution and social skills Study skills (*n* = 13), including strategies to acquire and demonstration knowledge Conflict resolution skills (*n* = 15), Productive Conflict Resolution Program; business-as-usual (*n* = 17). Teachers taught study skills groups, and school counselors taught conflict resolution group, both providing daily instruction as part of these elective classes; students in control condition were in study halls, taught by teachers Intervention groups received 31 lessons, including 30 minutes of instruction and 20 minutes of applied practice (15.5 hours of explicit instruction)	Identified using schoolwide data collected at end of 1 academic year to identify returning students: Academic: Quarter 4 GPA ≤2.7 or 1+ failing grade Behavior: moderate or high risk on SRSS Spring screening or ≥ one ODR during Spring semester	Randomized trial: longitudinal random coefficients analysis applied to three repeated measurements: preintervention, postintervention, maintenance Proximal: Knowledge of study skills Knowledge of conflict resolution skills Distal: Study Habit Inventory (Jones & Slate, 1990); ConflictTalk (Kimsey & Fuller, 2003); Social Skills Rating System (Gresham & Elliott, 1990) Treatment integrity Social validity	Students in both groups improved knowledge of study skills scores, with study skills groups' scores showing significance relative to conflict resolution skills group; however, still below 80% accuracy
Lane, Eisner, et al. (2009)	*N* = 2 first-grade students (one general education and one receiving special education services for emotional disorders) One general education classroom, where teachers job-shared, in middle Tennessee	Behavior intervention: FABI (Umbreit, Ferro, Liaupsin, & Lane, 2007) Identified students received intervention designed (1) based on function of undesirable behavior (2) to improve environment as both students were capable of performing the tasks, but environment could benefit from modifications; interventions included (1) antecedent adjustments, (2) reinforcement adjustments, and (3) extinction components	Teacher nominations were confirmed by behavior screening data Behavior: SSBD (externalizing) or SRSS (high risk)	Withdrawal design Behavior: off-task and AET behaviors using direct observation procedures Treatment integrity Social validity	Results indicated functional relation between introduction of intervention and changes in AET, with increased AET sustaining into maintenance phase

(cont.)

TABLE 4.5. *(cont.)*

Study	Participants and setting	Support and description	Schoolwide data: entry criteria	Design and monitoring procedures	Results
Lane, Rogers, et al. (2007) (Note that this study includes 2 students, only 1 of whom is presented here)	*N* = 1 student in grade 8 receiving special education services for SLD; white Middle school in middle Tennessee	Behavior intervention: FABI (Umbreit, Ferro, Liaupsin, & Lane, 2007) Identified students received intervention designed (1) based on function of undesirable behavior (2) to improve environment as student was capable of performing the tasks, but environment could benefit from modifications; interventions included (1) antecedent adjustments, (2) reinforcement adjustments, and (3) extinction components	Nonresponsive to secondary intervention as having continued academic and behavioral concerns: Academic: GPA 2.17 Behavioral: SRSS score of 14; nine ODRs	ABABB withdrawal Behavior: noncompliance using direct observation procedures Treatment integrity Social validity	Results indicated functional relation between introduction of intervention and changes in target behavior
Diken & Rutherford (2005)	*N* = 2 kindergarteners and 2 first graders, all Native American Elementary school of a southwestern Indian tribe in Arizona	Behavior intervention: FSS early intervention program 1. CLASS (Contingencies for Learning Academic and Social Skills) 2. HomeBase	SRSS	Multiple baseline Modified Parten's Social Play Scale, observations, Revised Behavior Problem Checklist, Teacher Rating of Behavior, interviews Treatment integrity Social validity	Results indicated intervention was effective in improving students' social play behaviors on playground

Note. AET, academic engaged time; CACL-TRF, Child Behavior Checklist Teacher Report Form; FSS, First Step to Success; LNF, letter-naming fluency; NSI, negative social interactions; NWF, nonsense word fluency; OF, onset fluency; ORF, oral reading fluency; PALS, Peer-Assisted Learning Strategies; TDB, total disruptive behavior; TOWL-3, Test of Written Language–3; SLD, specific learning disabilities; SRSD, self-regulated strategy development; WJIII, Woodcock–Johnson-III tests of achievement.

supports be implemented (i.e., who is going to do what to whom and under what conditions; Lane, Wolery, Reichow, & Rogers, 2006)? How will you monitor progress? How will you know if the intervention is effective? How will you make decisions about when and how to fade this extra support, return to primary prevention, or seek other, more intensive supports?

In addition, there are other applications of the SRSS for use within three-tiered models of prevention. For example, the SRSS can be used descriptively to illustrate how a school's risk shifts over time. Lane and Menzies (2002) used SRSS Fall and Winter scores to describe how risk shifted 4 months after implementing a schoolwide program, including literacy and behavioral components. They used bar graphs to

show the percentage of students scoring in the low-, moderate-, and high-risk categories between Fall and Winter (see Figure 4.2). They also included another graph
to describe movement between these categories, noting the percentage of students
remaining stable, improving, or declining. Lane and Menzies (2005) conducted similar analyses to report year-end findings and described (1) how risk shifted over the
course of 1 academic year and (2) how information was used to place students into
targeted supports.

More recently, Lane, Kalberg, Bruhn, and colleagues (2008) published an article examining a primary prevention program implemented in elementary schools in
middle Tennessee. They addressed issues related to measuring treatment integrity,
reinforcement, and systematic screening. This is a another useful article for practitioners because it illustrates techniques for using the SRSS (as well as the SSBD) when
implemented as part of regular school practices to (1) assess the overall index of risk
evident in a school-site building and (2) determine how different types of students
respond to primary prevention efforts, with an emphasis on identifying students for
secondary (Tier 2) and tertiary (Tier 3) supports.

Lane, Oakes, and Menzies (2010), Lane, Kalberg, and colleagues (2011), and
Kalberg and colleagues (2010) are other sources of information you might find useful
as you construct these types of supports in your school or research project because
they offer recommendations on how to use data from multiple sources (e.g., academic
and behavioral screening tools) to identify and support students for whom primary
prevention efforts are insufficient.

Strengths and Considerations

After you have reviewed these various applications, we encourage you to think about
how you might use the information in your own work. To assist with this endeavor,
we present an evenhanded discussion of the strengths and challenges associated with
using the SRSS.

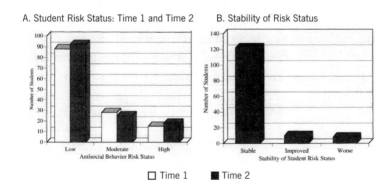

FIGURE 4.2. Using the SRSS to show change over time. From Lane and Menzies (2002, Figures 1
and 2, p. 31). Copyright 2002 by Taylor & Francis. Reprinted by permission.

Strengths

As previously mentioned, the SRSS has strengths in the areas of feasibility, psychometric rigor, and utility. In this section, we briefly discuss these features.

First, from a practitioner perspective, a key strength of its SRSS rests in its feasibility or simplicity. It is user friendly and cost-effective because it requires limited resources (e.g., time, money, and personnel) in all key aspects. Namely, it costs nothing to obtain the instrument, it is simple to prepare (e.g., importing student names and identification number), easy to complete (e.g., seven responses required per student), quick to score (e.g., add seven numbers together), and easy to interpret (e.g., place students into one of three categories). Other instruments provide more detailed information on specific areas of concern such as the SDQ (Goodman, 1997), the Social Skills Improvement System Performance Screening Guide (SSiS-PSG; Elliott & Gresham, 2007b), and the BASC™2-BESS (Kamphaus & Reynolds, 2007a), with the later two offering direct guidance as to how to assist students with given areas of concern. However, the SSiS-PSG costs approximately $4 per class for each screening time point ($12 per class for the year), and the BESS costs approximately $100 for a class of 25 students, including the manual, and approximately $1 per student thereafter for each screening time point ($175 per class for the year for three screenings). Although the SDQ is free of charge (like the SRSS), it is more cumbersome to score by hand or requires online scoring.

Second, the SRSS is psychometrically sound. It is both reliable and valid. School-site teams can be confident that, when the SRSS is implemented as intended, decisions about identifying which students require additional supports in the form of secondary (Tier 2) and tertiary (Tier 3) practices are accurate (Kauffman & Brigham, 2009; Lane, Oakes, Ennis, et al., in press). Like the SSBD, it can be used in conjunction with other data (e.g., attendance, curriculum-based measures; see Illustration 1) to efficiently link students to available supports (Lane, Kalberg, & Menzies, 2009).

Third, the SRSS can be used to systematically monitor school adjustment and behavioral performance of students within a given school and across multiple school years. As demonstrated in Illustrations 2 and 3, this information can be quite useful for school-site leadership teams in monitoring the overall level of risk in a school over time to use a data-based approached to determine patterns of responsiveness (Lane, Kalberg, et al., 2011) and the effectiveness of any interventions.

In sum, the SRSS is a feasible, accurate, and useful instrument for detecting students with antisocial behavior patterns. In the following section, we examine some limitations of this tool.

Considerations

In terms of limiting factors, there are a few key considerations. First, the SRSS was not designed to detect students with internalizing behaviors. Although it does demonstrate some utility in identifying these students (Lane, Little, et al., 2009), it is important to note that the SRSS is highly useful for identifying students with externalizing behaviors but less so identifying those with internalizing behaviors. However, currently, research is underway to add additional items to the SRSS to expand this instrument to detect the second domain (Lane, Oakes, Harris, et al., 2011).

Second, the SRSS does not offer information about how to intervene with students; it does not come with an intervention component that links students to specific supports. Thus, some might say it lacks functional utility. However, there are articles (Kalberg et al., 2010; Lane, Kalberg, et al., 2011), book chapters (e.g., Lane, Oakes, & Menzies, 2010), and a book (Lane, Kalberg, & Menzies, 2009) that offer guidelines for using data-based decision making. In addition, we offer illustrations in the subsequent sections of this chapter as well.

Third, although preliminary evidence supports the utility of the SRSS for elementary-age students, additional inquiry is needed in middle schools and, particularly, high schools to support the reliability and validity of the SRSS for use beyond the elementary school setting (Lane, Bruhn, et al., 2010; Lane, Kalberg, Parks, et al., 2008; Lane, Oakes, Ennis, et al., in press; Lane, Parks, et al., 2007).

Despite these limitations, the SRSS is a feasible, accurate, and useful tool for detecting students with antisocial behavior. We encourage readers to evaluate these cautionary features (e.g., population of interest, functional utility, and accuracy with middle and high school students) when considering using the SRSS as part of regular school practices or in scientific inquiry.

In the next section, we provide illustrations for further guidance in using the SRSS as part of your regular school practices to monitor overall student progress and in identifying and supporting students who require additional supports.

Illustrations

In this section, we offer three illustrations: one each for the elementary school, middle school, and high school settings. These illustrations are adapted from actual studies conducted as part of ongoing collaborations with Vanderbilt University and Arizona State University and several school districts. We emphasize that these are adaptations and refer readers interested in learning more about the actual applications to the original studies.

An Illustration in a Suburban Elementary School: Crafton Elementary School

Crafton Elementary School (CES) is located in a suburb of Phoenix, Arizona, with approximately 552 PreK–6 students in grades pre-kindergarten through sixth grade. The school offers a variety of programs, including supports for English learners, students with special needs, and additional academic supports through Title 1 funding. The school qualified as a comprehensive Title 1 school, with the majority (56.42%) of its students eligible for free or reduced-price lunch (Arizona Department of Education, 2008). The students were predominantly white (49%) and Hispanic (40%), with 23% speaking Spanish as a first language. Nineteen percent of students were served by special education programs (Individuals with Disabilities Education Improvement Act [IDEA], 2004).

Building a CI3T Model of Prevention

CES was in the process of building a CI3T model of prevention for students (Lane, Menzies, Kalberg, & Oakes, in press). Their efforts began with a districtwide character education program (social skills component) in 2005. They added an academic component in 2006 to address early reading and a behavior component in 2008.

SOCIAL SKILLS COMPONENT

CES taught a schoolwide character education program, Character Counts!® (Josephson Institute Center for Youth Ethics). Their program focused on six pillars of character (trustworthiness, respect, responsibility, fairness, caring, citizenship), which were taught in a variety of ways, including monthly lessons, large murals in the school's main hallway and on the outside of the building, weekly quotes and short character biographies in students' planners, and assemblies. It included an equally diverse reinforcement system with activities such as public recognition at awards assemblies, on bulletin boards, and through other schoolwide-designed reinforcement systems (e.g., ticket system in which students earned prizes and recess). Although this program was a school and district priority, the school did not implement a behavior screening tool as part of regular school procedures.

ACADEMIC COMPONENT

CES established a response to intervention (RTI) model in 2006. RTI for reading had three goals: (1) Identify students in need of reading intervention and provide instruction as necessary, (2) inform decisions about special education eligibility for specific learning disabilities (SLD; IDEA, 2004), and (3) monitor the effectiveness of the reading instruction offered in kindergarten through third grade.

At CES the RTI team members (special education team leader, school psychologist, speech and language pathologist, reading specialist, administrator, and classroom teachers) reviewed the reading level and progress for all kindergarten through sixth-grade students using the Dynamic Indicators of Basic Early Literacy Skills (DIBELS; Good & Kaminski, 2002) benchmark assessment, which was administered to all students three times per year. Evidence-based reading programs were reviewed by the district and purchased for CES to provide rigorous reading interventions for students requiring secondary and tertiary levels of support.

BEHAVIOR COMPONENT

The principal of CES attended a Safe and Civil Schools (R. Sprick) professional development seminar as part of a district initiative to integrate behavior monitoring and instruction at all school sites. In the first year, CES's model included a description of expected behaviors in all school settings outside of classrooms (e.g., bathrooms, hallways, cafeteria, playground, bus). All adults in the building were given paper cutouts of the school's mascot to award to students (paired with behavior-specific praise) who demonstrated the specified behaviors. Students wrote their name and their teacher's name on the paper and turned it in to the principal's office. Once a week the principal drew one of the names and awarded a prize to the winning student. Prizes ranged from a new bicycle or skateboard to stuffed animals, games, and extra time with friends. Teachers designed and implemented individual classroom procedures. In brief, teachers established routines and procedures to support their instruction as well as systems for monitoring adherence to schoolwide expectations.

Measures

The school's RTI team was established as the school leadership team to look at all available data on student performance. Several measures beyond the DIBELS (Good & Kaminski, 2002) reading benchmark assessments were examined for students who were not responsive the secondary reading interventions. Other data sources included attendance rates, office disciplinary contacts, report card grades, and patterns of comments by teachers (see Table 4.1).

CES's second grade participated in a research study to examine the effect of adding a behavior support component to their existing secondary reading instruction for students with and without behavioral risk (Oakes, Mathur, et al., 2010). The second-grade team completed the SRSS in Fall (6 weeks after the start of the year) and Winter (corresponding with the DIBELS Winter benchmark). This information was used to answer the following questions:

How Are Data Used to Determine Placement in Supplemental Supports?

The study examined the additive effect of behavior screening and supports to current school practices in reading. As such, reading (DIBELS) and behavior (SRSS) screening data were used to identify students who met the criteria for placement in the supplemental intervention (see Table 4.6). Figure 4.3 shows the Fall 2008 screening data used as part of the criteria for participation in the study and the Winter data used by the school to determine response to reading. The first bar represents the percentage and number of students who scored in the three risk ranges (low, moderate, or high) on the SRSS in Fall. The second bar represents the percentage and number of students in the three risk ranges (low risk, some risk, and at-risk) on DIBELS in Fall. Students who were at risk on DIBELS ($n = 19$) were initially considered for participation in the secondary intervention. The second set of bars appearing after the vertical dashed line represents the risk level of students on the SRSS and DIBELS Winter 2009 screening. Because of a transient population at the school, it should be noted that four new students were identified during the screening process in Winter

TABLE 4.6. CES Secondary Intervention Grid

Support	Description	Schoolwide data: entry criteria	Data to monitor progress	Exit criteria
Fundations: Wilson Language Basics for K–3© small-group reading intervention	Content: Reading instruction: evidence-based program with systematic and explicit instruction to teach basics of reading and spelling Multisensory approach with high rates of opportunities for students to practice and apply learned skills Focus skills (Wilson, 2002): • Letter formation • Phonological and phonemic awareness • Sound–symbol • Phonics • Irregular words • Fluency Behavioral supports: establish expectations daily, provide behavior-specific praise through assigning points to student, teacher earns points for providing behavioral redirection Students earn proximal and distal reinforcement (daily sticker if more points earned than teacher; small prize after eight stickers earned) 30-minute instruction 4 days/week with reading specialist (in addition to 90-minute classroom reading instruction)	*All the following criteria must be met: 1. For students in grades K–3 2. Fall DIBELS (Good & Kaminski, 2002) benchmark scores indicating need for intensive intervention (at-risk range) 3. Participation in small-group reading intervention provided by classroom teacher, in addition to core reading instruction (30 minutes 4 days/week) 4. Classroom instruction meeting at least 80% procedural fidelity on a procedural checklist. (Is the instruction taught as planned?) 5. Not making adequate progress with supplemental classroom instruction according to biweekly progress monitoring—trend and level	1. DIBELS weekly progress monitoring probes 2. SRSS (Drummond, 1994) behavior screening data 3. Transfer of skills to classroom instruction (spelling tests, weekly vocabulary, comprehension assessments)	DIBELS benchmark scores indicating core reading instruction is appropriate (low risk) Four consecutive DIBELS progress monitoring data points above the aim line (set to meet end-of-year benchmark goal) Follow-up: biweekly progress monitoring to ensure growth is continuing with lower intensity of instruction

Note. From Lane, Kalberg, and Menzies (2009, Table 6.1, pp. 130–131). Copyright 2009 by The Guilford Press. Adapted by permission.

and 14 students who were present for the Fall screening left the school prior to the Winter screening.

A data-driven process was used to determine students' participation in the secondary intervention (see Figure 4.4). First, all students were considered for participation based on their Fall DIBELS reading benchmark assessment. Students determined to be at risk for reading problems were monitored in reading using the DIBELS progress monitoring passages during 6 weeks of instruction in the primary prevention curricula and classroom-based supplemental instruction (extra 30 minutes/day in a

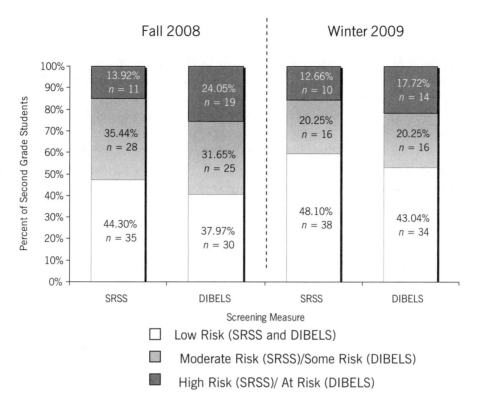

FIGURE 4.3. CES second-grade behavior (SRSS; Drummond, 1994) and reading (DIBELS; Good & Kaminski, 2002) screening data for Fall 2008 and Winter 2009.

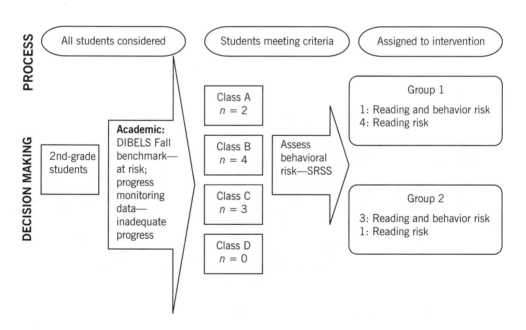

FIGURE 4.4. CES's process and decision making for determining secondary prevention: targeted reading instruction and behavioral support for second-grade students in 2008–2009. This model illustrates the process for determining participation in a research study (see Oakes, Mathur, & Lane, 2010).

small group). Student progress was reviewed at the end of the interval, and those students who were nonresponsive to the current program (not reaching level or trend to meet end-of-year benchmark) were assigned to intervention groups in addition to their current program. The secondary intervention groups were taught by the reading specialist. In Week 6, the teachers completed the SRSS for all enrolled second-grade students. Of the nine students identified as nonresponders in reading, four had co-occurring behavioral risk (rated in the high-risk category of the SRSS). All nine students began secondary reading interventions with the reading specialist in Week 7 in two small groups (*n* = 5 and *n* = 4; see Oakes, Mathur, et al., 2010, for intervention outcomes).

How Can These Data Be Used to Make Classwide Instructional Decisions?

DIBELS and the SRSS screening data can be used by classroom teachers to determine the types and intensity of supports needed. Figure 4.5 illustrates one second-grade classroom at CES. The graph allowed the classroom teacher to look at reading and behavioral growth for individual students. Each dot on the graph represents a student in the class. The *x*-axis displays the Fall correct words read per minute on DIBELS and the *y*-axis represents the Winter DIBELS score. Solid circles are used to identify

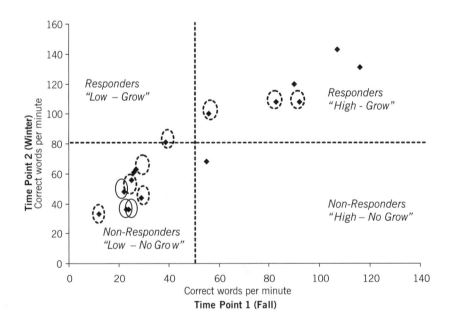

FIGURE 4.5. CES second-grade class B's (*N* = 18) reading and behavior scores at Fall (time point 1) and Winter (time point 2). Each dot represents one student's DIBELS oral reading fluency scores. The solid circles indicate students who were rated on the SRSS as at high risk in Fall. The dotted circles represent students who were at moderate risk on the SRSS in Fall. Only students who were screened at both time points are represented on the graph. From Kalberg, Lane, and Menzies (2010, Figure 1, p. 570). Copyright 2010 by the authors. Adapted by permission.

which students were at high risk in Fall on the SRSS, and dotted circles represent students with moderate behavioral risk scores. Figure 4.5 highlights the need for pairing behavioral interventions for students at high risk for antisocial behavior who also are at high risk for reading problems in the Fall. These students remained low on the reading screening in the Winter despite supplemental classroom reading interventions. Some students require both academic and behavioral intervention in order to make academic growth.

Summary

CES illustrates how elementary schools can implement a CI3T model to support students. Over the course of 4 years, the school was able to introduce new structures, programs, and procedures as schoolwide practices. This comprehensive approach resulted in slow but meaningful changes. With a shift in thinking and practice from reactive (e.g., ODRs) to proactive (e.g., providing interventions as soon as potential difficulties can be detected) policies, systematic screening tools (DIBELS and SRSS) offered a feasible and reliable way to find students who could benefit from the supports the school had to offer. With all three components in place (academics, behavior, and social skills), CES offered a comprehensive education to all students.

An Illustration at an Inclusive Rural Middle School: Foster Middle School

Foster Middle School (FMS) is a rural middle school located in middle Tennessee with approximately 500 sixth- through eighth-grade students in a fully inclusive environment. In other words, all students with special needs received their core curriculum in the general education setting. The vast majority of students were white (> 95%). Approximately 20% of students received special education services, with the largest percentage identified with SLDs. The economic disadvantage rate was 30.8%.

Building a CI3T Model of Prevention

The middle school established a positive behavior support team that included an administrator, two general education teachers, a special education teacher, a parent, and a student. This team attended a year-long training hosted by Vanderbilt University. The intent of this privately funded training series was to design and implement a three-tiered model of prevention, with an emphasis on positive behavior supports and using data-driven procedures to (1) monitor the overall level of risk present in a school and (2) identify students who might need secondary (Tier 2) or tertiary (Tier 3) levels of prevention.

The overall primary plan included three core components (academic, behavior, and social) to meet students' multiple needs. The plan outlined clear expectations for students and teachers for each component; procedures for teaching and reinforcing expectations; and a plan for monitoring student progress, program implementation (treatment integrity), and consumer-opinion social validity. The leadership team administered a survey to determine the academic and behavioral expectations the teachers thought were "critical for student success." The social skills component included a program called Character under Construction. They developed an implementation manual for all adults in the building that included the full plan (as well as procedures for teaching and reinforcing schoolwide expectations), the expectation matrix that described the expectations for each school setting, a grid listing all secondary supports (see Table 4.7 for examples), a grid listing all tertiary supports (see Table 4.8 for one example), as well as an assessment schedule (see Table 4.2) to monitor treatment integrity, social validity, and student performance.

Measures

Treatment fidelity data were collected on the primary prevention plan using teacher-completed component checklists. Direct observations were conducted by research assistants for teachers who gave permission to be observed. Social validity data were collected by surveying teachers before the program began; they were asked their opinions about the significance of the goals, the acceptability of the procedures in the plan, and the likelihood that the plan would yield important outcomes. This same survey was given at the end of each year of program implementation. The assessment plan also involved monitoring student performance on measures that were collected as part of regular school practices, including ODRs, grades, attendance and tardiness, referrals (e.g., special education, counseling, alternative learning center, prereferral interventions), and the SRSS (behavioral screener). Homeroom teachers completed the SRSS at three points over the course of the school year: 6 weeks into the school year (Fall), prior to Winter break (Winter), and 6 weeks prior to year end (Spring). Information from the SRSS was used in conjunction with other data to identify students for secondary (see Kalberg et al., in press; Robertson & Lane, 2007) and tertiary (see Lane, Rogers, et al., 2007) prevention efforts.

The SRSS was first completed by teachers during a regularly scheduled faculty meeting at the onset of the school year to familiarize them with the purpose of the instruments and to explain how to complete them. Thereafter, the school-site team distributed the forms to teacher mailboxes along with instructions on how to complete the forms and contact information should questions arise. This information was used to answer questions such as the following.

How Is Risk Shifting Over Time at FMS?

One important question the school-site team wanted to answer was, "How is risk shifting over time, after having implemented the plan for 6 years?" To answer this question, they made a graph of their SRSS data for each Fall administration beginning in 2004 through the current year. In Figure 4.6 you see the overall level of risk during Fall for each year represented by six bars. The white portion of this first bar reflects the percentage of students who received scores of 0–3 on the SRSS during the

TABLE 4.7. FMS Secondary Intervention Grid

Support	Description	Schoolwide data: Entry criteria	Data to monitor progress	Exit criteria
Study skills	Content: Study skills curriculum of skills and strategies used to gain and demonstrate knowledge Goals: • Gain knowledge from text, class discussions, and teacher-led instruction • Demonstrate knowledge on formal and informal assessments (test, quizzes, homework, presentations, projects) Topics include: • Note-taking strategies • Use of graphic organizers • Organization • Goal setting • Test-taking strategies • Writing process (planning/drafting/editing) Scheduling: 50-minute class (30 minutes instruction, 20 minutes applied practice) 56 lessons (Robertson & Lane, 2007, p. 9)	Academic: 1. GPA ≤ 2.7; or 2. One or more course failures in a quarter (D or F/E) and 3. Not participating in Read 180 reading intervention and Behavior: 1. SRSS (Drummond, 1994) score in moderate (4–8) or high (9–21) risk; or 2. One or more ODR within 4-month period	Schoolwide data: GPA Course grades (9 weeks) SRSS ODRs Proximal measures: 1. Criterion-referenced assessment—acquiring knowledge, demonstrating knowledge, and conflict resolution (Lane, 2003b) 2. Knowledge of study skills 3. Knowledge of conflict resolution skills Distal measures: 1. Study Habits Inventory (Jones & Slate, 1990) 2. ConflictTalk (Kimsey & Fuller, 2003)	Academic (for the quarter): 1. GPA > 2.7; or 2. No course failures (D or F/E) and Behavior: 1. SRSS screening low risk (0–3) or 2. No ODRs within the quarter Students participate in this class for one semester; if exit criteria are not met, further interventions are considered for following semester
Study skills plus conflict resolution	Content: Note. The study skills curriculum is described above. Students received instruction in conflict resolution skills in addition to study skill component Generalization and maintenance lessons and activities were replaced with conflict resolution curriculum Productive Conflict Resolution Program (School Mediation Center, 1998) Goals: "(a) Empower students and teachers with the skills necessary to resolve conflicts productively, (b) develop emotional intelligence, (c) create and uphold social justice, (d) aid in the development of responsible citizenship, and (e) create a caring and cooperative whole school environment" (School Mediation Center, p. B-3).	Academic: 1. GPA ≤ 2.7; or 2. One or more course failures in a quarter (D or F/E) 3. Not participating in Read 180 reading intervention and Behavior: 1. SRSS screening moderate (4–8) or high (9–21) risk; or	Schoolwide data: GPA Course grades (9 weeks) SRSS ODRs Proximal measures: Criterion-referenced assessments 1. Knowledge of study skills 2. Knowledge of conflict resolution skills Distal measures: 1. Study Habits Inventory (Jones & Slate, 1990)	Academic (for the quarter): 1. GPA > 2.7; or 2. No course failures (D or F/E) and Behavior: 1. SRSS screening low risk (0–3) or 2. No ODRs within the quarter Students participate in this class for one quarter; if

(cont.)

TABLE 4.7. (cont.)				
Support	Description	Schoolwide data: Entry criteria	Data to monitor progress	Exit criteria
Study skills plus conflict resolution (cont.)	Topics include understanding: • Conflict • Cooperation • Conflict styles • Valuing diversity • Communication skills (listening and expression) • Problem solving • Forgiveness • Reconciliation Scheduling: 50-minute class (30 minutes instruction; 20 minutes applied practice) 56 lessons (Robertson & Lane, 2007, p. 10)	2. One or more ODRs (within a specified time, e.g., 4 months)	2. ConflictTalk (Kimsey & Fuller, 2003)	exit criteria are not met, further interventions are considered for following quarter

Note. From Lane, Kalberg, and Menzies (2009, Table 6.2, pp. 132–133). Copyright 2009 by The Guilford Press. Adapted by permission.

TABLE 4.8. FMS Tertiary Intervention Grid				
Support	Description	Schoolwide data: Entry criteria	Data to monitor progress	Exit criteria
Functional assessment-based intervention	Individualized intervention is developed 1. Information collection from review of student records, student interview, teacher interview, parent interview, direct observation of target behavior, and Social Skills Rating System (Gresham & Elliott, 1990) is used to identify target behavior and inform intervention 2. Information is placed in function matrix (Umbreit, Ferro, Liaupsin, & Lane, 2007) 3. Function of behavior is identified with decision model (Umbreit et al., 2007) 4. Intervention is developed with three components: antecedent adjustments, reinforcement, and extinction Data are collected daily; procedural fidelity is assessed, and data are graphed to determine effect of the intervention (Lane, Rogers, et al., 2007)	1. Met criteria for secondary interventions (see Table 4.7) 2. Participated in secondary interventions used between screenings with documentation of lack of success for academic and behavioral performance • GPA remaining below secondary criteria ≤ 2.7 • Continued course failures • Earning ODRs • SRSS (Drummond, 1994) moderate or high risk 3. Parent permission to conduct functional assessment	Direct observation and recording of target student's behavior Graphing of data to determine changes in behavior across four phases: 1. Baseline (before intervention is implemented) 2. With intervention in place—fidelity that plan is being implemented as planned is needed 3. Withdrawal (remove intervention to ensure that it is the reason for the change) 4. Reinstate intervention	Measurable changes in target behavior using the graphed data for all four phases • GPA > 2.7 • No course failures • No ODRs • SRSS low risk

Note. From Lane, Kalberg, and Menzies (2009, Box 6.4, pp. 136–137). Copyright 2009 by The Guilford Press. Adapted by permission.

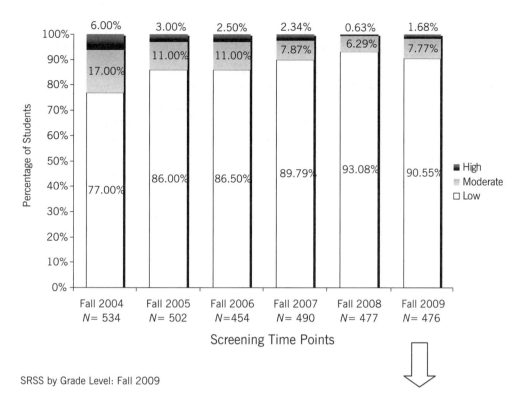

Screening Time Points

SRSS by Grade Level: Fall 2009

Grade Level	Number of Students Screened	Low	Moderate	High
6	163	149 (91.41%)	12 (7.36%)	2 (1.23%)
7	159	144 (90.57%)	10 (6.29%)	5 (3.14%)
8	154	138 (89.61%)	15 (9.74%)	1 (0.01%)

Treatment Integrity

	04–05	05–06	06–07	07–08	08–09	09–10
Fall	85.54%		89.46%	92.86%	80.35%	
Winter						86.61%
Spring			93.75%	93.75%	92.68%	

FIGURE 4.6. SRSS scores for FMS from 2004 through 2009. For Fall 2009, numbers and percentage of students in each risk category are reported. Means are reported for treatment integrity using the SET (Sugai et al., 2001). From Lane, Kalberg, and Menzies (2009, Figure 6.7, p. 142). Copyright 2009 by The Guilford Press. Adapted by permission.

first administration (77%), suggesting a low level of risk for antisocial behavior. The gray portion reflects the percentage of students who received scores of 4–8 (17%), signifying moderate risk. Finally, the black portion reflects the percentage of students who received scores of 9–21 (6%), suggesting a high level of risk.

By Fall 2008, there had been clear changes in the levels of risk present, with 93% of the study body scoring in the low-risk category, 6% in the moderate-risk category, and less than 1% in the high-risk category. However, in Fall 2009, there was a slight increase of risk. After graphing these data and looking at the levels of risk, the team met to discuss the treatment integrity data and noticed a decrease in the level of implementation. The percentage of implementation as measured by the School-wide Evaluation Tool (SET; Sugai et al., 2001) had decreased from 93.75% during the Spring of 2007–2008 academic year to 80.35% during Fall 2008–2009, which may have impacted risk, as reported during the start of the 2009–2010 school year. Upon further discussion, it became clear a booster session was needed to rejuvenate the primary prevention plan. The leadership team realized they would need to reteach the plan regularly as new teachers and staff joined FMS. After 6 years of implementation, the positive behavior support practices were such a natural part of the school's culture that training new faculty and staff had diminished over time.

Which Students Need Support Beyond the Primary Program?

The leadership team determined that both secondary and tertiary levels of support were needed in addition to the primary plan.

SECONDARY SUPPORTS

The team met during the first semester of implementation to examine the behavior data (SRSS and ODR) in conjunction with academic data (GPA and course failure). The assistant principal noticed that many students (grades 6–8) had co-occurring behavior and academic difficulties. FMS invited researchers from Vanderbilt University to discuss this concern (see Robertson & Lane, 2007). The meeting focused on how best to assist students who were not responding to the primary prevention plan. Some of the school-site team members indicated students would do a better job if they improved their ability to negotiate conflicts with peers and adults. Other team members thought students were struggling as a result of poor study skills. There was a lack of consensus about how to best support students.

Together, the school leadership team and the researchers from Vanderbilt University developed an intervention to address the specific behavioral and academic needs of students at FMS. Based on data the school already collected, a secondary intervention was developed and then added to the school's secondary intervention grid (see Table 4.7). The collaborative team determined that instruction in study skills would address the academic needs; they also decided that many of their students did not have the skills to resolve interpersonal conflicts that often resulted in ODRs. So the question became, "What is the additive benefit of conflict resolution skills over and above improving study skills?" Two interventions were developed to address these needs: (1) instruction in study skills and (2) instruction in both study skills and conflict resolution. These interventions were written in column 1 of the secondary intervention grid. A description of each intervention was developed and written in column 2 of the grid.

These interventions were developed based on key skills and strategies (Deshler et al., 2001) previously validated for students with academic and behavior problems (Bos & Vaughn, 2002). The interventions were scheduled for a 50-minute instructional block to be part of students' schedules in the second semester and were taught by four teachers (one teacher volunteered to teach all three of the study skills intervention groups) who volunteered. Schoolwide data were used to determine the criteria for identifying which students would be offered this class (intervention; see column 3 of the grid). An academic need was defined as students earning a GPA of 2.7 or less or one or more course failures (D or F/E) in the second quarter. A behavioral need was defined as students rated as moderate or high risk on the SRSS or who had earned one or more ODR in the first 4 months of school. Students who met one academic and one behavioral criterion were invited to participate. Data to measure students' progress were also chosen (and listed in column 4 of the grid). Finally, a criterion was used to decide when students were no longer in need of additional support. If students did not meet the criteria by the end of the semester, they would be considered for further supports.

In the first year of implementation, all students in grades 6 through 8 were considered for this intervention. Figure 4.7 illustrates the process and decision making for determining students in need of the study skills or the study skills plus conflict resolution. All students who met criteria were invited to participate in this course. Parent permission was secured and then students were invited. Those who agreed were scheduled into the course for the Spring semester. The students with parent permission who agreed to take the course ($N = 65$) were randomly assigned by grade level to one of the two interventions. One class of each intervention was taught for each grade level (see Robertson & Lane, 2007, for further detail). The students whose parents did not provide parental consent remained in the class, but their assessment data were not collected for purposes of the study.

In Year 2 of their three-tiered model, the school decided to continue the intervention class as part of their regular course offerings. All students were scheduled for one of three classes: study skills, conflict resolution, or focus (study hall). This time, study skills or conflict resolution skills relative to regular school practices were compared to determine the isolated benefits of each intervention. In order to offer support for students at the start of the school year, schoolwide data from Quarter 4 of the previous school year were used for placement. Therefore, only rising seventh and eighth graders were considered for these courses. Students who met the criteria were randomly assigned to one of each of the three class options. Figure 4.8 illustrates the process and decision making for determining the placement of students by the school. The first step in the process was to screen all students in the seventh and eighth grades to determine who met the criteria. The second step was to determine which students met

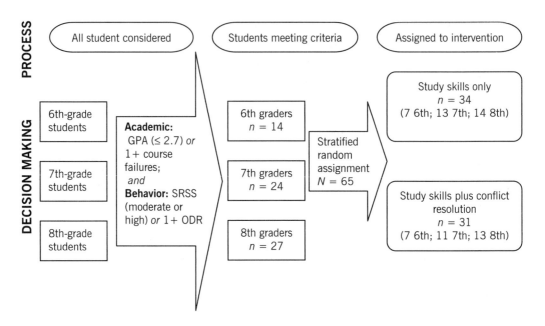

FIGURE 4.7. FMS's process and decision making for determining the secondary prevention: study skills and study skills plus conflict resolution for students in grades 6–8 in the 2004–2005 school year. Year 1 of implementing a three-tiered prevention model (Robertson & Lane, 2007).

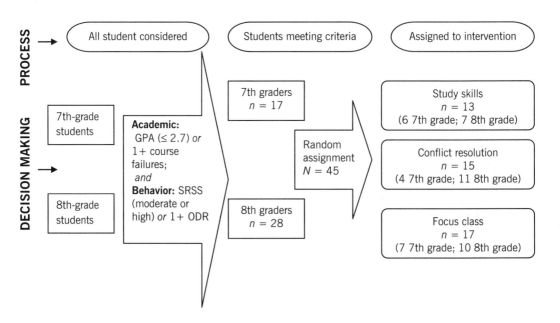

FIGURE 4.8. FMS's sequence of using schoolwide data to identify students in need of secondary academic and behavioral intervention. Seventh- and eighth-grade students meeting the criteria received one of three interventions: study skills instruction, conflict resolution instruction, or a focus class during Year 2 of implementing a three-tiered prevention model (Kalberg, Lane, & Lambert, in press).

the academic and behavior criteria (seventh grade, n = 17; eighth grade, n = 28). The third step was to assign each student randomly to one of the three course offerings for the first quarter. The Vanderbilt University research team assisted in analyzing student responses to the interventions for students who agreed and whose parents gave permission (see Kalberg et al., in press, for further detail).

TERTIARY SUPPORTS

Students who exhibited persistent academic and behavior difficulties were considered for tertiary supports. Schoolwide data were monitored to determine responsiveness to the primary (as described previously) and secondary (see Table 4.7) programs. At FMS, functional assessment-based interventions (FABI; Umbreit et al., 2007) were developed for students who continued to meet the criteria for academic and behavioral need after participation in the primary and secondary preventions (see Table 4.8; see also Lane, Rogers, et al., 2007, for a step-by-step example of the FABI process).

FABI are developed through a systematic process of identifying the antecedent (A) conditions in a classroom that set the stage for the undesirable behavior (B, referred to as the target behavior—that needs to be defined very specifically) to occur as well as the consequences that maintain the occurrence (C; e.g., what reinforces the behavior or keeps it going; Umbreit et al., 2007). Several tools and procedures were used, such as interviews with teachers, parents, and students; direct observations of behavior in the classroom to collect A-B-C data; as well as a review of records to determine why the behavior occurs. All behaviors will occur to either access (positive reinforcement) or avoid (negative reinforcement) attention, tasks or tangibles, or sensory experiences (Umbreit et al., 2007). Next, a new and more desirable replacement behavior is identified, one that works better than the target behavior, and operationally identified. Finally, a three-part intervention is developed: (1) adjustments to the antecedent conditions, (2) increased rates of reinforcement for the replacement (desired) behavior, and (3) extinction procedures to eliminate or reduce the occurrence of the target behavior. Single-case methodology is used to see how well the intervention works in increasing the occurrence of the replacement behavior and reducing the occurrence of the target behavior. For example, in a withdrawal design, data are collected on the target behavior prior to the intervention, during the intervention, after withdrawal of the intervention, and again after the intervention is reinstated to test the effect of the intervention on the target and replacement behaviors (Lane, Weisenbach, Phillips, & Wehby, 2007). This level of support is reserved for the students with the most intensive needs because of the time and resources to implement this individual approach.

Summary

FMS illustrates how to use schoolwide data for multiple purposes. First, they monitored the level of student risk in their building through systematic screening procedures conducted three times per year. The school leadership team utilized measures of program fidelity along with student data to monitor the need for training faculty and staff. The screening data, along with other schoolwide data sources (i.e., ODR, GPA, referrals), were used to develop specific secondary interventions based on observations and information provided by teachers. Because of the strength of the primary and secondary prevention plans, fewer students needed the most intensive, tertiary, supports (FABI). Therefore, school personnel were able to address the needs of this small group of students. This school implemented all three levels of support within the first 2 years of designing their CI3T model. It was a large undertaking, but they were committed to slow (1 year to fully develop a plan with faculty and staff feedback) and meaningful change, which is evidenced in their SRSS screening data (see Figure 4.6).

An Illustration in a Suburban High School: Liberty High School

Liberty High School (LHS) is located in a suburban area of middle Tennessee. It is a growing high school with approximately 2,000 students in ninth through 12th grades in an inclusive environment. The students are predominantly white (> 88%). Approximately 7% of students received special education services (IDEA, 2004). Thirteen percent of students were considered economically disadvantaged. The graduation rate at LHS was approximately 91.5%.

Building a CI3T Model of Prevention

LHS designed a CI3T model of prevention during a year-long training series. Through a privately funded training series at Vanderbilt University, the school leadership team (the assistant principal, two general education teachers, and one special educator) designed a plan that integrated academics, behavioral supports, and social skill instruction. During the development of the schoolwide plan, the team identified academic, behavior, and social skill responsibilities for administrators, teachers, students, and parents. There was an emphasis on positive behavior supports (establishing and defining behavioral expectations, teaching and reinforcing expectations, monitoring outcomes) because of concern that student behavior was negatively impacting instruction. Expected behaviors and social skills (Elliott & Gresham, 1991) were explicitly taught to students. Social validity (faculty perception of the feasibility, acceptability, and importance of the goals and practices of the plan) and treatment integrity (the degree to which the plan was implemented as planned) measures were collected. The goal was to increase prosocial behaviors and reduce problem behaviors, in turn increasing the quantity and quality of instructional time. The team began by identifying supports that already existed for students who needed additional assistance (secondary and tertiary grids; Lane, Kalberg, & Menzies, 2009). Then they coordinated the academic, social, and behavioral expectations with existing programs. This allowed the team to see what they could offer students who needed help in meeting the various expectations. Then the team used schoolwide data sources to determine students' current level of academic and behavioral risk and how students would be identified for targeted supports.

The school met with several challenges within the first 2 years of implementing their three-tiered model of prevention. Several teachers did not want to complete the behavior screeners for their students. This made it difficult to determine an accurate picture of risk status in the building and to ensure that students who needed targeted supports were being considered. Multiple data sources were used so that students who demonstrated need would not be overlooked. The leadership team put all of the information into a manual for teachers and staff to access when they had a question about the program.

Measures

Included in the school's implementation manual was an assessment schedule (see Table 4.3). The schedule listed all of the data collected on student performance as well as measures used to evaluate the implementation of their three-tiered prevention plan. Data sources were grouped by outcome type—academic, behavior, and referrals—and the month they were collected was marked in the grid. For example, the SRSS is completed 6 weeks into the school year (September), at the end of the first semester (December), and approximately 6 weeks before the end of the year (April). Students were screened by two teachers, second period and seventh period, at each time point. Teachers were given time to complete the SRSS at a regularly scheduled faculty meeting in the first year. They intended to have teachers complete the SRSS on the password-protected district server; however, technical problems interfered, and the team spent a considerable amount of time collecting the screeners individually. In the second year, the technical issues were addressed, and screenings were completed with greater ease and accuracy. Other measures monitored by the school's leadership team were GPA (semester and year end), course failures (quarterly), ODRs, attendance (absences and tardies), and referrals to student support services such as counseling and the school resource officer. LHS elected to participate in a partnership with the research team at Vanderbilt University for support in evaluating their plan; therefore, the team had confidential program measures (social validity, treatment integrity) to evaluate and revise their plan over the Summer. Social validity data were collected from teachers who agreed to provide the information. The school leadership team used the Primary Intervention Rating Scale (PIRS; Lane, Robertson, et al., 2002) to survey the staff about the acceptability of the practices, feasibility of the procedures, and acceptability of the goals and procedures. They administered it before the start of the school year, but after the plan was fully explained. Then, in mid-March, the PIRS was used again to measure how the practices, procedures, and goals met initial expectations. Treatment integrity was measured in three ways. First, the SET (Sugai et al., 2001) was used to measure overall implementation. Second, teachers self-rated their participation in the plan such as whether they offered multiple opportunities for students to participate during instruction, provided behavior-specific praise when giving out the positive behavior support tickets, and modeled the positive behaviors they expected from students. Teachers rated each item on a 4-point Likert type scale (0 = *not at all*, 1 = *some of the time*, 2 = *most of the time*, 3 = *all of the time*) based on their use of the practice or procedure for the current school year. Finally, 25% of the faculty was randomly selected for direct observation. The same treatment integrity checklists were used to evaluate a 30-minute instructional block from two perspectives, the teacher and an outside observer (research assistant). The observation tool included a response rating to indicate no opportunity to observe that item in the 30-minute observations window (7 = *no opportunity*). Together, these three measures provided a picture of the faculty and staff opinions about the plan and the level of its use. The information was aggregated and provided to the leadership team to inform revisions of their plan over the Summer. Teacher names or identifiers were not attached to the program data provided to the schools.

The student outcome and program measures were used to answer the following questions:

How Is Risk Shifting over Time at LHS?

The LHS school leadership team was interested in changes in risk during the first 2 years of implementing their plan (Lane, Oakes, Ennis, et al., 2011). Furthermore, they were concerned that not all teachers were participating in screening their classes. They wanted to know whether the CI3T model they designed especially for their school site was having a positive impact on their school culture. They graphed the percentage of students at risk at the Winter time point for each of the 2 years (see Figure 4.9). The school leadership team chose to have two raters for each student, the

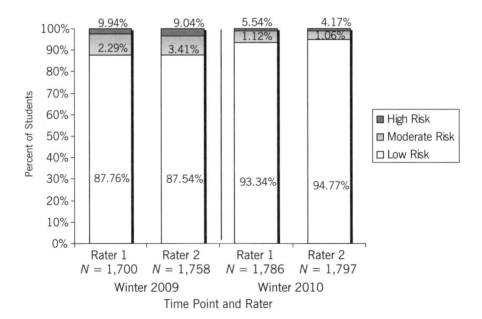

FIGURE 4.9. LHS screening data for Winter 2009 and Winter 2010. Rater 1 is the second-period teacher and Rater 2 is the seventh-period teacher. Each student was screened by two teachers.

second-period and seventh-period teachers, so that two perspectives were considered when determining which students were in need of additional supports. The Winter time point was used because the Fall 2009 time point was prepared with only the first six items on the scale; therefore, the data were not usable by the team. The data in Figure 4.9 shows the percentage of students rated in each risk category: low (0–3) in white, moderate (4–8) in light gray, and high (9–21) in dark gray. The first bar shows the percentage of students in each category as rated by the second-period teachers. The second bar shows the ratings for the seventh-period teachers for Year 1. The third and fourth bars represent Year 2 for each rater (second and seventh periods, respectively). The ratings between the second-period and seventh-period teachers were fairly consistent for each risk category at the same time points. Year 2, compared with Year 1, reveals decreases in the percentage of students at high risk, from 9.94% to 5.54% for second-period and 9.04% to 4.17% for seventh-period teachers, and at moderate risk, from 2.29% to 1.12% for second-period and 3.41% to 1.06% for seventh-period teachers. It should be noted that the student body would also have changed with a new freshman class coming in and a senior class leaving; however, the reductions in risk were seen across all grade levels. These data were shared with the faculty, and an increase in participation in the three-tiered model was seen by the growing number of teachers willing to participate in the program evaluation component from 77.3% in 2008–2009, 86.5% in 2009–2010, and 82.4% at the start of the 2010–2011 school year.

How Can This Information Be Used to Support Students and Teachers?

SUPPORTING STUDENTS

As part of identifying students with increased risk, the school leadership team, led by the assistant principal, wanted to create a system that would provide them with appropriate supports in a timely way. Because of LHS's collaborative ongoing relationship with the Vanderbilt University research team, another study was designed to use the schoolwide data to make decisions about which students to consider for the secondary supports. Figure 4.10 displays the decision-making process that LHS and the research team designed. First, data for all the students in 10th or 11th grades were examined. This was done by using the SRSS screening data and reviewing course failure (D or F) data for the first semester. Students were considered eligible if they scored in the moderate-risk or high-risk category on the SRSS, had two or more course failures, and had a study hall period in their schedules. The 11 students who met these criteria were invited to participate in an 8-week class on self-determination skills, which was offered during their study hall (see Table 4.9) To test the effect of the intervention on students' grades and behavioral risk status, a multiple baseline design across participants was used. The secondary intervention grid (Table 4.9) describes this intervention, the criteria for accessing the intervention, the data used to monitor the effects, and the exit criteria (in this case completion of the 8-week curriculum).

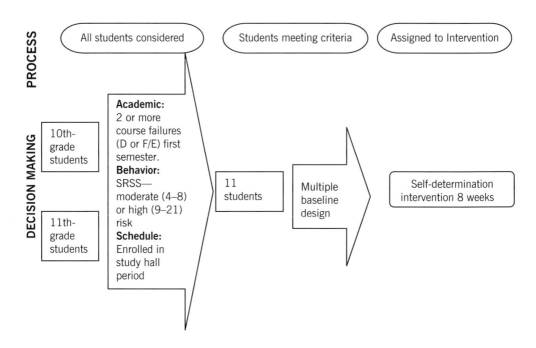

FIGURE 4.10. LHS's process and decision making for determining student participation in the secondary intervention: project self-determination. Students who met the criteria in grades 10 and 11 participated in the Spring semester Year 1 implementation of the primary prevention plan.

TABLE 4.9. LHS Secondary Intervention Grid				
Support	**Description**	**Schoolwide data: Entry criteria**	**Data to monitor progress**	**Exit criteria**
Project Self-Determination 3 days per week; 30-minute lesson; 8 weeks	Direct instruction of self-determination skills taught in small groups during students' study hall class. Tell, Show, Do lesson format to teach the following skills: • Organizational skills • Study skills • Note taking • Participating in discussions • Decision making • Asking for help Treatment integrity monitored through daily completed component checklist of critical lesson elements; 25% of lessons observed for reliability by second rater.	1. Students in grades 10 or 11 2. Academic: 2+ course failures (D or F/E) in first semester 3. Behavior: SRSS—moderate (4–8) or high (9–21) risk 4. Schedule: enrolled in study hall period	1. AIR Self-Determination Scale (pre- and postintervention) 2. SRSS (Gresham & Elliott, 1990; pre and post) 3. Student and classroom teachers completed checkout form with seven items related to the self-determination skills taught (weekly) 4. Attendance rates 5. ODRs Social validity of intervention (teacher and student completed)	Completion of Project Self-Determination (8-week course—one quarter)

Note. From Lane, Kalberg, and Menzies (2009, Table 6.2, pp. 132–133). Copyright 2009 by The Guilford Press. Adapted by permission.

Other secondary interventions were eventually added to the grid in this same format.

SUPPORTING TEACHERS

The school team was also interested in deciding how to focus mentoring opportunities for new teachers as well as professional development for current staff. Table 4.10 illustrates a secondary support grid for teachers. The first column details the data used to determine whether the teacher might benefit from professional development to support classroom behavior. For example, teachers rating 20% or more of their class at moderate risk or high risk on the SRSS may indicate that they need strategies to increase opportunities to respond during instruction or to adjust the pace of lessons. Both of these strategies increase students' engagement and allow less time for disruptions (Lane, Menzies, et al., 2011). In another example, if teachers rate more than 20% or their class to be at moderate or high risk for behavior problems on the SRSS and 20% or more of students receive low test grades, this might indicate that teachers are losing instructional time to managing behavior. Increasing rates of reinforcement might help such teachers regain instructional time and reduce the need for behavioral redirection (Lane, Menzies, et al., 2011). Goal setting is another technique that offers students a purpose for learning and also serves as an advanced organizer so students know what is to be accomplished (Schunk, 2001).

TABLE 4.10. LHS Secondary Intervention Grid for Supporting Teachers		
Data used for instructional decision making	**Strategy**	**Data to monitor progress**
SRSS: 20% of students are at moderate or high risk	**Pacing:** Moving through a lesson with appropriate momentum facilitates student involvement	**SRSS:** less than 10% of students at moderate/high risk
Class grades: 20% or more of students are receiving lower than a C on progress report or report card	**Opportunities to respond:** Providing students with a high number of opportunities to answer or actively respond to academic requests	**Class grades:** 5% or fewer students receive lower than a C on progress report or report card
SRSS: 20% of students are at moderate or high risk	**Provide precorrections:** begin each class by setting a goal. Tell students exactly what is to be accomplished that day and post the objectives on the board. Also set behavioral expectations by referring to the three schoolwide expectations (Be Prompt, Show Respect to Yourself and Others, Be Responsible)	**SRSS:** less than 10% of students at moderate/high risk
Class grades: 20% or more of students are receiving lower than a C on test grades		**Class grades:** 5% or fewer students receive lower than a C on test grades
ODRs: two or more ODRs written in a quarter	**Increase use of reinforcement:** Increase the use of the schoolwide reinforcement system: the positive behavior support tickets. Suggestions include reinforce students for being in class and in their seats with materials ready when the bell rings, reinforce students who have homework completed and in class, reinforce students who work collaboratively when appropriate, reinforce students who participate in class discussions	**ODRs:** one or fewer ODRs written in a quarter

Summary

LHS is an illustration of a CI3T model that provided early detection through screening. They also implemented a primary program for academics, behavior, and social skills. Despite the challenges faced with the initially low levels of teacher participation, the leadership team persisted in putting practices in place to support students and teachers. Social validity data were important to ensure that teachers had a voice in the formulation and revision of LHS's plan.

Summary

This chapter introduced a very brief, no-cost, user-friendly screening tool—the SRSS—and offered step-by-step directions on how to complete it. Research conducted with the SRSS was synthesized to (1) examine the reliability and validity of this tool for use in the elementary school, middle school, and high school settings as well as (2) demonstrate how to use the SRSS to identify students who might require secondary (Tier 2) or tertiary (Tier 3) supports. Then an evenhanded discussion of the strengths and considerations associated with preparation, administration, scoring, and interpreting findings of the SRSS was provided. The chapter closed with illustrations of how to use the SRSS as part of regular school practices at the elementary school, middle school, and high school levels.

In the next chapter, we introduce another no-cost screening tool: the SDQ (Goodman, 1997). We encourage you to read on to learn about a tool that provides even more information on different types of behavior challenges (e.g., conduct problems, emotional symptoms, peer problems, and hyperactivity) as well as strengths (e.g., prosocial behavior).

CHAPTER 5

Strengths and Difficulties Questionnaire

In this chapter, we introduce the Strengths and Difficulties Questionnaire (SDQ; Goodman, 1997). The SDQ is an extensively researched, no-cost behavior screening questionnaire designed for use with students ages 3 to 16. The SDQ is an internationally utilized set of screening tools, providing the educational and clinical communities with a relatively brief (25-item) measure. They are briefer instruments than others designed to measure similar behavior patterns, such as the 118-item (five demographic and 113 actual items) Teacher Report Form (the teacher version of the well-known Child Behavior Checklist [CBCL]; Achenbach, 1991).

Whereas the screening tools discussed in the previous chapters have focused on internalizing and externalizing behaviors (see Chapter 2 for the Systematic Screening for Behavior Disorders [SSBD; Walker & Severson, 1992] and Chapter 3 for the Early Screening Project [ESP; Walker et al., 1995]), the SDQ assesses a broad set of behavioral domains, namely four problem behavior domains: conduct problems, hyperactivity, peer problems, and emotional symptoms, which are combined into an overall total difficulties score. The SDQ also includes one measure of desirable behavior: prosocial behavior.

Whereas the SSBD, ESP, and Student Risk Screening Scale (SRSS; Chapter 4) focus on teacher perspectives of characteristic behavior patterns (although the ESP does have a parental component), the SDQ considers input from different stakeholders. Forms are available to assess a given individual's behavioral performance from teacher, parent, and student perspectives, providing input from key adults (e.g., teachers and parents) in a student's life as well as the student him- or herself (provided the student is at least 11 years of age).

In this chapter, we begin with an overview of the SDQ, including step-by-step directions for how to complete and score this screening tool. Next, we highlight some of the supporting research conducted with the SDQ, including studies (1) examining the reliability and validity as well as (2) demonstrating how to use the SDQ to identify students who might require secondary (Tier 2) or tertiary (Tier 3) supports.

Then we provide a balanced discussion of the strengths and considerations associated with preparation, administration, scoring, and interpreting findings of the SDQ. Finally, we offer three illustrations, the first of which demonstrates how a small-town preschool's leadership team (Child's Play Preschool) used the SDQ to inform their primary prevention plan and monitor the need for secondary and tertiary supports. The second illustration highlights an urban public school, New Haven Elementary School, and their use of the SDQ to monitor the level of risk during the implementation of their primary plan and to inform secondary prevention efforts. The third illustration shows how the leadership team of a rural public school, Finn High School, used the SDQ behavior screening data to evaluate the impact of the primary prevention plan on overall levels of risk and to consider secondary (Tier 2) supports to better address the specific needs of individual students.

An Overview of the SDQ

In this section, we begin by describing the SDQ. Then we provide information on logistical considerations such as preparing, administering, scoring, and interpreting the SDQ.

Description

Like the SRSS (Drummond, 1994), the SDQ is a no-cost, factor-analytical-derived, one-stage universal screening tool (*www.sdqinfo.org*), with several versions available for use by the research, teaching, and clinical communities (Table 5.1) and published (and studied) in a variety of languages (Table 5.2).

Each version contains 25 items equally distributed across five scales: Emotional Symptoms (five items), Conduct Problems (five items), Hyperactivity/Inattention (five items), Peer Relationship Problems (five items), and Prosocial Behavior (five items). The items are statements about behavior, some of which are phrased positively (e.g., "Considerate of other people's feelings," "Generally liked by other children") and others negatively (e.g., "Fears or easily scared," "Often lies or cheats"). Items are rated on a 3-point Likert-type scale, ranging from 0 = *not true*, 1 = *somewhat true*, or 2 = *certainly true*, to determine the occurrence of each described behavior during the last 6 months or the current school year. The ratings on the first four scales are added together to form an overall total difficulties score (20 items).

The teacher and the parent versions of the SDQ for 4- to 16-year-olds contain the same 25 items, and the teacher and parent report assessing 3- (and 4-) year-olds is a modified version: It includes 22 of these 25 items, two other items addressing antisocial behavior are changed to measure oppositional behavior, and Item 21 assessing reflectiveness is modified. Likewise, the wording of the 25 items on the adolescent self-report version (ages 11–16) has been slightly modified.

Positively stated items are reverse-scored, so that higher numbers indicate higher levels of concern. Subscale scores range from 0 to 10 and total scores range from 0 to 40. These scores are compared with cut scores provided for each scale (and these are

TABLE 5.1. SDQ Versions Available

Rater	Age groups	One-sided informant-rated version 25 items (3-point Likert-type scale)	SDQ and impact supplement 25 items (3-point Likert-type scale) *and* 5 items (Likert-type scale of intensity)	SDQ, follow-up questions, and impact supplement *and* 6 items (Likert-type scale of frequency)
Teacher	3- and 4-year-olds	✓	✓	✓
	4- to 10-year-olds	✓	✓	✓
	11- to 17-year-olds	✓	✓	✓
Parent	3- and 4-year-olds	✓	✓	✓
	4- to 10-year-olds	✓	✓	✓
	11- to 17-year-olds	✓	✓	✓
Student	11- to 17-year-olds	✓	✓	✓

different for each scale), and the total difficulties score falls into one of three categories: normal, borderline, or abnormal.

An extended, two-sided version, intended to inform intervention efforts (Goodman, 1999), is also available, and includes not only the 25 behavior items but also an impact supplement. The rater (teacher, parent, or student) answers additional items to provide more information regarding level of distress, chronicity of the concern, social implications, and relative impact on others.

Finally, there are follow-up versions of the SDQ, containing two additional questions (beyond the 25 items and the impact supplement), designed to evaluate intervention outcomes. The two questions are (within the last month), "Has the intervention reduced problems?" and "Has the intervention helped in other ways such as making the problem more tolerable or bearable?"

TABLE 5.2. Languages of the SDQ

Afrikaans	English (UK)	Hmong	Maltese	Slovene
Amharic	English (US)	Hungarian	Norwegian (Bokmal)	Somali
Arabic	Estonian	Icelandic	Norwegian (Nynorsk)	Spanish
Basque	Farsi	Indonesian	Pashto	Spanish (Rio de la Plata)
Bengali	Finnish	Irish	Polish	Swahili
Bulgarian	French	Italian	Portuguese (Brazil)	Swedish
Catalan	Gaelic	Japanese	Portuguese (Portugal)	Tamil
Chinese	Gallego	Kannada	Punjabi	Thai
Croatian	German	Khmer	Romanian	Turkish
Czech	Greek	Korean	Russian	Ukranian
Danish	Greenlandish	Lithuanian	Sami	Urdu
Dari	Gujarati	Macedonian	Serbian	Welsh
Dutch	Hebrew	Malay	Sinhalese	Xhosa
English (Austral)	Hindi	Malayalam	Slovak	Yoruba

Logistical Issues

In this section, we address a number of logistical considerations. Each is framed in the form of a question, followed by recommendations based on our 5 years of experience using the SDQ in our school-based intervention and professional development work.

When Should We Administer the SDQ?

If your school-site leadership team elects to implement the SDQ as part of regular school practice, it should be completed by teachers after they have had sufficient time to become familiar with the website and directions for completing the SDQ.

In our work with elementary, middle, and high schools, we recommend teachers complete the SDQ more than one time per year so the information can be used to identify students for additional supports such as secondary (Tier 2) and tertiary (Tier 3) supports following each screening period (see Illustrations 2 and 3). The concern associated with once-yearly screening (e.g., Fall) is that students' characteristic behavior patterns may shift as the content becomes more differentiated and the academic tasks become more demanding. Also, students may be exposed to new risk factors such as changes in family status (e.g., parents separating), traumatic events (e.g., being a victim of a violent crime), medical conditions (e.g., childhood-onset diabetes), or other events that could trigger a shift in behavioral performance patterns. Furthermore, in schools with high mobility, one screening time point would overlook some students for additional supports (remember that teachers should know students at least 30 days prior to screening). Those who attend multiple schools may be at increased risk (Walker, Block-Pedego, Todis, & Severson, 1991) and could need supports to transition between schools. By screening more than once, changes in performance patterns and individual needs can be detected and supported.

In addition to supporting individual students, data from the SDQ can be used as a snapshot view in time to examine the level (and types) of risk evident in a school. Data can be aggregated so the school-site leadership team can examine the percentage of students in the building (or in a grade level) who have abnormal levels of hyperactivity, peer problems, emotional symptoms, conduct problems, or limited prosocial skills. This information can be used to inform primary prevention efforts and to plan targeted supports (see Illustration 2). For example, if a large percentage of the student body is struggling with peer problems and conduct problems, the leadership team might consider an empirically valid primary prevention program (e.g., Positive Action, Inc., 2008) to address this schoolwide concern.

In our technical assistance work with schools developing assessment plans, we encourage school-site teams to conduct systematic screenings three times per year (if resources permit): approximately 6 weeks after the onset of the school year, before Winter break, and again prior to the end of the academic year (Kalberg et al., 2010; Lane, Kalberg, Bruhn, et al., 2008; Lane, Kalberg, Parks, et al., 2008). Samples of these assessment schedules are presented in the illustrations at the end of the chapter

TABLE 5.3. NHES Assessment Schedule

Measure	Aug	Sept	Oct	Nov	Dec	Jan	Feb	Mar	Apr	May
School demographics	×	×	×	×	×	×	×	×	×	×
Academic measures										
CBM-reading: DIBELS (Good & Kaminski, 2002)		×			×				×	
CBM-writing: district writing			×							
CBM: ThinkLink (ThinkLink Learning, 2000)		×			×			×		
TCAP (state achievement assessment)									×	
Course failures (report cards)			×			×		×		×
Behavior measures										
SDQ (Goodman, 1997)		×			×				×	
SRSS (Drummond, 1994)		×			×				×	
Attendance: tardies/absences	×	×	×	×	×	×	×	×	×	×
ODRs Suspensions/expulsions	×	×	×	×	×	×	×	×	×	×
Referrals										
Special education/student support team/ counseling referrals	×	×	×	×	×	×	×	×	×	×
Program measures										
Social validity (Primary Intervention Rating Scale: Lane, Kalberg, Bruhn, et al., 2009; Lane, Robertson, et al., 2002)	×					×				
Treatment integrity: SET (Sugai et al., 2001)						×				

Note. CBM, curriculum-based measurement; TCAP, Tennessee Comprehensive Assessment Program. From Lane, Kalberg, and Menzies (2009, Table 5.1, p. 105). Copyright 2009 by The Guilford Press. Adapted by permission.

(see Table 5.3 for New Haven Elementary School's assessment schedule) to demonstrate how the school-site team monitored all assessments occurring as part of regular school practices over the course of a school year.

How Do We Prepare Materials to Conduct the SDQ?

The SDQ is free of charge and can be completed either online at *www.sdqinfo.org* or by hand on a printed-out form. One form is needed for each student rated. The length varies depending on the specific instrument selected (refer back to Table 5.1). As discussed in previous chapters, accuracy is very important—please be certain to select the appropriate form (and in its entirety and without changing any of the individual items to retain the validity of the SDQ) before having teachers complete it.

How Do We Administer the SDQ?

The SDQ can be administered and scored either electronically or using a hard copy and hand scoring. To assist you in making a decision about which method to use, we have provided step-by-step guidelines for both: Table 5.4 provides directions for preparing, administering, and scoring electronically, and Table 5.5 offers directions for the paper-and-pencil method. We encourage school-site teams to develop similar checklists or guidelines to share with the teachers completing the SDQ. Also, we recommend that time be devoted to answering all questions in a whole-group format before administering the SDQ to make certain teachers are clear on the procedures (i.e., ensuring all items are completed).

TABLE 5.4. Preparing, Administering, and Scoring the SDQ Electronically

Preparing:

Step 1. Go to *www.youthinmind.info*.

Step 2. Choose the United States link and either the Spanish or English version.

Step 3. Choose the rater: parent or teacher.

Step 4. Click on the item "What, if anything, should I be concerned about?"

Administering:

Step 5. Read the limitations and then click on the bar at the bottom of the screen to continue "*I want to continue with the computerized assessment despite its limitations.*"

Step 6. Complete the brief demographic questions (gender, age, name if you chose to include this information—we suggest using student initials or the first name and first two letters of the last name).

Step 7. Complete the 25 items by clicking on the blue button corresponding with *Not True, Partly True, Certainly True*. The option chosen will turn green. If you change your mind, simply choose the new response.

Step 8. When all items are completed, click Continue at the bottom of the page. Please note that all items must be completed before you will be allowed to proceed.

Step 9. If you chose Yes—minor, Yes—definite, or Yes—severe on the overall question, then the next page contains the supplemental questions, detailed in the description section.

If you chose No on the overall question, go to Step 10.

Step 10. You have completed the screening measure. Click Continue for report options.

Scoring:

Step 11. There are two types of reports with a link at the top of each report page to take you to the other report:

Readable report—(1) offering level of concern (close to average, slightly raised, high, very high) for categories of overall stress; worries, fears, or sadness; troublesome behavior; overactivity and lack of concentration; difficulties with other children; kind and helpful behavior; (2) overall level of concern; (3) likelihood of a diagnosis; (4) overall impression; (5) what next? Offers options for support such as book finder, Internet resources, and additional screening options; and (6) a caution statement.

Technical report—(1) specific scores and the corresponding bands (close to average, slightly raised, high, very high) for categories of overall stress, emotional stress, behavioral difficulties, hyperactivity and attentional difficulties, difficulties getting along with other children, kind and helpful behavior; (2) likelihood of diagnosis in areas of any diagnosis, emotional disorders, behavioral disorders, hyperactivity, or concentration disorder; (3) a caution statement.

Print the page of whichever report you find most useful.

Step 12. Click on the tab for Teacher at the top of the page to rate the next student.

Step 13. Complete Steps 4–12 until all students are rated.

TABLE 5.5. Preparing, Administering, and Scoring the SDQ Using Paper-and-Pencil Method

Preparing:

Step 1. Go to *www.sdqinfo.org/b1.html*.

Step 2. Click on the tab at the top labeled "Questionnaires etc. View & Download."

Step 3. Choose the preferred language for the screener. (Remaining instructions are for English [U.S.].)

Step 4. All of the available screeners (see description section) are listed. Click on the golden dot next to the form you would like to administer.

Step 5. The screening measures (one or two pages) will open in a pdf format. Click Print and choose the number of screeners needed (or copy them)—one per student.

Administering:

Step 6. Write the student's information at the top of the screener (name, date of birth).

Step 7. Complete the 25 items by marking the corresponding box in the column labeled *Not True, Somewhat True, Certainly True*. If you change your mind on an item, clearly erase it so that it does not interfere with scoring.

Step 8. Make sure to complete every item (do not leave any blank).

Step 9. Complete one form for each student in your class (or who you are rating).

Scoring:

Step 10. Begin at the homepage *www.sdqinfo.org/b1.html* or click on the back button to return to the listing of versions.

Step 11. Click on the tab at the top labeled "Scoring the SDQ."

Step 12. There are two options for hand scoring: hand calculations (see Step 13, Option A) and transparency overlays (see Step 13, Option B).

Step 13(A). *Option A: Hand Calculations:* Click on the golden dot for "Instructions in English" for informant-rated (parent and teacher) SDQ or self-rated SDQ. Proceed with scoring directions for the rater who completed the SDQ you are scoring.

Step 14(A). Read the directions for scoring and then write the point value for each one.

Likert-type rating (0 = *Not True*, 1 = *Somewhat True*, 2 = *Certainly True*). Score each item by writing the corresponding point value to the item's rating. For example, if I rated "Many fears, easily scared" as *Not True*, next to my rating of that item I would mark it a 0. *Please note the items that are reverse-scored (e.g., 2 = *Not True*). Check each item for scoring.

Step 15(A). Once all items are given a score, the items for each scale are totaled. Use caution as the domain items are not together on the screener. Read each item carefully and match it to the score sheet provided. (Each individual scale range, 0–10.)

Step 16(A). To obtain the total difficulties score, add each subscale total *except* for the Prosocial Behavior scale (range, 0–40).

Step 17(A). Once items are totaled for each scale, use the interpreting scale on page 2. There are score ranges for teacher and parent versions.

Step 18(A). Locate the student's score for each scale and the total difficulties score to obtain a category score (normal, borderline, abnormal).

Step 19(A). Impact scores are obtained by assigning a numeric value to each response: 0 = *Not at All*, 1 = *Only a Little*, 2 = *Quite a Lot*, 3 = *A Great Deal*. A score of 2 or higher on an item indicates performance in the abnormal range. A score of 1 indicates behavior in the borderline range.

Step 13(B). *Option B: Transparency Overlays:* Click on the golden dot for "Black-and-white transparent overlays for hand scoring."

Step 14(B). Print a set of the transparencies (five pages—one per subscale)

Step 15(B). Return to the previous page and click on the golden button labeled "A record sheet."

(cont.)

TABLE 5.5. *(cont.)*

Scoring *(cont.)*:

Step 16(B). The record sheet will be in pdf format. Print one per student to be screened.

Step 17(B). Complete the information at the top of the record sheet for each student. Be sure to indicate the rater and use the corresponding line for each scale. For example, if the teacher completed the SDQ, then the line beginning with T for each scale will be used for scoring.

Step 18(B). Next, lay the Emotional Symptoms Scale transparency on top of the rating scale. Add the values assigned to the marked items that are identified on that scale's transparency and circle the total on the record sheet. Repeat for each scale with the appropriate transparency overlay.

Step 19(B). Add all scale scores together *except* Prosocial Behavior to obtain the total difficulties score. Circle that score on the record sheet. The record sheet indicates the level of rated performance for each scale.

For scoring the impact items, follow the scoring in Step 19(A).

Include procedures that will ensure the accuracy of the results. For example, you might want to have each teacher assigned to a colleague to confirm the accuracy of the completion and scoring procedures and verify that all students have been screened (provided they have been enrolled at the school site for a sufficient length of time).

How Do We Score and Interpret the SDQ?

Each subscale contains five items. These five item scores are summed to create a total score for each subscale. Then the four problem area subscale scores are combined to create a composite score (total difficulties). Subscale scores and the total difficulties score are used to classify students into one of three risk categories: normal, border-line, or abnormal. The cut scores for each subscale vary according to the age group of the students rated (3- to 4-year-olds; 4- to 10-year-olds; 11- to 17-year-olds) and the rater (teacher, parent, or student). Cut sores are provided on the website.

The scoring and interpretation of the SDQ are straightforward when completed electronically; subscale and total scores are automatically generated for each student. When scoring by hand, the process is more cumbersome because each student's form must be scored using a series of overlays, as described in Table 5.5. As illustrated later in this chapter, results can be used to make decisions regarding how to (1) focus efforts of the primary plan, (2) identify and support students who require supports beyond primary prevention efforts, and (3) monitor the overall level of performance over time at a given school.

How Can We Use This Information at Our School Site?

First, the SDQ can be used to identify students who may require additional supports. Students scoring in the borderline and abnormal categories should be considered for secondary or tertiary supports. Second, the information can be used to monitor risk over time for the school as a whole and for individual students. Furthermore, the information can be used to evaluate needs of the primary prevention plan (see Illustration 2), such as social skills programming to address areas of need for a large percentage of the student body (i.e., peer problems). In the illustrations presented at the end of this chapter, we provide three examples (one each at the preschool, elementary, and high school levels) adapted from actual schools whose school-site leadership teams elected to implement the SDQ as part of regular school practices. The illustrations provide concrete examples of how to (1) monitor the overall level of risk present over time at a given school (Illustrations 1, 2, and 3), (2) analyze data from the SDQ in conjunction with academic data to identify students for secondary and tertiary levels of prevention within the context of three-tiered models (Illustration 2), and (3) determine program needs at the primary prevention level (Illustrations 1 and 3).

How Much Does the SDQ Cost, and Where Can I Order It?

The SDQ (as with the SRSS) is free. If you have a moment, please refill your cup of coffee and log onto *www.sdqinfo.org* and take a look the instrument and user-friendly information provided on the website. We encourage you to complete the administration and scoring for a hypothetical student (student information is not stored on the site), so you can experience the ease and limitations of completing this screening tool.

In the next section, we provide an overview of the supporting research for the SDQ, specifically information on the psychometric features of the SDQ as well as how the tool has been used in research studies to describe the behavior patterns of different groups of children to better understand specific issues (e.g., bullying, siblings of persons with autism).

Supporting Research

Reliability and Validity

Extensive research has been conducted to establish the reliability and validity of the parent, teacher, and youth self-report versions of the SDQ. In fact, if you log on to *www.sdqinfo.org*, you will notice that reliability and validity studies have been conducted worldwide, with normative data available for six countries: Australia, Britain, Finland, Germany, Sweden, and the United States. Studies from around the world include people from numerous cultural and linguistic backgrounds. Some of the countries include Australia (Hawes & Dadds, 2004; Mellor, 2005; Mellor & Stokes, 2007), Bangladesh (Mullick & Goodman, 2005), Britain (Goodman, 2001; Goodman & Goodman, 2009), the Netherlands (Crone, Vogels, Hoekstra, Treffers, & Reijneveld, 2008; van Widenfelt, Goedhart, Treffers, & Goodman, 2003), Finland (Koskelainen, Sourander, & Vauras, 2001), France (Capron, Therond, & Duyme, 2007; Shojaei, Wazana, Pitrou, & Kovess, 2009), Germany (Becker, Woerner, Hasselhorn, Banaschewski, & Rothenberger, 2004; Woerner, Becker, & Rothenberger, 2004), Japan (Matsuishi et al., 2008), Norway (Ronning, Handegaard, Sourander, & Morch, 2004), Russia (Ruchkin, Koposov, & Schwab-Stone, 2007), Sweden (Smedje, Broman, Hetta, & von Knorring, 1999), as well as the United States (Bourdon,

Goodman, Rae, Simpson, & Koretz, 2005; Hill & Hughes, 2007; Palmieri & Smith, 2007), to name yet a few.

In Table 5.6 we highlight just a few of the more than 25 reliability and validity studies conducted to date, with an emphasis on some of the original work by the developer (Goodman), initial studies involving teachers, and those conducted in the United States. In terms of reliability of the teacher version of the SDQ, results suggest high internal consistency, with Cronbach's alpha coefficients of .87 (total difficulties), .78 (Emotional Symptoms), .74 (Conduct Problems), .88 (Hyperactivity/Inattention), .70 (Peer Problems), and .84 (Prosocial Behavior; Goodman, 2001). Analyses also suggest the SDQ has high concurrent validity with the CBCL (Achenbach, 1991) and the Rutter Questionnaires (Goodman & Scott, 1999; Rutter, 1967). The SDQ has the ability to detect students whose behavior patterns differ from normative behavior; it identified individuals as abnormal who had a previous psychiatric diagnosis with a specificity (please see the definitions of these statistical terms in provided in Chapter 1 if you'd like a refresher!) of 94.6% (95% confidence interval 94.1–95.1%) and sensitivity of 63.3% (59.7–66.9%; Goodman, 1997). In essence, the SDQ ratings yield very low rates of false-positive results—those identified as having difficulties when indeed they do not (although there were differences in clinical and community samples; Goodman, Renfrew, & Mullick, 2000).

More recent studies, conducted in the southern region of the United States, also support the validity of the SDQ. For example, a series of studies were conducted at the elementary school (Ennis et al., in press), middle school (Lane, Parks, et al., 2007), and high school (Lane, Kalberg, Parks, et al., 2008) levels to examine the convergent validity of the SRSS (Drummond, 1994) and the SDQ. Specifically, Pearson correlation coefficients suggest convergent validity between total SRSS scores and all SDQ subscales scores and total difficult scores.

Identification of Nonresponders

In this section, we typically highlight a few applications of how a screening tool is utilized within the context of tiered models of prevention. We use examples from peer-reviewed, treatment–outcome studies to demonstrate how this screening tool has been used by the research community to identify and assist students who require targeted supports when primary prevention efforts are not enough. However, the SDQ has not been used in this manner.

Despite the absence of applications in three-tiered models of prevention, there have been several interesting descriptive and treatment–outcome studies of students with behavioral challenges. For example, the SDQ has been used in a number of descriptive studies to better understand existing problems and issues. For example, it has been used to examine (1) issues related to bullying by looking at the behavior patterns of persons involved in various aspects of bullying (e.g., direct and relational bullying; Wolke, Woods, Bloomfield, & Karstadt, 2000; Woods & White, 2005; Yang, Kim, Kim, Shin, & Yoon, 2006) and (2) the relation between physical activity

TABLE 5.6. Partial Listing of Reliability and Validity Studies of the SDQ

Citation	Purpose	Description of participants	Description of schools	Reliability	Validity
Goodman (2001)	Describe psychometric properties of the SDQ as completed by teachers, parents, and students in Britain	9,998 parents (96%), 7,313 teachers (70%), and 3,983 students (11–15 years; 91%)	Total sample of 10,438 children recruited through child benefit records as part of 1999 survey conducted by Office for National Statistics in Britain	Factor analyses yielded five-factor solution Internal consistency estimate ranges were satisfactory, with a mean of .73, and total difficulty scores of .80 and higher Interrater agreement was better than average level of agreement reported for comparable measures (Achenbach) Test–retest stability (4–6 months) yielded mean scores of .62, with teacher means most stable (.73).	Validity was established by reporting extent to which various scales were associated with presence or absence of psychiatric disorders
Bourdon et al. (2005)	Describe psychometric properties of SDQ in U.S. national sample	9,878 parents of 4- to 17-year-olds in 2001 National Health Interview Survey	Children and parents were randomly selected from each family respondent Parents (92%), grandparents (4.4%), other primary caregivers (4.6%) of 4- to 17-year-olds participating in 2001 National Health Interview Survey completed surveys	Good acceptability and internal consistency: total difficulties (.83) Normative bands were similar to the original British bands	Service contact or use was used as validation criteria Variables predicted to be correlates of risk for child mental health problems were statistically significantly associated with results of three scoring methods
Lane, Parks, et al. (2007)	Provide initial evidence to support use of SRSS at middle school level	Study 1: $N = 500$ students in grades 6–8; 97.60% white; rated by 38 teachers	Study 1: One rural middle school in middle Tennessee; 30.8% economic disadvantage rate; 20% special education		Study 1: Convergent: Pearson correlation coefficients suggest convergent validity between the SRSS (Drummond, 1994) and all SDQ subscale scores and total score at each time point

(cont.)

TABLE 5.6. (cont.)

Citation	Purpose	Description of participants	Description of schools	Reliability	Validity
Lane, Kalberg, Parks, et al. (2008)	Provide initial evidence to support use of SRSS at high school level	$N = 674$ students in grades 9–12; 96.67% white; rated by 41 teachers	One rural high school in middle Tennessee; 17.2% economic disadvantage rate; 12.02% special education		Convergent: Pearson correlation coefficients suggest convergent validity between SRSS and all SDQ subscale scores and total score at each time point for both raters, with more pronounced effects for noninstructional raters
Ennis et al. (in press)	Psychometric properties (validity and reliability) of SRSS for urban elementary schools Convergent validity of SRSS with SDQ and SSBD (Walker & Severson, 1992) over three administrations per year across 2 school years; predictive validity of SRSS with year total suspension rates (K–4) and state achievement test outcomes (grade 3)	Study 1: $N = 448$ (2006–2007) and $N = 497$ (2007–2008) students in grades K–4; 50% white	Study 1: One diverse, urban, elementary school in middle Tennessee; 9.80% and 9.46% received special education; 32.4% and 27.2% economically disadvantaged		Study 1: Pearson correlation coefficients suggest convergent validity between SRSS and SDQ subscales and total scale for all administrations

and mental health (Sagatun, Sogaard, Bjertness, Selmer, & Heyerdahl, 2007). Also, the SDQ has been used to describe behavior patterns of students with various types of special needs such as cerebral palsy (Dickinson et al., 2006), intellectual disabilities (Kaptein, Jansen, Vogels, & Reihneveld, 2008), speech and language difficulties (Dockrell & Lindsay, 2001), hyperactivity (e.g., Adams & Snowling, 2001; Sayal, Taylor, & Beecham, 2003), narcolepsy (Stores, Montgomery, & Wiggs, 2006), and even recurring headaches (Strine, Okoro, McGuire, & Balluz, 2006). The SDQ has been used in descriptive studies of the behavioral performance of siblings of children with autism (Hastings, 2003), children who have spent time in foster and residential care (Goodman, Ford, Corbin, & Meltzer, 2004), and even students who have varying degrees of acne (Smithard, Glazebrook, & Williams, 2001).

In addition, there have been interesting studies examining characteristic behavior patterns of children born to mothers with various natal practices and conditions such as those who (1) had material anxiety during the antenatal period (O'Connor, Heron, Glover, & Alspack Study Team, 2002); (2) had depression, partnerships, and social support systems during the postpartum period (Herwig, Wirtz, & Bengel, 2004); and (3) consumed vitamin D (Gale et al., 2008), iron supplements (Zhou, Gibson, Crowther, Baghurst, & Makrides, 2006), antibiotics (Kenyon et al., 2008), and alcohol (Sayal, Heron, Golding, & Emond, 2007) during pregnancy. These studies examined the relationships between these conditions or exposures and children's behavioral performance. The SDQ has even been used in studies of the behavioral performance of children conceived through in vitro fertilization (Golombok, MacCallum, & Goodman, 2001; Rice et al., 2007), those with very premature gestation (before 29 weeks; Gardner et al., 2004), and children spent time in pediatric intensive care units (Rees, Gledhill, Garralda, & Nadel, 2004) to study issues of adjustment from multiple perspectives. This is a widely utilized instrument in screening, intervention, and descriptive inquiry.

We do want to emphasize information from descriptive studies cannot be used to draw causal inferences, meaning you cannot say that a certain practice (e.g., taking antibiotics during pregnancy) led to a given behavior problem (e.g., higher SDQ total difficulty scores). However, such data can help researchers determine where to focus their intervention efforts.

There have also been intervention studies conducted involving the SDQ. For example, one study explored the relation between parents' functioning at work and the capacity to manage parenting as well as other home-based responsibilities (Martin & Sanders, 2003). Forty-two staff members (general and academic) at a major university in a metropolitan area in Australia who self-reported difficulty balancing work and home responsibilities—thus experiencing high levels of stress—and whose children were showing behavioral challenges were randomly assigned to (1) a group version of the Triple-P Positive Parenting Program or (2) a wait-list control condition. Parents in the treatment condition reported increased self-efficacy at work and home as well as decreased dysfunctional parenting practices and levels of behavior problems for their children.

Similarly, Jones, Daley, Hutchings, Bywater, and Eames (2007) conducted an efficacy study of the Incredible Years basic parent training program (Webster-Stratton & Hancock, 1998). This study involved a community-based sample of families with preschool-age children with conduct problems who were at risk for attention-deficit/hyperactivity disorder as measured by the SDQ Hyperactivity/Inattention subscale. Children were randomly assigned to the treatment or wait-list control condition. Results suggest that the Incredible Years program facilitated favorable outcomes for students, according to postintervention scores measuring hyperactivity and inattention.

We encourage the research and teaching communities to consider using the SDQ within the context of three-tiered models of prevention as a method for identifying and supporting students for whom primary prevention efforts are insufficient. In the illustrations presented at the end of this chapter, we present several suggestions for using the SDQ as a screening tool within the school context.

Strengths and Considerations

At this point, we encourage you to think about the extent to which the SDQ might be used in your work. To assist you in considering its potential applications, we present an evenhanded discussion of the strengths and considerations associated with using the SDQ.

Strengths

Three strengths of the SDQ are its psychometric rigor, accessibility, and multiple uses. Numerous studies have established the reliability and validity of the SDQ, with normative data available from Australia, Britain, Finland, Germany, Sweden, and the United States. In addition to the information we provided in the previous section, we encourage you to look at the list of relevant publications provided by Youthinmind at *www/sdqinfo.org/f0.html*. The site includes links to each publication's abstract.

The SDQ is available to practitioners and researchers at no cost and has been translated into 69 different languages (see Table 5.2), some of which are currently in draft form. We respectfully point out that the questionnaires (in English or any other language) are copyrighted documents and, consequently, cannot be modified in any way—you cannot change any of the items to better fit your context. The website explicitly states that print versions can be downloaded and photocopied at no cost by individuals or nonprofit organizations provided that they do not charge families or other individuals for their use. You will need Acrobat Reader (which is available free of charge online) to access the questionnaires that are in Adobe Acrobat. Youthinmind is the only entity authorized to create or distribute electronic versions.

The SDQ is versatile, usable in a variety of ways. It can be used as part of an initial clinical assessment to obtain multiple perspectives (e.g., teacher, parent, and student [if the student is older than 11 years]) to obtain a comprehensive view of student strengths and areas of concern. Also, the SDQ can be used as a pre–post intervention measure to determine how students have responded to various types of supports (e.g., Tier 2 supports to improve self-regulation skills—might this be your thesis or dissertation work? ☺). Data from the SDQ can be analyzed in conjunction with other variables and using more sophisticated data analytic techniques to determine how intervention outcomes are moderated by initial child characteristics (e.g., hyperactivity, conduct problems). Finally, as we have highlighted in this chapter, the SDQ is an excellent screening tool that can predict the presence of a disorder in community samples with adequate sensitivity and good specificity (Goodman, Ford, Simmons, Gatward, & Meltzer, 2003).

In sum, the SDQ is a psychometrically rigorous, accessible instrument, with multiple uses not only for practitioners but also the research community. In the following section, we suggest some issues to consider.

Considerations

In terms of limiting factors, there are a few key considerations. First, whereas some of the more comprehensive screening tools, such as the Social Skills Improvement System—Performance Screening Guide (Elliott & Gresham, 2007b) and the BASC™-2 Behavior and Emotional Screening System (Kamphaus & Reynolds, 2007a) have information available to directly link screening results to appropriate intervention efforts, the SDQ does not offer this feature. Yet the absence of an explicit connection to intervention options in no way limits the utility of the SDQ as a screening instrument.

Second, in our work with elementary, middle, and high schools, teachers whose school-site leadership team adopted the SDQ as a screening tool often expressed concerns about the time requirements. Although teachers appreciated the specific information available on multiple domains (e.g., hyperactivity, peer problems, conduct problems, emotional symptoms, and prosocial behavior), they also felt overwhelmed with the task of rating each student on 25 items. We do recognize the length of the SDQ as a vast improvement compared to the TRF and CBCL tools. However, teachers did cite specific concerns regarding the time needed to complete the instrument and, for those completing the SDQ using the paper-and-pencil method, the resources (e.g., paper) and time required to prepare (one page per student) and score each questionnaire. These latter concerns can be addressed by completing the surveys online; however, even with the electronic method, in order to have a copy of the students' results one page per student would need to be printed (one option is to confirm that all were screened but only print a selection, e.g., those in the abnormal or borderline range). A class score report does not currently exist.

Despite these considerations, the SDQ is a well-researched, accurate, and accessible tool with multiple uses, one of which includes systematic screening. We encourage readers to evaluate these cautionary features when considering using the SDQ as part of regular school practices or in scientific inquiry.

We now provide three illustrations for further guidance in using the SDQ as part of regular school practices to monitor overall student risk, inform the primary prevention plan, and identify and support students who require additional assistance.

Illustrations

An Illustration at a Small-Town Preschool: Child's Play Preschool

Child's Play Preschool (CPP) serves a small-town community in a midwestern state. Approximately 280 students (ages 3–5) attended CPP in Fall 2010. CPP had a diverse student population. Approximately 41% of students were black, 21% Hispanic, 19% white, and 11% Asian. The economic disadvantage rate was nearly 27%. Children with special educational needs represented 32% of the student body. The school environment was inclusive, and all service providers (e.g., speech pathologists, occupational therapists, physical therapists, behavior specialists) worked with identified students in the general education classroom. Providers worked closely with faculty and staff to facilitate appropriate educational experiences for all students.

Building a CI3T Model of Prevention

CPP was located in a public school district that had adopted a CI3T model of prevention across all schools (five elementary, one middle). The CPP leadership team worked with the leadership teams of the feeder elementary schools during Summer 2010. Because they had a relatively small staff (20 classroom teachers and teaching assistants, related services specialists, and special areas teachers—approximately 50 adults in total) and worked on 12-month contracts, they felt committed to plan during the summer months to begin implementation in Fall 2010 along with the feeder schools (the other schools designed their plans over the 9-month school year). The CPP leadership team received guidance from the leadership teams at the feeder schools, published resources (see Lane, Kalberg, & Menzies, 2009), onsite and remote support of national experts, and resources available through the National Center for Positive Behavior Interventions and Supports (PBIS; *www.pbis.org*), the National Center for Response to Intervention (*www.rti4success.org*), and the Center on the Social and Emotional Foundations for Early Learning (*csefel.vanderbilt.edu*). They developed a CI3T model of prevention that included components to teach, reinforce, and monitor social skills, behavioral expectations, and preacademic skills.

The school team began with their mission and purpose statements to ensure that a consistent message was shared with their community and families. They decided to adopt the schoolwide expectations used by the feeder elementary schools: Respect, Responsibility, and Cooperation. The first step was for the team was to define the key behaviors in each setting of their school. To make sure that all of the adults in the school had an opportunity to share their opinions about the selected critical behaviors, the team drafted an expectation grid listing the three expectations vertically and the key settings (classroom, bus, snack table time, playground, gym, library, bathroom, nap time) horizontally. Then the behaviors were listed in each corresponding cell for each expectation across all settings (e.g., respect on the playground). The team asked for faculty and staff input on the initial set of behaviors as well as additional suggestions. Two volunteer team members collected and combined all of the feedback and presented it to the team at the next meeting. Once all ideas were combined, the team distributed the matrix one final time to the full faculty. The faculty was asked to rate each of the behaviors as *not important* (0), *important* (1), or *critical* (2) for students to learn for success in that setting. The same two volunteers compiled the information and the team worked to create the final matrix, which included the behaviors marked as critical by 50% or more of the adults.

Next, the school team defined the roles and responsibilities for all stakeholders across the social skill, behavior, and academic components. For example, administrators were responsible for supporting faculty and staff with events such as an open house to discuss the schoolwide prevention plan. Teachers were responsible for age-appropriate instruction and learning opportunities focused on language, social, physical, and cognitive development. Students were responsible for respect, responsibility, and cooperation (the three expectations, all of which were directly taught). Parents were asked to be partners with the teachers and school personnel, keeping open communication, sharing concerns as they arose, and attending family events when possible. Families were asked to access community and school supports (with help) as needed to ensure healthy food options and medical, dental, and mental health care for the children and families.

The team selected specific curricula for academic and social instruction. Teacher teams created lesson plans to introduce all students to the behavioral expectations of each setting. This was a common practice for preschool teachers, but extra attention was given to consistency in teaching the language of respect, responsibility and cooperation in every classroom. Multiple evidence-based strategies were used, such as establishing consistency procedures (What do you do when you first arrive? What happens when the students return from recess? What happens if students arrive to school late? Where do materials go that students need to take home to their families?); proximity (using the teacher's physical presence to redirect students); and strategic use of praise (using behavior-specific praise to change another student's behavior—Josh is scooting around the rug at storytime, Justin is sitting as taught by the teacher. The teacher says to Justin, "Justin, thank you for sitting crisscross applesauce. I see that you are ready for storytime." Josh then hears the teacher and is cued to sit appropriately. See Lane, Menzies, et al., 2011, for additional details and strategies). Both examples and nonexamples of the desired behavior and social skills were provided. The use of these strategies occurred across all settings to eliminate (or at least drastically reduce) the confusion of hearing different expectations from different teachers.

Measures

CPP had measures of academic and social performance already in use (see Table 5.7). For academics they used screening measures at school entry and in January prior to transitioning to kindergarten to ensure readiness. The initial screening was used to design instruction. For example, if students arrived with limited language skills, they were placed in classrooms where the speech and language pathologist was assigned. For students who enrolled and were ready for prereading (or even reading) instruction in preschool, they were scheduled into classes where others needing this instruction were already placed. This does not mean that students were grouped by ability, only that multiple screening measures were used to determine appropriate placement.

The school-site leadership team learned about behavior screening tools from their feeder schools. Prior to this, teachers evaluated academic and social performance to

TABLE 5.7. CPP Assessment Schedule

	July	Aug	Sept	Oct	Nov	Dec	Jan	Feb	Mar	Apr	May
Student demographics											
Student demographics, special education eligibility	×	×	×	×	×	×	×	×	×	×	×
Screening measures											
Developmental Assessment of Young Children (Voress & Maddox, 1998)	×	×	×	×	×	×	×	×	×	×	×
	Upon school registration										
Peabody Picture Vocabulary Test–4 (Dunn & Dunn, 2007)			×	×	×	×	×	×	×	×	×
SDQ (Goodman, 1997) (age 4 and older)			×				×				×
Measures of development and growth											
Progress on language development (narrative with benchmark indicators)	×	×	×	×	×	×	×	×	×	×	×
Progress on social skill goals—report card	×	×	×	×	×	×	×	×	×	×	×
Health, hearing, and vision screening	×	×	×	×	×	×	×	×	×	×	×
School attendance		×	×	×	×	×	×	×	×	×	×
Program measures											
Treatment integrity: SET (Sugai et al., 2001)							×			×	
Social validity surveys	×	×					×			×	

Note. From Lane, Kalberg, and Menzies (2009, Table 5.1, p. 105). Copyright 2009 by The Guilford Press. Adapted by permission.

report progress. The school team learned to augment their current practices by using screeners to measure the level of behavioral risk early in the school year. With this information, teachers could evaluate students with increased risk after they had the benefit of the preschool experience to see if they made progress in acquiring prosocial skills. Teachers could also monitor how students responded overall to the primary prevention plan. The school leadership team chose to add the SDQ to their screening procedures as part of their primary prevention plan for students who had been enrolled for at least 30 days and had reached their fourth birthday. For the first year, they decided to use only the teacher-completed version. Once they established how the data were used in conjunction with their other measures, they would reconsider using the parent version as well.

They staff also chose two program measures: (1) a treatment integrity measure, the School-wide Evaluation Tool (SET; Sugai et al., 2001) and (2) social validity measures to seek the opinions of all stakeholders (parents, teachers, and even students).

What Was the Level of Risk at the First Time Point in Year 1 of Implementation?

The school-site leadership team visited the SDQ website to learn the procedures for administering and scoring the SDQ. They thoroughly researched and practiced with this tool (three volunteers from the team took the lead on this task). The team decided to use the paper-and-pencil SDQ screeners and score with the overlays (see Table 5.5 for detailed directions) because they wanted to keep actual hard copy of the completed screener for each student with the accompanying risk levels (normal, borderline, abnormal) across all five domains (see description of the SDQ in this chapter for domains). The faculty (primary classroom teachers) met during a faculty meeting to conduct the screening. A team member gave a presentation of the purpose of the screener, how it was to be completed, information it would provide, and how the results would be used. The faculty then completed the screeners, one per student, for each student who had been enrolled for at least 30 days and had reached his or her fourth birthday. The leadership team scored and graphed the data for the first time point (Fall 2010). They shared the graph with the full faculty and staff to assess the current level of risk for each domain and to set the focus of the primary prevention plan. Figure 5.1 displays the data for the first time point. Each bar represents a

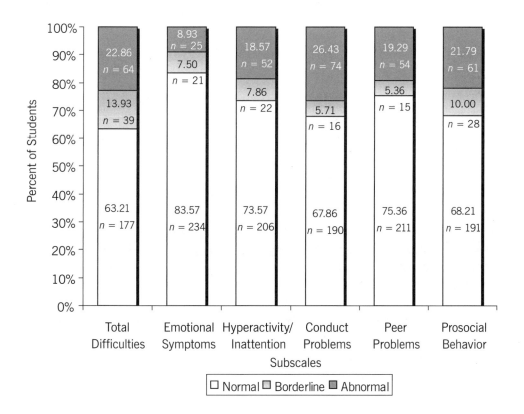

FIGURE 5.1. CPP behavior screening data (SDQ), Fall 2010, Year 1 of implementation of the schoolwide three-tiered model of prevention, $N = 280$.

domain. Total difficulties is presented first and is the composite score for the next four domains (Emotional Symptoms, Hyperactivity/Inattention, Conduct Problems, Peer Problems). The last domain is Prosocial Behavior. The bars are divided into three sections representing the percentage of students in each risk category. The white portion of the bar represents students rated in the normal range. For example, 63.21% (*n* = 177) of students were evaluated to be within the normal risk for behavioral concerns in Fall 2010 in terms of total difficulties scores. The light gray portion represents the borderline category: 13.93% (*n* = 39). The dark gray portion represents the abnormal range: 22.86% (*n* = 64) of students fell into this category at the first time point. The school-site leadership team reviewed these data to determine the focus of the primary plan for Year 2 of implementation. They decided to look for programs and supports addressing two areas: (1) increasing prosocial behaviors and (2) decreasing conduct problems. Because more than 30% of students needed additional supports in these two key areas, it was critical that the primary plan include this instruction rather than pursuing secondary supports with so many students.

How Are the Screening Data Used to Revise the Primary Prevention Plan and Reduce the Need for Secondary and Tertiary Supports?

The team elected not to make any changes to the new primary prevention plan in the first year; they wanted to evaluate changes that occurred with the implementation of the current plan. They also felt that the structure and procedures for teaching behavior and social skills would reduce the number of students at risk on the SDQ. They took the opportunity to research and preview programs to address the two areas identified as concerns on the SDQ. They wanted to be proactive by identifying these programs so that if their Spring screening showed similar results, they could put these programs in place in the following school year (Fall 2011). They also wanted to take the time to plan for professional development.

After consulting resources such as the Office of Juvenile Justice and Delinquency Prevention, and U.S. Department of Health and Human Services, and Substance Abuse and Mental Health Services Administration's National Registry of Evidence-Based Program and Practices, CPP decided on Al's Pals: Kids Making Healthy Choices (Wingspan, n.d.) program. The benefit of Al's Pals was that it was preventive in nature, focusing on building protective skills. It targeted the school's expectations of Respect, Responsibility and Cooperation. Research showed students participating in this program had fewer aggressive behaviors (e.g., hitting, name calling, destroying others belongings) and increases in prosocial behaviors (e.g., appropriate expression of feelings, exhibiting self-control, and using prosocial means of problem solving; Lynch, Geller, & Schmidt, 2004).

The team's long-term plan was to strengthen the primary prevention plan in Year 2 as well as to develop secondary prevention supports for Year 3. These interventions would be chosen based on Year 2 SDQ results after students had the time to benefit from the primary plan.

Summary

CPP is one illustration of a public preschool that coordinated primary prevention efforts to align with the schools their students would attend in kindergarten. Consistent expectations facilitated these smooth transitions. Additionally, this preschool chose to institute behavioral screening measures (SDQ) to establish the level of risk during the first year of the primary prevention plan. The SDQ results were used to monitor the primary plan and make decisions about the schoolwide program and individual student needs.

An Illustration at an Urban Elementary School: New Haven Elementary School

New Haven Elementary School (NES) is a small public school in a large southern city. NES serves approximately 350 K–4 students. The majority of students attending this Title 1 school were black ($n = 342$). The economic disadvantage rate at NES was greater than 99%. The attendance and promotion rates exceeded state averages at 95.4% and 98.8%, respectively. Ten percent of the students at NES were eligible for special education services, which included a variety of delivery models (e.g., inclusion, resource, self-contained programs).

Building a CI3T Model of Prevention

NES staff attended a year-long training series at a local university in the 2008–2009 school year. The school was in a restructuring phase under school improvement mandates; therefore, a large portion of the staff and the administrators were new to the school. This offered a unique opportunity to assess teachers' expectations for students (academically, behaviorally, and socially) and to build a CI3T model of prevention. A school leadership team was established to attend all of the trainings, complete the design of the CI3T model, share the plan with faculty and staff, make revisions based on staff feedback, and start the program on the first day of school in the 2009–2010 school year. The team consisted of the principal, the behavior specialist, and general and special education teachers. The team began by revising their mission statement with a focus on providing a secure learning environment where faculty worked together to develop successful students. Their purpose was to create an environment that valued respect, responsibility, and safety to encourage lifelong learning and responsible citizenship. To achieve this mission, the school designed a plan based on three expectations: Be Respectful, Be Responsible, and Be Safe. The plan included academic, behavior, and social procedures and responsibilities.

ACADEMIC COMPONENT

The leadership team identified core expectations for all stakeholders for the academic component. Teachers were responsible for designing engaging lessons to teach state and district standards, providing differentiated instruction according to student needs, establishing specific procedures for supporting students who have missed instruction, and including starter and closing activities to ensure that academic time was maximized. Teachers were asked to model positive interactions with all staff and students. They were also expected to keep parents informed of school activities and student progress through the consistent use of a parent communication system. Administrators were responsible for ensuring teachers had the resources to facilitate instruction. Parent responsibilities included participating in communication with the school, encouraging their child to give their best effort, providing a place for their child to do their homework, and accessing homework tutoring and assistance programs offered at the school. Student responsibilities were to arrive on time to school with all materials, including the return of parent communications, and participate in and complete all classroom activities and work to the best of their ability. Together, these responsibilities were designed to meet the school's mission.

BEHAVIORAL COMPONENT

Behavioral expectations (Be Respectful, Be Responsible, and Be Safe) were further described for each school setting (classrooms, hallways, cafeteria, playground, bathroom, walking to/from school) in the expectation matrix. For example, to show respect on the playground, students would use positive words and actions. Responsibilities were identified for all stakeholders, as with the academic component. Faculty and staff responsibilities included displaying, modeling, and teaching the expectations to all students; providing behavior-specific praise and reinforcement for students when demonstrating expectations; and consistently using the school's reactive plan (consequence system) as appropriate. All responsibilities were designed to foster a safe environment for students and staff. Administrators were responsible for implementing the school reactive and proactive plans. Parents were asked to review the proactive and reactive (disciplinary) procedures, post the expectation matrix at home, and keep open communication with teachers and administrators. Students were responsible for meeting schoolwide expectations, taking responsibility for their actions' effects on others, and telling adults about any unsafe behaviors. The behavioral expectations and responsibilities were designed so that all stakeholders had a common set of expectations to teach and reinforce.

SOCIAL SKILLS COMPONENT

The social skills component added an additional instructional layer to support students in meeting behavioral expectations. The schools' expectations matrix and social skills lessons were determined by a faculty survey where teachers rated behaviors that were critical to student success (i.e., arrives to class prepared, controls temper in conflict situation). This information was compiled, and then social skill lessons (Elliott & Gresham, 1991) were prepared by the training team for the school's use. Lessons were taught to the entire school within a short window of time so that all staff and faculty could reinforce behaviors and use common language with students.

Responsibilities for teachers included teaching the monthly lessons, modeling the social skills, and providing behavior-specific praise connected to the lessons taught and identified expectations (e.g., "Rose, you were showing respect to your friend by sharing the playground equipment"). Students were responsible for participating in the lessons and meeting expectations. Parents and administrators were responsible for supporting the social skills lesson content. The social skills component provided instruction to support the learning of the expected behaviors.

Measures

To evaluate the effect of implementing a schoolwide plan of prevention on student performance, the school leadership team identified key sources of data to monitor. They chose specific academic and behavior measures to examine. Student academic performance was monitored with Dynamic Indicators of Basic Early Literacy (DIBELS; Good & Kaminski, 2002) for reading, ThinkLink formative assessments in math, course failures, and the state achievement assessment for all academic areas. Student behavioral performance was monitored through attendance, office discipline referrals (ODRs), referrals to support team (prereferral), and special education referrals. During the training series, the school's team learned about the utility of behavior screeners in the early identification of students who may be in need of additional instruction. After learning about several options, they decided on the SRSS (Drummond, 1994) and the SDQ (Goodman, 1997). The leadership team initially planned to use both screeners, but decided to only use the SRSS because it was more time efficient. The Fall screening results revealed high numbers of students at moderate and high risk. This was unexpected, so the leadership team decided to administer the second screener (SDQ) as originally planned to gather more specific information about the types of behavioral issues. The SDQ would help them better focus their available resources for supporting students with behavior problems.

The behavior screening data were used with other school information. The assessment schedule listed the types of data available for decision making and time points in the year when the team would collect and review the results (Table 5.3). Additionally, the team worked with the research assistants from the university training team to collect information about the program by surveying teachers and staff for their perceptions about the plan (social validity) and measuring the degree to which the components of the plan were implemented (treatment integrity). The NES leadership team used their SDQ data to determine changes needed for the primary plan given the large percentage of students at elevated risk and to inform secondary intervention decisions.

How Are SDQ Data Used to Evaluate and Support the Primary Prevention Efforts?

The NES Winter screening data for the SDQ are displayed in Figure 5.2. The bars on the graph display the percentage of students in each risk category (normal, borderline,

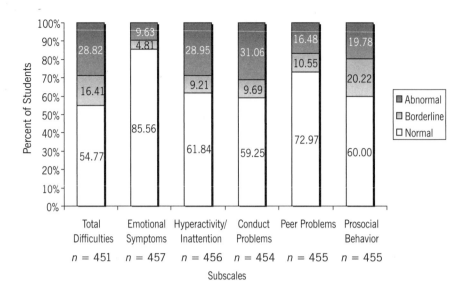

FIGURE 5.2. NHES behavior screening data (SDQ), Winter 2009, Year 1 of implementation of the schoolwide three-tiered model of prevention; *N* = 491.

abnormal) across all of the subscales and total difficulties. The total difficulties score is derived from a composite of all subscales except Prosocial Behavior. According to these data, large percentages of students scored in the borderline or abnormal range on the Hyperactivity/Inattention and Conduct Problems subscales. The principal was also concerned with the large number of students who were quick to react to situations with anger and, often, violence. Because 40.75% of students were rated at risk for conduct problems (borderline and abnormal), a schoolwide anger management program would be added to the social skills component of the primary prevention plan. The number of students, approximately 185, was too many to serve in secondary intervention programs with the school's current resources; therefore, the school team decided to strengthen the primary plan to include this instruction for all students. Programs considered by the team that would address this schoolwide concern were Promoting Alternative THinking Strategies (PATHS®; Kusche & Greenberg, 1994), which focuses on the development of self-control, emotional awareness, peer relations, and problem-solving skills, and Second Step: Violence Prevention (Committee for Children, 2003), which focuses on reducing impulsive and aggressive behaviors of students at the elementary level. Both programs have been reviewed by the Institute of Education Sciences What Works Clearinghouse and were determined to have strong effect for "teaching new skills to increase appropriate behaviors" (Epstein, Atkins, Cullinan, Kutash, & Weaver, 2008, p. 64). The school-site leadership team reviewed these programs and related research for evidence of use and effectiveness in their school context to determine the best program for use at their school. The program chosen would then be started the following school year. This allowed time for decision making about the program, professional development for teachers, and determining the logistics of scheduling of the program into the school day.

How Are SDQ Screening Data Used to Inform Secondary Prevention Efforts?

The SDQ data from the Winter 2009 screening revealed 16.48% ($n = 75$) of students had high levels of peer problems. Because the school staff felt they did not have the resources to intervene at the secondary support level (Tier 2) with all 75 students, they used additional school data to determine which students had multiple risk factors. They were confident that schoolwide practices (the PBIS component and social skills lessons) would meet the needs of the majority of students. Therefore, they used their data to identify students who, by the Winter screening, continued to be at risk on the SDQ for peer problems and had earned two or more ODRs and were struggling in math or reading (see Table 5.8 for the secondary intervention grid). These students would be supported with Peer-Assisted Learning Strategies (Fuchs & Fuchs, 1998; Fuchs, Fuchs, Hamlett, et al., 1997) taught and monitored by specialists (e.g., literacy and math support teachers) during the school's 30-minute/day intervention block. The SDQ screening data would also be used with other data (ODR, academic measures) to determine which students benefited from the intervention, to monitor their progress, and as part of the intervention exit criteria.

Summary

NHES provides an illustration of how schools might use the SDQ screening data to inform schoolwide primary and secondary support efforts. The SDQ behavioral screening data were used within the structure of a CI3T model of prevention targeting academic, behavioral, and social skill outcomes for students. When larger numbers of students are at risk for academic, behavioral, or social difficulties, schoolwide efforts may be the best first step. Once primary plans are in place and implemented with fidelity, then resources can be used to support students for whom primary prevention plans are inadequate.

An Illustration at a Rural High School: Finn High School

Finn High School (FHS) is a rural high school in middle Tennessee. FHS served approximately 670 students in grades 9 through 12. The majority of students were white (96%), and approximately 12% received special education services, most of whom qualified for services in high-incidence disability categories. The economic disadvantage rate at FHS was almost 17%, and the graduation rate was approximately 98%.

Building a CI3T Model of Prevention

FHS participated in a year-long training series during which a school leadership team (an administrator, general educator, special educator, counselor, parent, and student) designed a CI3T model of prevention. The prevention plan integrated academic

TABLE 5.8. NHES Secondary Intervention Grid

Support	Description	Schoolwide data: entry criteria	Data to monitor progress	Exit criteria
PALS (Fuchs, Fuchs, Hamlett, et al., 1997)—math	PALS strategies are taught to peer partners by math specialist and then monitored closely to encourage and reinforce practice and positive relationships 30-minute instruction 3 days/week with instruction and monitoring by math specialist (student pairs)	*All the following criteria must be met 1. Students in K–4 2. Voluntary participation by student and parent permission Academic: 3. Math CBM in the strategic range (some risk) Behavior: 4. SDQ—peer problems: abnormal range *and* 5. Two or more ODRs *Peer partners* Academic: 3. At benchmark on math assessments Behavior: 4. 0 ODRs 5. Normal range on SDQ and low risk on SRSS	1. Math progress based on CBM administered by teacher 2. SDQ behavior data at Spring screening (peer problems reduced, prosocial behaviors improved) 3. Weekly participation report—self- and partner ratings (e.g., Did I participate in the math activities with my partner? Did my partner participate in the math activities with me?) Rated on Likert scale: 0 = *never*, 5 = *all of the time.* Average of 3 or higher needed for week	Math CBM benchmark score improvements Improved prosocial behaviors and decreases in peer problems and ODRs Successful peer pairs will be offered participation in monthly privileges (e.g., lunch bunch, special recess, buddy math games time) to maintain gains Participation is gained by earning preset number of schoolwide Bear Bucks PBIS tickets
PALS (Fuchs, Fuchs, Mathes, et al., 1997)—reading	PALS strategies are taught to peer partners by literacy specialist and then monitored closely to encourage and reinforce practice and positive relationships 30-minute instruction 4 days/week with instruction and monitoring by the literacy specialist (student pairs)	*All the following criteria must be met 1. Students in K–4 2. Voluntary participation by student and parent permission Academic: 3. Winter DIBELS benchmark scores indicating need for intensive intervention (strategic range) Behavior: 4. SDQ—peer problems: abnormal range *and* 5. Two or more ODRs	1. DIBELS weekly progress monitoring probes by classroom teacher 2. SDQ behavior data at Spring screening (peer problems reduced, prosocial behaviors improved) 3. Weekly participation report—self- and partner ratings (e.g., Did I participate in the reading activities with my partner? Did my partner participate in the reading activities with me?) Rated on Likert scale: 0 = *never*, 5 = *all of the time.* Average of 3 or higher needed for week	DIBELS benchmark scores indicating shift in level or trend to project meeting end-of-year benchmark Improved prosocial behaviors and decreases in peer problems and ODRs Successful peer pairs will be offered participation in monthly privileges (e.g., lunch bunch, special recess, buddy reading times) to maintain the gains Participation is gained by earning preset number of schoolwide Bear Bucks PBIS tickets

(cont.)

Support	Description	Schoolwide data: entry criteria	Data to monitor progress	Exit criteria
TABLE 5.8. *(cont.)*				
PALS (Fuchs, Fuchs, Mathes, et al., 1997)—reading *(cont.)*		*Peer partners* Academic: 3. At benchmark on reading assessments (DIBELS) Behavior: 4. 0 ODRs 5. Normal range on SDQ and low risk on SRSS		

Note. CBM, curriculum-based measurement; ODR, office discipline referrals; PALS, Peer-Assisted Learning Strategies; PBIS, positive behavior intervention and support. From Lane, Kalberg, and Menzies (2009, Table 6.1, pp. 130–131). Copyright 2009 by The Guilford Press. Adapted by permission.

instruction, behavioral supports, and social skills instruction. In addition, the school faculty and staff identified three primary schoolwide expectations (Be on Time and Ready to Learn; Show Respect for Yourself, Peers, and Adults; and Be Proud of Your School). These expectations provided the core expectations across all three areas (academic, social skills, and behavior plan) of FHS's primary intervention plan.

ACADEMIC COMPONENT

The academic program was driven by state and district standards as well as program standards for advanced placement courses and other college requirements. A high percentage of students transitioned from high school into higher education (community colleges, technical schools, and universities); therefore, the school faculty and administration had a strong commitment to rigorous coursework that prepared students for this next level of education. Thus, the primary plan's expectations focused on teaching students to be prepared with necessary materials, complete assignments in a timely manner, remain on task, and be receptive to others' ideas. Teachers were expected to have entry activities prepared for all lessons so that engaging and meaningful activities were waiting for students when they arrived on time. In addition, teachers were asked to model appropriate behavior, reinforce students' appropriate behavior, and keep schoolwide expectations posted in their classroom. Administrators were expected to be fair and consistent in the application of school and district policies and to communicate clear expectations to faculty, staff, and students.

BEHAVIORAL COMPONENT

The behavioral expectations were designed to facilitate a safe and orderly environment where students could explore new interests and excel in their areas of strengths. Students were expected to arrive to class on time, follow directions the first time asked, and show affection in appropriate ways. Teachers were asked to teach the behaviors they wanted students to use. To facilitate this, all faculty taught the expectations for each area of the school, including all instructional areas, the parking lot, common areas, physical education locker rooms, and hallways. Posters were used in all areas to prompt use of the expectations.

SOCIAL SKILLS COMPONENT

To further extend the instructional and behavioral expectations, social skills instruction occurred on a monthly basis. The school-site team chose key skills that they felt were needed based on ODR (e.g., conflict resolution) and faculty feedback about areas of concern. Targeted skills included demonstrating respect by listening and responding appropriately to others and appropriately transitioning between classes. Meanwhile, teachers participated in a beginning-of-the-year assembly to introduce the schoolwide effort.

Measures

FHS elected to monitor several types of data throughout the school year, which included both behavioral (ODRs, alternative learning center referrals, attendance, tardies, SRSS, SDQ) and academic (ACT scores, GPA) sources. The two behavior screening measures were completed by teachers three times during the school year (6 weeks after the onset of the school year, prior to Winter break, and 6 weeks before the end of the school year). The team chose to have two perspectives of each student's behavior with instructional and noninstructional (study hall teachers) raters. Schoolwide data were used to monitor school progress as well as to determine which students needed additional support.

Which Behavioral Difficulties (Emotional, Conduct, Hyperactivity, Problems with Peers) Are the Most Prevalent at Our School?

Figure 5.3 displays the Fall 2005 SDQ data (the percentage of students who obtained a score exceeding normal limits for each of the four difficulty categories—emotional symptoms, conduct problems, hyperactivity, peer problems—and the percentage of students whose prosocial behavior was a strength). At FHS, between 72 and 80% of students were determined to exhibit prosocial behaviors. The team was encouraged by this relatively high percentage. As the literature suggests, 80% of students are likely to respond to a primary prevention plan (Gresham, Sugai, Horner, Quinn, & McInerney, 1998; Sugai & Horner, 2006). Within each of the five difficulty categories, two bars are displayed, each representing the percentage of students in that category from two perspectives. The first bar shows results from the instructional class period rater and the second bar results from the noninstructional class period rater (further explanation to follow). According to this graph, hyperactivity was the most common problem, exhibited by nearly 16% of students, followed by problems

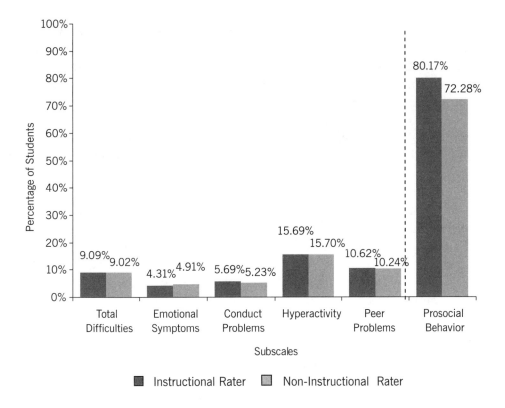

FIGURE 5.3. FHS SDQ schoolwide data, Fall 2005. Subscales represent the percentage of students rated at risk (risk category: abnormal) by instructional and noninstructional raters. The Prosocial Behavior subscale represents students with low risk (risk category: normal) skills.

with peers, affecting approximately 10%. Conduct problems and emotional symptoms involved the lowest percentage of students. The school-site team used these data to identify building- and student-level needs. First, they chose to identify strategies to support students with hyperactivity as well as classroom strategies for teachers to support students in class. Second, the team decided to capitalize on the large percentage of students with prosocial behaviors to support students with peer problems. They were hoping to find an evidence-based program to address these needs, ideally one they could plan during the Fall semester and be ready to offer to students and teachers in the Spring semester.

What Type(s) of Secondary Interventions Would Address the Needs Identified by the SDQ Screening Data?

To prepare for supporting students in peer relationships and strategies for supporting students with hyperactivity, the leadership team divided into two subcommittees. The first was led by the school counselor, who obtained a list of the students identified as demonstrating peer problems. The subcommittee drafted a letter to the parents of these students with the intent of explaining the support that would be offered to their child. Second, they planned to meet at the department meetings with teachers to confirm that the chosen program or support would be appropriate for the students' needs. Finally, the counselor would meet with the students to offer them this support. The second committee, led by the school psychologist, worked to identify programs and supports that would meet student needs, work with the high school schedule, and be within their resources (monetary).

After a review of available mentoring programs for purchase, the second sub-committee decided to design a mentoring program to fit their needs. The majority of students with peer problems were freshmen and sophomores, so the school leadership team chose to invite seniors to be mentors for the freshmen and sophomores who met the criteria for this support (see Table 5.9 for the secondary intervention grid). The focus of the mentoring program was planning for higher education; thus, activities included taking online aptitude and interest surveys; researching careers and voca-tions of interest; planning and conducting interviews with professionals in the field; looking at colleges, technical schools, and universities for programs of study; and identifying entrance requirements. Each mentor pair would also meet with the guid-ance counselor to ask questions about the application process and the 3- and 4-year

TABLE 5.9. FHS Secondary Intervention Grid

Support	Description	Schoolwide data: Entry criteria	Data to monitor progress	Exit criteria
Freshmen and sophomore peer mentoring club (senior mentors)	The goal was to facilitate positive peer relationships focused on positive school outcome; content focus of mentoring program was to be planning for higher education Activities included: • Taking online aptitude and interest surveys • Researching careers and vocations of interest • Planning and conducting interviews with professionals in the field • Looking at colleges, technical schools, and universities for programs of study • Identifying entrance requirements Each mentor–mentee pair would also meet with guidance counselor to ask questions about application process and 3- and 4-year planning guide Meet during club time 50 minutes once per week; monitored by the guidance counselors	Mentees: Freshmen and sophomores SDQ: elevated risk on Hyperactivity subscale Mentors: Full-time senior volunteers: 1. SDQ low risk for prosocial behavior 2. Passing grades in all classes 3. Meeting attendance requirements (< 3 days absent)	Mentees: Course grades—monitored through electronic grade book by counselor, ODRs, counseling referrals Mentors: Monitor grades and attendance (weekly check-in with counselor with sheet signed by all teachers indicating good standing in class)	Mentees: End of semester: may requalify for club next semester based on entry criteria Mentors: Completion of semester Graduation

Note. From Lane, Kalberg, and Menzies (2009, Table 6.2, pp. 132–133). Copyright 2009 by The Guilford Press. Adapted by permission.

planning guide. The goal was to facilitate peer relationships focused on a positive school outcome.

To address concerns about hyperactivity, the team identified strategies teachers could use. These included offering choice in classroom and homework projects, facilitating multiple learning styles, and using procedures that minimized disruption to instruction. Furthermore, schoolwide procedures would be implemented to provide additional and consistent structure for students (such as posting the standards and objective for the lesson, having specific procedures common to all classrooms for turning in work, finding work that was missed [teacher webpages have become a valuable resource for parents and students], and providing advanced organizers, to name a few). Professional learning opportunities as well as schoolwide procedures were shared at Fall semester faculty meetings. The administrators provided recognition to teachers who immediately implemented the new procedures, although they were not required by all faculty until the start of the Spring semester.

Summary

FHS is an illustration of one rural high school's implementation of a schoolwide primary prevention plan that included the use of SDQ behavioral screening data. The SDQ was used to plan secondary supports, which included strategies teachers could use in their classrooms and a student mentoring program.

Summary

This chapter introduced a no-cost screening tool—the SDQ—and offered step-by-step directions on how to complete it. Research conducted with the SDQ was synthesized to examine the reliability and validity of this tool for use in the elementary, middle, and high school settings as well as provide information on how the SDQ has been used in descriptive research. Then an evenhanded discussion of the strengths and considerations associated with preparation, administration, scoring, and interpreting findings of the SDQ was provided. The chapter closed with illustrations of how to use the SDQ as part of regular school practices, from preschool to high school.

In the next chapter, we introduce another screening tool: the BASC-2 Behavioral and Emotional Screening System (Kamphaus & Reynolds, 2007a), including a brief overview of the BASC-2 family of products, which together provide a comprehensive system for meeting students' behavioral needs as well as detailed information about the BASC-2 BESS.

CHAPTER 6

BASC-2 Behavioral and Emotional Screening System

This chapter introduces the BASC™-2 Behavioral and Emotional Screening System (BASC-2 BESS; Kamphaus & Reynolds, 2007a). The BASC-2 BESS is a systematic screener intended for use with students from preschool (beginning age 3) to grade 12. It was designed to identify children who may be experiencing behavioral or emotional issues that negatively impact their academic achievement or social relationships.

As we have discussed in other chapters, students with emotional and behavioral disorders (EBD) are recognized for behavioral challenges that manifest in terms of externalizing (e.g., noncompliance, aggression, delinquency) and internalizing (e.g., anxiety, depression, somatic complaints) behaviors (Achenbach, 1991; Walker et al., 2004). Students with EBD also have academic challenges in core academic areas such as reading, written expression, and mathematics as well as other content areas (e.g., social students and science; Greenbaum et al., 1996; Mattison, Spitznagel, & Felix, 1998; Nelson, Benner, Lane, & Smith, 2004; Scruggs & Mastorpieri, 1986; Wagner, 1995; Wilson, Cone, Bradley, & Reese, 1986). Unfortunately, students with EBD do not tend to improve over time, and their behavioral excesses and deficits tend to become more resistant to intervention efforts (Bullis & Walker, 2004). Their academic deficits are likely to remain stable or even intensify (Greenbaum et al., 1996; Mattison et al., 2002; Nelson et al., 2007). There are now several studies to suggest a strong association between students' emotional and behavioral performance and academic performance (Gutman, Sameroff, & Cole, 2003; McEvoy & Welker, 2000; Morgan, Farkas, Tufis, & Sperling, 2008). For example, Rapport, Denney, Chung, and Hustace (2001) found that depression and anxiety negatively influenced academic achievement after controlling for the cognitive ability.

Collectively, the research establishes the importance of early and accurate detection given that (1) behavioral and academic performance are related and (2) students with EBD pose significant challenges to their teachers, parents, and peers as well as to society as a whole (Kauffman, 2001; Walker, 2003), not to mention the struggles they face within and beyond the school setting. Although other types of screening procedures are part of regular school practices (e.g., vision, hearing, and academic performance), less than 2% of U.S. school districts screen for emotional or behavioral problems (Jamieson & Romer, 2005).

This chapter offers a brief overview of the BASC-2 family of products, which together provide a comprehensive system for meeting students' behavioral needs. Then we supply detailed information about the BASC-2 BESS, including step-by-step directions for how to administer, score, and interpret this measure. Next, we highlight some of the supporting research conducted, with the studies focusing on the reliability and validity of the BASC-2 BESS. Then we present a balanced discussion of the strengths and considerations in using the BASC-2 BESS, offering information to assist school sites or individual teachers in determining whether this measure is right for the purposes they have in mind. The chapter concludes with three illustrations that will help leadership teams decide how information from the BASC-2 BESS can be used to improve student outcomes. The first illustration demonstrates how one school used the screening data to allocate resources. The second features a middle school that used a Web-based program to quickly identify students for Tier 2 supports. The last illustration presents a high school that used screening data to assess schoolwide risk and to then plan professional development.

An Overview of the BASC-2 Family of Products

The BASC-2 BESS is a newer item in the BASC-2 family of products. In brief, the BASC-2 family offers a comprehensive system designed to identify and manage emotional and behavioral strengths in students across the PreK–12 continuum (see Figure 6.1). This set of tools provides an integrated behavioral system to screen, assess, intervene, and monitor progress. The original tool, the BASC, was expanded to include new components to work within the context of three-tiered models of prevention such as response to intervention (RTI), positive behavior intervention and support (PBIS), and comprehensive, integrated three-tiered models of prevention (CI3T; Lane, Kalberg, & Menzies, 2009). There are four sets of tools that can be used independently or as part of an integrated system.

BASC-2 Behavioral and Emotional Screening System

The first tool is the universal screener using the BASC-2 BESS, which is the focus of this chapter. Few screeners (e.g., the Strengths and Difficulties Questionnaire) provide parent, teacher (or other supervising adults), and student reports. The BASC-2 BESS offers an advantage over screeners that include only one perspective of an individual's behavior. Multiple informants allow for a comprehensive understanding of students' strengths and weaknesses, thereby taking into account that people tend to behave differently with different people and in different contexts (Kazdin, 1977; Kamphaus & Reynolds, 2007a).

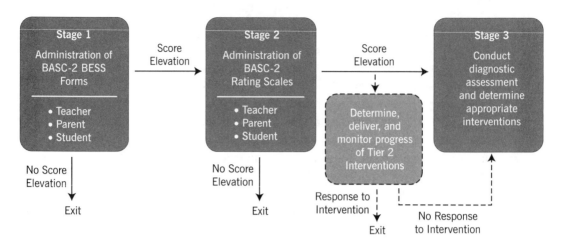

FIGURE 6.1. The BASC-2 BESS framework for integrating the BASC-2 screening and assessment tools into a multi-tiered model. From Kamphaus and Reynolds (2007a, Figure 1.1, p. 4). Copyright 2007 by NCS Pearson, Inc. Reprinted by permission.

The BASC-2 BESS includes a teacher form, a parent form, and a student self-report form. The teacher and parent forms are available in two levels: one for preschool (ages 3–5) and one for grades K–12. The student form is available for students in grades 3–12. Parent and student forms are available in Spanish and in English, with a CD available for parents and youth who may have difficulty with reading. The overall score (which is discussed in more detail later) places the student into one of three risk categories: normal, elevated, or extremely elevated. Kamphaus and Reynolds (2007a) clarify that classification as "normal" does not mean a student has absolutely no risk. Everyone has some risk for emotional or behavioral challenges. However, the risk may be very small or within normal expectations.

BASC-2 Targeted Assessment Tools

The second set of tools includes targeted, complementary components, as follows: BASC-2 rating scales (Reynolds & Kamphaus, 2004; teacher, parent, and student versions), student observation system (SOS), structured developmental history (SDH), and the Parenting Relationship Questionnaire (PRQ; Kamphaus & Reynolds, 2006). The BASC-2 rating scales are lengthier assessment tools design to measure adaptive and problematic behaviors from teacher, parent, and student perspectives. The BASC-2 Teacher Rating Scale (TRS) contains forms for use at three age levels: preschool (ages 2–5), child (ages 6–11), and adolescent (ages 12–21). Teachers rate specific behaviors on a 4-point Likert-type scale ranging from *never* to *almost always*. The BASC-2 TRS contains validity indexes to help determine the quality of the information provided. The parent version, the BASC-2 Parent Rating Scale, measures adaptive and problematic behaviors in the home and community settings. The student version, the BASC-2 Self-Report Personality, can be used to gain comparable information from students at three levels: child (ages 8–11), adolescent (12–21), and adult

(18–25). There is also an interview-format version for children ages 7–8 called the Self-Report Personality—Interview. An examiner asks the child a series of questions that require yes–no answers. Each of these measures was normed on a representative sample closely matching the U.S. Census population characteristics.

The SOS is an efficient system for conducting direct observations of behavior. Qualified observers can code and record direct observations of students' behavior in a classroom setting using momentary time-sampling procedures. The SOS assesses adaptive (e.g., positive social interactions with peers) and maladaptive (e.g., repetitive movement) behaviors. Also note there is the Portable Observation Program (POP) designed to simplify behavior observations by recording information directly onto a laptop. The POP is a computer program that removes some of the challenges of direct observations (e.g., requires no paper, pencils, stopwatches) but still allows the collection of SOS data.

The SDH is a comprehensive survey of a student's background. This tool provides a structure for collecting a student's social, psychological, developmental, educational, and medical information. This is also available in Spanish.

The PRQ (Kamphaus & Reynolds, 2006) provides information on several dimensions of the parent–child relationship such as attachment, communication, discipline practices, involvement, parenting confidence, satisfaction with school, and relational frustration. This can be administered to parents of children between ages 2 and 18 and takes approximately 10–15 minutes to complete. Information from the PRQ can be used to develop an intervention program that involves the parents.

BASC-2 Intervention Guide

The third tool is the BASC-2 Intervention Guide (Vannest, Reynolds, & Kamphaus, 2008), designed to support targeted interventions. The Intervention Guide is a comprehensive step-by-step guide for selecting and implementing evidenced-based interventions. It offers a breadth of information on the most common behavioral and emotional issues, focusing on academic problems, adaptability, aggression, anxiety, attention problems, conduct problems, depression, functional communication, hyperactivity, leadership, social skills, and somatization. School psychologists and other treatment agents will find this book helpful in informing intervention efforts because it provides explicit details on 60 interventions, including the theoretical framework and practical information for each. Each chapter includes (1) characteristics of the condition, (2) theoretical framework, and (3) a list of available evidence-based interventions for the given condition. To assist with the design, implementation, and evaluation of each intervention, the chapters also provide an overview of recommended interventions, step-by-step procedures for implementing the intervention, references to the appropriate research conducted to support the intervention, and factors that might facilitate or impede implementation. There are also classroom intervention guide sets, which are targeted workbooks for teachers, one for externalizing behaviors and school problems and another for internalizing behaviors and adaptive skill problems. Each workbook contains a description of the problem area, examples of behaviors typically occurring as a result of this problem, and a discussion of causes. Then, for each intervention, there is information on the strategies provided, including step-by-step procedures for how to implement the strategy as well as an illustration. There are also parent tip sheets and document checklists. The parent tip sheets offer useful information regarding each category along with specific strategies parents can use to assist school- and home-based interventions. The documentation checklists are simple, convenient worksheets designed to monitor treatment integrity, which is essential to drawing accurate conclusions about intervention outcomes (Lane & Beebe-Frankenberger, 2004). There is an ASSIST™ software upgrade available for purchase that can add intervention information to the computer-generated reports.

BASC-2 Progress Monitor

The fourth tool focuses on progress monitoring to determine the effectiveness of interventions for specific areas of concern. Once the interventions are in place, it is important to monitor student progress to see how they are responding to secondary or tertiary supports. The BASC-2 Progress Monitor (Reynolds & Kamphaus, 2009) system is designed to perform this task. Teachers and parents can complete one of two forms (one for preschool ages 2–5 and one for children/adolescents grades K–12) specific to the behavior being addressed. The specific progress monitoring content areas include externalizing and attention-deficit/hyperactivity disorder (ADHD) behaviors, internalizing behaviors, social withdrawal, and adaptive skills. There is also a student form available for students in grades 3–12. These progress monitoring forms can be scored using the ASSIST software, providing individual rater reports, multirater reports, and progress reports.

Summary

In looking at this set of tools, Kamphaus and Reynolds created the BASC-2 BESS—the focus of this chapter—to be a starting point. This instrument is easy to use, quickly administered, and psychometrically sound, making it appropriate for screening large groups of students. As they explain in the BASC-2 BESS manual, the terms *screening* and *assessment* should not be considered synonymous. Screening tools can be used to determine whether additional assessment is necessary, but only an in-depth assessment can be used to diagnose or confirm the presence of a particular concern (Hills, 1987; Kamphaus & Reynolds, 2007a). Screening should be implemented within the context of a system prepared to conduct additional assessments, provide supports based on student needs, and monitor progress.

The BASC-2 BESS can be used with the BASC-2 (Reynolds & Kamphaus, 2004) to provide a three-stage framework to screen, identify, and support students with emotional and behavioral challenges (see Figure 6.1). In Stage 1, the BASC-2 BESS can be completed by one or more respondents (teachers, parents, students [self-report]) to identify students with elevated scores. In Stage 2, the BASC-2 rating scales and other tools mentioned can be used as an assessment tool for students who exceed normative criteria on the BASC-2 BESS. Students with elevated scores can receive targeted interventions in the form of secondary (Tier 2) supports, including progress monitoring, as part of a three-tiered model of prevention. In Stage 3, additional diagnostic assessment can be conducted and the appropriateness of additional supports determined.

When implementing any systematic screening process, it is important for a school-site or district-level leadership team to have a framework in place so that screening tools are used effectively. Issues related to preparing, administering, scoring, and interpreting the measure must be worked out in advance. It is important to have the necessary structures in place to be able to respond to students who require additional assessments or supports (Lane, Oakes, & Menzies, 2010). If assessment tools are used to gather additional information beyond the screening measure, parent permission must be secured according to district and state procedures.

Although we discuss how to use the BASC-2 BESS in the school setting, it was also intended to be used by researchers, community health centers, pediatric clinics, and other agencies who have an interest in screening for EBD (Kamphaus & Reynolds, 2007a).

In this chapter we focus on the universal screening component. Readers interested in learning more about the tools in the BASC-2 family are encouraged to attend one of their Webinars and see the extensive array of materials online at *www.PsychCorp.com*.

An Overview of the BASC-2 BESS

As previously described, the BASC-2 BESS is a mass screening instrument that can be completed by teachers, parents, and students (depending on their age). The BASC-2 BESS offers a number of core features:

1. Assessment of behavioral strengths and concerns inclusive of externalizing problems, internalizing problems, school problems, and adaptive skills
2. One total score predictive of important emotional, behavioral, and academic outcomes
3. Brief forms that require 5–10 minutes to complete per student
4. Spanish versions of parent and student forms
5. Norming samples that closely parallel the U.S. population
6. Validity indexes to determine whether the rater was overly negative (F index) or inconsistent in their responding (consistency index) or whether patterned responses were provided (response pattern index)
7. Two types of normative scores: *T*-scores and percentiles, with two norm group options (combined-gender norms and separate-gender norms)
8. Different reporting options that include group-level reports, which can be used to monitor risk over time, or individual reports to determine which students require secondary (Tier 2) and tertiary (Tier 3) prevention efforts (Kamphaus & Reynolds, 2007a, 2007b)

The next section of the chapter describes the BASC-2 BESS and provides information on logistics such as administering, scoring, and interpreting the measure. Before we begin, we want to mention that the BASC-2 BESS manual provides information on hand scoring and computer scoring software (ASSIST). Since the publication of the technical manual, a Web-based version of the BASC-2 BESS has also become available through the new (released Fall 2010) behavior component of the AIMSweb[r] assessment and data management system. The authors recommend hand scoring only if there is no access to a computer or if results are needed immediately (see p. 7 of the BASC-2 BESS technical manual).

Description

Each of the three forms of the BASC-2 BESS is a four-page booklet (a single 14½″ × 11″ sheet folded in half). They are also Scantron® forms, so that their data can be electronically scanned and scored using the ASSIST software program, which can be purchased separately. This makes screening large numbers of students a more efficient process. The form can also be scored by hand and, most recently, can also be completed as part of the AIMSweb Web-based assessment and data management system (Pearson Education, 2008).

On each paper form, the first page displays the name of the instrument and indicates the type of report: teacher, parent, or student. The front page also includes spaces (and Scantron bubbles) for the student's name, date of birth, grade level, and gender and the date of administration. There is a small box that has directions on how to mark the Scantron (e.g., use a no. 2 pencil).

The next page (inside cover) has a space and Scantron bubbles for the name of the person administering the form as well as space (and Scantron bubbles) to indicate how long the person administering the instrument has known the student and whether the rater is a general or special education teacher (or other professional). The parent version has spaces to indicate the rater's gender and relationship to the child. The student self-report is blank on the inside cover. There is no other information on the second page.

The third page lists the items on which the teacher (or parent or student) will be rating the student. Depending on the form, there are 25–30 items. For example, the first item on the parent and teacher forms is "Pays attention." All forms use a 4-point rating scale: *never, sometimes, often,* and *almost always.* The bubble with the descriptor that best matches the student's behavior in relation to the item is filled in.

The last page has spaces to include additional information if desired (e.g., the student's identification number or other codes). There is also a box to summarize the scoring if it is completed by hand. The form is simple to read and easy to fill out.

The Web-based AIMSweb tool has a function to upload all classroom students' names and data into the system, although this information can also be entered individually by hand. A class roster is created, and teachers can screen their entire class simply by clicking on the Assess Now link next to each student's name. Once teachers choose that option, they are taken to a screen that displays the online version of the

BASC-2 BESS. The teacher (using the teacher version) completes the form by clicking on the Likert-type scale choice (*never, sometimes, often,* or *almost always*) that best describes the student in relation to the item. The online formatting looks similar to the paper version. Once the screener is completed, the score is instantly entered in a space next to the student's name. The total score, scoring date, and color coding of the risk category are recorded in that space. Reports can be generated for the individual student, class, school, or district, as desired.

Once teachers are familiar with the form and the scoring process, it should take them approximately 4–6 minutes to complete per student. As with other screeners, teachers should have several weeks (5–10) of contact with students before evaluating them.

Logistical Issues

In this section, we address a number of logistical considerations, each framed in the form of a question. We also provide information about each method of scoring (ASSIST software, hand scoring, and Web-based option).

When Should We Administer the BASC-2 BESS?

Deciding when to administer the BASC-2 BESS depends on the school's purpose in using the measure. Some schools may want a yearly, one-time screening of all students so that they can identify those who are at high risk. (Students identified as being at high risk should receive an intervention.) Screening can be conducted 5–10 weeks after the school year starts. By this time, teachers will know their students well enough to accurately evaluate their behaviors. It is also early enough that students who need additional help can be provided with an appropriate intervention.

Some schools may also want to use the measure as a benchmarking or progress monitoring tool. As discussed in detail in Chapter 4, an assessment schedule (see Table 6.1 for an example) can be created. Screening two to three times a year allows the leadership team to evaluate the effectiveness of their primary (Tier 1) prevention plan by examining the percentage of students who move to a lower risk status. Three screening points (Fall, Winter, Spring) are recommended by the AIMSweb system developers. At the second time point, the BASC-2 BESS can be used to decide whether interventions the students received were effective.

How Do We Prepare Materials to Conduct the BASC-2 BESS?

The BASC-2 BESS is a commercially produced screener, so there is minimal preparation involved. The first step is to determine which form the school site will need. Most schools will need the teacher form for grades K–12. If the site is a preschool, the teacher form for preschool can be ordered. For those sites who want additional input, the parent (for either preschool or K–12) or student forms (grades 3–12) can be ordered in English or Spanish. If a school prefers to have the forms electronically

TABLE 6.1. EES Assessment Schedule				
Measure	Quarter 1	Quarter 2	Quarter 3	Quarter 4
School demographics				
Student demographic information	×	×	×	×
Screening measures				
Behavior screeners: BASC-2 BESS	×	×		×
Student measures—academic				
Curriculum-based measure—reading AIMSweb reading (Pearson Education, 2008)	×	×		×
Progress reports	×	×	×	×
District measures: math and language arts	×	×	×	×
Report cards	×	×	×	×
Student measures—behavior				
ODRs	×	×	×	×
BASC-2 BESS progress monitoring component	×	×		×
Program measures				
Social validity (Primary Intervention Rating Scale: Lane, Kalberg, Bruhn, et al., 2009; Lane, Robertson, et al., 2002)	×		×	
Treatment integrity: Schoolwide Evaluation Tool (Sugai, Lewis-Palmer, Todd, & Horner, 2001)			×	

Note. From Lane, Kalberg, and Menzies (2009, Table 5.1, p. 105). Copyright 2009 by The Guilford Press. Adapted by permission.

scored to automatically generate individual or group reports, the ASSIST software must also be purchased. If the school has elected to purchase the AIMSweb management system, no other materials need to be purchased. All screening and scoring functions are included in the purchase of the AIMSweb behavior component, as are the intervention tools.

How Do We Administer the BASC-2 BESS?

We suggest that the first school-site administration of the BASC-2 BESS be done at a faculty meeting. Teachers can be briefed on the procedures for administering the BASC-2 BESS and provided time to complete a form for each student. Then all forms can be submitted for scoring at the end of the meeting. This is more efficient than having teachers complete them on their own. Everyone will have received the same information, and questions can be answered as they arise. It also ensures that all data are collected in a timely manner. As teachers become familiar with the process, it may not be necessary to have them meet together to complete the screening. However, if there are new faculty members or if it becomes difficult to collect all the forms, a meeting designated for the sole purpose of completing the screening is recommended.

The student and teacher information must be filled in on the front page and inside cover of every form. Teachers will need to have a list of their students and their birth dates. To complete the instrument, teachers read each of the 25–30 items (e.g., "is fearful," "worries," "has good study habits") and darken the bubble response (*never, sometimes, often, almost always*) that best describes the student in relation to the item. It is important that every single item be scored. Once all the student and teacher information has been entered and each item scored, the form is complete.

How Do We Score and Interpret the BASC-2 BESS?

The BASC-2 BESS is a norm-referenced instrument, which means it can provide a comparison of an individual's performance with that of a statistically calculated "average" student. It provides both *T*-scores and percentiles to be used for comparison, with the option to use combined- or same-gender norms depending on the intent of the screening (see the technical manual for additional information on which norms to select). BASC-2 BESS scoring reports generate cut points that are related to risk classification levels: Normal, Elevated, and Extremely Elevated. These scores can be calculated with the ASSIST software or by hand using the manual that accompanies the instrument, or they can be automatically generated through the Web-based system.

ASSIST SOFTWARE

The software produces both individual and group reports. The completed form is scanned, or can be keyed by hand, and the report parameters selected using either a Windows or Macintosh platform. ASSIST can create reports that demonstrate a school's or an individual's progress over time. The software has the capacity to combine data from the teacher, student, and parent forms in a single report. It is also possible to create customized cut scores based on a desired *T*-score or a specific number of students in a particular level (e.g., the top 25% of students with the highest risk level). Individualized student reports can provide data across multiple screenings. This allows teachers to compare performance over a year's time or more.

HAND SCORING

Scoring the forms by hand is more time consuming. Each raw score is converted to either a percentile or a *T*-score, as desired. The raw score can also be used to determine risk levels of Normal, Elevated, and Extremely Elevated. (Raw scores must first be converted to a *T*-score to find a cut score because each age group is separately normed.) The publishers provide three types of norm group comparisons: females, males, and combined. This offers increased possibilities for interpretation of scores depending on one's purpose.

In order to score by hand, it is necessary to access the tables in the technical manual. Each item selection (*never, sometimes, often, almost always*) is related to a particular value; however, items that are positively worded are reverse-scored, so the values can change depending on the item's wording. For example, the values for the item "Pays attention" are *never* = 3, *sometimes* = 2, *often* = 1, *almost always* = 0, and the values for the item "Disobeys" are *never* = 0, *sometimes* = 1, *often* = 2, *almost always* = 3. Once every item has been assigned a value, all the values are summed. This is the raw score, which is entered in the Score Summary section on page 4 of the screener.

Using Appendix B in the manual, the raw score and the student's age are used to find the corresponding percentile rank. First, the appropriate table is located for the form used (e.g., Table B.1 is Teacher, Preschool, Table B.2 is Teacher, Child/Adolescent). Second, the norm group used as a comparison must be chosen (female, male, or combined). The student's raw score in the first column is located. Once the raw score is located, move across the columns to the student's age (e.g., ages 5–9, ages 10–14, or ages 15–18 for the child/adolescent form) and norm group. Each raw score, age group, and norm group is associated with a corresponding *T*-score and percentile. Once these values are determined, they can be recorded on the last page of each student's form. For example, if Raymond's teacher wants to find the *T*-score and percentile for his parent form, he or she would turn to Table B.5 (Parent, Preschool), look up his raw score of 61 in the first column, and then move across to the column for his age (choose the age group under Combined or Male depending on which norm group is preferred). Raymond is 4 years old, so his *T*-score (for Combined) is 81 and his percentile rank is 99%. These values can be written on the last page of Raymond's form in the boxes provided for the scores.

The risk levels can be determined by using the *T*-scores listed in the manual's Appendix B. Each *T*-score corresponds to the following risk levels:

- Risk level Normal includes *T*-scores of 60 and below (no more than 1 *SD* above the mean of 50)
- Risk level Elevated includes scores ranging from 61 to 70 (1–2 *SD* above the mean)
- Risk level Extremely Elevated includes any score of 71 or higher (> 2 *SD* above the mean)

Using Raymond's *T*-score of 81, his risk level is Extremely Elevated.

WEB

Teachers can access their entire class on one screen. They click on the Assess Now link next to each student's name and proceed to rate each item. The item values are assigned by the program as the teacher chooses the responses. As mentioned, once the teacher evaluates the student on the Web-based BASC-2 BESS screener, the scores are instantly generated by the program. The raw score and screening date appear in the box next to the student's name. The box is color coded to represent the action recommendation (red = consult with behavior specialist, yellow = consider need for individualized instruction, green = meets or exceeds basic expectations).

How Can We Use This Information at Our School Site?

The BASC-2 BESS is one of the few measures that includes a preschool version. Not only will preschools want to consider it, but so will sites that serve preschool and other grade levels on the same campus. This allows for a comparable measure across all grades. The BASC-2 BESS can be used as a screener to identify students at risk who may need additional support (such as secondary or tertiary intervention), who require additional monitoring, or who should be assessed in further depth. The BASC-2 BESS can also be used to produce a snapshot view of student risk at a particular point in time so that the site can monitor its overall status. For example, each year the school may screen their students and analyze the aggregated data to see what their population's risk status looks like in Fall as they begin the school year. This can help them determine whether their schoolwide plan is working as they would like it to or whether their population's characteristics may be changing. It also provides useful information for professional development planning.

The Web-based version creates action item recommendations to aid teachers in planning supports for identified students. Students scoring in the red (consult with behavior specialist) or yellow (consider need for individualized instruction) categories are automatically flagged by the system for an action plan. Then teachers or school teams can choose the best interventions (which are included in the cost of the Web-based version) based on student need and available resources. Progress monitoring tools can then be used to determine how students respond to these supplemental supports and instruction.

In the illustrations at the end of this chapter, we provide examples of how to use the BASC-2 BESS to identify students for secondary supports, how to progress monitor their growth, and how to use screening data to inform professional development.

How Much Does the BASC-2 BESS Cost, and Where Can I Order It?

The BASC-2 BESS is sold in kits or as individual items. There are two versions of the kit: preschool and child/adolescent. The preschool kit includes the manual and 25 each of the teacher and parent forms and costs approximately $100. The child/adolescent kit includes the manual and 25 each of the parent, teacher, and student forms and costs approximately $125. The forms can also be purchased in packages of 25 or in packages of 100 for approximately $1 per form. The manual costs approximately $70. The ASSIST software package costs less than $600, and the header sheet for group scanning can be purchased for about $20. All of these items can be ordered from Pearson Assessment at *www.pearsonassessments.com*.

The Web-based system can be purchased through NCS Pearson, AIMSweb at *www.aimsweb.com* for $4 per student per year. The system includes BASC-2 BESS screening and Social Skills Improvement System (SSiS) screening (motivation and prosocial scales, to be described in Chapter 7) and all of the resources and tools to design, implement, and evaluate a range of behavioral interventions. If the AIMSweb data management system has already been purchased by the school or district, the behavioral component can be added for an additional $1 per student per year.

The next section of the chapter examines the psychometric features of the BASC-2 BESS.

Supporting Research

Reliability and Validity

Because the BASC-2 BESS is a relatively new instrument, few peer-reviewed studies are available. However, the initial studies conducted to develop the preschool (DiStefano & Kamphaus, 2007) and elementary (Kamphaus, Thorpe, Winsor, Kroncke, Dowdy, & VanDeventer, 2007) versions of the BASC-2 BESS provided initial evidence of the utility of these screening tools. See Table 6.2 for results of these studies.

The technical manual provides extensive information on the reliability and validity of the preschool, elementary, and secondary versions of the BASC-2 BESS, which we discuss next, along with the results of the first peer-reviewed study of the elementary-level teacher-completed BASC-2 BESS. The authors analyzed data from a sample taken from the 4-year longitudinal study conducted with the three versions (teacher, parent, and student) of the BASC-2. (The authors used items from the BASC-2 to create the BASC-BESS. This gave them the ability to create a shorter screener with items that had already been validated with the first measure.) Overall, the sample approximated the U.S. population.

According to the technical manual, test–retest reliability studies were performed for all levels (preschool, child, and adolescent) of each form (parent, teacher, and student) with sample sizes that ranged from 78 to 227 (BASC-2 BESS; Kamphaus & Reynolds, 2007a). The adjusted reliability coefficients ranged from .80 to .91 depending on the form and the level (see Table 6.3). The most reliable scores are for children/adolescents who are rated by teachers.

The interrater reliability of the BASC-2 BESS was also examined. Specifically, interrater reliability on the BASC-2 BESS compared mothers and fathers who completed separate parent forms as well as two teachers who completed separate teacher forms for the same group of children. The sample sizes ranged from 112 for teacher ratings of the child/adolescent to 31 for the parent preschool ratings. Reliability coefficients ranged from .71 to .83. The most reliable interrating is between teachers of students in grades 3–12.

The technical manual also provides evidence of criterion and predictive validity. Specifically, Kamphaus and Reynolds (2007a) reported the degree of similarity between the BASC-2 BESS and other established instruments that measure the same construct (emotional and behavioral characteristics). Second, they looked at the predictive power of the BASC-2 BESS: Did it accurately identify students' later pattern of behavioral strengths and weaknesses? The findings for each of these types of validity are discussed next.

TABLE 6.2. Reliability and Validity Studies of the BASC-2 BESS

Citation	Purpose	Description of participants	Description of schools	Reliability	Validity
DiStefano & Kamphaus (2007)	Develop short behavioral screener for preschoolers Establish predictive and concurrent validity	Study 1: *N* = 564 preschoolers; 316 (56%) boys and 248 (44%) girls Study 2: *N* = 423 kindergartners; 221 (52%) boys and 202 (48%) girls	Study 1: BASC TRS-P (4–5 years) norming data base. Data were collected from across U.S. (116 sites) and included a diverse sample: 58% white; 22% black; 18% Hispanic; 2% Asian, Pacific Islander, and multiracial Study 2: School in one Georgia district that participated in Project A.C.T. Early grant; independent sample	Study 1: Analyzed the 109 TRS-P items to determine which would provide adequate psychometric integrity for a screener. Using several analyses (e.g., exploratory factor analysis, ROC), 23 items were chosen for screening tool Internal consistency: .91	Study 1: ROC analysis: .70; sensitivity and specificity results suggested a cut score of 47 Study 2: Concurrent validity established between TRS-P and five items on Georgia Kindergarten Assessment Program. Predictive validity established between TRS-P short-form scores and behavioral infractions in second grade. Also, a negative relationship established between TRS-P short-form scores and academic outcomes. Higher scores on TRS-P short form were related to a lack of behavioral readiness for school context and lower grades and test scores in second grade
Kamphaus et al. (2007)	Investigate psychometric properties and reduce number of items on original measure	*N* = 637 students in grades K–5 (approximately half boys); <300 students had data available for predictive validity analyses	Participating district served high population of students receiving free and reduced-price lunch (70%) and with less than 50% graduation rate. Part of federally funded longitudinal study that examined students' adjustment to school, Project A.C.T. Early; 52% black, 29% white	Results of a principal-components analysis to create a 23-item BASC TRS-C to reduce number of items (148) in original full-length version; results suggest strong initial reliability (.97)	TRS-C was an adequate predictor of behavioral and academic outcomes (e.g., math and reading scores, work habits, social development, conduct) Coefficients were robust for reading and math test scores and report card grades (range –.48 to –.58) and slightly lower for special education placement (.31) and prereferral intervention (.31) Moderate correlation between BASC screener and work habit grades (–.43)
Renshaw et al. (2009)	Examine concurrent validity of BESS with report card outcomes	26 third and 22 fourth graders	Participants were from two suburban schools located on California's central coast; 78% Hispanic/Latino, 18% white, 6% other or multiple ethnic groups; 68% economically disadvantaged, 40% English learners, 14% students with disabilities		BESS risk level classifications of normal or at risk were significantly correlated with academic and behavioral composites created from report card scores. Discriminant function analyses indicated that the measure is an effective discriminator of risk status

Note. ROC, receiver operating curve; TRS-P, Teacher Rating Scale–Preschool; TRS-C, Teacher Rating Scale–Child.

TABLE 6.3. Reliability Coefficients for the BESS		
Form	Level	Adjusted reliability coefficient
Test–retest reliability		
Teacher	Preschool Child/adolescent	.83 .91
Parent	Preschool Child/adolescent	.81 .84
Student	Child/adolescent	.80
Interrater reliability		
Teacher	Preschool Child/adolescent	.80 .71
Parent	Preschool Child/adolescent	.83 .82

Note. Data from Kamphaus and Reynolds (2007a).

To examine criterion validity, the authors compared the BASC-2 BESS with several other instruments to determine whether it measured the same types of behavioral and emotional issues. One broad-based measure used for comparison was the original measure from which it was developed: the BASC-2. The BASC-2 purports to measure a wide variety of behavioral functioning, including externalizing and internalizing problems, school-related problems, and adaptive skills. Total scores on the student, teacher, and parent forms of the BASC-2 BESS are highly correlated with the global scores for each form of the BASC-2, with coefficients ranging from .86 to .94. The BASC-2 forms include a teacher and a parent rating scale and a self-report of personality form. The grade 3–12 teacher report form of the BASC-2 BESS had a correlation of .90 with the global composite score of the teacher rating scale of the BASC-2, which indicates that these versions of the two measures are closely related. In other words, it is likely that the BASC-2 BESS identifies the same types of problems as the BASC-2. Because the BASC-2 has been independently validated, this information strengthens the validity claims of the BASC-2 BESS.

Another broad-based measure that the BASC-2 BESS has been compared with is the Achenbach System of Empirically Based Assessment (ASEBA; Achenbach & Rescorla, 2000). This measure also has several forms. Correlations among the BASC-2 BESS and the ASEBA Teacher Report Form, Child Behavior Checklist, and the Youth Self-Report Form were examined. The relation between the ASEBA forms, although still moderately high, was not as strong as that between the BASC-2 BESS and the BASC-2. Correlations ranged from .71 to .77. The grade 3–12 teacher report form of the BASC-2 BESS had a correlation coefficient of .76 with the ASEBA teacher form.

Measures that focused on a narrower range of behaviors were also examined. For example, the Conners Rating Scales–Revised (CRS-R; Conners, 1997) are used to assess ADHD in children and adolescents. The CRSR has three forms: parent, teacher, and student. Correlations among various composite scores ranged from .51 to .87 with the teacher forms of the BASC-2 BESS, and the CRS-R correlated at .79

on the ADHD index. This indicates that the BASC-2 BESS most likely measures some aspect of ADHD.

The relation between the Vineland-II, which measures adaptive behavior, and the BASC-2 BESS was relatively weak, with correlations of –.69 and –.50 on the composite scores of the teacher form and the parent form, respectively. This suggests the BASC-2 BESS does measure limited aspects of adaptive behavior.

Since the publication of the technical manual, one peer-reviewed study (Renshaw et al., 2009) looked at the relation between teacher measures of academic performance and the BASC-2 BESS. The researchers examined report cards for 26 third graders and 22 fourth graders in two suburban schools. Using the scores on academic, engagement, and behavioral indicators from the report cards, three composites were created to align with each of these conceptual categories. Students' risk level categories on the BASC-2 BESS (Normal, Elevated, and Extremely Elevated) were then correlated with the category composites (academic, engagement, and behavioral performance). Teacher ratings using the BASC-2 BESS were strongly related to students' report card scores. Correlations between the BASC-2 BESS and the composite scores were –.55 for academic achievement, –.61 for engagement, and –.51 for behavioral performance. This indicates there is concurrent validity for the BASC-2 BESS with teachers' observations of students' academic and behavioral skills. Renshaw and colleagues (2009) also offered some evidence that the BASC-2 BESS does accurately discriminate between students who do and do not have behavioral problems. Results of an analysis of variance conducted between the mean composite scores of students identified at risk by the BASC-2 BESS compared with those not at risk indicated significant group differences. This means the BASC-2 BESS accurately identified students who did, in fact, have behavioral and academic issues, as defined by their teachers.

Kamphaus and Reynolds (2007a) provided evidence of the BASC-2 BESS's ability to predict reading and math achievement, grade point average (GPA), and days tardy and absent from school. These are not behavioral issues, but are strengths when a screener can also predict which students are not likely to succeed academically. Although the study had a limited number of participants, the BASC-2 BESS did appear to predict student performance 4 years later on some of the variables. Correlations were strongest for the relation between teacher and student forms and GPA, ranging from the mid-.40s to the upper-.60s. There was some relation between the BASC-2 BESS teacher, parent, and student forms and reading and math scores. The correlations ranged from the high-.30s to the mid-.40s. There was no relation between the BASC-2 BESS and days absent or tardy.

Validity Indexes

The authors developed three indexes that protect the integrity of the measure, which are related to another type of validity. It ensures that students are accurately assessed on the skills or behaviors that the instrument claims to measure. These indexes check the quality of the completed forms and account for the possibility that the rater has been careless, has been overly negative about a student, or does not understand the items.

The Response Pattern Index was developed to determine whether a rater scored the items with the same descriptor without carefully reading each of the items. For example, it can detect forms that have too many successive items scored the same way (e.g., too many items in a row scored *almost always*) and forms that have an alternating or cyclical pattern (e.g. O, O, O, A, O, O, O, A). This index can be applied to decide whether the rater may have been careless, did not take the time to read the items fully, or answered untruthfully.

The Consistency Index is used to determine whether a rater has given a different rating to items that would typically be rated similarly. This can happen for several reasons, including mistakenly rating another child partway through the form, changing one's mind about a student's behaviors, or having different raters complete the same form. Classification ranges are provided in the technical manual and can be used to help decide whether the form has been scored with consistency.

The F Index can be applied to examine whether a rater has been overly negative in rating a child. It compares high ratings of negative items with low ratings of positive behaviors. The authors provide the following descriptors for F Index raw scores: 0–2, acceptable; 3, interpret with caution; 4 or higher, interpret with extreme caution.

Summary

The BASC-2 BESS is a reliable and valid instrument that identifies students who may be at risk for low academic achievement and challenging behaviors. In the few studies conducted to date, the BASC-2 BESS is strongly correlated with test scores in reading and math, teachers' report card grades, and teachers' reporting of behavioral infractions. In addition, these studies indicate that students who "screen in" are most likely to be those who will benefit from additional support.

Identification of Nonresponders

Given that this instrument has only recently been available to the research and teaching communities, to date there have been no studies published using the BASC-2 BESS as part of a three-tiered model of prevention. However, we are confident that inquiry will be conducted in this area in the near future. We provide illustrations to help inform practice and research in this area after we review the strengths and considerations of the BASC-2 BESS. The next section of the chapter looks at the unique strengths and considerations that schools will want to examine before deciding whether the BASC-2 BESS is a good fit with the needs of their site.

Strengths and Considerations

Strengths

The BASC-2 BESS is a multiform, multilevel screener (preschool–12) that identifies students with both internalizing and externalizing behavior patterns. Although relatively new, the BASC-2 BESS was developed from items on the extensively validated

BASC-2 to create an efficient screener that can be used to detect students who may be at risk for behavioral issues.

One of the main strengths of the BASC-2 BESS is that it is easy to administer. The items are brief, and teachers and parents are likely to feel confident that they can make a judgment on each item. Although there are between 25 and 30 items (depending on the form), it takes only a few minutes to complete a screener for each student once one is familiar with the measure.

Another strength is that the BASC-2 BESS covers a wide range of ages from multiple perspectives. Students from ages 3 to 18 can be screened using the age-appropriate version. In addition, it offers the ability to look at a student from multiple perspectives because it has teacher, parent, and self-report forms.

Third, the BASC-2 BESS does appear to accurately identify both internalizing and externalizing behavior patterns that are likely to interfere with students' ability to do well in school. Although the measure has not yet been widely used in peer-reviewed studies, it does have relatively strong criterion validity with the BASC-2, which is a well-researched and frequently used instrument. Because it was developed directly from the BASC-2, the authors were able create a screener using items that had already been extensively field tested (DiStefano & Kamphaus, 2007; Kamphaus et al., 2007).

Fourth, the Web-based option offers ease of scoring with a direct link to recommended interventions. Strategies, tools (check-in, check-out data collection sheets, self-monitoring forms), and management of data, including a method to analyze academic and behavior data together, are accessed in one location. The data management tool offers administrators the ability to monitor risk levels and intervention outcomes for individual students as well as school and districtwide changes in risk levels.

The BASC-2 BESS is an easy-to-administer measure covering preschool through grade 12 that can be used to screen students for internalizing or externalizing behaviors. It includes both hand-scoring and computer-scoring options in addition to a new Web-based scoring platform.

Considerations

Although the BASC-2 BESS is one of the few screeners that includes preschoolers as well as older children, some considerations should be taken into account before deciding to use it at the school site. We focus specifically on issues related to scoring and validity.

The BASC-2 BESS may be challenging to score at least initially because of the time required to score each student's protocol. Although software is available to electronically score the measure, it is relatively expensive. If a site decides to hand score the screeners, all teachers should be trained to accurately calculate a student's raw score. This is both slightly difficult and time consuming. Once each student's raw score has been determined, it can be changed to a percentile, a T-score, or risk level using the manual appendix. Again, teachers would require training in how to do this accurately. If a school site felt that the expense of machine scoring was reasonable, then the process of scoring and analyzing the data is quick and efficient.

Another consideration is the lack of empirical studies to validate and demonstrate its use. We feel confident these studies will be conducted; however, the knowledge base is not yet established. When a measure has been used in intervention studies, those studies provide additional information for a school site to consider when deciding which screener to select. For example, although the instrument may have adequate reliability and validity overall, an intervention study may have been used at a school that sounds much like yours. This may provide greater confidence that the screener is the right one for your site. Until the BASC-2 BESS is more widely used by researchers, such information will not be available.

Although the Web-based option offers schools a potentially useful tool to evaluate, monitor, and intervene with students, it does require training to benefit from the intervention options. There are a large number of options to choose from and multiple steps involved to access the resources that can be tailored to each child. This may be cumbersome for a classroom teacher to navigate without extended time to become familiar with the options. Free Webinars with facilitators are available to acquaint professionals with the new component of the AIMSweb system, but to fully learn the system additional training would be needed. Training can be costly (3-day onsite training on the full product costs up to $6,600 for 30 participants) when the professional development fee is added to the expense of hiring substitute teachers. The screening portion only (at about $.33 per student per screening, Fall, Winter, Spring) could be purchased as schools initially learn to access the other resources. Keep in mind that if students are screened and determined to be at risk, the school site must have options for supporting them even as they transition to full use of the Web-based system.

We now present illustrations that may help you decide whether the BASC-2 BESS can be used to monitor overall student progress at your school site or to identify students who will benefit from additional supports. The first illustration takes place in a rural elementary school setting, the second in a middle school in a suburban area, and the third in a high school in a small town.

Illustrations

An Illustration at a Rural Elementary School: Eleanor Elementary School

Eleanor Elementary School (EES) is located in a small rural town of nearly 4,000 residents on the East Coast. This public school served 372 students (190 boys, 182 girls) from preschool to grade 5. The student ethnic and racial composition was approximately 70% white, 22% Hispanic, and 8% black. There were two classes for each grade level, with about 30 students in each class. There were also two special education classes: one for students in grades 3–5 (three students) and one for students in preschool–grade 2 (four students). There was one instructional aide, who split her time between the two special education classrooms. All related special education services such as speech and language and adaptive physical education were delivered by itinerant specialists who visited the school two to three times a week.

Building a CI3T Model of Prevention

EES was designated a "high-priority" school because its statewide testing scores did not show adequate growth. The principal and staff felt that one of their challenges was addressing the behavior issues that many students were experiencing. Not only did teachers feel frustrated by what they felt was a lack of respect, but they knew too much time was being spent responding to inappropriate behavior rather than focusing on teaching and learning. Teachers were also worried that their approach to supporting students was not as systematic as it should be. They thought that students who could have benefited from additional assistance did not always get referred for extra support. The staff at EES was ready to take action to improve their school climate.

The principal met with a district support specialist, who suggested the school consider developing at CI3T model to coordinate social, behavioral, and academic supports. This would address their concern about behavior and also offer a systematic approach to intervening with at-risk students.

Although it was near the end of the school year, the principal convened a leadership team that included one primary and one upper grade teacher, one special education teacher, the Parent–Teacher Association president, and herself. The team attended two inservices, one day-long training before summer vacation started and one a month later to receive feedback on the plan they had put together in the interim, which they would implement during the following school year. Although a longer planning process is recommended, the principal, staff, and leadership team agreed that they would do their best to get started in September. They decided that, despite not having the entire plan ready for the first day of school, it was still important to begin with a universal component and to continue planning so they could phase in the secondary supports by January.

The school leadership team worked with the staff to establish their schoolwide expectations of Responsibility, Organization, and Respect. The teachers agreed to teach the expectations during the first week of school. The leadership team put together lessons for all teachers to use. The first lesson introduced the schoolwide expectations and involved students in a discussion of why they were important. Subsequent lessons involved modeling each of the expectations and explaining what they would look like in the cafeteria, playground, bus, hallway, classroom, and restroom (see Table 6.4) settings. Students were also told how they would receive reinforcers when they demonstrated responsibility, organization, and respect. Specifically, they would be given tickets paired with verbal praise. These tickets could be saved and exchanged for small, tangible items (e.g., pencils, pens) or events (e.g., eating lunch with a friend in a preferred location at the school) or entered into lotteries for larger prizes (e.g., iPod Shuffle).

The staff worked hard to implement the schoolwide expectations while the leadership team started on the next component of their plan: screening to detect students at risk and providing secondary supports. They decided to use a variety of measures to locate students who were at academic or behavioral risk as well as those who had difficulties in both domains (see Table 6.1).

TABLE 6.4. EES Expectation Matrix

Expectations		Settings					
	Hallway	Classroom	Cafeteria	Restroom	School Bus	Playground	Dismissal
Responsible	• Walk on the right side of the hallway • Keep hands and feet to self	• Bring completed assignments to class • Always follow rules	• Get everything you need (e.g., napkins, silverware, condiments) before going to your seat	• Stay on task • Exit the bathroom when finished • Turn water off when finished	• Sit facing forward • Keep hands and feet to yourself	• Follow directions • Report any play equipment in need of repair	• Walk quietly to car rider area • Car riders sit/stand quietly until your name is called
Organized	• Face forward and walk in a straight line	• Come to class with needed supplies • Keep classroom area neat and organized	• Quietly wait your turn in the food line • Clean area and throw away trash when told	• Wash hands and put paper towels in the trash can	• Remain in your seat • Watch for your stop and be ready to exit • Keep materials in your backpack	• Stay in designated area • Line up with your class when the whistle is blown	• Leave with everything you need to take home • Pack up when asked by your teacher
Respectful	• Stay quiet • Follow your teacher's directions	• Raise hand for permission to speak • Be courteous to others	• Use polite manners when speaking to cafeteria staff • Talk quietly at your table and eat your lunch	• Wait quietly for your turn, and use quiet voices in the restroom • Respect the privacy of others	• Listen to the bus driver • Use quiet voices	• Take turns and play with others • Keep hands, feet, and objects to yourself	• Keep hands and feet to yourself • Remain quiet and wait for your name or bus number to be called

Note. From Walker, Ramsey, and Gresham (2004, Figure 2.4, p. 138). Copyright 2004 by Wadsworth, a part of Cengage Learning, Inc. Reproduced by permission. *www.cengage.com/permissions.*

ACADEMIC COMPONENT

EES used an RTI model in reading. The district-adopted text had been reviewed by a state panel to ensure that its content was based on empirical evidence. Teachers received training in how to use the text and ancillary materials for whole-group instruction. The statewide testing results were used to identify students whose achievement was below the 45th percentile. Progress monitoring was conducted for these students during the first 8 weeks of school. Scores on AIMSweb reading (Pearson Education, 2008) were graphed. After 8 weeks, each student's graph was examined to make decisions about secondary supports. If the trend line showed adequate upward growth, students remained in Tier I instruction. If the trend line was stable but too low or had a downward trajectory, the students received small-group instruction provided by a reading specialist.

BEHAVIOR COMPONENT

In addition to the primary plan, the leadership team decided on two interventions they could offer as secondary supports: behavior contracting and self-monitoring (Lane, Menzies, et al., 2011). The special education teachers were familiar with each of these interventions, so they provided the entire staff with an inservice on how to use them. Once students were identified as at risk at the end of the first or second quarter of the school year, they would be referred for one of these supports. The leadership team was also exploring character and social skills programs so that they could add a social component to their comprehensive model. Once the academic (RTI) and behavior (schoolwide expectations) plans were firmly in place, the leadership team would introduce a social skills curriculum. EES staff knew it would have been better to have a year to design their CI3T model before implementation, but because they felt immediate action was necessary they decided to introduce it on a shortened time line. They had the advantage of a cohesive, motivated staff who agreed with the direction the principal and leadership team had suggested.

Measures

The team felt it was important to make use of the academic assessment information teachers already collected. This was part of the school's strategy to be more systematic. These assessments included progress reports that went out after the first 6 weeks of the quarter, a districtwide language arts and math test given near the end of each quarter, report cards that were completed quarterly, and AIMSweb reading screening for all students. The team decided to use the data from these measures as well as the progress monitoring graphs. They would review the information at the end of each quarter to identify students at risk for academic failure.

The leadership team decided to use the BASC-2 BESS as well as office discipline referrals (ODRs) for behavioral data. Because ODRs can be subject to great variability, the principal dedicated a staff meeting to reviewing the schoolwide consequences that teachers were to implement for behavioral infractions (see Table 6.5). The staff

TABLE 6.5. EES Consequences

Offense	Consequence
First	Verbal warning
Second	Miss half of recess and parent phone call
Third	After school detention
Fourth	Principal's office
First instance of any severe offense: bad language, fighting, destroying property, out of control, etc.	Principal's office

agreed to be more consistent in how they applied consequences, which made them feel more confident that when a student was referred to the principal the infraction was serious enough to warrant it. The team liked the fact that the BASC-2 BESS allowed them to screen all of their students, including the preschoolers, with a single measure. They also knew that using a screener in addition to ODRs would ensure that all students were objectively screened for behavioral issues. Despite their efforts at using ODRs uniformly, they felt a standardized mass screener would give them more reliable information.

Another advantage of using the BASC-2 BESS is that parent and student self-report forms were available. Although the leadership team did not have immediate plans to use either of those forms, they thought they might be useful in the future.

How Are BASC-2 BESS Data Used to Evaluate and Compare the Level of Risk in Two Kindergarten Classrooms?

The EES principal was especially interested in understanding risk level in the two kindergarten classrooms. She had been trying to decide where resources could be used most effectively to improve the school climate and student achievement. One idea that she and the leadership team had discussed was funding a behavioral assistant for the kindergarten classrooms. They thought that tackling behavioral issues early and intensively would pay off in fewer problems in subsequent grades.

Using the BASC-2 BESS data (Figure 6.2) allowed the principal and teachers to clearly see the overall levels of risk in kindergarten in addition to the challenges that each classroom faced. The percentage of students (in both classes A and B) in the Extremely Elevated risk category ranged from 4 to 12.5%. Specifically, class B had a greater proportion of students who were in the Extremely Elevated risk category (12.5%, $n = 3$) compared with class A, where 4% ($n = 1$) of the 25 students met the criteria. The percentage of students in the Elevated Risk category was also higher in class B (29.17%, $n = 7$) compared with class A (16%, $n = 4$). A greater proportion of students ranked in the Normal risk category in class A (80%, $n = 20$) than in class B (58.33%, $n = 14$).

How Are BASC-2 BESS Screening Data Used to Inform Instruction and Provide Support in Kindergarten Classrooms?

The principal used the screening data (see Figure 6.2) to verify that additional behavioral supports were needed in the kindergarten classrooms. Given that behavior issues are most amenable to intervention in the very early grades, dedicating resources to support prosocial behavior in kindergarten was an effective use of resources. A behavioral assistant could provide social skills lessons for students at risk and lower the student–adult ratio so that students would receive more individual attention.

Examining the data at the individual classroom level (in addition to the grade level) allowed the principal to consider whether the teachers might benefit from professional development. Some behaviors are remediable by using effective classroom procedures or high-engagement instructional practices; it may be that the kindergarten teacher needed coaching or help with classroom management strategies. The high rate of risk in class B could be related to the teacher's skill level or low levels of implementation of the primary plan. The principal planned for the teacher in class B to participate in professional development to build on her repertoire of classroom management practices. Furthermore, the teacher and principal discussed the critical

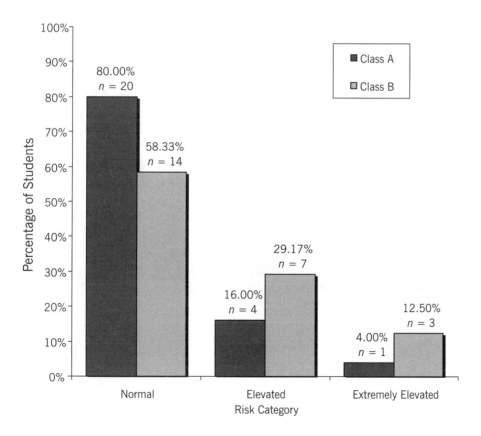

FIGURE 6.2. EES illustration of BASC-2 BESS screening data, kindergarten, Fall 2010, time point 1.

elements of the primary plan and assigned a peer mentor to serve in a supportive role by offering feedback to assist the teacher in consistent implementation.

To support the teacher in class A, the leadership team chose to purchase a program to target improving the identified students' behaviors. First Step to Success (FSS; Walker et al., 1997), an evidence-based program aimed at reducing or eliminating the development of antisocial and aggressive behaviors in young students (see Table 6.6 for a description of the program). The new kindergarten assistant would receive training to implement FSS with students in class A, with support of the school psychologist as the consultant. At the next screening time point, the progress in class B would be reviewed, and students in that class would also be offered this individual support.

Summary

Using the BASC-2 BESS data to assess risk level in a particular grade was critical in directing resources to where they would have the greatest impact. Screening data can be aggregated at the school level to examine overall risk or at the individual grade or classroom level, as in this illustration. As EES moved forward with implementing its schoolwide plan, the leadership team was able to use their academic and behavioral data to make decisions about support programs for students and professional development for teachers. In addition, teachers gained a more nuanced perspective on their students' achievement and were able to adjust their instructional practices to support and increase student success.

TABLE 6.6. EES Secondary Intervention Grid				
Support	**Description**	**Schoolwide data: Entry criteria**	**Data to monitor progress**	**Exit criteria**
First Step to Success (Walker et al., 1997)	Teacher and assistants work together to establish target behaviors for each eligible student School intervention (CLASS—Contingencies for Learning Academic and Social Skills): establish behaviors, direct feedback for desired target behaviors (green card), and corrective feedback for undesired behaviors (red card). Proximity and feedback faded as behavior is shaped Implemented by classroom teachers and kindergarten assistant with support from school psychologist, who served as consultant	Kindergarten students Parent permission Behavior: BASC-2 BESS rating of Elevated or Extremely Elevated *or* ODRs, two or more earned in a 6-week time frame	Behavioral measures: Daily goals met for target behavior as recorded on FSS card	Successful completion of the program (approx. 30 school days) Behavior: BASC-2 BESS in normal range No ODRs earned over a 4-week period

Note. From Lane, Kalberg, and Menzies (2009, Table 6.1, pp. 130–131). Copyright 2009 by The Guilford Press. Adapted by permission.

An Illustration at a Suburban Middle School:
Cesar Chavez Middle School

Cesar Chavez Middle School (CCMS) is located in a suburban area of southern California. It has 717 seventh and eighth graders, who made up a mostly Latino (65.44%) population. Other ethnic groups included white (21.11%), black (9.37%), Asian and Pacific Islander (2.64%), Filipino (.53%), and American Indian (.53%). A large percentage of the school population was considered socioeconomically disadvantaged (71%). The school had one special day class for students with moderate to severe disabilities. Students with mild disabilities attended all general education classes and one support class, where they received help with their general education assignments.

Building a CI3T Model of Prevention

The staff at CCMS had established schoolwide expectations of Empathy for Others, Learning as a Priority, and Community Membership. These expectations were taught to students at the beginning of the school year and were reinforced—whenever teachers or staff members saw them displayed—with the use of tickets paired with behavior-specific praise. Initially, the school did not have a social skills program but added one when they become more knowledgeable about CI3T models of prevention. They chose the Building Decision Skills (Institute for Global Ethics, 2008) curriculum, which is designed for middle and high school students. The staff felt confident about the districtwide curriculum in all the core content areas and their ability to offer academic support to students who required remediation; however, they were looking for a way to quickly identify students who had behavioral problems so they could be offered support programs as early as possible.

ACADEMIC COMPONENT

CCMS used the district-adopted Holt Literature Series (Holt, Rinehart & Winston, 2002) in both seventh and eighth grades. When the series was initially adopted, all language arts teachers were trained in how to use the text and support materials. Textbooks by Holt, Rinehart and Winston were also used in math, science, and history. With the adoption of each series, inservices were provided for all content area teachers in the district. When new teachers joined the district, they attended a special inservice, and their department chairperson worked closely with them to ensure they were knowledgeable about the core curriculum.

The district conducted quarterly assessments in reading comprehension, writing, and mathematics. These assessments were used to identify struggling students and to improve instructional strategies. CCMS used a problem-solving approach; teachers met in grade-level teams to discuss student progress. All students were assigned to a team where the language arts, history, mathematics, and science teachers shared the same group of students. A team structure allowed teachers to communicate with one another about a student's progress in all of their classes. It also facilitated communication with parents when there were concerns about student behavior or completing homework. At quarterly team meetings, teachers met to review each student's achievement and decide whether additional academic supports were needed. Students could be referred to a study skills homeroom or attend a special elective that focused on the academic area of concern.

BEHAVIORAL COMPONENT

The behavioral component consisted of teaching and emphasizing the schoolwide expectations (Empathy for Others, Learning as a Priority, and Community Membership). The school staff created an expectation matrix to clarify expectations in each school setting (e.g., classroom and hallway), and these were taught during the first week of school using lessons prepared by their school-site leadership team. Students were reinforced with behavior-specific praise or Cougar Coupons when they displayed instances of Empathy for Others, Learning as a Priority, or Community Membership. Students could write their name on the coupon, which were collected daily in homerooms. Each month a drawing was held and a prize winner announced on the public address system during the morning announcements. Prizes included items such as coupons for free pizza, certificates for iTunes, books, and small electronics.

SOCIAL SKILLS COMPONENT

In the second year, the school site added the Building Decision Skills program. This curriculum focused on improving students' awareness of others, building their leadership skills, and strengthening their critical decision-making skills. It included 10 lessons, which were taught in language arts classes over the course of 5 months; this ensured that all students would receive the lessons.

Measures

CCMS was concerned about their ability to identify students who had behavioral challenges. They decided to use AIMSweb because it offered a Web-based platform for screening with the BASC-2 BESS. The Web-based system allowed teachers to log on to the AIMSweb site, pull up their class roster, complete the BASC-2 BESS teacher form for each of their students, and immediately receive a choice of reports. The class roster itself is the first report. Once the data are entered for a student, there is a color-coded box with the date the screening was conducted. The color indicates the student's risk level. For example, Solis Mendoza's screening date of 10/2010 is coded green, which indicates normal risk. However, further down on the roster, Heather Grey's screening date is coded red, which indicates Extremely Elevated risk. The teacher can choose a more detailed report that shows where the student's score falls relative to the other risk categories and includes an evaluative comment such as "consult with behavior specialist" or "meets or exceeds basic expectations." Reports that rank students by risk group can also be generated.

The AIMSweb program also provides the option of generating progress monitoring reports. Once an intervention is chosen, one of three progress monitoring forms can be selected: frequency, interval, or a rating scale form. The data from these forms are also entered and saved electronically. In addition, teachers can archive anecdotal notes about each student by clicking on a link in the roster and entering comments.

How Did CCMS Use BASC-2 BESS Data to Offer Tier 2 Support?

The school staff knew the primary program was not sufficient for students who were at elevated risk. The seventh-grade counselor created a graph that showed the number of students in each category of risk at the October screening (see Figure 6.3). Approximately 25% of seventh and eighth graders were at either Elevated or Extremely Elevated risk. Teachers decided to use the SSiS: Intervention Guide (SSiS-IG; Elliott & Gresham, 2008a) to create a personalized curriculum to address the behaviors they felt were essential for students to know. The SSiS-IG includes 20 lessons that address the following domains: communication, cooperation, assertion, responsibility, empathy, engagement, and self-control. Each lesson includes six steps for teaching the

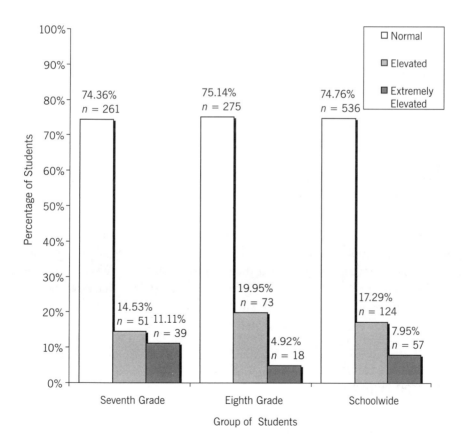

FIGURE 6.3. CCMS BASC-2 BESS screening data, Fall 2010, comparing the number of students in each risk category by grade and whole school.

skill: tell, show, do, practice, monitor progress, and generalize. The staff came to consensus on 10 lessons that centered on self-control, responsibility, and cooperation. The lessons were offered twice a week for 45 minutes per session as recommended in the SSiS–IG manual (Elliott & Gresham, 2008a). Because all students lived within walking distance of school and did not have to worry about busing, the program was offered as additional instruction during zero period and after school. Teachers did not want students to miss any regularly scheduled instruction in content and elective courses. Every student in the Elevated or Extremely Elevated risk category was invited to participate in the intervention and offered a choice of morning or afternoon sessions. Parents were also notified about the opportunity and were provided with information about the curriculum.

How Did CCMS Monitor the Effectiveness of Their Secondary Supports?

Using the AIMSweb program, teachers created progress monitoring forms using items from the BASC-2 BESS. The CCMS staff used items that most closely represented their behavioral concerns such as "listens to directions," "pays attention," "gets into trouble." Each item was rated on a Likert-type scale of *never, sometimes, often,* and *almost always.* Language arts teachers rated intervention students every 2 weeks and turned the rating forms into the counselors, who facilitated the social skills groups. This feedback was used to modify the intervention lessons or to review concepts. After 10 weeks, students' overall progress was evaluated and a decision was made to either exit them from the intervention or invite them to participate in another 10 weeks of instruction.

Summary

CCMS is an example of a school that used systematic behavioral screening to form Tier 2 groups and to monitor student progress in acquiring the targeted skills. Using the BASC-2 BESS allowed teachers to see exactly how many students were at Elevated or Extremely Elevated risk. It was a powerful motivator for deciding to move ahead with secondary supports. The AIMSweb program made it possible for teachers to quickly and easily screen students and then immediately analyze the data. The progress monitoring option provided a simple tool for tracking the success of the secondary support and deciding when to exit students. These features allowed the school to rapidly collect and respond to screening data.

An Illustration at a Small-Town High School: McNaughton High School

McNaughton High School (MHS) is located in a small town in a southern state. It served approximately 1,200 students in grades 9 through 12, making up a population that was 49.54% white, 48.35% black, and 1.43% Hispanic. Of the total student body, 59% qualified for free or reduced-price lunches. MHS had a retention rate of 5.2%. Sixteen percent of students participated in special education programs (inclusive general education classes, resource classes, and a self-contained program for students with moderate disabilities). MHS had an honors program; however, no advanced placement courses were offered. The average attendance rate was 92% and the graduation rate 94%, both above the state average. The state conducted a yearly satisfaction survey, and the results for the 2005–2006 school year indicated that MHS parents and teachers were satisfied with the learning environment. However, parents and students were somewhat dissatisfied with the social and physical environment. This was the impetus to create a primary prevention plan in the 2006–2007 school year.

Building a CI3T Model of Prevention

The high school's leadership team met regularly to discuss school issues and concerns. They consulted with their district coordinator, who suggested they look at the National PBIS Center's website (*www.pbis.org*). There they found contact information for a technical assistance partner offering training to help them develop a CI3T model of prevention (see Lane, Kalberg, & Menzies, 2009) free of charge. After a year-long planning process, the team presented the final schoolwide plan to the full faculty and staff (including permanent substitute teachers, cafeteria staff, bus drivers, and every adult who worked at the school) at the end of the school year. The primary prevention plan was based on three core expectations: Be Engaged, Be Your Best, and Show Pride. The team explained the details of the big kickoff that would be held in September to teach students and parents about the new program.

ACADEMIC COMPONENT

The academic component of the plan was informed by the student responses on the satisfaction survey. Student concerns included consistency about homework policies, procedures for making up work when absent, and inconsistencies in teacher responses to class tardiness. As a result, teachers decided to use starter activities that reviewed concepts or provided practice opportunities before the tardy bell rang. Teachers also agreed on common policies and worked together to apply them consistently.

The school supplied each student with a daily planner embossed with the school logo that included pertinent dates and information. Teachers posted assignments, content, and announcements on their websites to make information about class easily accessible, especially when a student was absent. The school purchased an online grading system so that parents could have frequent access to their child's progress in each class.

BEHAVIORAL COMPONENT

The behavioral component of the primary plan included written procedures for teaching, modeling, and reinforcing the schoolwide expectations. The school leadership team developed an expectation matrix that detailed each expectation in various school settings (see Table 6.7). Teachers were also given a set of four lesson plans to

TABLE 6.7. MHS Expectation Matrix

		Settings				
		Classroom	Hallway/Lockers	Cafeteria	Gym/assemblies	Bathroom	Arrival/dismissal
Be Engaged		• Make up work when absent • Participate in class activities • Be on time, seated, and ready to learn when class begins • Bring all necessary materials to class, including school planner • Complete assignments on time	• Use quiet voices • Keep hands, feet, and objects to yourself • Walk • Quickly get all needed materials	• Use a conversational tone of voice • Eat in assigned locations	• Keep hands, feet and objects to yourself • Participate in all activities • Listen for directions • Be appropriately dressed for the activity	• Use facility between classes quickly and quietly and return to class • Return to class promptly	• Be ready when buses arrive • Carry on all personal belongings when needed • Watch for others when driving on campus
Be Your Best		• Listen to and follow teacher instructions • Ask questions • Listen to classmates presenting work or ideas • Follow the dress code • Use kind words • Listen to and follow directions • Be truthful	• Keep hands, feet and objects to yourself • Avoid gossip • Use kind words	• Share lunch tables with others • Follow directions first time asked • Eat your own food • Clean up area	• Listen to speaker • Remain quiet between speakers	• Take care of your own business • One person per stall • Minimize chatting	• Be kind to the bus driver • Listen to and follow the bus driver's directions the first time given • Speak in a quiet voice • Remain seated after boarding the bus
Show Pride		• Complete all assignments to the best of your ability • Keep desk area clean • Use classroom supplies and books appropriately • Take all of your belongings when leaving class	• Keep clean • Respect displays (e.g., posters and artwork)	• Keep cafeteria and tables clean • Clear any trash • Recycle	• Support all people being recognized	• Keep bathroom clean • Throw trash away properly	• Keep bus clean • Take off all personal belongings

Note. From Walker, Ramsey, and Gresham (2004, Figure 2.4, p. 138). Copyright 2004 by Wadsworth, a part of Cengage Learning, Inc. Reproduced by permission. *www.cengage.com/permissions.*

teach all students about the primary plan and the three schoolwide expectations during the first week of school. The school created McNaughton Money, their reinforcer tickets. When students earned a ticket by demonstrating any of the expectations, they wrote their name on it and placed it in one of the ticket boxes in the school. During monthly drawings, tickets were randomly selected and prizes awarded. The school later added a surprise drawing for additional reinforcement after they looked at their schoolwide screening data. This drawing was for more extravagant items such as a prom package (tickets to the prom, flowers, and tuxedo rental). One time the prize was a used car, which had been donated to the school (talk about motivating!).

SOCIAL SKILLS COMPONENT

The social skills component of the MHS primary plan was conducted by the school guidance counselors. Each month the four guidance counselors chose one social skill, which was selected based on suggestions from teachers and staff as well as schoolwide data (e.g., ODRs, screening data). The guidance counselors taught a 30-minute lesson on the target skill in each study hall during the first week of the month.

Measures

In addition to attendance records, report cards, and ODRs, MHS elected to use the BASC-2 BESS to evaluate behavior and social skill performance. Behavioral screeners were completed three times throughout the school year: Fall (4 weeks after the onset of school), Winter (before Winter break), and Spring (6 weeks prior to the end of the school year). To monitor academic progress, all teachers used an online notification system that was part of the electronic grading program. Counselors were notified when any student was failing a class; the criterion was set at 70%. Then they reviewed other student information to see what supports should be offered. For example, if a student was failing a first-period class, the counselor checked to see if the student was arriving late to school. If so, the first support would be to help the student get to school and class on time. If that was not sufficient, another support would be provided. Academic progress was monitored weekly as online notifications were received.

How Can BASC-2 BESS Screening Data Be Used to Monitor Schoolwide Progress?

The MHS leadership team was interested in the schoolwide progress over time because the survey responses indicated low student satisfaction with the school's social and physical environment. They were also interested in monitoring changes within the school year so they could improve the comprehensive plan over the summer. Graphs were created to illustrate changes and trends in student risk across the school year (e.g., Figure 6.4). Figure 6.4 shows the Fall and Spring screening results for 4 consecutive school years. The school-site team graphed changes in normal levels of risk

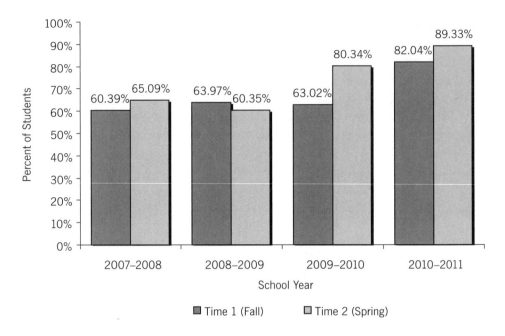

FIGURE 6.4. MHS BASC-2 BESS screening data, Fall and Spring 2007–2011, showing the percentage of students scoring in the Normal risk category across 4 consecutive school years.

to explore trends. For example, during the 2007–2008 school year, 60.39% of the MHS student body met criteria for normal level of risk during the Fall assessment. By the end of that school year (Spring 2008), an additional 5% were identified with normal risk. The following school year demonstrated similar levels of performance during Fall and Spring assessments, with scores of 63.97 and 60.35%, respectively. This lack of growth led administrators to ask questions about the effectiveness of their schoolwide plan.

How Can BASC-2 BESS Screening Data Inform Schoolwide Professional Development?

Figure 6.4 provided important information that prompted the school leadership team to think about how schoolwide professional development might improve their ability to support students. They also decided to revise the schoolwide primary plan. Procedures for teaching the schoolwide expectations were reexamined, and the team looked at treatment integrity data (information on the extent to which the plan was put in place as designed). They realized it was necessary to clarify the use of McNaughton Money and added procedures for teaching and reinforcing the schoolwide expectations. Videos about the expectations were created by the school media team and the special drawings were added. Furthermore, the leadership team decided to dedicate some of the summer teacher inservice to training teachers in the consistent use of the schoolwide primary plan. Administrators adapted their interview format so prospective faculty could read the school's primary plan and discuss its content during their employment interview. The administrators hired teachers who were philosophically aligned with a schoolwide approach to positive behavior support. These changes were all prompted by the data shared in the graph shown in Figure 6.4.

Summary

MHS serves as an example of how a school-site leadership team sought training to address concerns about the effectiveness of their comprehensive plan. They chose to use the BASC-2 BESS systematic screening tool to monitor schoolwide progress during and across school years to evaluate their plan. Data were used by the leadership team to make changes and improvements for supporting their school community.

Summary

This chapter introduced the BASC-2 BESS, which is a screener for children ages 3–18. The reliability and validity of the BASC-2 BESS were examined. The strengths and considerations associated with preparation, administration, scoring, and interpreting the findings of the measure were discussed. The chapter closed with illustrations of how to use the BASC-2 BESS in elementary, middle, and high schools, with one example featuring use of the AIMSweb assessment and data management system.

In the next chapter, we introduce a multicomponent program—the SSiS, which includes a systematic screening tool: the SSiS Performance Screening Guide (Elliott & Gresham, 2007b). The family of tools includes a universal screener, a social skills curriculum, a diagnostic tool, and an intervention component.

CHAPTER 7

Social Skills Improvement System: Performance Screening Guide

This chapter introduces the Social Skills Improvement System: Performance Screening Guide (SSiS-PSG; Elliott & Gresham, 2007b). The SSiS-PSG is a systematic universal screening tool for gathering information about preschool through secondary students in four areas: prosocial behavior, motivation to learn, reading skills, and math skills. It can be used to collect baseline information about students' social *and* academic behavior as well as monitor their progress over the course of the academic year.

Whereas many educators are clear on the importance of and instructional techniques for teaching academic skills, less attention is devoted to social skills. Social skills are learned behaviors that guide us in our social interactions with one another (Gresham, 1990). People typically learn how to perform these actions by observing those around them. They are also guided by influential adults in their lives. Social interactions are communicated through verbal and nonverbal behaviors. Some are subtle, such as knowing when to smile or nod your head during a conversation. Others, like saying "please" or "thank you," are more obvious. Students who are adept at understanding and using prosocial behaviors are more likely to be successful in school (Caprara, Barbaranelli, Pastorelli, Bandura, & Zimbardo, 2000; Elliott & Gresham, 2008a).

Schools require a particular set of social behaviors to facilitate the instructional process, referred as to academic enablers (Elliott & Gresham, 2008a). These skills include paying attention to the teacher, working well with others, behaving responsibly, and knowing how to get the teacher's attention in an acceptable way. Students who will not or cannot perform these actions may be perceived of as a behavioral challenge. When students lack these important social skills, it negatively impacts their ability to successfully negotiate relationships with teachers and peers (Walker et al., 1992). In addition, research suggests that poor social skills may influence long-term academic achievement (Caprara et al., 2000; Malecki & Elliott, 2002; Wentzel, 1993). In a longitudinal study examining social and academic skills of students in third grade and again in eighth grade, social skills in third grade were more predictive of performance on eighth-grade academic achievement tests than were academic skills in third grade (e.g., Caprara et al., 2000). Although we certainly recognize the pressure teachers are under to produce high-achieving students (e.g., No Child Left Behind Act, 2001), taking the time to explicitly teach critical social skills can facilitate the instructional process by affording teachers the time to focus on academic instruction rather than responding to problem behaviors (Elliott & Gresham, 2008a; Lane, Kalberg, & Menzies, 2009).

As in Chapter 6, which described the BASC™-2 family of products, this chapter provides an overview of all components constituting the SSiS program, which together make up a comprehensive system for developing students' social skills. Then we offer detailed information about the SSiS-PSG, including step-by-step directions for its use. Supporting research covering issues such as reliability and validity and the instrument's strengths and considerations are examined. The chapter ends with illustrations of how to use the SSiS-PSG data in a three-tiered model of prevention in an elementary school setting and a middle school setting. The illustrations also include information about using the screening data for specific instructional purposes such as designing secondary (Tier 2) and tertiary (Tier 3) supports. The first illustration demonstrates how to use screening data to implement targeted interventions. The second demonstrates using the screening data to evaluate the effect of the primary three-tiered model of prevention on student risk levels. It also provides information on how the school improved their program by implementing a schoolwide social skills curriculum.

An Overview of the SSiS Family of Products

Like the BASC-2 BESS, the SSiS-PSG is part of a multicomponent program. The SSiS family of tools provides a comprehensive system for use within the context of three-tiered models to support the development of social skills (see Figure 7.1). The program includes materials to (1) screen students for behavioral and motivation issues, academic performance, and prosocial behavior; (2) provide a primary prevention (Tier 1) program to teach 10 core social skills that can be led by classroom teachers; (3) monitor student progress on targeted skills; (4) conduct in-depth assessments of students' academic and social behaviors; (5) identify areas for intervention; and (6) offer interventions (secondary and tertiary) customized to each student's area of need. Depending on your purpose, it is not necessary to use all components. Each component can be used collectively or on a stand-alone basis.

The SSiS includes several products. In addition to the universal screener (SSiS-PSG; Elliott & Gresham, 2007b), the SSiS includes the Classwide Intervention Program (SSiS-CIP; Elliott & Gresham, 2007a), the Rating Scales (SSiS-RS; Gresham & Elliott, 2008), and the Intervention Guide (SSiS-IG; Elliott & Gresham, 2008a). These can be used together to implement a comprehensive system of monitoring and intervention for students with behavioral issues (see Figure 7.1).

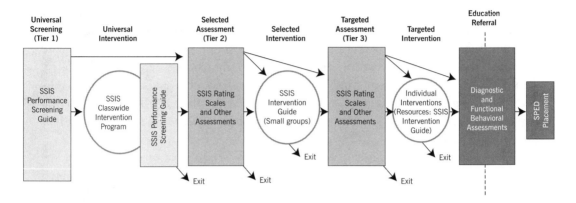

FIGURE 7.1. SSiS multi-tiered assessment and intervention model. From Gresham and Elliott (2008, p. 5). Copyright 2007 by NCS Pearson, Inc. Reprinted by permission. All rights reserved.

SSiS Performance Screening Guide

There are three versions of the SSiS-PSG: preschool, elementary, and secondary. Each is criterion referenced and can be used for universal screening and the more frequent monitoring of social and academic performance. All versions include the following four domains: prosocial behavior, motivation to learn, math skills, and reading skills. The preschool form is scored using a 1–4 rating scale while the elementary and secondary forms use a 1–5 rating scale. A color coding system is used to facilitate scoring and interpretation. For the preschool scale, a score of 1 (red band) indicates elevated risk, 2 moderate risk (yellow band), and 3 or 4 (green band) adequate performance. On the elementary and secondary scales, a score of 1 (red band) indicates students who experience significant difficulty, 2 or 3 (yellow band) identifies students who may be experiencing moderate difficulty, and 4 or 5 (green band) indicates adequate performance. Teachers rate each student in their classroom in each domain. The screener is administered after at least 3–4 weeks of classroom experience with students. This allows the teacher time to establish a complete picture of students' skill level in each area. Once the rating has been completed, teachers can use the information to monitor student performance or to intervene if necessary. Additional administrations of the screener can be used to track student progress. Detailed information about the screener is provided later in the chapter. The next section discusses the other components of the SSiS family.

SSiS Classwide Intervention Program

The SSiS-CIP is a social skills curriculum that teachers can use for individual or whole-class instruction. The curriculum includes 10 lessons, identified by the authors as essential for success according to their decades of research in social skills. The individual lessons include topics such as how to listen to others, following the rules, and getting along with their peers. Each lesson has six steps: tell, show, do, practice, monitor progress, and generalize.

The SSiS-CIP can be used as a schoolwide primary prevention program. In a comprehensive integrated three-tiered (CI3T) model of prevention that includes academics, behavior, and social skills (Lane, Kalberg, & Menzies, 2009), the SSiS-CIP would serve as a schoolwide program to teach all students the social skills that facilitate a successful academic environment. In conjunction with the SSiS-PSG, a school could monitor changes in the overall level of risk. The individual performance of students identified at risk could also be monitored. Together, the SSiS-PSG and the SSiS-CIP offer readily available, easy-to-use tools for designing and implementing a schoolwide primary prevention program.

SSiS Rating Scales

The SSiS-RS is a diagnostic tool that provides detailed information about students' social behaviors. It is a recently updated version of the Social Skills Rating System (Gresham & Elliott, 1990). This norm-referenced measure can be used with students ranging in age from 3–18 years and has three versions: parent, teacher, and student self-report (ages 8–18). It is a more sensitive measure of students' strengths and weaknesses in the areas of behavior and interpersonal skills than the SSiS-PSG, so it can be used to inform a secondary intervention. The SSiS-RS identifies the specific skill areas in which students may require intervention and more fully describes students' behavioral, social, and academic profile. Whereas the SSiS-PSG identifies students who may be at risk, the SSIS-RS more fully describes students' needs and strengths. The SSiS-RS is directly linked to the SSiS-IG, which provides targeted interventions that can be used with small groups (secondary, Tier 2) or with individual students (tertiary, Tier 3).

SSiS Intervention Guide

The SSIS-IG is a curriculum that addresses an extensive array of social skills in seven prosocial areas: communication, cooperation, assertion, responsibility, empathy, engagement, and self-control. This curriculum can be used for small groups or for individual students. The ASSIST™ software uses the data from the administration of the SSiS-RS to provide recommendations for the lessons appropriate for a particular student's areas of need. Specifically, the SSiS-RS ASSIST (Elliott & Gresham, 2008b) Standard Report provides scores, demographic information, test administration information, a social skills intervention planning guide, and a tabular summary of all item-level data. The social skills intervention planning guide uses a model of social behavioral strengths and weaknesses to look at social skills strength (what students do well), social skills performance deficits (won't do problems), social skills acquisition deficits (can't do problems), and competing problem behavior (interfere with using a learned social skill). This information is used to identify specific social skills and problem behavior items to focus on during secondary or tertiary intervention (see p. 18 of the SSiS-IG). The report also specifies the corresponding lesson in the SSiS-IG that can be taught to address specific social skills in need of improvement.

The SSIG lessons follow the same format as the SSiS-CIP lessons. The six steps to the lesson plan are as follows: tell, show, do, practice, monitor progress, and generalize. The SSiS-IG manual includes case studies that provide detailed examples of how to use the various tools associated with the curriculum. The manual comes with ancillary materials such as treatment integrity forms, parent letters, and video examples of the skills featured in each lesson.

Summary

In looking at this set of tools, Elliott and Gresham created the SSiS-PSG—the focus of this chapter—to be a starting point. This teacher-completed instrument is easy to use, quickly administered, and psychometrically sound, making it appropriate for screening large groups of students. The SSiS-PSG can be used to determine how students respond to the SSiS-CIP (10 social skills lessons taught either classwide or schoolwide) to make decisions as to whether or not additional assessment is necessary. If additional assessment is necessary, the SSiS-RS can be completed by teachers, parents, and, in some cases, students. Information from these rating scales can be used to develop secondary (Tier 2) interventions using the SSiS-IG, with intervention efforts clearly linked to assessment results. If students are not responsive to secondary support, tertiary (Tier 3) supports can also be customized using data provided as part of the SSiS family of tools (see Figure 7.1).

As mentioned in Chapter 6, when implementing any systematic screening process, it is important for a school-site or district-level leadership team to have a framework in place so that screening tools are used effectively. Issues related to preparing, administering, scoring, and interpreting the measure must be worked out in advance. It is important to have the necessary structures in place to respond to students who require additional assessments or supports (Lane, Oakes, & Menzies, 2010). If assessment tools are used to gather additional information beyond the universal screening measure, parent permission must be secured according to district and state procedures. One of the benefits of the SSiS family of tools is that this program is well conceptualized and provides all the assessment and intervention materials necessary to design, implement, and evaluate three-tiered models of prevention, including secondary and tertiary prevention efforts for students requiring instruction beyond that offered as part of the SSiS-CIP (primary plan).

In this chapter, we focus on the universal screening component. If you are interested in learning more about the tools in the SSiS family, we encourage you to attend one of their Webinars and see the extensive array of materials online at *www.Psych-Corp.com*.

An Overview of the SSiS-PSG

Universal screeners are used to identify students with elevated risk for behavior problems and who may benefit from intervention. Efficiency is a critical consideration in choosing a screener because teachers and school-site personnel have limited time to devote to screening. Balancing the need for efficiency are considerations related to the reliability and validity of an instrument. The screener must reliably and accurately identify students who are at risk. The PSG attempts this balance by (1) creating separate screeners for preschool, elementary, and secondary students; (2) using a criterion-referenced approach to determining students' behavioral performance; and (3) rating behaviors directly related to student performance in the school setting. In 30-minutes this screener collects data that can be used to evaluate a classroom of students on prosocial behavior, motivation to learn, reading skills, and math skills. A class should be rated only after the teacher has several weeks (3–4 minimum) of experience with students. This screener can be used for classwide screening, program evaluation, and progress monitoring.

Description

PSG: Preschool

The preschool version of the PSG is an 8½″ × 11½″ booklet of 12 pages (six double-sided). Inside the front cover is an overview of the purpose of the SSiS-PSG, instructions for completing the SSiS-PSG, and considerations when evaluating students. The back cover includes spaces to enter the teacher's name, school name, grade level, number of students in the class, completion date, and purpose of the evaluation (e.g., classwide screening, progress monitoring, program evaluation). Inside the booklet are four separate pages with performance descriptors for each area (prosocial behavior, motivation to learn, early reading skills, and early math skills) that line up with a column where each student's name is entered. Next to each name is a 4-point scale the teacher (or rater) uses to indicate (by crossing or circling) the student's level of performance in the area under consideration.

For example, in the preschool version, the first performance descriptor is prosocial behavior. The following definition of prosocial behavior is provided:

> Prosocial behavior is behavior directed toward other people that involves effective communication skills, cooperative acts, and self-control in difficult situations. For example, children who consistently act in a prosocial manner compromise in conflict situations, invite others to join activities, volunteer to help others, and listen when others are speaking. (Pearson Education, 2007)

Adjacent to the definition is a four-level rubric that defines each level of prosocial behavior. Level 4 is defined as follows:

> Students at this performance level demonstrate most of the following:
>
> - Effective skills to communicate and/or cooperate with others.
> - Effective skills to initiate and sustain conversations/interactions with others.
> - A high level of self-control and/or concern for others.

Students at this performance level generally do not need additional instruction to improve their social skill level, and their current skill level is considered to be high for their age. (Pearson Education, 2007)

The SSiS-PSG provides a detailed description for each of the remaining three levels of prosocial behavior.

After entering all students' names into the class roster scoring summary sheet (which is simply the column for students' names and the accompanying 4-point scale for each domain), the rater starts by reading the definition of the first performance skill area and each of the accompanying rubric levels. Once familiar with the performance skill definition and the descriptions of each rubric level, the rater evaluates each student's current level of functioning and circles the level (1–4) that most directly corresponds to the student's ability in that area (e.g., behavior, motivation to learn, early reading skills, or early math skills).

The teacher (or other rater) flips the page to the next performance skill area (motivation to learn) and follows the same procedure. First, he or she reads the definition of motivation to learn and the descriptions for each of the four rubric levels. The pages are designed so that it is not necessary to reenter all the students' names every time the rater considers a new performance skill area. (The pages vary in size so that when the page is turned the rating scale that accompanies it is revealed.) Again, once the rater is familiar with the definition and performance levels, each student's level (1–4) can be circled quickly. The same steps are followed for math and reading skills.

After all students have been rated in the final areas—reading and math skills— the page is turned, and each student's level for all of the performance areas is visible on the same page. The columns can be rapidly scanned to see which students have scores of 1 or 2 in any of the performance areas. On this same page (where all students' names have been entered and the rating scale levels are circled), there are two additional boxes. One box is for entering the names of all students who have a 1 in any of the four areas. The other box is for entering the names of students who have a 2 in any of the four areas. Each box also includes a line for recording what action will be taken to assist students who have ratings of 1 or 2. Interpretations are provided for each of the ratings on the opposite page. For example, in the preschool version, the description for a rating of 1 is as follows:

Ratings of 1 in any of the four skill performance areas indicate students who are experiencing significant difficulty. They may need instruction beyond what is currently provided. List students who received this evaluation in the appropriate space provided on the class roster scoring summary page. Follow school or district procedures for indicating any concerns for specific students to appropriate school personnel. (Pearson Education, 2007)

Descriptions are also provided for ratings of 2, 3, and 4. By rating each domain, a student at risk for poor performance in any of the areas has been systematically and objectively identified.

The two boxes that are filled in with the names of students who scored a 1 or a 2 in any of the domains are the mechanism for identifying which students are at risk and the areas of risk. At this point one of two actions can be taken. Students initially identified as at risk can be monitored for a specific period of time (perhaps a month or until the Winter screening time point) and then be reassessed using the SSiS-PSG. If the student is no longer at risk, he or she should continue to be monitored and reassessed periodically. Alternately, school sites may decide to take immediate action and provide an appropriate intervention as part of the schoolwide secondary or tertiary prevention program, as illustrated in Figure 7.1.

PSG: Elementary and Secondary

There are additional PSG versions for the elementary and secondary levels. They are formatted in exactly the same way as the preschool version, but the definitions for each of the performance skill areas (prosocial behavior, motivation to learn, reading and math skills) are age appropriate. One difference in the elementary and secondary screening guides is that the scores range from 1 to 5. The names of students who have performance skill scores of 1, 2, or 3 are entered in the boxes on the form for consideration of additional supports or monitoring. A score of 1 indicates students who are experiencing significant difficulty and a 2 or 3 signals students who may be experiencing moderate difficulty.

There is an option to complete the SSiS-PSG prosocial behavior and motivation to learn domains online in conjunction with the BASC-2 BESS as part of the Web-based screening process available through AIMSweb®.

Logistical Issues

In the next section, we discuss the logistical issues related to preparing, administering, and scoring the SSiS-PSG. Each is framed in the form of a question.

When Should We Administer the SSiS-PSG?

As with the BASC-2 BESS, deciding when to administer the SSiS-PSG depends on the intent of the evaluation. Is it being completed as a classwide or schoolwide screening? To monitor progress? To evaluate a program?

We recommend the SSiS-PSG be completed three times per year: after the onset of the academic year, prior to Winter break, and again at year end. This information can be used to monitor the overall level of student risk in the four areas of prosocial skills, motivation to learn, reading skills, and math skills, which can then be used to inform decision making regarding the primary prevention plan. For example, if 60% of the elementary student body is scoring in the yellow (2 and 3) and red (1) levels in terms of reading skill, this suggests the primary plan needs improvement.

Data from the first and second time points can be used to inform secondary (Tier 2) and tertiary (Tier 3) intervention efforts for the first and second semesters, respectively. Spring screening data can be used to prepare for the following school year so that secondary and tertiary supports are in place for students when they return from Summer break (see Lane, Oakes, Ennis, et al., 2011, for an illustration at the high school level). Data from the SSiS-PSG can also be used to assess how students respond to each level of prevention. For example, the data can be used to decide whether a student has benefited from a secondary (e.g., small-group social skills intervention) or tertiary (e.g., functional assessment-based intervention to increase positive social interactions) plan and can now return to only the primary prevention plan.

Elliott and Gresham (2007b) recommend that teachers have at least 3–4 weeks of experience with the students they will be screening. The intent is to ensure that teachers have a thorough knowledge of the students and will be able to accurately rate students' performance on all items. The SSiS-PSG requires teachers to be knowledgeable about academic performance as well as students' social behavior.

How Do We Prepare Materials to Conduct the SSiS-PSG?

The directions for use are printed on the inside cover of the SSiS-PSG booklet. Each rater needs one copy of the 12-page booklet for every 25 students; if a class has more than 25 students, another booklet will be needed. The first time a school site completes a screening, it is preferable to conduct it during a regularly scheduled staff meeting. Meeting together is more efficient because everyone can be given directions at the same time and all questions can be answered. Once the staff is comfortable with completing the screeners, teachers can complete the screener within a given time period, providing them some flexibility. The school-site team or administrator in charge will want to set a deadline for completing and turning in the screeners to ensure that all students are screened within the designated assessment window.

How Do We Administer the SSiS-PSG?

As mentioned, we recommend the screening be administered during a regularly scheduled faculty meeting during the first one or two administrations. The school-site leadership coordinating the screening procedures can orient the teachers on the SSiS-PSG and answer any questions. During subsequent screenings, teachers can refamiliarize themselves with the performance skill definitions and rubric descriptions. Then each student's performance in prosocial behavior, motivation to learn, reading skills, and math skills is rated using a scale of 1–4 for preschool or 1–5 for elementary and secondary. The names of all students who scored a 1 (red band) in any of the performance skill areas are entered in a box on the form. These students are considered high risk for either academic or social failure for the given domain (prosocial behavior, motivation to learn, reading skills, or math skills). The students who received a 2 (yellow band) on the preschool measures or a 2 or 3 (yellow band) on elementary or secondary scales are identified as being at moderate risk. Their names are entered in another box to indicate that they should receive continued monitoring to determine whether additional assessment or intervention may be warranted at a later date.

How Do We Score and Interpret the SSiS-PSG?

As previously discovered, the SSiS-PSG contains specific language explaining how to interpret and take action according to ratings provided. Any preschool, elementary, or secondary students who earn a rating of 1 (red band) are identified at high risk, experiencing significant difficulty. Their name is entered in the box for high-risk students, and an intervention should be provided. The intervention may be academic or behavioral, or both, depending on the area in which the students have high-risk status. Teachers are instructed to follow school or district procedures for students with high-risk status. Any preschool students who earn a score of 2 (yellow band) or elementary or secondary students who earn a score of 2 or 3 (yellow band) suggests the student is experiencing moderate difficulty and thus are at *possible* risk. As mentioned, these students may not currently warrant an intervention but should be monitored for signs of declining performance. It is possible these students many also be in need of extra supports beyond primary prevention efforts. Preschool students who earn a score of 3 or 4 (green band) or elementary or secondary students who earn a score of 4 or 5 (green band) are functioning at an average or above-average level for their grade or age. These students are responding to primary prevention efforts and do not require additional supports at this time.

How Can We Use This Information at Our School Site?

Once a school has the capacity to identify students at risk, the teacher or school-site team must be able to provide an intervention or some type of support in the area of need. Because the SSiS-PSG screens four separate domains (prosocial behavior, motivation to learn, reading skills, and math skills), some consideration will have to be given to each area. Ideally, students would be screened approximately 2 months into the school year. Prior to this time, school-site personnel could plan for students who will be identified at risk. Schools should first consider the resources they already have in place. Is there a homework club, a school counselor who meets with groups of students, or inclusive delivery of special education services that also provides assistance to at-risk students? Do teachers provide small-group instruction using evidenced-based practices? Each of these could be potential resources for supporting students in addition to the SSiS-IG, which includes ready-made lessons and materials for social skills interventions (secondary [Tier 2] and tertiary [Tier 3]). School teams should also consider the data already collected at the school site to determine which students would benefit from each support. For example, teams could use oral reading fluency (ORF) scores collected from a curriculum-based measure along with the screening data from the SSiS-PSG. Students who score in the at-risk range on ORF and are at-risk on the SSiS-PSG in prosocial, motivation to learn, or reading skills would be provided with a small-group reading intervention with a behavioral component (e.g., self-monitoring; see Kalberg et al., 2010). Screening students does not necessarily mean that a school will have to establish a whole new set of programs. They can use supports within their existing framework and then supplement current supports with other evidenced-based programs and practices. The advantage of using a universal screener like the SSiS-PSG is that student achievement and prosocial behavior are evaluated systematically.

If a school site implements the SSiS-PSG, all teachers would be able to identify which students are having difficulty in the target areas after the 3- to 4-week period. Some schools may create a team to look at the list of at-risk students and suggest interventions as prescribed in the school's secondary intervention grid. The team may comprise teachers, the counselor, and an administrator. However, other sites may use grade-level teams to make recommendations for students identified at their respective grade level. In either case, a system should be created to (1) screen students, (2) identify those at risk, (3) systematically determine how to support those identified, and (4) monitor progress to determine whether the supports are effective. The teams will need to reconvene at regular intervals to review progress monitoring data.

How Much Does the SSiS-PSG Cost, and Where Can I Order It?

The SSiS-PSG is published by Pearson and and can be ordered online at *psychcorp. pearsonassessments.com.* The elementary and secondary screeners cost less than $50 for a package of 10 forms. Each form can be used to screen 25 students. The preschool package costs less than $20 for a package of four forms. In addition to its ease of administration, the technical strength of the instrument should be reviewed before making a final decision as to which screener will become a part of schoolwide practice.

In the next section, we discuss the validity and the reliability of the instrument which are important considerations when determining which screener to choose.

Supporting Research

Reliability and Validity

The SSiS-PSG is a new screening measure first published in 2007 (Elliott & Gresham, 2007b). Development and field testing of the SSiS-PSG occurred during the standardization of the SSiS-RS, providing information on the usability, reliability, and validity of the SSiS-PSG. A total of 138 teachers in the United States completed the SSiS-PSG for students in their class: 30 preschool teachers, 76 elementary teachers, and 32 high school teachers. This yielded data on 2,497 students: 439 preschool, 1,475 elementary, and 583 secondary. Results of these studies are reported in the technical manual and are discussed next.

First, a usability study was conducted to determine what teachers thought about the quality and utility of the SSiS-PSG. Results suggested that it took teachers approximately 30 minutes to rate all students in their class. Teachers also found the instrument to be acceptable; 98% indicated that the behaviors included in the screening tool were important. They viewed the SSiS-PSG as clearly written and easy to use, providing information that could be readily used to inform intervention efforts.

Two types of reliability were examined: test–retest and interobserver. The field test of the PSG's test–retest reliability included 25 teachers who assessed 543 students

(64 preschool, 302 elementary, and 177 secondary), with an average of 74 days between the two administrations. Intraclass correlations were used to measure reliability because they are believed to be more accurate when using observer (or rater) data (Landis & Koch, 1977). Table 7.1 reports the reliability coefficients (intraclass correlations because of the nested nature of the data—important information for researchers!) for each level and skill area. Coefficients of .20 or less are considered weak, .50 adequate, and .80 or higher strong (Hatcher & Stepanski, 1994). As evident in Table 7.1, there is some variability among the different skill areas and levels. For example, the preschool-level SSiS-PSG is somewhat less reliable than the elementary or secondary levels, and the reliability for math tends to be lower than the other skill areas. Overall, the early data on the SSiS-PSG suggest it has adequate test–retest reliability for a screener, with a moderate to strong level of test–retest reliability. It is likely to *consistently* identify a student who is experiencing difficulty in one of the performance skill areas.

Interrater reliability refers to whether two different observers would arrive at the same score. The field test for interrater reliability included 44 teachers who evaluated 434 students in 22 classrooms. The sample included 79 preschool students, 215 elementary students, and 140 secondary students. The second rater in the preschool classrooms was usually a team teacher (or colleague). At the elementary level, the second rater was a team teacher, teacher's aide, or reading specialist. At the high school level, the second rater was usually a different content area teacher who taught the same students. Both sets of teachers (the first and second raters) completed their scorings within 12 days. Intraclass correlations (ICCs) were calculated for each skill area for each level. Table 7.1 reports the ICCs for each skill area. Correlations are generally lower for interrater reliability than for test–retest reliability

TABLE 7.1. Reliability Coefficients (Intraclass Correlations) for the SSiS-PSG			
	Test–retest reliability		
	Level		
Skill area	Preschool	Elementary	Secondary
Math skills	.53	.68	.56
Reading skills	.62	.74	.72
Motivation to learn	.58	.74	.73
Prosocial behavior	.53	.69	.72
	Interrater reliability		
Math skills	.72	.68	.57
Reading skills	.73	.57	.60
Motivation to learn	.71	.62	.59
Prosocial behavior	.60	.55	.37

of this measure, except of the preschool level, where they are relatively high. The authors suggest that this may be because the preschool observers had shared classroom experience with the same students, while at the secondary level the observers may not have spent any time together in the same classroom. Prosocial behavior had low correlations compared with the other skill areas. Observers may have different tolerances for behavior, which, despite providing a definition of prosocial behavior in the SSiS-PSG, results in higher variability for this skill area. Overall, ICCs were moderate to strong.

Elliott and Gresham (2007b) established the concurrent validity of the SSiS-PSG by obtaining a sample of students who were evaluated on both the SSiS-PSG and the SSiS-RS (teacher version). The total sample included 22 preschoolers and 63 elementary or secondary students. The demographic information of the sample is presented in the technical manual (Elliott & Gresham, 2007b, Table 9.5). In all cases, the SSiS-RS teacher version was completed before the SSiS-PSG. In brief, correlations between the SSiS-RS mean scale (Social Skills, Problem Behaviors, and Academic Competence) and subscale (Communication, Cooperation, Assertion, Responsibility, Empathy, Engagement, Self-Control, Externalizing, Bullying, Hyperactivity/Inattention, Internalizing, Autism, and Academic Competence) scores across forms and ages (3–5 and 5–18) were computed. Results suggested average levels of behaviors for Social Skills and Problem Behaviors. For example, the preschool sample showed a .63 correlation between the SSiS-RS Social Skills and SSiS-PSG Prosocial Behavior scores. There was a .70 correlation between these scores with the 5- to 18-year-old sample. Overall, students with higher SSiS-RS Social Skills scores tend to have higher scores on the SSiS-PSG reading, math, and motivation to learn scores. There was a negative relation between SSiS-RS Problem Behaviors and SSiS-PSG scores. Collectively, these findings support criterion validity.

Further evidence of criterion validity and new evidence of predictive validity are offered in Kettler, Elliott, Davies, and Griffin's (2009) paper presented at the American Educational Research Association's annual meeting (see Table 7.2). In this study of 536 elementary students in Australia, concurrent validity was again established between SSiS-RS (teacher version) and SSiS-PSG scores. There was also evidence of predictive validity, with SSiS-PSG scores predicting a criterion measure of performance of year-end achievement tests.

Collectively, these findings support the reliability and validity of the SSiS-PSG, a criterion-referenced screening tool. When interpreting these findings, it is important to keep in mind that this is not a norm-referenced screening tool. Norm referenced means that an individual student's performance is compared with a statistically constructed "average" student based on the mean scores of other students. The ability to compare with an average helps with interpretation. If a student is significantly below average, then it is clear that he or she requires additional support. The SSiS-PSG is not norm referenced. Instead, the authors have constructed a criterion-referenced instrument, which means they have determined how acceptable performance is measured. In this case, acceptable performance is a 3 or 4 on the preschool scale and a 4 or 5 on the elementary and secondary scales.

TABLE 7.2. Reliability and Validity Studies of the SSiS-PSG					
Citation	Purpose	Description of participants	Description of schools	Reliability	Validity
Kettler et al. (2009)	Compare predictive validity of SSiS-PSG (Elliott & Gresham, 2007b) with predictive validity of SSiS-RS (Gresham & Elliott, 2008), with a criterion measure of performance on year-end achievement tests	$N = 536$ elementary students (second, third, and fifth grades); rated by 30 teachers; SSiS-PSG was completed on all students, and SSiS-RS was completed on a subsample ($n = 178$), 6 students per classroom	Australian elementary school students		Concurrent validity: Correlations between SSiS-PSG and SSiS-RS subscales were varied; measures in academic and social behavior areas shared greater correlations with each other relative to correlations across areas. Predictive validity: SSiS-PSG yielded high sensitivity (.95) in predicting academic test performance and high negative predictive value (.99); SSiS-PSG had low specificity (.44) and low positive predictive power (.18) This profile is appropriate for a screening system, with false negatives being a more serious error than false positives

Identification of Nonresponders

Given that this instrument has only recently been available to the research and teaching communities, to date there are no published studies using the SSiS-PSG as part of a three-tiered model of prevention. However, we are confident that inquiry will be conducted in this area in the near future. We provide illustrations to help inform practice and research in this area following a review of the strengths and considerations of the SSiS-PSG, presented next.

Strengths and Considerations

Strengths

One of the most attractive features of the PSG is that it is simple to score. This is due to the straightforward rating scale in combination with the easy-to-understand academic and behavior items. This makes the scoring time relatively short. An entire class (of approximately 25 students) can be screened in about 30 minutes.

Another strength of the SSiS-PSG is that it combines academic and social skill items, whereas most screeners only include behavioral and social skill items. Schools that implement a CI3T model of prevention may prefer a screener like the SSiS-PSG because it includes an academic component. This may reduce the need for additional measures and can streamline data collection and analysis.

The items in each of the domains are based on observable classroom skills. This is important because these are skills directly related to teachers' expectations. For example, the definition of reading achievement in the elementary measure defines adequate performance (level 4) as

> Good attending behaviors and appropriate participation in grade-level reading activities; an adequate number and variety of grade-level reading skills; and very good grade-level reading comprehension skills in a variety of situations. A teacher will readily know which students do not meet this criterion and can easily identify the students' risk status as it is based on their every day academic performance. (Pearson Education, 2007)

The same is true for the definition of prosocial behaviors (level 4): "a general competence when communication or cooperating with others; adequate skills to initiate and sustain conversations/interactions with others; and adequate self-control and/or an appropriate level of concern for others" (Pearson Education, 2007). This definition consists of behaviors teachers would expect their students to demonstrate, and teachers will easily know whether students are using them.

Finally, because the screener is part of the Social Skills Improvement System, it is linked directly to a curriculum (e.g., SSiS-IG) that can provide either secondary or tertiary interventions for students who need support beyond the primary prevention plan (SSiS-CIP lessons). This offers school sites a resource for designing more intensive social skills supports. In addition, the SSiS-RS includes an in-depth diagnostic measure that can be used for further assessment. As we mentioned at the onset of this chapter, the SSiS family of tools is a multicomponent package that offers a universal screener (SSiS-PSG), a primary prevention program (SSiS-CIP), and a diagnostic assessment for students who are screened at risk (SSiS-RS), which are all linked to a secondary intervention program: the SSiS-IG. All components work together, and the lesson plan format is the same for both the SSiS-CIP and the SSiS-IG. This cohesive assessment and programming reduces the need for schools and school systems to evaluate multiple elements to find the answer to their assessment and instructional needs.

Considerations

The primary consideration with the SSiS-PSG is that it is a new instrument, so there is a lack of peer-reviewed studies examining its validity and reliability. Although the authors have conducted reliability and validity tests, it is important that measures be subjected to independent research studies to fully examine their psychometric properties. We are confident this inquiry is underway, and we look forward to you reading the results of these future studies as they become available following the peer-review process.

Second, a small disadvantage associated with the screener is that a class of more than 25 students requires a second form. This is slightly cumbersome as well as slightly more expensive than measures that allow you to screen an entire class regardless of its size.

Finally, although this system offers one-stop shopping for assessment and intervention, the cost may be prohibitive for some schools. The screening tool (SSiS-PSG) requires a new form each time a class is rated. Duplicating the forms is not offered as an option; therefore, the cost is ongoing even after the initial purchase.

The next section includes two illustrations of how to use the PSG at the elementary and middle school levels. The examples demonstrate how to monitor overall progress in decreasing student risk status as well as identifying and supporting students who require additional assistance.

Illustrations

An Illustration Identifying Students at Risk for Both Behavioral and Academic Issues in a Midsized Elementary School: Harrison Elementary School

Harrison Elementary School (HES) is located in a midsized city in southern California. It had approximately 700 students in kindergarten through grade 6. The demographic makeup of the school is 67% Latino, 20% white, 9% black, 2% Asian or Pacific Islander, and 2% other. The school had a large percentage of English learners (26%). Students with individualized education programs for mild disabilities attend general education classes and a resource class, where they receive extra assistance. There are two special education classrooms for students with moderate disabilities: one for K–3 students and one for grade 4–6 students. Over 70% of students are socioeconomically disadvantaged and receive free and reduced-price lunch.

Building a CI3T Model of Prevention

HES had a primary prevention plan that focused on the expectations Work Hard and Be Kind. Each Fall, teachers introduced the school expectations and encouraged students to follow them. Teachers and staff reinforced students for demonstrating the expectations with Caught Being Good tickets. Students could put their tickets in a box, and each month there was an assembly where tickets were drawn from the box and students won prizes. However, not all teachers participated in the program as it was designed. Nor did the staff make an expectation matrix and teach students what working hard and being kind looked like in various school settings. Some teachers used other reinforcement methods such as sticker charts, Popsicle sticks, and marbles in a jar. Because this was a schoolwide plan, the principal felt strongly that only one system should be used by the whole school. She worked with teachers to transition them to the schoolwide system.

Planning for Supports

Although HES had a primary plan in place, they did not regularly analyze any data to measure its effectiveness. When the principal noticed an increase in office discipline referrals (ODRs), she asked the grade-level team leaders to work with her on the problem. The school systematically collected ODRs and number of suspensions, so the team leaders examined these data from the past 3 years. They created a graph that showed an increase in ODRs and suspensions for students who refused to complete class work and homework. This made the principal question whether all teachers were implementing the primary plan. She shared her concerns with the staff, who agreed they needed to work together to reduce the behavior issues that had become prominent over the past few years. The team leaders worked with the principal during the Summer to reconsider the primary plan. They realized their approach to improving behavior had been piecemeal and ineffective. They looked at all the components of the SSiS and decided that implementing all four parts would streamline the process for putting together a CI3T model of prevention. Using the SSiS-CIP as the social skills component of their primary prevention plan would provide the consistency across the school that was currently lacking. The SSiS-PSG would be used to evaluate whether the social skills curriculum was making a difference and to identify at-risk students. The SSiS-RS (teacher version) would be used with the SSiS-IG to provide secondary, small-group interventions for students at risk. The principal and team leaders also created an expectation matrix for operationalizing the school rules of Work Hard and Be Kind in all areas of the school and on the bus. Teachers were asked to give up all other reinforcement systems and use only the Caught Being Good tickets to reinforce students for demonstrating the school rules or the new social skills.

Measures

The SSiS-PSG (elementary) was an instrument that could quickly identify students who were at risk because of dual deficits in academics and social skills. The staff believed this was a good tool for them because they wanted to use more than one data source to identify students at risk for academic failure. They decided they would use the SSiS-PSG in conjunction with the districtwide assessments in language arts and mathematics that were administered three times a year. The first district measure was given in late October, so the principal reserved an October faculty meeting for completing the SSiS-PSG. Because HES had adopted all parts of the SSiS, they could also look at the data from the SSiS-RS and SSiS-PSG to see whether students in Tier 2 supports were making progress. The principal decided to collect ODR and suspension data on a regular basis. This provided several data sources that would help create a detailed picture of student performance.

How Were Screening Data Used to Make Decisions about Targeted Supports?

During the last faculty meeting in October, the kindergarten team leader walked the staff through each step of the screening process with the SSiS-PSG. Teachers were given 30 minutes to complete the screener. When finished, the teachers turned in their class booklet to another team leader, who checked them for accuracy (e.g., all students rated on each domain and all students' names entered in the boxes on the last page). The team leaders, who had agreed to take responsibility for the schoolwide plan, prepared a presentation for the next faculty meeting, where they shared students' risk status according to the SSiS-PSG and the districtwide assessments in language arts and mathematics. First, they looked at the results from the PSG. Figure 7.2 shows the number of students in each risk category in reading, mathematics, prosocial behavior, or motivation to learn who placed in the green, yellow, and red band levels. HES had the best profile in reading: 610 students were at or exceeded average performance (scored a 4 or 5), 70 were at moderate risk (scored a 2 or 3), and 20 were in the high-risk category (scored a 1). Performance in mathematics was not quite as strong, with only 525 students reaching or exceeding average performance. HES teachers were especially interested in the numbers of students at risk in the prosocial behavior and motivation to learn categories. Although 200 students were at either moderate or high risk for motivation to learn, the total number of students at risk for prosocial behavior was slightly lower (187), indicating that students may not be motivated but this does not necessarily mean they demonstrate problem behaviors in the classroom. However, risk status in this category is likely to impact both students' behavior and academic achievement. The SSiS-PSG provided an easy way to quantify and view risk status across the school and across several areas. Next, the staff looked at the number of students who were below proficiency on the mathematics portion of the district assessment *and* had high- or moderate-risk status for mathematics on the SSiS-PSG. These students were referred to Homework Club, where they could receive free help from math tutors after school. All students who earned a 1 (high risk) on the prosocial domain of the SSiS-PSG were referred for social skills intervention. In addition to looking at subsequent administrations of the SSiS-PSG, the school site would also have the ODR and suspension numbers to use in assessing whether the interventions were working.

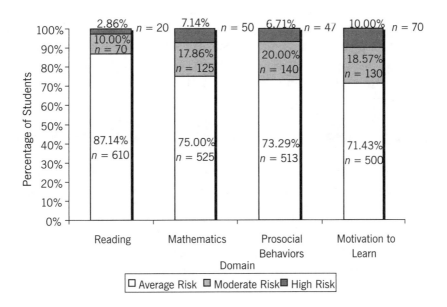

FIGURE 7.2. HES SSiS-PSG data: for all domains.

What Did the Tier 2 Interventions Look Like?

Students who were experiencing academic failure attended the after-school Homework Club. The team leaders, with faculty input, created Homework Club to be a Tier 2 support. Before students began the intervention, teachers held conferences with parents to communicate their concerns and describe how Homework Club would work. It was structured to support both behavior and academics. To support behavior, the Homework Club teachers decided to emphasize the school's positive behavior support plan, which included clear expectations and reinforcing students when they demonstrated them. For example, the teachers taught students to come to Homework Club with their assignments and the materials they would need to complete them. Students were reinforced with a Caught Being Good ticket and behavior-specific praise: "Here is a ticket, Tyler. I noticed you came to Homework Club ready to work." Similarly, teachers provided extra instruction that helped students complete their homework or review concepts introduced in class. There was a focus on math homework and skills because of the high number of students at risk in that area. Teachers taught students to set goals for completing homework with better accuracy and to self-graph their progress.

Students at high risk in the prosocial domain of the SSiS-PSG were invited to attend a social skills group. This was provided in small groups twice a week for 45 minutes after lunch. Teachers of the students who attended social skills groups were asked to complete the SSiS-RS for each student after obtaining parent consent. This helped determine which skills would be taught. After 10 sessions, students were evaluated again on the SSiS-RS and either exited the program or were invited to attend another round of sessions.

HES staff planned to screen students again before the Spring break. They would use the district assessment and another administration of the SSiS-PSG to make decisions about students who attended Homework Club. They also planned to look at their ODR and suspension rates and the SSiS-PSG scores on the prosocial domain to monitor changes in those patterns. HES staff was confident that their improved focus on an integrated, schoolwide approach to academic and behavior support would result in better student outcomes.

Summary

HES serves as an example of how a school-site leadership team used information from the screening data to made decisions regarding targeted supports. They then focused their initial efforts on secondary (Tier 2) interventions.

An Illustration Using Screening Data to Determine Secondary Academic and Behavioral Support Needs in an Urban Middle School: Jamison Middle School

Jamison Middle School (JMS) is an urban school on the edge of a major southwestern U.S. city. JMS had 880 students in sixth through eighth grade. The majority of students were Hispanic (64%), and 90% indicated that Spanish was their home language; 25% of JMS students received services for English learners. The school offered special education classes in all academic areas as well as self-contained programs for students served under the emotional disturbance (Individuals with Disabilities Education Improvement Act, 2004) category and a life skills program for students with multiple learning and behavioral needs eligible under a variety of special education categories. The economic disadvantage rate was 75%. After several years of high suspension rates, low attendance rates, and poor test scores, the district installed a new principal at the school and replaced the majority of the faculty and staff. Since that time, attendance, suspension rates, and test scores have steadily improved. JMS students met or exceeded the standard on most areas of the state achievement assessment; however, reading achievement was below the state average in all grades.

Starting a Primary Prevention Model

JMS took a proactive stance after the change in staff. They began by focusing on math and writing (districtwide goal for that year). The principal made sure teachers had all necessary curriculum materials (e.g., textbooks, teachers' guides with resource materials, and supplies, such as paper, calculators, access to computers, and so on). Professional development on teaching strategies was a high priority for the new principal, who supported teachers to attend trainings, planned faculty meetings where they could share the new ideas with the entire faculty and staff, and organized in-district opportunities. The principal also created a leadership team that included a special educator, a counselor, one teacher each from the sixth, seventh, and eighth grades, and himself. The team's charge was to design and implement a primary prevention model. The leadership team started the work of creating a schoolwide behavior plan and investigated how the school site could use data to examine their effectiveness in supporting students' behavioral and academic skills. They also were looking at various character programs that would fit with the school goals of developing students' ability to work with effectively with others. They felt this would enhance students' problem-solving skills as well as improve the school climate.

ACADEMIC COMPONENT

Although JMS students had made gains in reading and math achievement, teachers were concerned with the large number of students who did not complete homework, which appeared to be a significant factor in course failures. The leadership team drew up plans for a Homework Tutoring Club (HTC). The language arts and math department chairs assumed responsibility for HTC, and it was staffed with teachers as well as volunteers from the local university. The school used Title 1 funding to provide a nutritious snack and transportation home for students. The club was offered Mondays through Thursdays. Parents of the students invited to participate were sent letters (in their home language) explaining the goals of HTC.

BEHAVIORAL COMPONENT

The leadership team also tackled behavior concerns teachers had raised in staff meetings. Teachers said they were spending too much time addressing minor behaviors such as not being prepared for class, disrespect toward teachers and students, and tardiness to class. A major problem for the staff was that teachers had different expectations for students, different approaches to discipline, and different tolerances for student behavior. The leadership team, with staff input, established three schoolwide expectations: Compassion, Justice, and Diligence. They developed an expectation matrix to use when teaching students what these ideals looked like in everyday life on their campus. All mathematics teachers agreed to devote one class period to teaching the expectations and reviewing the expectation matrix. All students had a math class, so every student would receive the schoolwide information. Any students who were absent that day would attend a special session led by the eighth-grade counselor.

Measures

JMS teachers wanted to be able to look at student behavior and academic performance from a schoolwide perspective (see Table 7.3 for their assessment schedule). This would let them see the progress they were making with their new initiatives. This was important to the staff because they were committed to the positive changes they had already brought about. Evaluating student performance would help staff track their success and would also provide an opportunity to make corrections if growth did not occur. Using a screening measure also fit with their prevention goal: finding students who need additional supports early. After reviewing several available tools, the leadership team chose the SSiS-PSG because it involved minimal screening time (30 minutes to screen an entire class) and provided them with academic as well as prosocial behavior information. The faculty and staff were also very interested in the motivation to learn domain because they believed student motivation was a critical element of academic success. This was the only screener they had seen that would let them measure this construct. Overall, the SSIS-PSG was the best fit for their purposes and resources.

The leadership team decided to administer the SSiS-PSG three times during the course of the school year to evaluate the effectiveness of the primary plan and their secondary supports. They also intended to use the screening data to establish a baseline for the overall level of student risk. That information would guide the development of any additional secondary supports. The SSiS-PSG would be used with other school data sources (number of students who meet and exceed state achievement assessment standards, ODR data, and suspension data) to make decisions about which students would benefit from each secondary support they designed.

With this in mind, the leadership team established three goals for the upcoming school year: (1) implement a systematic method for measuring the overall level of students' academic and behavioral risk, (2) identify students in need of additional supports, and (3) establish consistency in the way behavioral infractions were reported.

TABLE 7.3. JMS Assessment Schedule

	Aug	Sept	Oct	Nov	Dec	Jan	Feb	Mar	Apr	May
		Quarter 1			Quarter 2			Quarter 3		Quarter 4
School demographics										
Student demographics		×			×		×			×
Academic measures										
California's Standardized Testing and Reporting Program							×			
AIMSweb reading—curriculum-based measurement (Pearson Education, 2008)		×			×					×
AIMSweb MAZE—curriculum-based measurement (Pearson Education, 2008)		×			×					×
AIMSweb math-computation (Pearson Education, 2008)		×			×					×
Behavior measures										
SSiS-PSG (Elliott & Gresham, 2007b)		×			×					×
ODRs		×			×		×			×
Suspensions (out of school)		×			×		×			×
Attendance: tardies/absences		×			×		×			×
Referrals										
Special education		×			×		×			×
Program measures										
Social validity (Primary Intervention Rating Scale: Lane, Kalberg, Bruhn, et al., 2009; Lane, Robertson, et al., 2002)		×					×			
Treatment integrity: School-wide Evaluation Tool (Sugai, Lewis-Palmer, Todd, & Horner, 2001)							×			

Note. From Lane, Kalberg, and Menzies (2009, Table 5.2, p. 106). Copyright 2009 by The Guilford Press. Adapted by permission.

To address the final goal, the leadership team designed an ODR form printed with operationally defined behaviors and a system for collecting this information so that the team could review it regularly.

What Is the Current Level of Risk at JMS?

The SSiS-PSG was purchased and administration procedures were reviewed by the leadership team. The principal scheduled time during the first professional development day for language arts and math teachers to fill out the screeners. The professional development day was held in early November, so teachers had adequate time to inter-act with their students and would be able to rate them on all the items. The language arts teachers completed the reading and prosocial behaviors items, and the math teachers completed the mathematics and motivation to learn items. Once the screener was finished (listed all students on the screener, rated each student in reading skills, math skills, motivation to learn, and prosocial behaviors), the teachers listed students rated a 1 (in the red band, at high risk) in the designated box on the last page and students rated a 2 or 3 (in the yellow band, at moderate risk) in the remaining box. The forms were collected by the school's leadership team to create a graph of the overall level of risk at the first screening (see Figure 7.3).

Fall screening data provided evidence that they were making good progress with the changes they had already put into place (the strong core curriculum for primary math instruction and the HTC addressing math skills). The first bars on the graph show the lower risk in math compared with the other domains. A large percentage of students (84.66%) had average or above-average performance in mathematics. The second group of bars confirmed teachers' concerns that reading was an area where students needed additional support. Only 72.73% had average or above-average per-formance. Teachers were encouraged that nearly 80% of students (79.66%) were in the average or above-average category for prosocial behavior. The behavior problems teachers experienced gave the impression that many more students were having dif-ficulties; however, the screening data show that it was a smaller group of students than they had believed. Finally, they were happily surprised to find that 81.02% of students were in the average or above-average category in the motivation to learn domain. The staff hoped that the focus on the expectations of Compassion, Justice,

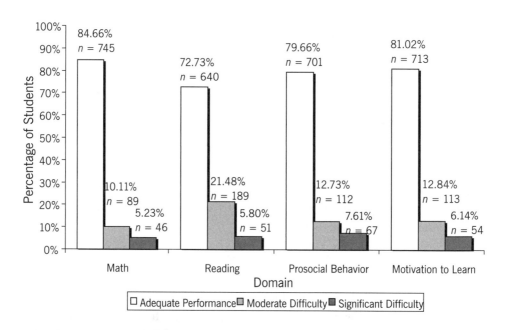

FIGURE 7.3. JMS SSiS-PSG data; $N = 880$.

and Diligence was creating a positive school climate that encouraged learning and mutual respect.

How Can This Information Be Used to Support Students and Teachers?

The data-sharing faculty meeting generated several new ideas. Although the leadership team was encouraged that the number of students at risk on prosocial behavior was lower than they had anticipated, it was still higher than they liked. They felt this should be addressed as primary prevention, so the SSiS-CIP was adopted as part of their homeroom program. Teachers were also interested in developing additional Tier 2 supports using the SSiS-IG. Over the course of the school year, the leadership team looked for new supports that could be sustained with their current resources, but would offer another option for addressing behavior concerns. A secondary supports grid (see Table 7.4) details what was already available at the school site. A faculty

TABLE 7.4. JMS Intervention Grid				
Support	Description	Schoolwide data: Entry criteria	Data to monitor progress	Exit criteria
Homework Tutoring Club	Students come to school library after dismissal bell, check in with two club monitors, and have a snack. After 20 minutes. the tutors arrive and work with individual students or small groups (≤ 3) on homework and unfinished class work—focus on math and language arts After 1 hour of tutoring, students have a 15-minute supervised recess and then board the buses for home	1. State achievement test—score of basic or below basic (not meeting the minimum criteria) on math or writing *and* 2. Parent permission to attend 3. Rated 1 on SSiS-PSG for math skills	1. Monitor math and language arts grades on progress reports and report cards 2. SSiS-PSG for math skills and motivation to learn	1. End-of-year state assessment scores meeting or exceeding criteria 2. Rated 4 or higher on SSiS-PSG for math skills and motivation to learn
Check-in/ check-out	Students are assigned to mentors (participating teachers and staff) Mentors greet students in the morning, provide a monitoring sheet for the day, and help them set expectations for the day At the end of the day students meet with their mentor to review the day's progress; mentor helps students make plans for any needed changes the next day (e.g., work completion, behavior, accuracy, preparedness)	Priority of criteria until all mentors were matched: 1. Rated a 1 on SSiS-PSG for motivation to learn *and* either math or reading skills 2. Rated 1 on SSiS-PSG for motivation to learn 3. Rated a 2 or 3 on SSiS-PSG for motivation to learn	1. SSiS-PSG for motivation to learn 2. Progress reports and report cards	1. Rated a 4 or 5 on SSiS-PSG for motivation to learn *or* 2. Grades above 80% in all academic areas with 85% of assignments completed on time

Note. From Lane, Kalberg, and Menzies (2009, Table 6.2, pp. 132–133). Copyright 2009 by The Guilford Press. Adapted by permission.

member suggested they work on designing a Check-In/Check-Out program (Crone et al., 2004). They thought the low-cost program was feasible, so it was added to their Tier 2 supports. The screening data made it possible to take a look at overall student performance in academics and behavior. It created a baseline performance that JMS teachers can use for comparison over the course of the current year as well as across future academic years.

Summary

JMS serves as an example of how a school-site leadership team sought used school-wide data to examine the overall level of risk at their school. They then used this information to support both students and teachers to better meet their respective needs by building in evidence-based practices in the Tier 2 supports.

Summary

This chapter introduced the SSiS-PSG, a screener with preschool, elementary, and secondary versions. The PSGs are part of a multicomponent program that includes a universal screener, a primary social skills curriculum, a diagnostic assessment, and an intervention curriculum. The reliability and validity of the SSiS-PSGs were examined, and the strengths and considerations associated with preparation, administration, scoring, and interpreting the findings of the measure were discussed. The chapter closed with illustrations of how to use the SSiS-PSGs in elementary and middle school settings to plan secondary and tertiary supports as well as to identify students with combined academic and behavioral risk.

In the next chapter, we offer some brief suggestions to assist you as you select a screening tool and begin this process. We provide information on how to select a screening tool that is psychometrically sound, socially valid, and responsive to the school's culture, needs, and values characteristic of their given context (e.g., an urban elementary school interested in identifying students with internalizing behavior patterns). We included a set of self-assessment questions to be used by school-site leadership teams to guide the decision-making process.

CHAPTER 8

Getting Started

A Few Concluding Thoughts to Guide the Decision-Making Process

First, we congratulate you on getting started! Making the decision to conduct behavior screenings is an excellent one, especially when we think about the fact that the general education teacher "is the primary link between a student who is in trouble and the necessary school-based evaluation and intervention services" (Walker & Severson, 1992, p. 1). In essence, the teacher is the gatekeeper to all types of support: academically, socially, and behaviorally.

The next step is to make an informed decision about which screening tool or system to select for implementation at your school or district. We hope you have found the contents of this book useful and that it has given you a thorough look at each potential screening tool. At this time, we think it might be helpful for you to consider the following questions to guide your decision-making process:

1. What grade (or age) levels are you working with? Are you working with preschool, elementary, middle, or high school students?
2. What types of concerns are you interested in identifying? Antisocial behavior? Internalizing or externalizing behavior patterns? Academic or motivational issues as well as behavioral concerns?
3. Who do you want to do the ratings? Are you interested in having teachers do the ratings? Would you also like to involve parents and students?
4. How much money, if any, do you have to spend? Are you interested in only those screening tools that are free of charge? Or do you have a more extensive budget?
5. How much time can you devote to the screening process? Do you have 10–15 minutes to rate an entire class? Or could you devote an hour of time for each administration?

6. Do you want to screen using paper-and-pencil or electronic techniques? Do you have access to computers? Do you have money for copying costs to prepare hard copies? What resources are available at your site to prepare, complete, score, and interpret?
7. Are you looking for a screening tool that provides information on what to do for students who have concerns? Do you want a comprehensive screening system that includes intervention materials?
8. What are your district and state policies surrounding screenings?

Clearly, there are a number of questions to consider when establishing screening practices and selecting a screening tool. To guide your decision-making process, we encourage you to review the information presented in Table 8.1. One option is for your school-site or district-site leadership team to make a comparable table that includes information on the key questions driving your own decision-making process. Then you can insert the answers to your questions for each screening tool you are considering by obtaining the information from the appropriate chapters. This table could be used in the same way a pro–con chart is used to inform other important decisions (e.g., which job to choose, which house to buy). For example, if you have no additional funds and your main focus is finding students with multiple facets of behavioral challenges, your team might select the Strengths and Difficulties Questionnaire. However, if funds are readily available and your main interest is looking for students with academic and social concerns, and you would like a comprehensive social skills intervention program, you might select the Social Skills Improvement System: Performance Screening Guide. If you have no funds available, very limited resources for scoring and preparing measures, just a few minutes to spare, and are primarily interested in identifying students with antisocial behavior patterns, you might select the Student Risk Screening Scale. In our work with schools, many school-site leadership teams elect to implement two screening tools in the first year. This allows teachers time to explore two tools so they can consider the cost–benefit ratio for each measure before they make a decision on which one to select as part of their comprehensive, integrated, three-tiered model of prevention.

This is an important decision and one we think teams should make carefully. In this next section, we offer a few concluding thoughts to consider as you move forward.

Concluding Thoughts

As we close this chapter, we have a few recommendations as you move toward selecting and implementing a systematic behavior screening tool for use within (or outside of) a three-tiered model of prevention: (1) build people's expertise, (2) develop the structures to sustain and improve practice, and (3) conduct screenings in a responsible fashion (Lane, Oakes, Menzies, & Altmann, 2011).

TABLE 8.1. Questions to Consider When Selecting a Behavior Screening Tool or System						
Questions to consider	Systematic Screening for Behavior Disorders (SSBD; Walker, & Severson, 1992)	Early Screening Project: A Proven Child Find Process (ESP; Walker, Severson, & Feil, 1995)	Student Risk Screening Scale (SRSS; Drummond, 1994)	Strengths and Difficulties Questionnaire (SDQ; Goodman, 1997)	BASC™-2 Behavioral and Emotional Screening System (BASC-2 BESS; Kamphaus & Reynolds, 2007b)	Social Skills Improvement System: Performance Screening Guide (SSiS-PSG; Elliott & Gresham, 2007b)
What grade level/student age was this measure designed for?	K–6	Preschool–K (ages 3–5 years)	K–6, with additional evidence to support use in 7–12	Preschool–12	Preschool–12	Preschool–12
What types of concerns does this measure detect?	Internalizing problems Externalizing problems	Internalizing problems Externalizing problems	Antisocial	Total difficulties: emotional symptoms, hyperactivity, conduct disorders, peer problems, prosocial behavior	Externalizing problems Internalizing problems School problems Adaptive skills	Prosocial behavior Motivation to learn Reading skills Math skills
Who may complete this tool?	Teachers	Teachers	Teachers	Teachers Parents Students (ages 11–17)	Teachers Parents	Teachers
Is this a no-cost instrument?	No	No	Yes	Yes	No	No
How much time does this measure take to complete?	Less than 1 hour per class	Less than 1 hour per class	10–15 minutes per class	Less than 1 hour per class	5–10 minutes per student	Approximately 30 minutes per class
Is there an online or computer-based scoring option?	No	No	Yes	Yes	Yes	Yes
Is there an intervention component?	No	No	No	No	Yes	Yes

Recommendation 1: Build People's Expertise

Three-tiered models, such those described previously, offer school-site and district-level teams a feasible, reliable method for preventing the development of concerns and responding efficiently to support students with current concerns (Lane, 2007). Central to these models is the accurate detection of students for whom primary prevention efforts are insufficient. Thus, reliable, valid, and practical systematic screenings of academic and behavioral performance patterns are an essential component of these models.

Because screening is a keystone feature, we strongly recommend resources such as professional development time be allocated to develop all key stakeholders' knowledge of screening practices. Administrators, teachers, support staff, related personnel, and parents must be aware of the benefits and consequences of screening practices. Screening should not be avoided, feared, or ignored. Data from screening tools allow schools an equitable, resource-efficient method of detecting students who require secondary (Tier 2) or tertiary (Tier 3) supports. Resources should be devoted to building people's understanding of the value, science, and mechanics of screening. Such topics would ideally include information on how to select, prepare, administer, score, and interpret findings from academic and screening tools. The ultimate goal is to implement evidence-based practices for behavioral support when the gap between current and desired levels of performance is most narrow (Lane, Oakes, & Menzies, 2010).

Recommendation 2: Develop the Structures to Sustain and Improve Practice

As former teachers, we are well aware of the enormous task demands facing today's administrators, teachers, and support staff. We know it is important to protect teachers' time and energy. Because we view systematic screening as absolutely germane to supporting teachers and students, and we recognize that time and effort are necessary to institutionalize screening practices, we feel strongly that time must be allocated to develop the structures necessary to sustain and improve screening procedures.

We recommend that time be allocated during the traditional school day, either during regularly scheduled faculty meetings or grade-level or department meetings, to prepare, administer, score, and interpret screening data (Lane, Kalberg, & Menzies, 2009). While the screening tools should be completed independently, we do recommend that teachers work with other school-site personnel (e.g., other teachers, literacy specialists, behavior specialists, school psychologists, mental health professionals) to attend to other facets of screening. For example, we recommend that teams of professionals be involved in scoring, analyzing data, selecting appropriate interventions for consideration, monitoring student responsiveness to the extra supports provided, and determining when supplemental supports should be concluded or modified.

Also, because the knowledge base changes with new research findings, it is important for administrators to provide ongoing professional development for school-site personnel as well as parents. Stakeholders need access to timely information so they can stay current with evidence-based practices. It is important that each school's three-tiered model of prevention be reevaluated, modified, and updated before each new academic year on new research findings, feedback from stakeholders, and student performance outcomes during the previous academic year. Revision efforts require time and money. However, we emphasize that a school or district's model should not be revised during an academic year. If plans are changed during a school year, it is not possible to draw accurate conclusions about program outcomes.

Recommendation 3: Conduct Screenings in a Responsible Fashion

Finally, screening carries with it huge responsibilities. Students identified as needing more support must be afforded it. It is essential school-site leadership teams have the systems and structures in place to support students identified with additional needs. Think of this from a medical perspective: It would be completely unacceptable for a physician to fail to treat early stages of a given disease (e.g., skin cancer). Similarly, it would be unprofessional for school-site leadership to fail to offer additional support to a student with below-average reading skills or interfering internalizing behaviors patterns (Lane, Oakes, & Menzies, 2010).

Throughout each of the illustrations offered in this book, we provided examples of how schools can organize existing resources using data from academic and behavior screening tools to connect students to appropriate resources. We also explained how to make decisions as to which evidence-based practices may be added to existing resources for students with common areas of concern. Each chapter offers examples of secondary and tertiary intervention support grids that provide a framework for organizing these supplemental programs and practices.

Finally, and perhaps most important, before you screen, be certain to review your federal, state, and local guidelines for determining what is allowed in terms of systematic screenings. You may want to read Individuals with Disabilities Education Improvement Act regulations Section D 300.301 through 300.311 (Assistance to States for the Education of Children with Disabilities and Preschool Grants for Children with Disabilities, 2006) and the Protection of Pupil Rights Amendment of 1978 (Kamphaus & Reynolds, 2007a, 2007b) to inform your decisions regarding systematic screenings. Also, be advised that guidelines are not consistent across states. Some states do not require parental consent for academic and behavioral screenings if they are conducted as part of regular school practices. Other states require parental consent before screenings are conducted. Some states require active consent, meaning that parents must return a letter giving their express written permission, whereas other states allow for passive consent. In this case, a letter would be sent home asking parents to return the form if they *do not* want their child to participate in the screening process. If secondary (Tier 2) or tertiary (Tier 3) supports are being considered, parents must be informed. It is not acceptable to provide extra support without informing parents and obtaining their permission.

Certainly, there are other issues that warrant attention before embarking on systematic screenings. However, we contend it is particularly important to develop expertise, create the necessary structures to sustain and refine practices, and screen responsibly. Again, we applaud you for your commitment to assisting students in meeting their multiple academic, behavioral, and social needs. We look forward to receiving your feedback and hearing about your successes!

References

Achenbach, T. M. (1991). *Manual for the Child Behavior Checklist/4-18 and 1991 profile.* Burlington: University of Vermont, Department of Psychiatry.

Achenbach, T. M. (1997). *What is normal? What is abnormal?: Developmental perspectives on behavioral and emotional problems.* New York: Cambridge University Press.

Achenbach, T. M., & Edelbrock, C. (1987). *Manual for the Teacher Report Form of the Child Behavior Checklist.* Burlington: Queen City Printers.

Achenbach, T. M., & Rescorla, L. A. (2000). *Manual for the ASEBA preschool forms and profiles.* Burlington: University of Vermont, Research Center for Children, Youth and Families.

Adams, J. W., & Snowling, M. J. (2001). Executive function and reading impairments in children reported by their teachers as "hyperactive." *British Journal of Developmental Psychology, 19,* 293–306.

Adams, M. J., Bereiter, C., McKeough, A., Case, R., Roit, M., Hirschberg, J., et al. (2002). *Open court reading.* Columbus, OH: McGraw-Hill.

Altmann, S. A. (2010). *Project Support and Include: The additive benefits of self-monitoring on students' reading acquisition.* Unpublished master's thesis, Vanderbilt University, Nashville, TN.

American Educational Research Association, American Psychological Association, & National Council for Measurement in Education. (1999). *Standards for educational and psychological testing.* Washington, DC: American Educational Research Association.

Arizona Department of Education. (2008). *www.ade.state.az.us.*

Barrera, M., Biglan, A., Taylor, T. K., Gunn, B. K., Smolkowski, K., Black, C., et al. (2002). Early elementary school intervention to reduce conduct problems: A randomized trial with Hispanic and non-Hispanic children. *Prevention Science, 3,* 83–94.

Beard, K. Y., & Sugai, G. (2004). First Step to Success: An early intervention for elementary children at risk for antisocial behavior. *Behavioral Disorders, 29,* 396–409.

Becker, A., Woerner, W., Hasselhorn, M., Banashewski, T., & Rothenberger, A. (2004). Validation of the parent and teacher SDQ in a clinical sample. *European Child and Adolescent Psychiatry, 13,* 11–16.

Behar, L., & Stringfield, S. (1974). *Manual for the Preschool Behavior Questionnaire.* Durham, NC: Behar.

Bos, C. S., & Vaughn, S. (2002). Written expression. In C. S. Bos & S. Vaughn (Eds.),

Strategies for teaching students with learning and behavior problems (5th ed., pp. 228–278). Boston: Allyn & Bacon.

Bourdon, K. H., Goodman, R., Rae, D. S., Simpson, G., & Koretz, D. S. (2005). The Strengths and Difficulties Questionnaire: U.S. normative data and psychometric properties. *Journal of the American Academy of Child and Adolescent Psychiatry, 44*, 557–564.

Brookes Publishing. (2009). *Ages and Stages Questionnaire.* Baltimore: Author.

Brophy, J. E., & Good, T. (1986). Teacher behavior and student achievement. In M.C. Wittrock (Ed.), *Handbook of research in teaching* (3rd ed., pp. 328–375). New York: MacMillian.

Brouwers, A., & Tomic, W. (2000) A longitudinal study of teacher burnout and perceived self-efficacy in classroom management. *Teaching and Teacher Education, 16*, 239–253.

Bullis, M., & Walker, H. M. (1994). *Comprehensive school-based systems for troubled youth.* Eugene: University of Oregon, Center on Human Development.

Caldarella, P., Young, E. L., Richardson, M. J., Young, B. J., & Young, K. R. (2008). Validation of the Systematic Screening for Behavior Disorders in middle and junior high school. *Journal of Emotional and Behavioral Disorders, 16*, 105–117.

Caprara, G. V., Barbaranelli, C., Pastorelli, C., Bandura, A., & Zimbardo, P. G. (2000). Prosocial foundations of children's academic achievement. *Psychological Science, 11*, 302–306.

Capron, C., Therond, C., & Duyme, M. (2007). Psychometric properties of the French version of the self-report and teacher Strengths and Difficulties Questionnaire (SDQ). *European Journal of Psychological Assessment, 23*, 79–88.

Carter, E. W., Lane, K. L., Pierson, M. R., & Stang, K. K. (2008). Promoting self-determination for transition-age youth: Views of high school general and special educators. *Exceptional Children, 75*, 55–70.

Chard, D. J., Ketterlin-Geller, L. R., Baker, S. K., Doabler, C., & Apichatabutra, C. (2009). Repeated reading interventions for students with learning disabilities: Status of the evidence. *Exceptional Children, 75*, 263–281.

Cheney, D., Flower, A., & Templeton, T. (2008). Applying response to intervention metrics in the social domain for students at risk of developing emotional or behavioral disorders. *Journal of Special Education, 42*, 108–126.

Coie, J. D., & Dodge, K. A. (1998). Aggression and antisocial behavior. In W. Damon (Series Ed.) & N. Eisenberg (Vol. Ed.), *Handbook of child psychology: Vol. 3. Social, emotional and personality development* (5th ed., pp 779–862). New York: Wiley.

Coie, J. D., Lochman, J. E., Terry, R., & Hyman, C. (1992). Predicting early adolescent disorder from childhood aggression and peer rejection. *Journal of Consulting and Clinical Psychology, 60*, 783–792.

Coie, J. D., Terry, R., Lenox, K., Lochman, J., & Hyman, C. (1995). Childhood peer rejection and aggression as predictors of stable patterns of adolescent disorder. *Development and Psychopathology, 7*, 697–714.

Colvin, G. (2004). *Managing the cycle of acting-out behavior in the classroom.* Eugene, OR: Behavior Associates.

Committee for Children. (2003). *Second Step: A violence prevention curriculum, grades 1–3.* Seattle, WA: Author.

Committee for Children. (2007). *Second Step: Violence prevention.* Seattle, WA: Author.

Conners, C. K. (1989). *Manual for the Conners' Rating Scales.* North Tonawanda, NY: Multi-Health Systems.

Conners, C. K. (1997). *Conners' Rating Scales–Revised*. North Tonawanda, NY: Multi-Health Systems.

Crick, N., Grotpeter, J., & Bigbee, M. (2002). Relationally and physically aggressive children's intent attributions and feelings of distress for relational and instrumental peer provocations. *Child Development, 73*, 1134–1142.

Crone, D. A., Horner, R. H., & Hawken, L. S. (2004). *Responding to problem behavior in schools: The Behavior Education Program*. New York: Guilford Press.

Crone, M. R., Vogels, A. G. C., Hoekstra, F., Treffers, P. D. A., & Reijneveld, S. (2008). A comparison of four scoring methods based on the parent-rated Strengths and Difficulties Questionnaire as used in the Dutch preventive child health care system. *BMC Public Health, 8*, 106–114.

Deschler, D., Schumaker, J., Bulgren, J., Lenz, K., Jantzen, J. E., Adams, G., et al. (2001). Making learning easier: Connecting new knowledge to things students already know. *Exceptional Children, 33*, 82–85.

Dickinson, H., Parkinson, K., McManus, V., Arnaud, C., Beckung, E., Fauconnier, J., et al. (2006). Assessment of data quality in a multi-centre cross-sectional study of participation and quality of life of children with cerebral palsy. *BMC Public Health, 6*, 273.

Diken, I. H., & Rutherford, R. B. (2005). First Step to Success early intervention program: A study of effectiveness with Native-American children. *Education and Treatment of Children, 28*, 444–465.

Dinwiddie, R. (n.d.). *Students taking a right stand*. Nashville, TN: Center for Youth Issues. Retrieved from *www.starsnashville.org*.

DiStefano, C. A., & Kamphaus, R. W. (2007). Development and validation of a behavioral screener for preschool-age children. *Journal of Emotional and Behavioral Disorders, 15*, 93–102.

Dockrell, J. E., & Lindsay, G. (2001). Children with specific speech and language difficulties: The teachers' perspective. *Oxford Review of Education, 27*, 369–394.

Drummond, T. (1994). *The Student Risk Screening Scale (SRSS)*. Grants Pass, OR: Josephine County Mental Health Program.

Drummond, T., Eddy, J. M., & Reid, J. B. (1998a). *Follow-up study #3: Risk screening scale: Prediction of negative outcomes by 10th grade from 2nd grade screening*. Unpublished technical report, Oregon Social Learning Center, Eugene.

Drummond, T., Eddy, J. M., & Reid, J. B. (1998b). *Follow-up study #4: Risk screening scale: Prediction of negative outcomes in two longitudinal samples*. Unpublished technical report, Oregon Social Learning Center, Eugene.

Drummond, T., Eddy, J. M., Reid, J. B., & Bank, L. (1994, November). *The Student Risk Screening Scale: A brief teacher screening instrument for conduct disorder*. Paper presented at the Fourth Annual Prevention Conference, Washington, DC.

Dunn, L. M., & Dunn, L. M. (1997). *Examiner's manual for the PVVT-III, Peabody Picture Vocabulary Test, third edition*. Circle Pines, MN: American Guidance Service.

Dunn, L. M., & Dunn, D. M. (2007). *Peabody Picture Vocabulary Test* (4th ed.). San Antonio, TX: Pearson.

DuPaul, G., McGoey, K. E., Eckert, T. L., & Van Brakle, J. (2001). Preschool children with attention deficit/hyperactivity disorder: Impairments in behavioral, social, and school functioning. *Journal of American Academic and Child Psychiatry, 40*, 508–515.

Elliott, S. N., & Gresham, F. M. (1991). *Social skills intervention guide: Practical strategies for social skills training*. Circle Pines, MN: American Guidance Service.

Elliott, S. N., & Gresham, F. M. (2007a). *Social Skills Improvement System: Classwide Intervention Program*. Bloomington, MN: Pearson Assessments.

Elliott, S. N., & Gresham, F. M. (2007b). *Social Skills Improvement System: Performance Screening Guides*. Bloomington, MN: Pearson Assessments.

Elliott, S. N., & Gresham, F. M. (2008a). *Social Skills Improvement System (SSIS): Intervention Guide*. Bloomington, MN: Pearson Assessments.

Elliott, S. N., & Gresham, F. M. (2008b). *The SSIS ASSIST: Scoring, interpretation, and report writing program*. Bloomington, MN: Pearson Assessments.

Ennis, R. P., Lane, K. L., & Oakes, W. P. (in press). Score reliability and validity of the Student Risk Screening Scale: A psychometrically sound, feasible tool for use in urban elementary schools. *Journal of Emotional and Behavioral Disorders*.

Epstein, M., Atkins, M., Cullinan, D., Kutash, K., & Weaver, R. (2008). *Reducing behavior problems in the elementary school classroom* (NCEE 2008-012). Washington, DC: National Center for Education Evaluation and Regional Assistance, Institute of Education Sciences, U.S. Department of Education. Retrieved from *ies.ed.gov/ncee/wwc/publications/practiceguides/behavior_pg_092308.pdf*.

Epstein, M. H., & Cullinan, D. (1998). *Scale for assessing emotional disturbance*. Austin, TX: Pro-Ed.

Epstein, M.H., Nordness, P.D., Cullinan, D., & Hertzog, M. (2002). Scale for Assessing Emotional Disturbance: Long-term test–retest reliability and convergent validity with kindergarten and first-grade students. *Remedial and Special Education, 23*, 141–148.

Epstein, M. H., Nordness, P. D., Nelson, J. R., & Hertzog, M. (2002). Convergent validity of the Behavioral and Emotional Rating Scale with primary grade-level students. *Topics in Early Childhood Special Education, 22*, 114–121.

Epstein, M. H., & Sharma, J. M. (1998). *Behavioral and Emotional Rating Scale: A strength-based approach to assessment*. Austin, TX: Pro-Ed.

Epstein, M. H., & Walker, H. M. (2002). Special education: Best practices and First Step to Success. In B. J. Burns & K. Hoagwood (Eds.), *Community treatment for youth: Evidence-based interventions for severe emotional and behavioral disorders* (pp. 179–197). New York: Oxford University Press.

Feil, E. G., & Becker, W. C. (1993). Investigation of a multiple-gated screening system for preschool behavior problems. *Behavioral Disorders, 19*, 44–53.

Feil, E. G., Severson, H. H., & Walker, H. M. (1995). Identification of critical factors in the assessment of preschool behavior problems. *Education and Treatment of Children, 18*, 261–271.

Feil, E. G., Severson, H. H., & Walker, H. M. (1998). Screening for emotional and behavior delays: The Early Screening Project. *Journal of Early Intervention, 21*, 252–266.

Feil, E. G., Walker, H. G., Severson, H. H., & Ball, A. (2000). Proactive screening for emotional/behavioral concerns in Head Start preschools: Promising practices and challenges in applied research. *Behavioral Disorders, 26*, 13–25.

Feil, E. G., Walker, H. M., Severson, H. H., Golly, A., Seeley, J. R., & Small, J. W. (2009). Using positive behavior support procedures in Head Start classrooms to improve school readiness: A group training and behavioral coaching model. *National Institute of Health Dialog, 12*, 88–103.

Flay, B. R., Allred, C. G., & Ordway, N. (2001). Effects of the Positive Action program on achievement and discipline: Two matched-control comparisons. *Prevention Science, 2*, 71–89.

Forrest, D. B. (2000). *Character under construction*. Chapin, SC: YouthLight.

Fuchs, D., & Fuchs, L.S. (1998). Researchers and teachers working together to adapt instruction for diverse learners. *Learning Disabilities Research and Practice, 13*, 126–137.

Fuchs, D., & Fuchs, L. S. (2006). Introduction to response to intervention: What, why, and how valid is it? *Reading Research Quarterly, 41*, 93–99.

Fuchs, D., Fuchs, L. S., Mathes, P. G., & Simmons, D. C. (1997). Peer-Assisted Learning Strategies: Making classrooms more responsive to diversity. *American Educational Research Journal, 34*, 174–206.

Fuchs, L.S., Fuchs, D., Hamlett, C.L., Phillips, N.B., Karns, K., & Dutka, S. (1997). Enhancing students' helping behavior during peer-mediated instruction with conceptual mathematical explanations. *Elementary School Journal, 97*, 223–250.

Gale, C. R., Robinson, S. M., Harvey, N. C., Javaid, M. K., Jiang, B., Martyn, C. N., et al. (2008). Maternal vitamin D status during pregnancy and child outcomes. *European Journal of Clinical Nutrition, 62*, 68–77.

Gardner, F., Johnson, A., Yudkin, P., Bowler, U., Hockley, C., Mutch, L., et al. (2004). Behavioral and emotional adjustment of teenagers in mainstream school who were born before 29 weeks' gestation. *Pediatric, 114*, 676–682.

Golly, A.M., Sprague, J., Walker, H., Beard, K., & Gorham, G. (2000). The First Step to Success program: An analysis of outcomes with identical twins across multiple baselines. *Behavioral Disorders, 25*, 170–182.

Golly, A. M., Stiller, B., & Walker, H. M. (1998). First Step to Success: Replication and social validation of an early intervention program. *Journal of Emotional and Behavior Disorders, 6*, 243–250.

Golombok, S., MacCallum, F., & Goodman, E. (2001). The "test-tube" generation: Parent-child relationships and the psychological well being of in-vitro fertilization children at adolescence. *Child Development, 72*, 599–608.

Good, R. H., & Kaminski, R. A. (Eds.). (2002). *Dynamic indicators of basic early literacy skills* (6th ed.). Eugene, OR: Institute for the Development of Educational Achievement. Available at *dibels.uoregon.edu*.

Goodman, A., & Goodman, R. (2009). The Strengths and Difficulties Questionnaire as a dimensional measure of child mental health. *Journal of the American Academy of Child and Adolescent Psychiatry, 48*, 400–403.

Goodman, R. (1997). The Strengths and Difficulties Questionnaire: A research note. *Journal of Child Psychology and Psychiatry, 38*, 581–586.

Goodman, R. (1999). The extended version of the Strengths and Difficulties Questionnaire as a guide to child psychiatric caseness and consequent burden. *Journal of Child Psychology and Psychiatry and Allied Disciplines, 40*, 791–801.

Goodman, R. (2001). Psychometric properties of the Strengths and Difficulties Questionnaire. *Journal of the American Academy of Child and Adolescent Psychiatry, 40*, 1337–1345.

Goodman, R., Ford, T., Corbin, T., & Meltzer, H. (2004). Using the Strengths and Difficulties Questionnaire (SDQ) multi-informant algorithm to screen looked-after children for psychiatric disorders. *European Child and Adolescent Psychiatry, 13*, 25–31.

Goodman, R., Ford, T., Simmons, H., Gatward, R., & Meltzer, H. (2003). Using the Strengths and Difficulties Questionnaire (SDQ) to screen for child psychiatric disorders in a community sample. *International Review of Psychiatry, 15*, 166–172.

Goodman, R., Renfrew, D., & Mullick, M. (2000). Predicting type of psychiatric disorder from Strengths and Difficulties Questionnaire (SDQ) scores in child mental health clinics in London and Dhaka. *European Child and Adolescent Psychiatry, 9,* 129–134.

Goodman, R., & Scott, S. (1999). Comparing the Strengths and Difficulties Questionnaire and the Child Behavior Checklist: Is small beautiful? *Journal of Abnormal Child Psychology, 27,* 17–24.

Graham, S., & Harris, K.R. (2005). *Writing better: Teaching writing process and self-regulation to students with learning problems.* Baltimore: Brookes.

Greenbaum, P. E., Dedrick, R. F., Friedman, R. M., Kutash, K., Brown, E. C., Lardierh, S. P., et al. (1996). National Adolescent and Child Treatment Study (NACTS): Outcomes for children with serious emotional and behavioral disturbance. *Journal of Emotional and Behavioral Disorders, 4,* 130–146.

Gresham, F. M. (1989). Assessment of treatment integrity in school consultation and prereferral intervention. *School Psychology Review, 18,* 37–50.

Gresham, F. M. (1990). Best practices in social skills training. In A. Thomas & J. Grimes (Eds.), *Best practices in school psychology* (pp. 181–192). Washington, DC: National Association of School Psychologists.

Gresham, F. M. (2002). Responsiveness to intervention: An alternative approach to learning disabilities. In R. Bradley, L. Danielson, & D. P. Hallahan (Eds.), *Identification of learning disabilities: Research to practice* (pp. 242–258). Mahwah, NJ: Erlbaum.

Gresham, F. M., & Elliott, S. N. (1990). *The Social Skills Rating System.* Circle Pines, MN: American Guidance Service.

Gresham, F. M., & Elliott, S. N. (2008). *Social Skills Improvement System: Rating Scales.* Bloomington, MN: Pearson Assessments.

Gresham, F. M., Lane, K. L., & Lambros, K. M. (2000). Comorbidity of conduct problems and ADHD: Identification of "fledgling psychopaths." *Journal of Emotional and Behavioral Disorders, 8,* 83–93.

Gresham, F. M., Sugai, G., Horner, R. H., Quinn, M. M., & McInerney, M. (1998). *Schoolwide values, discipline, and social skills* (synthesis report for American Institutes of Research and Office of Special Education Programs). Washington, DC: American Institutes of Research and Office of Special Education Programs.

Gunn, B., Feil, E., Seeley, J., Severson, H., & Walker, H. (2006). Promoting school success: Developing social skills and early literacy in Head Start classrooms. *National Institute of Health Dialog, 9,* 1–11.

Gutman, L. M., Sameroff, A. J., & Cole, R. (2003). Academic growth curve trajectories from 1st grade to 12th grade: Effects of multiple social risks and preschool child factors. *Developmental Psychology, 39,* 777–790.

Hammill, D., & Larsen, S. (1996). *Test of Written Language–3.* Austin, TX: Pro-Ed.

Hamre, B. K., & Pianta, R. C. (2001). Early teacher-child relationships and the trajectory of children's school outcomes through eighth grade. *Child Development, 72,* 625–638.

Harris, L. (1991). *The Metropolitan Life Survey of the American Teacher, 1991: The first year. New teachers expectations' and ideals.* New York: Metropolitan Life Insurance Company.

Hasselbring, T. S., & Goin, L. I. (1999). Read 180 [Computer software]. New York: Scholastic.

Hastings, R. P. (2003). Brief report: Behavioral adjustment of siblings of children with autism. *Journal of Autism and Developmental Disorders, 33,* 99–105.

Hatcher, L., & Stepanski, E. J. (1994). *A step-by-step approach to using the SAS system for univariate and multivariate statistics.* Cary, NC: SAS Institute.

Hawes, D. J., & Dadds, M. R. (2004). Australian data and psychometric properties of the Strengths and Difficulties Questionnaire. *Australian and New Zealand Journal of Psychiatry, 38*, 644–651.

Herwig, J. E., Wirtz, M., & Bengel, J. (2004). Depression, partnership, social support, and parenting: Interaction of maternal factors with behavioral problems of the child. *Journal of Affective Disorders, 80*, 199–208.

Hiebert, E. H., & Raphael, T. B. (1998). *Early literacy instruction*. Fort Worth, TX: Harcourt Brace.

Hill, C. R., & Hughes, J. N. (2007). An examination of the convergent and discriminant validity of the Strengths and Difficulties Questionnaire. *School Psychology Quarterly, 22*, 380–406.

Hills, T. W. (1987). *Screening for school entry* (ERIC Identifier ED281607). Urbana, IL: ERIC Clearinghouse on Elementary and Early Childhood Education.

Holt, Rinehart & Winston. (2002). *Holt literature and language arts: Mastering the California standards and core resource package, grade 7*. Austin, TX: Harcourt School.

Hops, H., & Walker, H.M. (1988). *CLASS: Contingencies for Learning Academic and Social Skills*. Seattle, WA: Educational Achievement Systems.

Horner, R. H., & Sugai, G. (2000). School-wide behavior support: An emerging initiative. *Journal of Positive Behavior Interventions, 2*, 231–232.

Individuals with Disabilities Education Improvement Act of 2004, 20 U.S.C. 1400 *et esq.* (Reauthorization of Individuals with Disabilities Act of 1990)

Institute for Global Ethics. (2008). *Building decision skills* (4th ed.). Rockland, ME: Author.

Jamieson, K. H., & Romer, D. (2005). A call to action on adolescent mental health. In D. L. Evans, E. B Foa, R. E. Gur, H. Hendin, C. P. O'Brien, M . E. P., Seligman, et al. (Eds.), *Treating and preventing adolescent mental health disorders: What we know and what we don't know* (pp. 617–624). New York: Oxford University Press.

Jentzsch, C. E., & Merrell, K. W. (1996). An investigation of the construct validity of the Preschool and Kindergarten Behavior Scales. *Assessment for Effective Intervention, 21*, 1–15.

Jones, C., & Slate, J. R. (1990). *Note taking, studying, and test taking: A survival manual for college students*. Unpublished manuscript, Arkansas State University.

Jones, K., Daley, D., Hutchings, J., Bywater, T., & Eames, C. (2007). Efficacy of the Incredible Years basic parent training programme as an early intervention for children with conduct problems and ADHD. *Child Care, Health, and Development, 33*, 749–756.

Josephson Institute Center for Youth Ethics. (2010). Character counts! Retrieved from *charactercounts.org*.

Kalberg, J. R., Lane, K. L., & Lambert, W. (in press). The utility of conflict resolution and social skills interventions with middle school students at risk for antisocial behavior: A methodological illustration. *Remedial and Special Education*.

Kalberg, J. R., Lane, K. L., & Menzies, H. M. (2010). Using systematic screening procedures to identify students who are nonresponsive to primary prevention efforts: Integrating academic and behavioral measures. *Education and Treatment of Children, 33*, 561–584.

Kamphaus, R. W., & Reynolds, C. R. (2006). *Behavior assessment system for children* (2nd ed.): *Parenting Relationship Questionnaire*. Minneapolis, MN: NCS Pearson.

Kamphaus, R. W., & Reynolds, C. R. (2007a). *BASC^{TM}-2 Behavior and Emotional Screening System (BASC^{TM}-2 BESS)*. San Antonio, TX: Pearson.

Kamphaus, R. W., & Reynolds, C. R. (2007b). *BASC-2 Progress Monitor*. Bloomington, MN: Pearson Assessments.

Kamphaus, R. W., Reynolds, C. R. (2008). *Behavior and Emotional Screening System*. Bloomington, MN: Pearson.

Kamphaus, R. W., Thorpe, J. S., Winsor, A. P., Kroncke, A. P., Dowdy, E. T., & VanDeventer, M. C. (2007). Development and predictive validity of a teacher screener for child behavioral and emotional problems at school. *Educational and Psychological Measurement, 67*, 342–356.

Kamps, D., Kravits, T., Rauch, J., Kamps, J. L., & Chung, N. (2000). A prevention program for students with or at risk for ED: Moderating effects of variation in treatment and classroom structure. *Journal of Emotional and Behavioral Disorder, 8*, 141–154.

Kamps, D., Kravits, T., Stolze, J., & Swaggart, B. (1999). Prevention strategies for at-risk students and students with EBD in urban elementary schools. *Journal of Emotional and Behavioral Disorders, 7*, 178–188.

Kamps, D. M., & Greenwood, C. R. (2005). Formulating secondary-level reading interventions. *Journal of Learning Disabilities, 38*, 500–509.

Kamps, D. M., Wills, H. P., Greenwood, C. R., Thorne, S., Lazo, J. F., Crockett, J. L., et al. (2003). Curriculum influence on growth in early reading fluency for students with academic and behavioral risks: A descriptive study. *Journal of Emotional and Behavioral Disorders, 11*, 211–224.

Kaptein, S., Jansen, C., Vogels, V., & Reijneveld, S. A. (2008). Mental health problems in children with intellectual disability: use of the Strengths and Difficulties Questionnaire. *Journal of Intellectual Disability Research, 52*, 125–131.

Kauffman, J. M. (2001). *Characteristics of emotional and behavioral disorders of children and youth* (7th ed.). Columbus, OH: Merrill.

Kauffman, J. M. (2005). *Characteristics of emotional and behavioral disorders in children and youth* (8th ed.). Upper Saddle River, NJ: Pearson Merrill Prentice Hall.

Kauffman, J. M., & Brigham, F. J. (2009). *Working with troubled children*. Verona, WI: Full Court Press.

Kazdin, A. E. (1977). Assessing the clinical or applied importance of behavior change through social validation. *Behavior Modification, 1*, 427–452.

Kazdin, A. E. (1985). *Treatment of antisocial behavior in children and adolescents*. Pacific Grove, CA: Brooks/Cole.

Kazdin, A. E. (1993a). Adolescent mental health: Prevention and treatment programs. *American Psychologist, 48*, 127–141.

Kazdin, A. E. (1993b). Treatment of conduct disorders: Progress and directions in psychotherapy research. *Development and Psychopathology, 5*, 277–310.

Kenyon, S., Pike, K., Jones, D. R., Brocklehurst, P., Marlow, N., Salt, A., et al. (2008). Childhood outcomes after prescription of antibiotics to pregnant women with spontaneous preterm labour: 7–year follow-up of the ORACLE II trial. *Lancet, 372*, 1319–1327.

Kern, L., & Manz, P. (2004). A look at current validity issues of school-wide behavior support. *Behavioral Disorders, 30*, 47–59.

Kettler, R. J., Elliott, S.N., Davies, M., & Griffin, P. (2009). *Using academic enabler nominations and social behavior to predict students' performance level on Australia's national achievement test*. San Diego, CA: American Educational Research Association.

Kimsey, W. D., & Fuller, R. M. (2003). CONFLICTALK: An instrument for measuring youth and adolescent conflict management message styles. *Conflict Resolution Quarterly, 21*, 69–78.

Koskelainen, M., Sourander, A., & Vauras, M. (2001). Self-reported strengths and difficulties in a community sample of Finnish adolescents. *European Child and Adolescent Psychiatry, 10*, 180–185.

Kusche, C. A., & Greenberg, M. S. (1994). *The PATHS curriculum: Promoting alternative thinking strategies.* Seattle, WA: Developmental Research and Programs.

Landis J. R., & Koch, G. (1977). The measurement of observer agreement for categorical data. *Biometrics, 33*, 159–174.

Lane, K. L. (1999). Young students at risk for antisocial behavior: The utility of academic and social skills intervention. *Journal of Emotional and Behavioral Disorders, 7*, 211–223.

Lane, K. L. (2003a). Identifying young students at risk for antisocial behavior: The utility of "teachers as tests." *Behavioral Disorders, 28*, 360–389.

Lane, K. L. (2003b). *Skills for Acquiring Knowledge, Demonstrating Knowledge, and Resolving Conflict: A Criterion Referenced Test.* Unpublished test, Vanderbilt University, Nashville, TN.

Lane, K. L. (2004). Academic instruction and tutoring interventions for students with emotional/behavioral disorders: 1990 to present. In R. B. Rutherford, M. M. Quinn, & S. R. Mathur (Eds.), *Handbook of research in emotional and behavioral disorders* (pp. 462–486). New York: Guilford Press.

Lane, K. L. (2007). Identifying and supporting students at risk for emotional and behavioral disorders with multi-level models: Data-driven approaches to conducting secondary interventions with academic emphasis. *Education and Treatment of Children, 30*, 135–164.

Lane, K. L., & Beebe-Frankenberger, M. E. (2004). *School-based interventions: The tools you need to succeed.* Boston: Allyn & Bacon.

Lane, K. L., Bruhn, A. L., Eisner, S. L., & Kalberg, J. R. (2010). Score reliability and validity of the Student Risk Screening Scale: A psychometrically-sound, feasible tool for use in urban middle schools. *Journal of Emotional and Behavioral Disorders, 18*, 211–224.

Lane, K. L., Eisner, S. L., Kretzer, J. M., Bruhn, A. L., Crnobori, M. E., Funke, L. M., et al. (2009). Outcomes of functional assessment-based interventions for students with and at risk for emotional and behavioral disorders in a job-share setting. *Education and Treatment of Children, 32*, 573–604.

Lane, K. L., Harris, K., Graham, S., Weisenbach, J., Brindle, M., & Morphy, P. (2008). The effects of self-regulated strategy development on the writing performance of second-grade students with behavioral and writing difficulties. *Journal of Special Education, 41*, 234 – 253.

Lane, K. L., Kalberg, J. R., Bruhn, A. L., Driscoll, S. A., Wehby, J. H., & Elliott, S. (2009). Assessing social validity of school-wide positive behavior support plans: Evidence for the reliability and structure of the Primary Intervention Rating Scale. *School Psychology Review, 38*, 135–144.

Lane, K. L., Kalberg, J. R., Bruhn, A. L., Mahoney, M. E., & Driscoll, S. A. (2008). Primary prevention programs at the elementary level: Issues of treatment integrity, systematic screening, and reinforcement. *Education and Treatment of Children, 31*, 465–494.

Lane, K. L., Kalberg, J. R., Lambert, W., Crnobori, M., & Bruhn, A. (2010). A comparison of systematic screening tools for emotional and behavioral disorders: A replication. *Journal of Emotional and Behavioral Disorders, 18*, 100–112.

Lane, K. L., Kalberg, J. R., Menzies, H., Bruhn, A., Eisner, S., & Crnobori, M. (2011). Using systematic screening data to assess risk and identify students for targeted supports: Illustrations across the K–12 continuum. *Remedial and Special Education, 32*, 39–54.

Lane, K. L., Kalberg, J. R., & Menzies, H. M. (2009). *Developing schoolwide programs to prevent and manage problem behaviors: A step-by-step approach.* New York: Guilford Press.

Lane, K. L., Kalberg, J. R., Parks, R. J., & Carter, E. W. (2008). Student Risk Screening Scale: Initial evidence for score reliability and validity at the high school level. *Journal of Emotional and Behavioral Disorders, 16,* 178–190.

Lane, K. L., Little, M. A., Casey, A. M., Lambert, W., Wehby, J. H., Weisenbach, J. L., et al. (2009). A comparison of systematic screening tools for emotional and behavioral disorders: How do they compare? *Journal of Emotional and Behavioral Disorders, 17,* 93–105.

Lane, K. L., Little, M. A., Redding-Rhodes, J. R., Phillips, A., & Welsh, M. T. (2007). Outcomes of a teacher-led reading intervention for elementary students at-risk for behavioral disorders. *Exceptional Children, 74,* 47–70.

Lane, K. L., Mahdavi, J. N., & Borthwick-Duffy, S. A. (2003). Teacher perceptions of the prereferral intervention process: A call for assistance with school-based interventions. *Preventing School Failure, 47,* 148–155.

Lane, K. L., & Menzies, H. (2005). Teacher-identified students with and without academic and behavioral concerns: Characteristics and responsiveness to a school-wide intervention. *Behavioral Disorders, 31,* 65–83.

Lane, K. L., & Menzies, H. M. (2002). The effects of a school-based primary intervention program: Preliminary outcomes. *Preventing School Failure, 47,* 26–32.

Lane, K. L., Menzies, H. M., Bruhn, A. L., & Crnobori, M. (2011). *Managing challenging behaviors in schools: Research-based strategies that work.* New York: Guilford Press.

Lane, K. L., Menzies, H. M., Kalberg, J. R., & Oakes, W. P. (in press). A comprehensive, integrated three-tier model to meet students' academic, behavioral, and social needs. In K. Harris, T. Urdan, & S. Graham (Eds.), *American Psychological Association educational psychology handbook.* Washington, DC: American Psychological Association.

Lane, K. L., Menzies, H. M., Munton, S., Von Duering, R. M., & English, G. (2005). The effects of a supplemental early literacy program for a student at-risk: A case study. *Preventing School Failure, 50,* 21–28.

Lane, K. L., Oakes, W. P., & Cox, M. (2011). *Functional assessment-based interventions: A university-district partnership to promote learning and success.* Manuscript submitted for publication.

Lane, K. L., Oakes, W. P., Ennis, R. P., Cox, M. L., Schatschneider, C., & Lambert, W. (in press). Additional evidence for the reliability and validity of the Student Risk Screening Scale at the high school level: A replication and extension. *Journal of Emotional and Behavioral Disorders.*

Lane, K. L., Oakes, W. P., Harris, P. J., Menzies, H. M., Cox, M. L., & Lambert, W. (2011). *Initial evidence for the reliability and validity of the Student Risk Screening Scale for internalizing and externalizing behaviors at the elementary level.* Manuscript in preparation.

Lane, K. L., Oakes, W. P., & Menzies, H. M. (2010). Systematic screenings to prevent the development of learning and behavior problems: Considerations for practitioners, researchers, and policy makers. *Journal of Disabilities Policy Studies, 21,* 160–172.

Lane, K. L., Oakes, W. P., Menzies, H. M., & Altmann, S. A. (2011). *Working in the context of three-tiered models of prevention: Using schoolwide data to identify elementary-age students for targeted supports.* Manuscript submitted for publication.

Lane, K. L., & Oakes, W. P. (2011). *The Student Risk Screening Scale for Early Childhood: An initial validation study.* Manuscript in preparation.

Lane, K. L., Parks, R. J., Kalberg, J. R., & Carter, E. W. (2007). Systematic screening at the middle school level: Score reliability and validity of the Student Risk Screening Scale. *Journal of Emotional and Behavioral Disorders, 15,* 209–222.

Lane, K. L., Robertson, E. J., & Wehby, J. H. (2002). *Primary Intervention Rating Scale.* Unpublished rating scale.

Lane, K. L., Rogers, L. A., Parks, R. J., Weisenbach, J. L., Mau, A. C., Merwin, M. T., et al. (2007). Function-based interventions for students nonresponsive to primary and secondary prevention efforts: Illustrations at the elementary and middle school levels. *Journal of Emotional and Behavioral Disorders, 15,* 169–183.

Lane, K. L., Walker, H., Crnobori, M., Oliver, R., Bruhn, A., & Oakes, W. P. (in press). Strategies for decreasing aggressive, coercive behavior: A call for preventative efforts. In M. Tankersley & B. Cook (Eds.), *Effective practices in special education.* Bloomington, MN: Pearson.

Lane, K. L., & Wehby, J. (2002). Addressing antisocial behavior in the schools: A call for action. *Academic Exchange Quarterly, 6,* 4–9.

Lane, K. L., Wehby, J., Menzies, H. M., Doukas, G. L., Munton, S. M., & Gregg, R. M. (2003). Social skills instruction for students at risk for antisocial behavior: The effects of small-group instruction. *Behavioral Disorders, 28,* 229–248.

Lane, K. L., Wehby, J. H., Menzies, H. M., Gregg, R. M., Doukas, G. L., & Munton, S. M. (2002). Early literacy instruction for first-grade students at-risk for antisocial behavior. *Education and Treatment of Children, 25,* 438–458.

Lane, K. L., Wehby, J. H., Robertson, E. J., & Rogers, L. (2007). How do different types of high school students respond to positive behavior support programs?: Characteristics and responsiveness of teacher-identified students. *Journal of Emotional and Behavioral Disorders, 15,* 3–20.

Lane, K. L., Weisenbach, J. L., Phillips, A., & Wehby, J. (2007). Designing, implementing, and evaluating function-based interventions using a systematic, feasible approach. *Behavioral Disorders, 32,* 122–139.

Lane, K. L., Wolery, M., Reichow, B., & Rogers, L. (2006). Describing baseline conditions: Suggestions for study reports. *Journal of Behavioral Education, 16,* 224–234.

Lanyon, R. (2006). Mental health screening: Utility of the Psychological Screening Inventory. *Psychological Services, 3,* 170–180.

Lewis, T. J., & Sugai, G. (1999). Effective behavior support: A systems approach to proactive school-wide management. *Focus on Exceptional Children, 31,* 1–24.

Lynch, K. B., Geller, S. R., & Schmidt, M. G. (2004). Multiyear evaluation of the effectiveness of a resilience-based prevention program for young children. *Journal of Primary Prevention, 24,* 335–353.

MacMillan, D., Gresham, F., & Forness, S. (1996). Full inclusion: An empirical perspective. *Behavioral Disorders, 21,* 145–159.

Malecki, C. K., & Elliott, S. N. (2002). Children's social behaviors as predictors of academic achievement: A longitudinal analysis. *School Psychology Quarterly, 17,* 1–23.

Mardell-Czudnowski, C., & Goldenberg, D. S. (1998). *Developmental indicators for the assessment of learning–third edition (DIAL-3).* Bloomington, MN: Pearson Assessments.

Martin, A. J., & Sanders, M. R. (2003). Balancing work and family: A controlled evaluation of the Triple P- Positive Parenting Program as a work-site intervention. *Child and Adolescent Mental Health, 8,* 161–168.

Matasuishi, T., Nagano, M., Araki, Y., Tanaka, Y., Iwasaki, M., Yamashita, Y., et al. (2008). Scale properties of the Japanese version of the Strengths and Difficulties Questionnaire (SDQ): A study of infant and school children in community samples. *Brain and Development, 30,* 410–415.

Mattison, R. E., Hooper, S. R., & Glassberg, L. A. (2002). Three-year course of learning disorders in special education students classified as behavioral disorder. *Journal of the American Academy of Child and Adolescent Psychiatry, 41,* 1454–1461.

Mattison, R. E., Spitznagel, E. L., & Felix, B. C. (1998). Enrollment predictors of the special education outcome for students with SED. *Behavioral Disorders, 23,* 243–256.

May, S., Ard, W., III, Todd, A. W., Horner, R. H., Glasgow, A., Sugai, G., et al. (2000). *School-wide Information System (SWIS©).* Eugene: University of Oregon, Educational and Community Supports.

McEvoy, A., & Welker, R. (2000). Antisocial behavior, academic failure, and school climate: A critical review. *Journal of Emotional and Behavioral Disorders, 8*(3), 130–140.

McGoey, K. E., & DuPaul, G. J. (2000). Token reinforcement and response cost procedures: Reducing the disruptive behavior of preschool children with attention-deficit/hyperactivity disorder. *School Psychology Quarterly, 15,* 330–343.

Mellor, D. (2005). Normative data for the Strengths and Difficulties Questionnaire in Australia. *Australian Psychologist, 40,* 215–222.

Mellor, D., & Stokes, M. (2007). The factor structure of the Strengths and Difficulties Questionnaire. *European Journal of Psychological Assessment, 23,* 105–112.

Menzies, H. M., & Lane, K. L. (in press). Validity of the Student Risk Screening Scale: Evidence of predictive validity in a diverse, suburban elementary setting. *Journal of Emotional and Behavioral Disorders.*

Moffitt, T. E. (1993). Adolescence-limited and life-course-persistent antisocial behavior: A developmental taxonomy. *Psychological Review, 100,* 674–701.

Mooney, P., Ryan, J. B., Uhing, B. M., Reid, R., & Epstein, M. H. (2005). A review of self-management interventions targeting academic outcomes for students with emotional and behavioral disorders. *Journal of Behavioral Education, 14,* 203–221.

Morgan, P. L., Farkas, G., Tufis, P. A., & Sperling, R. A. (2008). Are reading and behavior problems risk factors for each other? *Journal of Learning Disabilities, 41,* 417–436.

Morris, R. J. Shah, K., & Morris, Y. P. (2002). Internalizing behavior disorders. In K.L. Lane, F. M. Gresham, & T. E. O'Shaughnessy (Eds.), *Interventions for children with or at risk for emotional and behavioral disorders* (pp. 223–241). Boston: Allyn & Bacon.

Mullick, M. S. I., & Goodman, R. (2005). The prevalence of psychiatric disorders among 5–10 year olds in rural, urban and slum areas in Bangladesh: An exploratory study. *Social Psychiatry and Psychiatric Epidemiology, 40,* 663–671.

Nelson, J. R., Benner, G. J., & Gonzalez, J. (2005). An investigation of the effects of a prereading intervention on the early literacy skills of children at risk for emotional disturbance and reading problems. *Journal of Emotional and Behavioral Disorders, 13,* 3–12.

Nelson, J. R., Benner, G. J., Lane, K., & Smith, B. W. (2004). An investigation of the academic achievement of K–12 students with emotional and behavioral disorders in public school settings. *Exceptional Children, 71,* 59–73.

Nelson, J. R., Benner, G. J., & Mooney, P. (2008). *Instructional practices for students with behavioral disorders: Strategies for reading, writing, and math*. New York: Guilford Press.

Nelson, J. R., Cooper, P., & Gonzalez, J. (2004). *Stepping Stones to Literacy*. Frederick, CO: Cambium Learning Group.

Nelson, J. R., Stage, S., Duppong-Hurley, K., Synhorst, L., & Epstein, M. H. (2007). Risk factors predictive of problem behavior in children at risk for emotional and behavioral disorders. *Exceptional Children, 73,* 367–379.

Nelson, J. R., Stage, S. A., Epstein, M. H., & Pierce, C. D. (2005). Effects of a prereading intervention on the literacy and social skills of children. *Exceptional Children, 72,* 29–45.

Nickerson, A. B., & Fishman, C. (2009). Convergent and divergent validity of the Devereux Student Strengths Assessment. *School Psychology Quarterly, 24*(1), 48–59.

No Child Left Behind (NCLB) Act of 2001, Pub. L. No. 107–110, § 115, Stat. 1425 (2002).

Oakes, W. P., Mathur, S. R., & Lane, K. L. (2010). Reading interventions for students with challenging behavior: A focus on fluency. *Behavioral Disorders, 35,* 120–139.

Oakes, W. P. Wilder, K., Lane, K. L., Powers, L., Yokoyama, L., O'Hare, M. E., et al. (2010). Psychometric properties of the Student Risk Screening Scale: An effective tool for use in diverse urban elementary schools. *Assessment for Effective Intervention, 35,* 231–239.

O'Connor, T. G., Heron, J., Glover, V., & Alspack Study Team. (2002). Antenatal anxiety predicts child behavioral/emotional problems independently of postnatal depression. *Journal of American Child and Adolescent Psychiatry, 41,* 1470–1477.

Olweus, D., Limber, S. P., Flerx, V. C., Mullin, N., Riese, J., & Snyder, M. (2007). *Olweus Bullying Prevention Program: Schoolwide guide*. Center City, MN: Hazelden.

Palmieri, P., & Smith, G. C. (2007). Examining the structural validity of the Strengths and Difficulties Questionnaire (SDQ) in a U.S. sample of custodial grandmothers. *Psychological Assessment, 19,* 189–198.

Parker, J., Rubin, K., Erath, S., Wojslawowicz, J., & Buskirk, A. (2006). Peer relationships, child development, and adjustment: A developmental psychopathology perspective. In D. Cicchetti (Ed.), *Developmental psychopathology: Vol. 2. Risk, disorder, and adaptation* (pp. 419–493). New York: Wiley.

Pashler, H., Bain, P. M., Bottge, B. A., Graesser, A., Koedinger, K., McDaniel, M., et al. (2007). Organizing instruction and study to improve student learning: A practice guide (NCER 2007-2004). Washington, DC: National Center for Education Research, Institute of Education Sciences, U.S. Department of Education. Retrieved from *ies.ed.gov/ncee/wwc/pdf/practiceguides/20072004.pdf*.

Patterson, G. R., Reid, J. B., & Dishion, T. J. (1992). *Antisocial boys*. Eugene, OR: Castalia.

Pearson Education. (2008). *AIMSweb*. Bloomington, IN: NCS Pearson.

Person, A. E., Moiduddlin, E., Hague-Angus, M., & Malone, L. M. (2009). *Survey of Outcomes Measurement in Research on Character Education Programs* (NCEE 2009-006). Washington, DC: National Center for Education Evaluation and Regional Assistance, Institute of Education Sciences, U.S. Department of Education.

Positive Action, Inc. (2008). *Positive Action: Positive development for schools, families and communities*. Twin Falls: ID: Author.

Protection of Pupil Rights Amendment. 20 U.S.C. 1232h; 34 C.F.R. Part 98 (1978).

Quinn, S. R., & Poirier, J. M. (2004). Linking prevention research with policy: Examining the costs and outcomes of the failure to prevent emotional and behavioral disorders. In

R.B. Rutherford, Jr., M. M. Quinn, & S. R. Mathur (Eds.), *Handbook of research in emotional and behavioral disorders* (pp. 78–97). New York: Guilford Press.

Rapport, M. D., Denney, C. B., Chung, K. M., & Hustace, K. (2001). Internalizing behavior problems and scholastic achievement in children: Cognitive and behavioral pathways as mediators of outcome. *Journal of Clinical Child Psychology, 30,* 536–551.

Reading Mastery. (1995). DeSoto, TX: SRA/McGraw-Hill.

Rees, G., Gledhill, J., Garralda, M. E., & Nadel, S. (2004). Psychiatric outcome following pediatric intensive care unit (PICU) admission: A cohort study. *Intensive Care Medicine, 30,* 1607–1614.

Reid, R., Gonzalez, J. E., Nordness, A. T., Trout, A., & Epstein, M. H. (2004). A meta-analysis of the academic status of students with emotional/behavioral disturbance. *Journal of Special Education, 38,* 130–143.

Renaissance Learning. (2010). Accelerated reader [Computer software]. Wisconsin Rapids, WI: Author.

Renshaw, T. L., Eklund, K., Dowdy, E., Jimerson, S. R., Hart, S. R., Earhart, J., et al. (2009). Examining the relationship between scores on the Behavioral and Emotional Screening System and student academic, behavioral, and engagement outcomes: An investigation of concurrent validity in elementary school. *California School Psychologist, 14,* 81–88. Retrieved from *findarticles.com/p/articles/mi_7479/is_200901/ai_ n52375546/?tag=content.*

Reynolds, C. R., & Kamphaus, R. W. (1992). *Behavior Assessment System for Children.* Circle Pines, MN: American Guidance Service.

Reynolds, C. R., & Kamphaus, R. W. (2004). *Behavior Assessment System for Children— second edition* (BASC-2). Circle Pines, MN: American Guidance Service.

Reynolds, C. R., & Kamphaus, R. W. (2009). *Behavior Assessment System for Children— second edition* (BASC-2): Progress Monitor (BASC-2 PM). Minneapolis, MN: NCS Pearson.

Rice, F., Lewis, A., Harold, G., VanDenBree, M., Boivin, J., Hay, D. F., et al. (2007). Agreement between maternal report and antenatal records for a range of pre and peri-natal factors: The influence of maternal and child characteristics. *Early Human Development, 83,* 497–504.

Richardson, M. J., Caldarella, P., Young, B. J., Young, E. L., & Young, K. R. (2009). Further validation of the Systematic Screening for Behavior Disorders in middle and junior high school. *Psychology in the Schools, 46,* 605–615.

Robertson, E. J., & Lane, K. L. (2007). Supporting middle school students with academic and behavioral concerns within the context of a three-tiered model of support: Findings of a secondary prevention program. *Behavioral Disorders, 33,* 5–22.

Robertson, S., & Davig, H. (2002). *Read with me: Stress-free strategies for building language and literacy.* Eau Claire, WI: Thinking Publications.

Ronning, J. A., Handegaard, B. H., Sourander, A., & Morch, W. T. (2004). The Strengths and Difficulties Self-Report Questionnaire as a screening instrument in Norwegian community samples. *European Child and Adolescent Psychiatry, 13,* 73–82.

Ruchkin, V., Koposov, R., & Schwab-Stone, M. (2007). The Strength and Difficulties Questionnaire: Scale validation with Russian adolescents. *Journal of Clinical Psychology, 63,* 861–869.

Rutter, M. (1967). A children's behaviour questionnaire for completion by teachers: Preliminary findings. *Journal of Child Psychology and Psychiatry, 8,* 1–11.

Sagatun, A., Sogaard, A. J., Bjertness, E., Selmer, R., & Heyerdahl, S. (2007). The association between weekly hours of physical activity and mental health: A three-year follow-up study of 15–16-year-old students in the city of Oslo, Norway. *BMC Public Health, 7,* 155–143.

Sayal, K., Heron, J., Golding, J., & Emond, A. (2007). Prenatal alcohol exposure and gender differences in childhood mental health problems: A longitudinal population-based study. *Pediatrics, 119,* 426–434.

Sayal, K., Taylor, E., & Beecham, J. (2003). Parental perception of problems and mental health service use for hyperactivity. *Journal of the American Academy of Child and Adolescent Psychiatry, 42,* 1410–1414.

Scholastic Inc. (1997). *Read 180.* New York: Author.

School Mediation Center. (1998). *Productive conflict resolution: A comprehensive curriculum and teacher's guide for conflict resolution education grades 6–8.* Boulder, CO: Author.

Schunk, D. H. (2001). *Self-regulation through goal setting.* Greensboro, NC: ERIC Clearinghouse on Counseling and Student Services.

Scruggs, T. E., & Mastropieri, M. A. (1986). Academic characteristics of behaviorally disordered and learning disabled students. *Behavioral Disorders, 11,* 184–190.

Serna, L., Nielson, E., Lambros, K., & Forness, S. (2000). Primary prevention with children at risk for emotional or behavioral disorders: Data on a universal intervention for Head Start classrooms. *Behavioral Disorders, 26,* 70–84.

Severson, H., & Walker, H. (2002). Proactive approaches for identifying children at risk for sociobehavior problems. In K. Lane, F. M. Gresham, & T. E. O'Shaughnessy (Eds.), *Interventions for children with or at risk for emotional and behavioral disorders* (pp. 33–54). Boston: Allyn & Bacon.

Shefelbine, J. (1998). *Phonics chapters books 1–6: Teachers guide.* New York: Scholastic.

Shojaei, T., Wazana, A., Pitrou, I., & Kovess, V. (2009). The Strengths and Difficulties Questionnaire: Validation study in French school-aged children and cross-cultural comparisons. *Social Psychiatry and Psychiatric Epidemiology, 44,* 740–747.

Sinclair, E., Del'Homme, M., & Gonzalez, M. (1993). Systematic screening for preschool behavior disorders. *Behavioral Disorders, 18,* 177–186.

Smedje, H., Broman, J. E., Hetta, J., & von Knorring, A. L. (1999). Psychometric properties of a Swedish version of the Strength and Difficulties Questionnaire. *European Child and Adolescent Psychiatry, 8,* 63–70.

Smithard, A., Glazebrook, C., & Williams, H. C. (2001). Acne prevalence, knowledge about acne and psychological morbidity in mid-adolescence: A community-based study. *British Journal of Dermatology, 145,* 274–279.

Sprague, J., & Perkins, K. (2009). Direct and collateral effects of the First Step to Success program. *Journal of Positive Behavior Interventions, 11,* 208–221.

Sprague, J., Walker, H., Golly, A., White, K., Myers, D. R., & Shannon, T. (2001). Translating research into effective practice: The effects of a universal staff and student intervention on indicators of discipline and school safety. *Education and Treatment of Children, 24,* 495–511.

Sprick, R. (n.d.). Randy Sprick's safe & civil schools: Practical solutions, positive results! Retrieved from *www.safeandcivilschools.com.*

Stang, K. K., Carter, E. W., Lane, K. L., & Pierson, M. R. (2009). Perspectives of general and special educators on fostering self-determination in elementary and middle schools. *Journal of Special Education, 43,* 94–106.

Stores, G., Montgomery, P., & Wiggs, L. (2006). The psychosocial problems of children with narcolepsy and those with excessive daytime sleepiness of uncertain origin. *Pediatrics, 118*, 1116–1123.

Strine, T. W., Okoro, C. A., McGuire, L. C., & Balluz, L. S. (2006). The associations among childhood headaches, emotional and behavioral difficulties, and health care use. *Pediatrics, 117*, 1728–1735.

Success for All Foundation. (1999). *Success for all*. Baltimore: Author.

Sugai, G., & Horner, R. H. (2002). Introduction to the special series on positive behavior support in schools. *Journal of Emotional and Behavioral Disorders, 10*, 130.

Sugai, G., & Horner, R. H. (2006). A promising approach for expanding and sustaining school-wide positive behavior support. *School Psychology Review, 35*, 245–260.

Sugai, G., Horner, R. H., & Gresham, S. (2002). Behaviorally effective school environments. In M. R. Shinn, H. M. Walker, & G. Stoner (Eds.), *Interventions for academic and behavior problems: II. Preventive and remedial approaches* (pp. 315–350). Washington, DC: National Association of School Psychologists.

Sugai, G., Lewis-Palmer, T., Todd, A., & Horner, R. H. (2001). *School-wide Evaluation Tool (SET): Version 2.1*. Eugene: University of Oregon, Educational and Community Supports.

Sutherland, K. S., & Wright, S. A. (in press). Students with disabilities and academic engagement: Classroom-based interventions. In K. L. Lane, M. Tankersley, & B. G. Cook (Series Eds.) & K. L. Lane (Vol. Ed.), *Effective practices in special education: Vol. 2. Strategies for improving outcomes in behavior*. Bloomington, MN: Pearson.

ThinkLink Learning. (2000). Nashville, TN: Discovery Education.

Todis, B., Severson, H. H., & Walker, H. M. (1990). The Critical Events Scale: Behavioral profiles of students with externalizing and internalizing behavior disorders. *Behavioral Disorders, 15*, 75–86.

Tomlinson, C. A. (2005). *How to differentiate instruction in mixed-ability classrooms* (2nd ed.). Upper Saddle River, NJ: Pearson Education.

Tomlinson, C. A., & McTighe, J. (2005). *Integrating differentiated instruction: Understanding by design*. Alexandria, VA: Association for Supervision and Curriculum Development.

Trout, A. L., Epstein, M. H., Nelson, J. R., Reid, R., & Ohlund, B. (2006). Profiles of young children teacher-identified as at risk for emotional disturbance: A pilot study. *Behavior Disorders, 31*, 162–175.

Trout, A. L., Epstein, M. H., Nelson, J. R., Synhorst, L., & Hurley, K. D. (2006). Profiles of children served in early intervention programs for behavior disorders: Early literacy and behavioral characteristics. *Topics in Early Childhood Special Education, 26*, 206–218.

Umbreit, J., Ferro, J., Liaupsin, C., & Lane, K. (2007). *Functional behavioral assessment and function-based intervention: An effective, practical approach*. Upper Saddle River, NJ: Prentice Hall.

Upshur, C., Wenz-Gross, M., & Reed, G. (2009). A pilot study of early childhood mental health consultation for children with behavior problems in preschool. *Early Childhood Research Quarterly, 24*, 29–45.

Van Widenfelt, B. M., Goedhart, A. W., Treffers, P. D. A., & Goodman, R. (2003). Dutch version of the Strengths and Difficulties Questionnaire (SDQ). *European Journal of Child and Adolescent Psychiatry, 12*, 281–289.

Vanderbilt, A. (2005). Designed for teachers: How to implement self-monitoring in the classroom. *Beyond Behavior, 15*, 21–24.

Vannest, K.J., Reynolds, C., & Kamphaus, R. (2008). *BASC-2 intervention guide for learning and behavior problems*. Minneapolis, MN: Pearson.

Voress, J. K., & Maddox, T. (1998). *Developmental assessment of young children*. Austin, TX: Pro-Ed.

Voyager Expanded Learning. (2004). *Voyager blast off to reading*. Dallas, TX: Author.

Vygotsky, L. S. (1978). *Mind in society*. Cambridge, MA: Harvard University Press.

Wagner, M., & Davis, M. (2006). How are we preparing students with emotional disturbances for the transition to young adulthood?: Findings from the National Longitudinal Transition Study-2. *Journal of Emotional and Behavioral Disorders, 14*, 86–98.

Wagner, M., Friend, M., Bursuck, D., Kutash, K., Duchnowski, A. J., Sumi, W. C., et al. (2006). Educating students with emotional disturbances: A national perspective on school programs and services. *Journal of Emotional and Behavioral Disorders, 14*, 12–30.

Wagner, M. M. (1995). Outcomes for youths with serious emotional disturbance in secondary school and early adulthood. *The Future of Children, 5*(2), 90–111.

Walker, B., Cheney, D., Stage, S., & Blum, C. (2005). School wide screening and positive behavior supports: Identifying and supporting students at risk for school failure. *Journal of Positive Behavior Interventions, 7*, 194–204.

Walker, H. M. (2003, February 20). *Comments on accepting the Outstanding Leadership Award from the Midwest Symposium for Leadership in Behavior Disorders*. Kansas City, KS: Author.

Walker, H. M., Block-Pedego, A., Todis, B., & Severson, H. (1991). *School archival records search*. Longmont, CO: Sopris West.

Walker, H. M., Golly, A., McLane, J. Z., & Kimmich, M. (2005). The Oregon First Step to Success replication initiative: State-wide results of an evaluation of the programs impact. *Journal of Emotional and Behavioral Disorders, 13*(3), 163–172.

Walker, H. M., Irvin, L., Noell, J., & Singer, G. (1992). A construct score approach to the assessment of social competence: Rationale, technological considerations, and anticipated outcomes. *Behavior Modification, 16*, 448–474.

Walker, H. M., Kavanagh, K., Stiller, B., Golly, A., Severson, H. H., & Feil, E. G. (1998). First Step to Success: An early intervention approach for preventing school antisocial behavior. *Journal of Emotional and Behavioral Disorders, 6*, 66–80.

Walker, H. M., McConnell, S. R., & Clarke, J. Y. (1985). Social skills training in school settings: A model for the social integration of handicapped children into less restrictive settings. In R. McMahon & R. D. Peters (Eds.), *Childhood disorders: Behavioral-developmental approaches* (pp. 140–168). New York: Brunner/Mazel.

Walker, H. M., Ramsey, E., & Gresham, F. M. (2004). *Antisocial behavior in school: Evidence-based practices* (2nd ed.). Belmont, CA: Wadsworth.

Walker, H. M., Severson, H., Nicholson, F., Kehle, T., Jenson, W. R., & Clark, E. (1994). Replication of the Systematic Screening for Behavior Disorders (SSBD) procedure for the identification of at-risk children. *Journal of Emotional and Behavioral Disorders, 2*, 66–77.

Walker, H. M., Severson, H., Stiller, B., Williams, G., Haring, N., Shinn, M., et al. (1988). Systematic screening of pupils in the elementary age range at risk for behavior disorders: Development and trial testing of a multiple gating model. *Remedial and Special Education, 9*, 8–20.

Walker, H. M., Severson, H., Todis, B. J., Block-Pedego, A. E., Williams, G. J., Haring N. G., et al. (1990). Systematic Screening for Behavior Disorders (SSBD): Further validation, replication, and normative data. *RASE: Remedial and Special Education, 11*, 32–46.

Walker, H. M., & Severson, H. H. (1992). *Systematic Screening for Behavior Disorders (SSBD): User's guide and technical manual.* Longmont, CO: Sopris West.

Walker, H. M., Severson, H. H., & Feil, E. G. (1995). *The Early Screening Project: A Proven Child Find Process.* Longmont, CO: Sopris West.

Walker, H. M., Sprague, J. R., Perkins-Rowe, K. A., Beard-Jordan, K. Y., Seibert, B. M., Golly, A. M., et al. (2005). The First Step to Success program: Achieving secondary prevention outcomes for behaviorally at-risk children through early intervention. In M. H. Epstein, K. Kutash, & A. J. Duchnowski (Eds.), *Outcomes for children and youth with emotional and behavioral disorders and their families: Programs and evaluation best practices* (2nd ed., pp. 501–523). Austin, TX: Pro-Ed.

Walker, H. M., Stiller, B., Golly, A., Kavanagh, K., Severson, H. H., & Feil, E. (1997). *First Step to Success: Helping young children overcome antisocial behavior.* Longmont, CO: Sopris West.

Webster-Stratton, C. (2000). *The Incredible Years training series.* Washington, DC: Office of Juvenile Justice and Delinquency Prevention, Juvenile Justice Bulletin.

Webster-Stratton, C., & Hancock, L. (1998). Parent training: Content, methods and processes. In E. Schaefer (Ed.), *Handbook of parent training* (2nd ed., pp. 98–152). New York: Wiley.

Wehmeyer, M. L., & Field, S. L. (2007). *Self-determination: Instructional and assessment strategies.* Thousand Oaks, CA: Corwin Press.

Wentzel, K.R. (1993). Motivation and achievement in early adolescence: The role of multiple classroom goals. *Journal of Early Adolescence, 13*, 4–20.

Wilson, B. A. (2002). *Fundations: Wilson language basics for K–3.* Oxford, MA: Wilson Language Training Corporation.

Wilson, L., Cone, T., Bradley, C., & Reese, J. (1986). The characteristics of learning disabled and other handicapped students referred for evaluation in the state of Iowa. *Journal of Learning Disabilities, 19*, 553–557.

Wingspan. (n.d.). *Al's Pals: Kids Making Healthy Choices—program kit.* Glen Allen, VA: Author.

Woerner, W., Becker, A., & Rothenberger, A. (2004). Normative data and scale properties of the German parent SDQ. *European Child and Adolescent Psychiatry, 13*, 3–10.

Wolf, M. M. (1978). Social validity: The case for subjective measurement or how applied behavior analysis is finding its heart. *Journal of Applied Behavior Analysis, 11*, 203–214.

Wolke, D., Woods, S., Bloomfield, L., & Karstadt, L. (2000). The relation between direct and relational bullying and behaviour problems among primary school children. *Journal of Child Psychology and Psychiatry, 41*, 989–1002.

Woodcock, R. W. (1988). *Woodcock Reading Mastery Test—Revised.* Itasca, IL: Riverside Publishing.

Woodcock, R. W., McGrew, K. S., & Mather, N. (2001). *Woodcock–Johnson III Tests of Achievement.* Itasca, IL: Riverside.

Woods, S., & White, E. (2005). The association between bullying behaviour, arousal levels and behaviour problems. *Journal of Adolescence, 28*, 381–395.

Yang, S., Kim, J., Kim, S., Shin, I., & Yoon, J. (2006). Bullying and victimization behaviors in boys and girls at South Korean primary schools. *Journal of the American Academy of Child and Adolescent Psychiatry, 45,* 69–77.

Zhou, S. J., Gibson, R. A., Crowther, C. A., Baghurst, P., & Makrides, M. (2006). Effect of iron supplementation during pregnancy on the intelligence quotient and behavior of children at 4 y of age: Long-term follow-up of a randomized controlled trial. *American Journal of Clinical Nutrition, 83,* 1112–1117.

Zigmond, N. (2006). Twenty-four months after high school: Paths taken by youth diagnosed with severe emotional and behavioral disorders. *Journal of Emotional and Behavioral Disorders, 14,* 99–107.

Index